LEGAL STUDIES

INTRODUCTION TO LEGAL ASSISTING

Vena Garrett
Saddleback College
Mission Viejo, CA

GLENCOE

Macmillan/McGraw-Hill

New York, New York
Columbus, Ohio
Mission Hills, California
Peoria, Illinois

Library of Congress Cataloging-in-Publication Data

Garrett, Vena.
Introduction to legal assisting / Vena Garrett.
p. cm.—(Legal studies series)
Includes index.
ISBN 0-02-800277-6 (pbk.)
1. Legal assistants—United States—Handbooks, manuals, etc.
2. Law—Study and teaching—United States—Outlines, syllabi, etc.
I. Title. II. Series.
KF320.L4G37 1993
340′.023′73—dc20 92-23569
CIP

Send all inquiries to:
GLENCOE DIVISION
Macmillan/McGraw-Hill
936 Eastwind Drive
Westerville, OH 43081

ISBN 0-02-800277-6

Printed in the United States of America.

1 2 3 4 5 6 7 8 9 0 POH 00 99 98 97 96 95 94 93

OTHER TITLES IN THE LEGAL STUDIES SERIES

Basic Law Office Management

Basic Legal Writing

Basic Legal Research

Basic Legal Research and Writing

Basic Family Law

Basic Civil Litigation

Defining the Law: A Basic Legal Dictionary

ABOUT THE AUTHOR

After holding positions as legal secretary, paralegal, and law office manager, Vena Garrett opened the first personnel agency in Orange County, California, to specialize in placing temporary and full-time law office personnel.

A decade later, Vena Garrett became an adjunct instructor in paralegal programs at Saddleback College in Mission Viejo, California, and the University of California at Riverside, where she authored curricula, classroom materials, and evaluation instruments.

Writing projects include her work as author of Basic Law Office Management (Glencoe: 1992), coauthor of Family Law (Glencoe: 1993), magazine columnist, and reviewer of textbooks for various publishers within the paralegal discipline. Her education background includes an M.B.A. (emphasis in human behavior) from National University and a B.S. (management) from Pepperdine University.

CONTENTS

PART TWO

CLIENT SERVICES

PART THREE

LAW OFFICE PROCEDURES AND SYSTEMS

PART FOUR

PERSONAL AND PROFESSIONAL CAREER DEVELOPMENT

PREFACE

Legal assistants are an integral part of the modern legal services team. To be successful in this growing, competitive field, a legal assistant must be dedicated to obtaining the highest quality education and to remaining a life-long student.

The goal of *Introduction to Legal Assisting* is to present to the student a variety of concepts and legal principles that will form the foundation on which to build a solid background of information for a career in the law. This text is appropriate for students who have little or no experience in a legal environment.

Organization of the Text

The text is composed of four parts. Part One, "Paralegals in the U.S. Legal System," includes five chapters, beginning with an overview of the U.S. legal system in general and a brief history of legal assistants within that system. Then students are introduced to general concepts of law, including how law is made in both the federal and state government systems and how the federal and state courts are organized. In addition, an extensive overview is provided of both the criminal justice system and civil law.

Part Two, "Client Services," consists of two chapters and focuses on the services typically provided to clients by legal assistants. These client services include interviewing and investigation skills, as well as legal analysis, legal research, and legal writing.

The two chapters in Part Three, "Law Office Procedures and Systems," introduce the student to basic law office procedures and systems, including how lawyers set their fees, billable hours, and records management. One chapter is devoted to information management in the law office and provides an overview of how computers work and a review of computer software used in today's offices.

Part Four, "Personal and Professional Career Development," consists of four chapters that are designed to acquaint students with some of the fields of law, as well as provide a blueprint for success as a legal assistant. The chapter on ethics for the legal assistant provides the foundation for professional success. The chapters on interpersonal communication skills and career development provide students with the framework for personal success along with practical skills and suggestions to help them find a job and to be successful on the job.

Text Design

Each chapter begins with a topic outline followed by a Commentary section that chronicles a fictitious entry-level legal assistant in a fictitious law firm, Dunn & Sweeney. This law firm was created solely for the purpose of illustrating the application of the concepts introduced in this text. Any reference to a law firm of the same name existing in either the past or present is purely coincidental.

This text is designed to be user-friendly. The lined margins provide ample space for both instructors and students to make notes within each chapter. Key terms are boldfaced and defined at first use, with an alphabetical list of these terms at the end of each chapter.

Each chapter contains photographs and figures to further illustrate concepts and information as it is presented. Some chapters contain assessment instruments to amplify the learning experience in a more personal way for the student. Students are encouraged to write in these books and to complete all assessments, activities, and review questions.

Other Learning and Teaching Resources

The accompanying *Study Guide* is designed as student support in the study of introductory concepts in legal assisting. Performing its numerous exercises will help the student achieve the objectives of this course.

Each chapter begins with a fill-in chapter outline, followed by a variety of exercises and activities designed to make the student think about and formulate other points of view on the principles presented in the text. Each activity reinforces the information presented and attempts to relate it to real-life situations. In addition, a systematic review and use of the *Study Guide* may help the student improve test scores and develop critical thinking skills.

To facilitate the teaching and learning processes, an *Instructor's Manual* accompanies this text. Included are more activities and problems to be solved by students, answer keys to all review and discussion questions contained in the text, and tests and answers for each chapter which include true/false, multiple choice, and short-answer problems.

Acknowledgments

The author wishes to gratefully acknowledge the contributions of the following reviewers, whose considerable efforts, suggestions, ideas, and insights made this text a more valuable learning tool:

Denise A. Hill, Esq., Instructor, Paralegal Studies, Metro Community College and the College of St. Mary, Omaha, Nebraska

Marni Pilafian Lee, Esq., formerly Director, Legal Assistant Institute, Barry University, Coral Gables, FL

Ronald G. Marquardt, Esq., Director/Professor, Paralegal Studies Program, University of Southern Mississippi, Hattiesburg, Mississippi

James P. O'Brien, Esq., Instructor, Paralegal Program, Harris School of Business, Cherry Hill, New Jersey

Francis D. Polk, Esq., Asst. Dean of Instruction, Paralegal Program, Department of Business and Computer Science, Ocean County College, Toms River, New Jersey

In addition, the author gratefully acknowledges the work of research assistant Bridgit Ostrand, humorist, friend; and editor Rick Adams; and the librarians at Western State University School of Law.

PART ONE

PARALEGALS IN THE U.S. LEGAL SYSTEM

NOTES

CHAPTER 1 Overview of the Legal Assisting Profession

OUTLINE

COMMENTARY

For some time now you have been considering a new career. Several possible careers interest you. Your interests are diverse and range from solving puzzles to working with computers. In addition, you would like to feel your work has meaning and you are in some way helping others. You like working with other very bright people and are not afraid of a challenge. Last week one of your neighbors told you that there is an opening for an entry-level legal assistant in the law firm where she works, Dunn & Sweeney. Mr. Dunn, to whom the legal assistant will report, is not only willing to hire an inexperienced legal-assisting student, but is also a great person to work with. You've read the statistics and have seen the reports. They all indicate that legal assisting is one of the fastest-growing occupations in the country. You have thought about becoming one yourself. You decide it's now or never and tell your neighbor that you are interested in scheduling an interview with Mr. Dunn. In the meantime, you want to find out as much about a career in legal assisting as you can.

OBJECTIVES

After studying the information in this chapter, you should be able to:

1. Define the terms *legal assistant* and *paralegal.*
2. Discuss the history of the U.S. legal profession.
3. List the states where reading for the law is acceptable.
4. Discuss how the paralegal profession was established.
5. Discuss the controversy surrounding the regulation of paralegals.
6. List employment opportunities for paralegals in the public sector.
7. List employment opportunities for paralegals in the private sector.
8. Compare and contrast the duties and responsibilities of the first legal assistants with those of the paralegals of the twenty-first century.
9. Discuss the factors in determining compensation.
10. Contrast the media-created fantasy of the legal profession with reality.
11. List characteristics of successful paralegals.

1–1 Historical Perspective

The terms ***legal assistant*** and ***paralegal*** are used interchangeably in this text and elsewhere. Both terms, however, refer to a person with legal skills beyond the secretarial level who works under the supervision of a lawyer. Legal assistants, or paralegals, are not licensed to practice law, nor are they allowed to give legal advice. Those who engage in the unauthorized practice of law are subject to criminal prosecution.

However, the differences between providing legal services and practicing law are often difficult to distinguish. This fine line of distinction has been and is currently an area of contention and concern among lawyers, paralegals, consumers, bar associations, and state legislatures.

A Brief History of the U.S. Legal Profession

When the United States of America was in its infancy and consisted of a handful of colonists, many people distrusted formal legal procedures used by lawyers. When disputes arose, the colonists either represented themselves or had someone else speak for them. In either case, the representative was not likely to be someone with formal legal training.

As the country grew, the colonists established their own systems of laws as need required. Consequently, one could become a lawyer or judge without formalized training. Illinois, Indiana, and other states permitted any voter with good morals and ethics to practice law in their courts. Judges were selected from the upstanding citizens of the community.

During the period from 1776 to about 1829, 17 states passed laws restricting entrance to the legal profession. Then, between 1830 and 1870, nearly all of these states removed their previously imposed restrictions. In 1850, for example, the state of Michigan declared, "Every person at the age of 21 years, of good moral character, shall have the right to practice in any court in this state."

Why did these states decide to remove the barriers to practicing law that they had previously imposed? The country was not yet well organized. The cities, towns, and villages were even less structured. People had to fend for themselves. Most were suspicious of others who had specialized education and were members of an organized profession that restricted everyone else's right to take care of themselves. So, for several decades anyone who wanted or needed to could represent himself and others in legal matters.

Many famous lawyers never went to law school. Abraham Lincoln, the 16th President of the United States, received his legal training by studying law on his own and working as an apprentice in a lawyer's office. Attorney Clarence Darrow received his legal education in much the same way as Lincoln and went on to establish his place in American history with the legendary Scopes "monkey trial," arguing for the right to teach Darwin's theory of evolution in the classroom. Today, California, New York, Vermont, Virginia, Washington, and Wyoming are the only states that still allow individuals to become lawyers without formalized training, a process called reading for the bar.

Formalized training for lawyers in this country began with the establishment of law schools around 1830. Today, the nationwide average of lawyers to population is about one lawyer for every 473 people.

As the number of lawyers increased, so did the need for structuring and organizing the profession. In 1870 the first bar association was organized in New York City. Subsequently, bar associations were formed throughout the country

Figure 1–1 States in Which Reading for the Bar Is Allowed

STATES IN WHICH READING FOR THE BAR IS ALLOWED	
California	Applicants may acquire training by completing four years of work in a law office, a California Judge's chambers, in a correspondence law school registered with the Committee of Bar Examiners, or any combination of the above. A total of 3456 hours of study is required and applicants must pass the first-year law students' examination (the Baby Bar) at the end of the first year of law study.
New York	Law training may be acquired by successfully completing the first year in a full-time program in an approved law school and thereafter pursuing study in a law office for a total of four years.
Vermont	Applicants may study in a law office for four years or combine law school with law office study for four years. The last two years of study must be in Vermont.
Virginia	Applicants may acquire legal training in a law office for 36 months or through a combination of law school and law office study. Registration with the state bar is required prior to commencement of study.
Washington	In lieu of law school, applicants may acquire training in a law office for four years, or, if an applicant studied in law school and did not receive a degree, s/he can supplement training by further study in law school or by training in a law office. Registration with the state bar is required for law office study.
Wyoming	Applicants may study for one year in an approved law school and two years in a law office.

Figure 1–2 Ratio of Lawyers to Population

LAWYERS TO POPULATION 1988

1. D.C.	1/40	14. Wash.	1/486	27. Ariz.	1/561	40. Iowa	1/664
2. N.Y.	1/295	15. Minn.	1/494	28. N.H.	1/565	41. Ky.	1/684
3. Mass.	1/318	16. Ore.	1/496	29. Maine	1/572	42. S.D.	1/719
4. Colo.	1/367	17. Fla.	1/501	30. N.M.	1/575	43. Tenn.	1/723
5. Conn.	1/375	18. Mont.	1/501	31. Mich.	1/591	44. N.D.	1/738
6. Alaska	1/387	19. Okla.	1/503	32. Wyo.	1/604	45. Ind.	1/765
7. N.J.	1/393	20. Vt.	1/507	33. Kan.	1/607	46. Ala.	1/777
8. Ill.	1/400	21. Texas	1/517	34. Va.	1/611	47. Miss.	1/790
9. Calif.	1/402	22. Pa.	1/520	35. Del.	1/612	48. S.C.	1/831
10. R.I.	1/474	23. Neb.	1/530	36. Nev.	1/612	49. W.Va.	1/838
11. Hawaii	1/475	24. Ohio	1/536	37. Utah	1/621	50. Ark.	1/872
12. La.	1/477	25. Mo.	1/541	38. Wis.	1/632	51. N.C.	1/886
13. Md.	1/477	26. Ga.	1/550	39. Idaho	1/647	**U.S. avg.**	**1/473**

Printed in *The Wall Street Journal; Source:* The American Bar Foundation. Reprinted with permission.

at both the state and local levels to organize and formalize the practice of law, to provide discipline guidelines for the lawyers, and to discourage nonlawyers from practicing law.

Early Legal Assistants

Before there were typewriters, lawyers employed apprentices who could write legibly to prepare pleadings, legal documents, and letters in longhand. These early legal apprentices also performed other routine clerical and secretarial duties. In addition to Lincoln and Darrow, many of these early legal assistants studied the law and went on to become lawyers.

Then, during the nineteenth century, the country experienced a period of intense industrialization. Emphasis was placed on organization and efficiency. Law firms and individual lawyers began hiring typists, switchboard operators, and other staff personnel to operate the new office machines, which were designed to increase the lawyers' productivity.

A major change in the legal profession was under way. Attorneys who were accustomed to doing everything themselves were now delegating some duties to staff members who were not lawyers. As might be expected, this shift was met with great resistance by some. However, as firms grew larger most lawyers could clearly see an advantage to increasing the size of the firm's nonlawyer staff and to delegating routine tasks to these staff members.

The services of legal secretaries were then and continue to be in great demand. Legal secretaries need typing skills and the ability to take shorthand, to work under pressure, and to communicate well with lawyers and clients. At the beginning of the twentieth century, these skills were possessed by only a few men and women who had been able to acquire more than a minimal level of education.

Over time, some legal secretaries took on more and more responsibilities, such as interviewing clients, drafting documents, and performing routine investigations and legal research. Legal secretaries who performed what are now considered paralegal functions were common during the 1950s and 1960s.

In the mid-1960s the first schools and programs were established to offer formalized classes in paralegal studies, largely in response to a new federal government program. The Office of Economic Opportunity (OEO) was established in 1964 to provide legal services to the poor through a national network of nonprofit corporations. The only way the OEO could make legal services affordable was to hire paralegals. Since the majority of legal work for the poor involved unemployment compensation claims and welfare or social security benefits, these legal services seemed ideal for paralegals who were trained to handle administrative law matters under the supervision of an attorney.

It was not long before the success of paralegals in administrative law matters caught the interest and attention of lawyers in private practice. Lawyers quickly realized how paralegals could increase the efficiency of their practices, as well as increase the firm's profit potential. As demand for trained legal assistants has continued to grow, so has the number of paralegal education programs. Throughout the country, enrollments have continued to increase in two-year and four-year public school programs as well as in private schools.

For the past decade, legal assisting has been at the top of the charts for job categories that will grow; as indicated by the predictions in the February 1992 issue of *Money* magazine, continued growth in this job category is expected well into the twenty-first century. But as far back as 1968, the American Bar Association recognized that paralegals were a valuable resource to the legal profession, and a special committee was formed to examine training programs for paralegals and to promote the use of paralegals. Nationwide, nearly 600 legal-assistant education programs have met the standards imposed by the American Bar Association and received that organization's approval.

In the 1970s, paralegals themselves began to organize. In 1974 the National Federation of Paralegal Associations (NFPA) was formed, and a year later, in 1975, the National Association of Legal Assistants (NALA) came into being. Throughout the country, paralegal associations at the national, state, and local levels provide continuing education, networking support, and other benefits to members.

Figure 1–3 Growth in Legal Assistants in U.S.

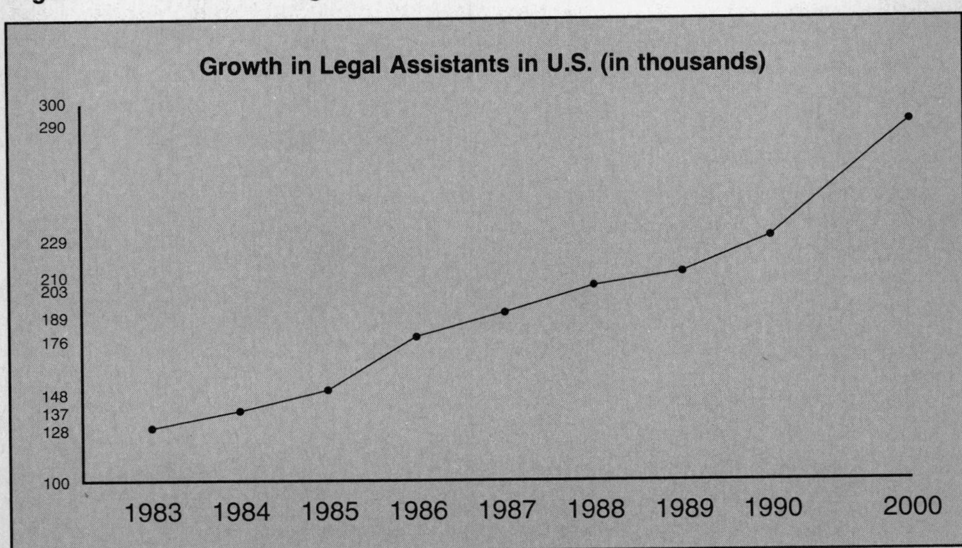

Source: U.S. Dept. of Labor, Bureau of Labor Statistics.

Figure 1–4 Job Categories That Will Grow

10 FOR THE LONG HAUL

JOB CATEGORIES THAT WILL GROW THE MOST BY THE YEAR 2005, WITH PERCENT INCREASE

LEGAL ASSISTANT	85%
COMPUTER ANALYST	79%
PHYSICAL THERAPIST	76%
PSYCHOLOGIST	64%
TRAVEL AGENT	62%
COMPUTER REPAIRER	60%
FLIGHT ATTENDANT	59%
MANAGEMENT CONSULTANT	52%
AD EXECUTIVE	47%
LOBBYIST	47%

Source: Reprinted from *Money* Magazine by special permission; copyright *1992* The Time Inc. Magazine Company.

Paralegals in the Twenty-first Century

In a relatively short period of time, the paralegal profession has come a long distance. The journey has not always been pleasant and it is far from over. However, there is no doubt that legal assistants have established themselves as an integral part of the legal community.

Before looking into the future for paralegals, it is important first to recall the past. In 1974, 10 years after the federal government had established the Office of Economic Opportunity to provide legal services to the poor by training and hiring paralegals, the U.S. Senate Subcommittee on Citizen Interests of the Committee on the Judiciary, known as the Tunney hearings, were held to determine whether the federal government should **regulate,** or control the conduct of, legal assistants. Although there was general agreement that paralegals must not be allowed to practice law, little else was determined in these hearings.

Many questions remain to be answered regarding regulation of paralegals. What purpose will be served by regulating paralegals? If paralegals need to be regulated, how will it be done? How much will it cost? Who will do it? What recourse would consumers have against possible malpractice claims? How can malpractice insurance be made affordable for freelance paralegals? Even though many issues remain unresolved on this controversial subject, the main question no longer appears to be whether the profession will be regulated, but when the first state will step forward and tackle the specifics of how regulation will be done.

Legal Technicians

A few years ago, a bill was introduced in the California Assembly by HALT (Help Abolish Legal Tyranny), a consumer-rights organization headquartered in Washington, DC, that would permit nonlawyers called **legal technicians** to provide out-of-court legal services to consumers in a broad range of areas without direct supervision of an attorney. Under the HALT bill, anyone could be licensed as a legal technician upon payment of a $25 fee, but licensing would be voluntary, not mandatory. For example, traditional legal assistants who work in law firms under the direct supervision of an attorney would not be required to be licensed, but if they wanted to provide services to friends or relatives outside the office, a license would be necessary.

In 1990, the California State Commission for the Licensing of Paralegals, which is composed of attorneys, judges, paralegals, and consumer advocates, countered with a bill of its own, Assembly Bill 168. A.B. 168 would require the state's Department of Consumer Affairs to discipline legal technicians and decree that a legal technician have 30 units of paralegal schooling or two years experience in the legal field and pass a day-long examination. Half the exam would be general in nature, and the other half focused on one of 16 specialty areas, such as immigration, bankruptcy, family law, or landlord-tenant law. These specialty recommendations are the result of a study conducted by the California State Bar Association, which found, for example, that during a two-month period one-third to one-half of all bankruptcy, family law, and landlord-tenant matters were filed ***in pro se*** or *in pro per,* both of which are Latin terms meaning that the parties bring a legal action on their own behalf without the representation of an attorney.

Because of the craziness of the California legislative situation in 1991—layoffs, staff reductions, budget crises, and other pending legislation with higher priority—A.B. 168 was doomed to an early death, but was expected to be revived in 1992 or 1993. Even though legislation initially faltered in California, many other states, including Oregon, Arizona, Florida, Ohio, Kansas, Minnesota, Illinois, and Wisconsin have formed task forces to study the legal technician issue and propose legislation.

Despite the nationwide ban on the unauthorized practice of law, there are approximately 3000 freelance paralegals providing legal help to consumers in landlord/tenant matters, administrative agency problems, simple divorces, drafting wills, filing for bankruptcy, and incorporating businesses. In addition to appearing on behalf of clients in administrative agency hearings, some states allow a paralegal to appear on behalf of someone else in magistrate courts or before a justice of the peace.

Although the primary objection to the concept of legal technicians has been a concern about the quality of service and the competency of the paralegal providing it, in the nearly 20 years that freelance paralegals have been operating in California, the Department of Consumer Affairs for that state reports that complaints about them have been almost nonexistent. Similarly, in a California bar survey, 76 percent of litigants who had used a freelance paralegal were satisfied with the service and would use one again.

Contrast these statistics with the bar's finding that only 64 percent of those who had used lawyers were satisfied and that nearly 100,000 complaints were filed against lawyers in California in 1989. These statistics suggest there is no quality-of-service or professional competency guarantee provided by the lawyers' exclusive license to provide legal services to consumers.

For paralegals, education is the key to competency in providing legal services directly to consumers. No doubt as the debates continue in California and other states, the central issue is whether allowing legal technicians to provide legal service directly to the public is likely to be more harmful than good. It is safe to assume that as the demand for paralegal services continues to grow, so, too, will the demand for more comprehensive educational programs.

The American Bar Association agrees with HALT and state bar associations throughout the country that there is a national crisis in providing legal services to middle- and lower-income consumers. Many people face evictions, problems with government benefits, consumer complaints, child-support problems, and other legal matters without the benefit of legal assistance. Legal technicians could provide these and other services. The question no longer is *if* nonlawyers will be licensed to provide services directly to consumers but *when* the first state will make this controversial move.

There seems to be little doubt that opportunities for paralegals will expand in coming decades. Look for nonlawyer providers of legal services to form separate organizations or businesses to contract with lawyers and law firms for services on an as-needed basis. Some futurists see the paralegal movement in the United States becoming more like the British model of barrister and solicitor, with the paralegal performing many of the solicitor's functions, namely, preparing cases for the lawyer (barrister) to try in higher courts and litigation before lower courts. Paralegals in the future may be allowed to appear in court to answer calendar calls and make simple motions and routine appearances on behalf of clients.

Whatever the future holds for today's paralegals, the key to future success will be a solid foundation of education and experience with an ongoing commitment to providing the highest quality services to employers, clients, and consumers.

1–2 Paralegals in the Public Sector

Paralegals typically find employment in private law firms and corporate legal departments, but opportunities exist in many other areas. Sometimes the lines of distinction are blurred between the public sector and the private sector. The **public sector** of law refers to legal problems that are not usually handled by a private attorney. Within the public sector, there are many opportunities for paralegals to find employment.

Lobbying and Governmental Relations

Paralegals are employed in lobbying and governmental relations work with trade associations and nonprofit organizations. In these positions, paralegals research and draft model legislation, serve as media liaisons to raise public awareness of their particular issues, provide reference and supporting materials to members of the legislature, aid in the preparation of testimony on topics of interest to their employer, and keep informed of developments on the issues.

Group Legal Services

Labor unions and other membership groups sometimes offer a prepaid legal-services plan to their members. Typical services offered through such a plan include an initial consultation, preparation of wills, handling of consumer complaints, family-law matters, real-estate transactions, bankruptcy, and tax matters. To keep the cost reasonable for these prepaid legal plans, paralegals are often employed by the service provider to interview clients, complete paper work, draft documents, or make recommendations to the supervising attorney.

Neighborhood Legal Services Outlets

The growth in legal services provided in convenient neighborhood outlets such as at shopping malls and legal clinics is made possible only through the employment of paralegals. Paralegals interview the clients and can often handle the problem themselves by referring the client to the appropriate government agency. When difficult issues arise, the paralegal prepares a memorandum to the supervising lawyer describing the case and outlining options. The lawyer then decides how best to handle the client's matter.

When administrative law matters are involved, such as problems with the Social Security Administration or unemployment and welfare benefits, the paralegal may accompany and represent the client before the administrative agency.

Public Advocacy

Recent attitude changes in federal, state, and local administrations toward providing low-cost legal services to the poor have resulted in a drastic cutback of services to this group of people. Church groups, foundations, paralegals, and others have worked hard to keep nonprofit, low-cost legal aid agencies from disappearing completely. Some of the services provided by paralegals include interviewing clients, outlining procedures and options, preparing forms, and accompanying and representing the client at administrative agency hearings. Payment for legal services is according to a sliding scale based upon the client's ability to pay.

Paralegals interested in public advocacy sometimes work for groups such as political lobbies. This area of the law includes all the various aspects of civil rights promised by our democratic form of government. Groups that sometimes use the services of public advocacy paralegals include the disabled, the elderly, consumer groups, children's rights groups, taxpayer groups, and racial and ethnic groups. Paralegals using their research, writing, and public relations skills help these and other groups clarify their rights and explore remedies available to them under the law.

Federal Government

The federal government was the first major employer of paralegals. The position of Paralegal Specialist was created to meet the needs of all the federal regulatory agencies, but most of the jobs are located in the Departments of Justice, Treasury, and Defense. For information on paralegal employment opportunities with the federal government, contact your local federal government Office of Personnel Management and ask for positions in the GS-950, GS-986, GS-954, and GS-960 series.

Paralegal positions with the federal government include performing legal research and analysis; summarizing statutes, treaties, contracts, and other legal documents; preparing cases for trial; and other related duties, which may or may not be performed under the direct supervision of an attorney.

State and Local Government

Paralegal positions are found in most offices of state attorneys general, district attorneys, and city attorneys. Job opportunities and duties in these offices vary widely. Generally, paralegals working in state and local government often handle various aspects of both criminal and civil matters, conduct investigation and research, and serve as liaisons with police departments and citizen committees. In addition, paralegals may work closely with attorneys in preparing cases for trial, including collecting and analyzing evidence and locating and interviewing witnesses.

Job opportunities for paralegals in the public sector vary from state to state and from one government agency to the next. By contacting the various government agencies in your area, attending job fairs, and networking with members of your local paralegal association, you will no doubt find there are many career opportunities for you in the public sector.

1–3 Paralegals in the Private Sector

The **private sector** of law refers to those services selected and fully paid for by individual or corporate clients. Within the private sector, many paralegals find employment with law firms and in the legal departments of major corporations.

Law Firms

Smaller law firms often employ paralegal generalists. A **generalist** is a paralegal who understands and is able to work in more than one field of law. For example, a generalist with a small firm might incorporate a small business, work in family law matters, and complete individual bankruptcy forms.

Most paralegals, however, tend to specialize both by function and by substantive law area. Since the law and procedures are revised and changed frequently, keeping up with all the changes in every area is virtually impossible. Specialization allows you to be more efficient and effective, as well as to maintain a high level of expertise in your specialty area.

Corporate Legal Departments

Even though some businesses use law firms to handle their complex legal transactions, most large corporations have their own in-house legal departments to handle routine legal matters and some litigation cases. Corporate paralegals perform a variety of duties including research, drafting documents, and serving as liaison between the corporate legal department and outside law firms. Many corporations have found hiring paralegals to be cost-effective. Consequently, the trend is toward hiring more in-house paralegals and making greater use of their skills throughout the organization.

Traditionally, the educational requirements for a corporate paralegal have been greater than for employment in other private-sector positions. However, the salary and benefits are usually substantially higher than in positions requiring less education.

Equipment Manufacturers

Paralegal jobs also exist in companies that provide equipment to the legal profession. For example, paralegals with knowledge of how computer systems are used in law offices are finding their skills in demand with computer-equipment manufacturers and software vendors.

Paralegals with an interest in sales are often hired by hardware manufacturers for their expertise in managing information in law firms and corporate legal departments. Likewise, paralegals who enjoy training others on software programs are finding instructional opportunities with software vendors and private training companies.

The list of opportunities for paralegals in sales and training positions is not limited to computer-related companies. It extends to companies that manufacture or sell photocopy equipment, microfilm equipment, and vendors of all types who provide services to lawyers.

Legal Research Assistants

Paralegals are employed to do research in the fields of journalism, advertising, and public relations. In addition, consulting firms, environmental agencies, writers, and companies that perform marketing and demographic studies often require the services of legal research assistants.

Finance

Paralegals work in accounting firms, brokerage houses, banks, and other financial institutions. In recent years, the banking industry has become one of the largest employers of legal assistants, who typically review loan applications, work with attorneys in litigation matters, or monitor bank-regulatory agencies and the actions of legislative committees.

Real Estate

Real-estate developers, property-management firms, escrow and title companies, and construction companies have found paralegals to be especially useful in transactions involving zoning regulations, drafting sales documents, ordering real property titles, organizing documents for and conducting closings, and assisting in arranging financing.

In addition, some paralegals have found their services to be in demand with *homeowners' associations,* groups of individual homeowners who are responsible for carrying out the conditions, covenants, and restrictions applicable to a particular housing tract or condominium.

Insurance Companies

Insurance companies employ paralegals as claims adjustors, claims processors, litigation assistants, researchers, and monitors of the activities of insurance-regulatory agencies and legislative committees. Within private law firms and corporate legal departments, many paralegals have expanded their roles in diverse directions, including paralegal supervisor or administrator, personnel assistant, office manager or administrator, litigation support manager, project case manager, and information-systems specialist.

This list of employment opportunities within the private sector is by no means exhaustive. It does illustrate, however, how diverse the opportunities are in the private sector and perhaps will help you realize that opportunities are virtually everywhere for paralegals. There is no doubt that what once may have been considered a career path lacking in opportunities is now viewed as a profession limited only by individual ambition.

1–4 Paralegal Duties and Responsibilities

Paralegal duties differ somewhat based upon area of specialization; the paralegal's level of experience, authority, and responsibility in the organization; and each attorney's willingness to delegate certain duties and responsibilities to the paralegal. Chapter 10 outlines in more detail the typical duties for a paralegal by area of specialization. However, there are some duties that are performed by the majority of paralegals, whether specialists or generalists.

Duties in General

The duties outlined in this section are intended as guidelines only and are not all-inclusive. They are merely examples of the duties a paralegal might typically perform. For instance, most paralegals perform the following duties, regardless of their area of specialization:

- Conduct client interviews to gather background information
- Refer clients to government agencies as required
- Correspond with clients, attorneys, and others on factual matters
- Draft correspondence, memoranda, documents, and pleadings
- Organize and maintain client files and form files
- Maintain calendar of court dates and other critical dates
- Assemble information, documents, and evidence related to case or client
- Prepare and file various forms, reports, and applications
- Review and summarize answers to interrogatories, depositions, police reports, medical records, documents, and transcripts

- Assist in maintaining law library and current binders of court rules
- Research procedural, administrative, and case law
- Track legislation that may affect clients
- Review legal periodicals and material related to area of interest

1–5 Compensation

According to information supplied by the U.S. Department of Labor, Bureau of Labor Statistics, the earnings of paralegals vary greatly, depending upon education, training, experience, type of employer, and the geographic location of the job. Paralegals who work for large law firms or in large metropolitan areas usually earn more than those who work for smaller firms or in less-populated regions.

In 1988 the last year for which the Department of Labor has information, the nationwide average annual salary for paralegals was about $24,900. Starting salaries averaged $20,900 for paralegals with no experience; those with three to five years of experience averaged $24,200 a year. Paralegals with more than 10 years of experience averaged $28,500 annually. Many paralegals received an annual bonus that averaged $1100, and the majority of employers provided life and health insurance benefits and contributed to a retirement plan on behalf of the paralegals.

In addition to experience, other factors contribute to determining salary. Firm size, city size, years of legal experience, and level of education have a relationship to compensation rates. Figure 1–5 illustrates the results of the 1991 National Utilization and Compensation Survey conducted by NALA, the National Association of Legal Assistants. According to their survey, although firm size and geographic location are important factors, years of experience and years with current employer have the strongest relationship to salary and compensation.

Factors in Determining Compensation

Salaries and hourly rates for paralegal services vary as much as the duties and responsibilities of the position. To help you understand why some people may feel they are not adequately compensated for their efforts, it is important to remember that in determining compensation for any position there are two points of view to consider: the employee's and the employer's. For the employee wages are, among other things, a tangible reward for services rendered. For the employer wages are the single greatest expense. Therefore, employers have the task of developing a compensation program that will satisfy and motivate employees, yet keep labor costs at an acceptable level.

In general, there are three major factors an employer considers when determining an employee's compensation.

Factor No. 1: Compensation Objectives Some law firms believe in compensating employees at or above the high end of the wage range in order to be able to choose from the best talent available. Other firms take a more conservative approach to compensation, hoping to attract employees who are motivated by needs other than money, such as working flexible hours or close to home.

Figure 1–5 Mean Salary and Compensation by Size of Firm

MEAN SALARY AND COMPENSATION BY SIZE OF FIRM

	Mean Salary	Mean Compensation
Sole Practitioner	24489	26337
2–5 Attorneys	26234	28348
6–10 Attorneys	25846	27224
11–15 Attorneys	27440	29154
16–20 Attorneys	26945	27777
21–30 Attorneys	27866	29351
31–35 Attorneys	28835	30743
36–40 Attorneys	28457	29700
41–45 Attorneys	29419	30767
46–50 Attorneys	30361	32603
51–55 Attorneys	28915	30415
56–60 Attorneys	29090	30133
61–65 Attorneys	29472	29194
66–70 Attorneys	29500	30486
71–75 Attorneys	31759	32210
76–80 Attorneys	30341	32408
81–85 Attorneys	31236	39200
86–90 Attorneys	29406	32808
91–95 Attorneys	30833	33000
96–100 Attorneys	29229	32615
Over 100 Attorneys	32095	35950

Source: Reprinted with permission of the National Association of Legal Assistants, Inc., Tulsa, OK.

Whichever approach to compensation the firm adopts, its general attitude and philosophy toward employees is often reflected in the way the employees are compensated. For example, a firm that highly values its employees and is interested in developing a loyal staff with little turnover will usually have a very competitive compensation program.

Factor No. 2: External Economic Conditions When determining employee compensation, the firm must also consider external economic conditions including:

1. Conditions of the labor market,
2. Wage rates for the area, and
3. Cost of living.

Labor Market Conditions Supply of and demand for qualified labor is reflected by the labor market. When demand for skilled labor is high and supply is low, not only do wages rise, but recruiting qualified employees becomes extremely difficult.

In recent years, the supply of paralegals has grown at an unprecedented rate, with supply exceeding demand in some areas, thus keeping wages for beginning paralegals lower than expected. At the same time, the supply of legal secretaries and legal word processors has decreased, although demand for these skills is at an all-time high. The basic economic law of supply and demand explains why some legal secretaries are currently paid more than paralegals—there are simply fewer of them and their skills are very much in demand.

Area Wage Rates The firm's wage structure should provide rates that are in line with those being paid by other firms in the area. If a firm's wage rates drift above existing area levels, labor costs, as a percentage of the firm's total expenses, may become excessive. When this condition occurs, the firm could be in danger of going out of business. On the other hand, if wages are allowed to drop below area levels, the firm will encounter difficulty in recruiting and retaining competent personnel.

Every industry and profession conducts wage surveys, usually on an annual basis. This information is then published by trade groups or professional associations. For example, salary information is available to paralegals who are members of either a local or national paralegal association. Employment agencies and personnel recruiters (commonly known as headhunters) are also reliable sources of information about prevailing wage rates in their geographical areas. In addition, your state's Department of Labor gathers wage, salary, and employee benefit statistics on a regular basis and should be able to provide you with current information for your area.

Cost of Living Factors Inflation makes it necessary to adjust compensation rates to keep up with purchasing power. In times of runaway inflation, *cost-of-living adjustments* (COLA), an index that considers the rate of inflation and its impact on purchasing power are usually made on a quarterly basis. At other times, these adjustments are made annually. COLA adjustments are based upon changes in the *consumer price index* (CPI), a measure of the average change in prices over time in a fixed "market basket" of goods and services including food, clothing, shelter, fuels, transportation fares, charges for medical services, and other day-to-day goods and services. COLA and CPI figures are compiled and published by both state and federal Departments of Commerce. Most employers, including law firms, consider one or both of these factors in determining base salary rates as well as annual increases.

Factor No. 3: Internal Considerations Internal factors that influence wage rates include:

1. The worth of the job to the firm,
2. The employee's relative worth, and
3. The employer's ability to pay.

Job Worth One major internal factor influencing wage rates is the worth of the job to the organization. Since paralegal time can be billed to clients, the relative worth of these billable hours to the firm should be considered when determining a paralegal's compensation. However, some firms have not yet shifted their viewpoint to seeing the paralegal as a revenue producer rather than an overhead expense.

Employee's Worth After determining the worth of the position to the firm, the next step in determining compensation is to evaluate the employee's relative worth to the firm in terms of meeting the job requirements. Education and experience are usually high on the list of factors in determining the value of a particular employee to the firm.

Ability to Pay Finally, the employer's ability to pay must be considered. All employers simply cannot afford to pay the same wages and benefits. There are differences in ability to pay, for example, between the public sector and the private sector, between large firms and small ones. In a district attorney's office, a public-sector employer, the amount of pay and benefits for paralegals and other employees is limited by the funds budgeted for this purpose and by the taxpayers' willingness to provide them.

In a private law firm, pay levels are determined by the amount of fees generated and the profits a firm can derive from the services they provide. Thus, in the private law firm, pay levels are determined in large part by the productivity of its employees and its ability to invest in labor-saving equipment to keep costs down.

Of course, economic conditions and competition from other firms for clients will also have a significant impact on the rates a firm can afford to pay. In the past, the practice of law was somewhat recession-proof. Today, however, a severe economic downturn can reduce law firm fee income much as losing a major client to a competitor might. Law firms feeling a recessionary squeeze may have little choice but to reduce wages, lay off employees, or go out of business.

In the final analysis, compensation is only one factor in choosing a career as a paralegal. Most people choose this profession because they love the law and the imperfect U.S. legal system and want to be a part of it.

1–6 Aptitude and Attitude

Why do you want to be a paralegal? Do you have the personal characteristics necessary to be successful? Is this the appropriate career choice for you? Your answers to these and other questions could help you in determining whether a career as a paralegal is suitable for you.

Fantasy and Reality

The public's fascination with the practice of law may be evidenced by the number of television shows and movies about lawyers, courtrooms, judges, private investigators, and good guys and bad guys. Unfortunately, all the excitement and drama that take place on the screen is often far from reality.

On a day-to-day basis, real life is boring. Most people live from one day to the next experiencing few, if any, dramatic moments. Hang around any law office or courtroom any day of the week and you will quickly see that much of what takes place is dull and routine. There is a conspicuous absence of the sophisticated, clever, and sometimes romantic repartee many have come to associate with the practice of law. Instead, you are more likely to find hardworking, dedicated professionals who still possess a degree of idealism and who are having a love affair with the law.

Characteristics of Successful Paralegals

Television shows and movies about the law focus on attorneys, judges, police, and criminals. Most fail to include legal assistants or, when they do include them, portray the role inaccurately.

If you are not familiar with the day-to-day workings of the typical law office, you could learn more about it by interviewing as many people as you can who are intimately familiar with the advantages and disadvantages of pursuing a career in this fascinating, frustrating, yet always challenging profession.

Figure 1–6 Personal Characteristics Assessment

PERSONAL CHARACTERISTICS ASSESSMENT

Respond to each statement by placing a check mark in the "Yes" or "No" column.

	Statement	Yes	No
1.	My life and my work are usually well organized.	____	____
2.	Methodical and meticulous are words used to describe me.	____	____
3.	I can make order out of chaos.	____	____
4.	I use logic to organize my thoughts and information.	____	____
5.	Following up on the smallest details does not annoy me.	____	____
6.	Most people would say I am patient and persistent.	____	____
7.	I am an assertive communicator.	____	____
8.	I am proud of my writing skills.	____	____
9.	Doing library research is a treat.	____	____
10.	I do not get upset when people are loud and angry.	____	____
11.	Resolving conflicts with others is a challenge to me.	____	____
12.	Everything about the law is interesting to me.	____	____
13.	I regularly set goals and attain them.	____	____
14.	Long hours and hard work are not a problem for me.	____	____
15.	I have learned to manage stress.	____	____
16.	My hobbies include reading.	____	____
17.	Problems are opportunities.	____	____
18.	I am willing to be held responsible and accountable for my decisions and actions, and in some cases, for the decisions and actions of others.	____	____
19.	I am dependable and consistent.	____	____
20.	I believe learning is a life long activity.	____	____

Scoring:
15–20 Yes answers—You should be very successful.
10–14 Yes answers—Success will come with a little extra effort.
5–9 Yes answers—You will be successful if you recognize your weaknesses and are willing to work hard.
Less than 5 Yes answers—Long hard road ahead; re-evaluate your career choice.

Pay particular attention to your "No" answers. They will not only provide you with insight regarding your attitude and aptitude towards a career as a paralegal, they are also indications of areas where you might want to place some extra emphasis to ensure success.

Complete the personal characteristics assessment in Figure 1–6, which may help you to determine whether being a paralegal is the career for you. Since you will be expending an enormous amount of time and energy in your studies and later in your work, you should be aware of the characteristics most likely required for success as a paralegal.

SUMMARY

1–1

When the United States was in its formative years, any man 18 years of age or older of good moral character could represent himself and others in legal matters. For the past 200 years, the U.S. legal system has been struggling to find answers to two important questions: what actions constitute practicing law, and who is qualified to do it. The question of whether legal assistants should be regulated was formally raised in 1974 in the Tunney hearings, 10 years after the federal government had established the Office of Economic Opportunity to provide legal services to the poor by hiring and training paralegals. The questions facing the profession today are not whether the paralegal profession will be regulated, but how regulation will be done and who will do it.

1–2

Many employment opportunities exist for paralegals in the public sector of law, including positions in lobbying and governmental relations work, providing prepaid group legal services, working in legal clinics and neighborhood outlets, and through public advocacy groups. Conventional public sector opportunities include positions with the federal, state, and local governments.

1–3

The largest source of employment for paralegals in the private sector is private law firms. However, opportunities also exist in corporate legal departments and with companies who manufacture or sell information management technology to law firms. In addition, the fields of consulting, journalism, advertising, public relations, and marketing require the services of legal researchers. Paralegals also work in banks, brokerage houses, real estate, and insurance companies. Employment opportunities for paralegals in the private sector are limited only by individual ambition.

1–4

Although the duties of an individual paralegal vary by area of specialization, level of experience, and the types of projects delegated by attorneys, most paralegals are expected to perform certain core duties including interviewing clients, corresponding with appropriate parties, drafting court documents, organizing client files, reviewing and summarizing legal documents, and assisting in maintaining the law library.

1–5

There are several factors to consider when determining compensation for a paralegal. Among them are the overall objectives of the firm; the external economic conditions of the labor market, area wage rates, and the cost of living for the area; and internal factors such as the worth of the job to the firm, the employee's relative worth, and the employer's ability to pay. Paralegals who stay in the field gaining experience and expertise are generally well compensated for their services.

1–6

The real life of a paralegal is often quite different from the fantasy of law portrayed on television and in movies. Successful paralegals need the ability to maintain a positive attitude toward themselves, their work, and others. In addition, successful paralegals are organized, methodical, logical thinkers, good communicators, good readers and researchers, and able to work hard for long hours under intense pressure.

REVIEW

Key Terms

Before proceeding, review the key terms listed below to be sure you understand each one. If necessary, read over the corresponding section of the chapter. When you are ready to test your understanding, answer the Review Questions.

generalist
in pro se
legal assistant
legal technician
paralegal
private sector
public sector
regulate

Questions for Review and Discussion

1. Compare and contrast the terms *legal assistant*, *paralegal*, and *legal technician*.
2. Discuss the history of the U.S. legal profession.
3. In which states is reading for the law still acceptable?
4. Discuss how the paralegal profession was established.
5. Discuss the controversy surrounding the regulation of paralegals.
6. List employment opportunities for paralegals in the public sector.
7. List employment opportunities for paralegals in the private sector.
8. Compare and contrast the duties and responsibilities of the first legal assistants with those of the paralegals of the twenty-first century.
9. What are the factors in determining a paralegal's compensation?
10. What characteristics are important to be a successful paralegal?

Activities

1. Invite a paralegal from the district attorney's office or other governmental agency to speak to the class on the subject of "A Day in the Life of a Paralegal."
2. Invite a paralegal from a private law firm and corporate legal department to describe a typical workday to the class.
3. Ask a member of the National Federation of Paralegal Associations (NFPA) and a member of the National Association of Legal Assistants (NALA) to debate the advantages and disadvantages of regulating paralegals before the class.
4. Ask members of the class to conduct a survey on compensation for paralegals in your area by contacting the local paralegal association, employment agencies, and the state Department of Labor.
5. Organize a field trip to the local courthouse and request permission to sit in on courtroom proceedings. Lead a discussion on the fantasy and the reality of a career in the legal profession.

CHAPTER 2 Law

OUTLINE

2–1 The Purpose and Function of Law
  Law
  Function of Law
2–2 Origins of the U.S. Legal System
  Common Law
  Statutory Law
  Substantive Law
  Procedural Law
2–3 How Federal Law Is Made
  The Federal Legislative System
  Federal Lawmaking in Action
  Constitutional Amendments
2–4 How State Law Is Made
2–5 How Local Law Is Made

COMMENTARY

Congratulations! Your homework paid off. Mr. Dunn wants you to begin working with him immediately as an entry-level legal assistant. Dunn & Sweeney is a well-known law firm in the community specializing primarily in business matters. After working at Dunn & Sweeney for a few weeks, you find that you are more intrigued by the law than ever. Since Mr. Dunn is involved in local and state politics, you have had the opportunity to meet the mayor, a state representative, and a U.S. Congressman from your state. Although you try to keep up with current issues and the various bills these politicians are sponsoring, you are not completely clear on the specifics of their jobs. So, you decide to look up information about the legal system and how laws are made.

OBJECTIVES

In the previous chapter you learned a little about the history of the U.S. legal system and the important roles that legal assistants play in it. After studying this chapter, you should be able to:

1. Define the terms *law*, *rules*, and *rights*.
2. Discuss what law does for people.
3. Discuss what law does not do for people.
4. Outline a brief history of the U.S. legal system.
5. Describe the common law system of jurisprudence.
6. Relate the principle of *stare decisis* to common law.
7. Distinguish the differences between substantive law and procedural law.

NOTES

8. Outline the federal legislative system.
9. Compare and contrast the federal legislative system and the state legislative system.
10. Describe the differences between a city governed by a mayor and by a city manager.

2–1 The Purpose and Function of Law

Some people think we have too many laws and others think there should be more. The side you take in this argument will no doubt have something to do with what you think laws are supposed to do and the reasons for them.

Law

Defining law is not an easy task. Many well-known legal scholars refuse to try and instead refer to the fact that many of their predecessors could not agree upon a definition. Nevertheless, Steven H. Gifis, Associate Professor of Law at Rutgers, makes an attempt in his *Law Dictionary* (New York: Barron's Educational Series, Inc., 1984) to define it.

Law, according to Prof. Gifis, is the legislative pronouncement of the rules that should guide one's actions in society; they are the official rules and principles of conduct established by legislative authority, court decisions, or local custom. Prof. Gifis even goes so far as to draw a distinction between *a* law and its plural *laws*, and *the* law. Laws refer to particular rules of action such as those of the Sherman Antitrust Act or the Civil Rights Act. *The law* refers to something more general, such as a recognized branch of law, for example, the law of **torts,** a private or civil wrong or injury. *The law* is often used also to refer to the institutions and people who represent and administer the law, such as courts, prisons, judges, lawyers, and police.

A federal or state **constitution** is the written instrument that sets forth the structure of laws by which a government is created and according to which a country or state is governed. The constitution is the basic source from which a government derives its power and under which governmental powers are both granted and restricted. It is the emphasis on restrictions that makes the U.S. Constitution different from those of other countries. In U.S. law, the Constitution gives permanence and stability to government, but it is not designed to protect majorities. The authors of the Constitution thought that majorities could protect themselves, but that minorities would need to have their rights preserved and protected against the arbitrary actions of those in power. The U.S. Constitution provides the basic laws to which everyone must conform; it is the supreme law of the land and cannot be repealed under any circumstances. It can, however, be amended, although this is so rarely done that only 27 times has the Constitution been amended in the past 200 years. Like the federal Constitution, a state constitution is the supreme law within the state and cannot be repealed, only amended.

The entire U.S. system of laws is derived from a combination of the divine or moral laws, the laws of nature, and human experience. To meet society's needs and to provide guidance for that society, laws must continually change as society's needs change. The continually challenging and often frustrating work for legal assistants is to stay informed of these changes in the laws.

Rules **Rules,** on the other hand, are quite different from laws. Rules are standards, regulations, guidelines, or methods of proceeding, and they are enforceable only by the institution, organization, agency, or entity that made them. For example, the American Bar Association has its Rules for Professional Conduct that members of the legal profession are expected to follow. Likewise, there are rules of civil and criminal procedure that the clerk of the court requires you to follow. Will you be thrown in jail if you do not follow the rules? Unlikely—although you will, no doubt, be reprimanded and perhaps punished in some way. Will you be thrown in jail if you do not follow the law? Perhaps—it would depend upon the law you violated. However, the punishment for breaking a law is likely to be more severe than the punishment for failing to follow a rule.

Throughout history one fact about the law has remained constant: the number of laws increases in direct proportion to the complexity of technology and to the number of people in the society. For example, most people agree that automobiles are more comfortable and provide a faster means of transportation than horses. They also create more hazards and problems requiring laws and rules to regulate their use. Likewise, few paralegals would willingly trade in a computer for a typewriter or pad and pencil. But the proliferation of computers has required new laws and rules to regulate the people who make them, the people who sell them, and the people who use them.

You do not have to be a futurist to see that the rate of change in technology and the continuing growth in population will lead to the creation of more laws and rules to regulate our society.

Rights U.S. law has another purpose in addition to guiding your actions in society. It spells out clearly what the government cannot do to you. In our legal system, laws cannot stop you from stating your opinion about anyone or anything, nor from assembling peacefully in a demonstration of protest or support. Neither will the law allow your home, automobile, or person to be searched without someone first convincing a judge that you are probably hiding something illegal. You cannot be arrested without a warrant or probable cause.

The first 10 amendments to the United States Constitution, known as the Bill of Rights, deal entirely with all the actions that the government cannot legally take against you. Legal **rights** are individual liberties either expressly provided for in the state or federal constitutions, or that have been found to exist as those constitutions have been interpreted. Legal rights are those that a person is entitled to have, or to do, or to receive from others within the limits prescribed by law. Former Attorney General of the United States Ramsey Clark put it this way: "A right is not what someone gives you; it's what no one can take away."

Function of Law

The law plays an important part in shaping the social environment. For example, the Supreme Court decisions on school segregation and abortion have had a significant effect on the nature of our lives. So, too, have congressional statutes on welfare and equal employment opportunity, as well as the decision to declare war.

Some laws are ineffective. Since the beginning of recorded history, there have been laws against killing and stealing. Yet these laws have often been unequally enforced. Noblemen of the Middle Ages were rarely punished for killing a serf, and in the last few decades only a few criminals on death row have been

Figure 2–1 The Bill of Rights

THE BILL OF RIGHTS

AMENDMENT I Congress shall make no law respecting an establishment of religion, or prohibiting the free exercise thereof; or abridging the freedom of speech, or of the press, or the right of the people peaceably to assemble, and to petition the Government for redress of grievances.

AMENDMENT II A well regulated Militia, being necessary to the security of a free State, the right of the people to keep and bear Arms, shall not be infringed.

AMENDMENT III No Soldier shall, in time of peace be quartered in any house, without the consent of the Owner, nor in time of war, but in a manner to be prescribed by law.

AMENDMENT IV The right of the people to be secure in their persons, houses, papers and effects, against unreasonable searches and seizures, shall not be violated, and no Warrants shall issue, but upon probable cause, supported by Oath or affirmation, and particularly describing the place to be searched, and the persons or things to be seized.

AMENDMENT V No person shall be held to answer for a capital, or otherwise infamous crime, unless on a presentment or indictment of a Grand Jury, except in cases arising in the land or naval forces, or in the Militia, when in actual service in time of War or public danger; nor shall any person be subject to the same offence to be twice put in jeopardy of life or limb, nor shall be compelled in any criminal case to be a witness against himself, nor be deprived of life, liberty, or property, without due process of law; nor shall private property be taken for public use without just compensation.

AMENDMENT VI In all criminal prosecutions, the accused shall enjoy the right to a speedy and public trial, by an impartial jury of the State and district wherein the crime shall have been committed; which district shall have been previously ascertained by law, and to be informed of the nature and cause of the accusation; to be confronted with the witnesses against him; to have compulsory process of obtaining witnesses in his favor, and to have the Assistance of Counsel for his defense.

AMENDMENT VII In Suits at common law, where the value in controversy shall exceed twenty dollars, the right of trial by jury shall be preserved, and no fact tried by a jury shall be otherwise reexamined in any Court of the United States, than according to the rules of the common law.

AMENDMENT VIII Excessive bail shall not be required, nor excessive fines imposed, nor cruel and unusual punishments inflicted.

AMENDMENT IX The enumeration in the Constitution of certain rights shall not be construed to deny or disparage others retained by the people.

AMENDMENT X The powers not delegated to the United States by the Constitution, nor prohibited by it to the States, are reserved to the States, respectively, or to the people.

The year 1991 marked the 200th anniversary of the adoption of The Bill of Rights to the United States Constitution.

executed even though the punishment for their crimes was death. Landlords collect rents on properties that do not meet health and safety codes while the tenants who must live in these filthy and unsafe buildings are evicted if they do not pay the rent.

What Law Does for People When you think about what laws are supposed to do for people, what is the first thing that comes to your mind? If you thought the purpose of law is to settle disputes, you would be right. Disputes occur between private parties, between units of government, and between private parties and the government. When parties engaged in a dispute cannot come to some resolution on their own, they often look to the law to help them solve their problems or resolve their differences.

If you thought laws are supposed to maintain order, you are also right. For example, because criminal laws carry the threat of imprisonment and/or fines if the laws are violated they do provide some degree of protection against violence to people and their property. Maintaining order through laws in our legal system includes the policing function, the court's role in trials and sentencing, and protection against the violent overthrow of the government. To maintain order, the law allows for certain uses of force by the government and its agencies but not by private parties, except in cases of unusual circumstance.

There is much more that the law does for people besides settling disputes and maintaining order. Laws provide a framework within which to live our daily lives. For example, we expect that those who have caused injuries will compensate others for those injuries; that those who have made promises will be held to their promises; that those who own property have exclusive rights in that ownership and are free to dispose of it as they wish. These expectations created by the framework of the law are another illustration of the interaction between law and society.

In addition, the law provides ways, in both constitution and statute, for the machinery of government to operate in balanced efficiency by allocating specific kinds of power to specific branches of government in an attempt to avoid overloading any one branch.

Another vital function of law is to protect the citizens against excessive or unfair government power. The Bill of Rights protects such basic rights as the freedom of speech, press, and religion, the right to a degree of privacy and against unreasonable searches and seizure, the privilege against self-incrimination, and the right to a jury trial for crime. Furthermore, the Fifth Amendment to the U.S. Constitution provides that no person shall "be deprived of life, liberty, or property, without due process of law." Although the interpretation of **due process** changes periodically to reflect changing times, the traditional meaning refers to a course of legal action according to rules and principles that have been established by our legal system for the protection and enforcement of private rights. In other words, the government cannot deprive you of your life, freedom, or property on a whim.

Likewise, our legal system is concerned with protecting people against excessive or unfair private power. Antitrust laws protect people against the monopolistic power of private corporations; minimum-wage laws and discrimination-in-employment laws curb an employer's power; and, a corporation's power in the sale of its securities is controlled by the Securities and Exchange Commission (SEC). Similar restrictions can be found in all levels of government and their myriad regulatory laws and administrative agencies.

Some laws are aimed specifically at assuring people an opportunity to enjoy life through the protection of their financial and physical health. Examples are unemployment and Social Security laws, bankruptcy and wage-garnishment statutes, Medicare, welfare, public housing, and antipollution legislation.

What Law Does Not Do for People Some people expect laws to do too much. Some expect that passing a law will change an attitude or feeling. Laws do not change attitudes and feelings, but they do change people's behavior. For example, some employers still hold the attitude that a woman's place is in the home. An employer with this attitude may be unhappy about hiring a qualified female applicant and may even look for reasons not to hire her. But the law says that an employer may not discriminate in employment because of sex. Further, the employer may not offer a woman lower pay or fewer benefits than a man in the same position. Although the law is specific about prohibiting discrimination

Figure 2–2 Government Pamphlets

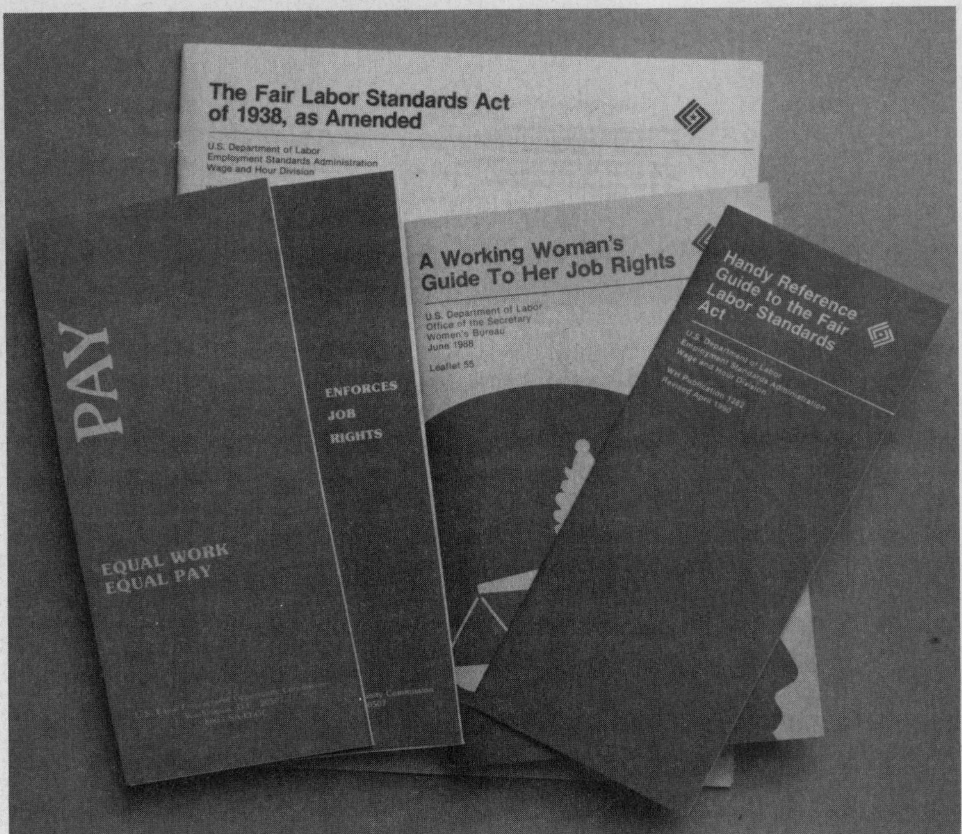

Pamphlets explaining fair labor practices are available through the U. S. Department of Labor. *Source*: Aaron Haupt.

in employment and can change behavior, it cannot do anything about changing attitudes and feelings.

In fact, any proposed law with the particular intention of changing attitudes or feelings is doomed from the start. People draw the line at having their feelings and attitudes legislated. Laws do, however, require people to act fairly and equitably regardless of their feelings about the situation or the individuals involved. However, oftentimes the passing of a law can cause people on their own to change their attitudes and feelings.

Restricting smoking in certain public areas is an example of how passing a law can change attitudes. Before smoking in restaurants, offices, and airplanes became a national health issue, many people had no particular feelings one way or the other about the matter. Nonsmokers may not have liked being around smokers, but few made an issue of it. As awareness of the health hazards resulting from smoking or breathing secondhand smoke became more prevalent, smokers and nonsmokers alike began to examine their attitudes and feelings about smoking in general. Since the passage of laws restricting smoking in public places, many lifelong smokers have kicked the habit, and many nonsmokers have become more assertive in standing up for their rights. Some people will continue to smoke and will dislike the restrictions placed upon them, but the laws that protect nonsmokers and smokers alike will have a lasting impact on behavior and attitudes about the use of tobacco and the industry as a whole.

Figure 2–3 A Typical Office

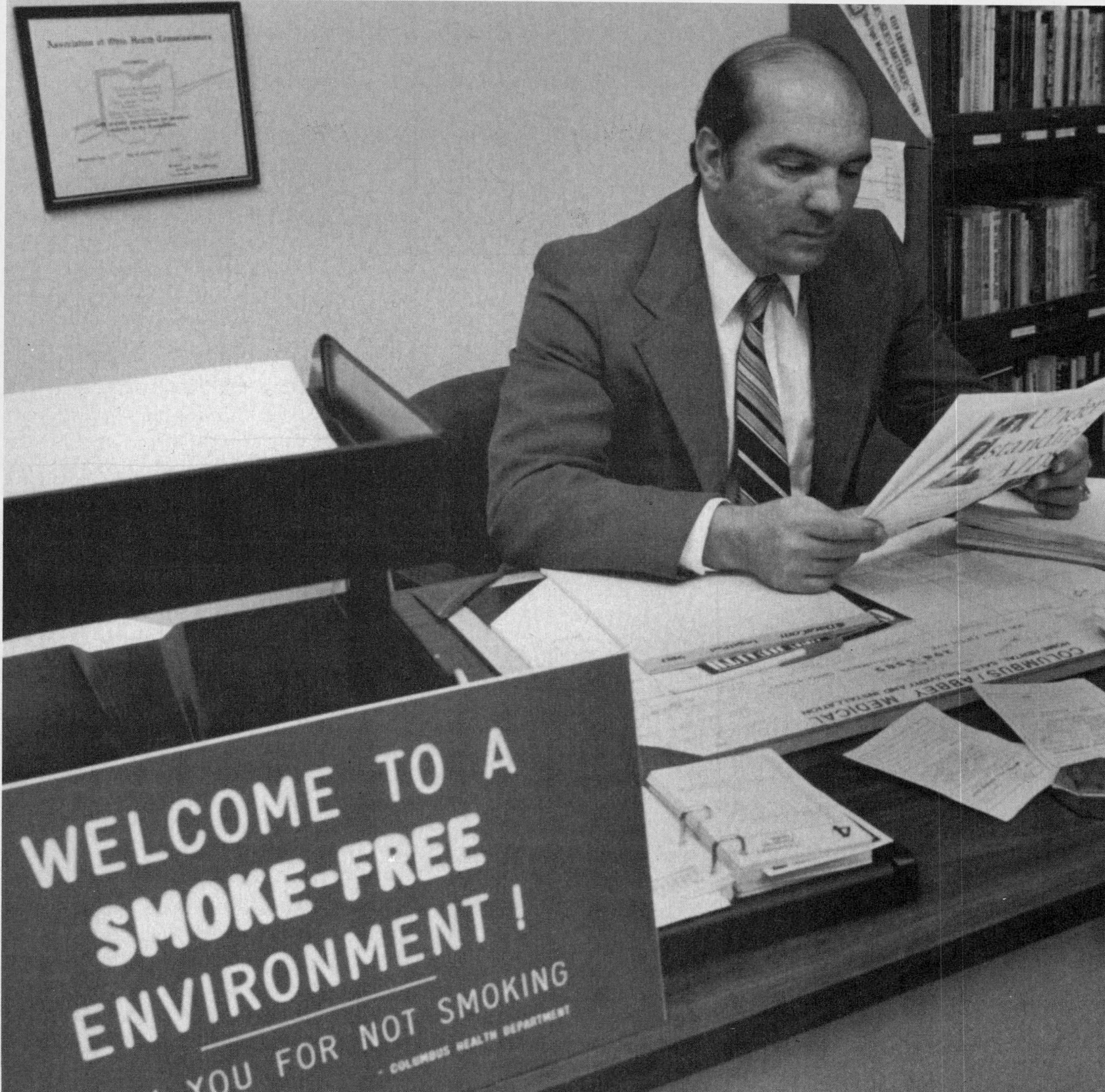

Public place alerts workers and visitors that it is a smoke-free environment. *Source*: File photo.

Ethics and Morals Does the law also have an ethical or moral function? It would appear that it does. In settling disputes the law attempts to reach solutions that are not only fair but socially desirable. For example, criminal laws carry out ethical rules of conduct, many of which are in the Ten Commandments. Likewise, the principles of tort law concerning negligent or intentional infliction of injury can be traced to the Golden Rule: treat others as you want and expect to be treated. Similarly, the obligation to keep promises is an ethical obligation. The standard phrases of legal conduct, such as "good faith," "fair and equitable," and "unjust enrichment" suggest that the law does have an ethical and moral function as well as the more pragmatic functions of providing a structure and rules for society.

Although some people argue that the American legal system is harsh and ineffective; that it is burdensome and cumbersome; that it favors the rich and ignores the poor; it is the system with which you will have to work. It is important for you to remember that laws, rules, and rights are not supposed to regulate feelings or attitudes. Rather, they are supposed to, and do, regulate actions within an ethical and moral framework. Therefore, your work as a paralegal is all about facts as they pertain to certain actions and behavior, not emotions.

2–2 Origins of the U.S. Legal System

Our Founding Fathers (and Mothers) had their hands full in adjusting to their new country. Establishing legal order takes time, and the early settlers were in no particular hurry. After all, they came to the new country to escape religious and legal tyranny, and they were not anxious to repeat past mistakes. When it came to settling disputes, making rules, and keeping the peace, they called upon a respected community member of good moral character to make decisions about how they should live (see Chapter 1, p. 3).

Common Law

As you might expect, since nearly all the early settlers of our country came from England, the U.S. legal system is based upon the common law of Medieval England and its predecessor, the 2000-year-old civil or Roman law. **Common law** is defined as the system of **jurisprudence,** a philosophy, science, or system of laws of a country, that originated in England during a time when judges in the small towns and villages resolved disputes by making decisions based upon common sense, fairness, and social custom.

Both ancient and modern common law are generally derived from principles rather than rules that are not absolute, fixed, or inflexible. From inception the principles of common law have been determined by the social needs of the community and have changed as required to meet those needs. Since decisions were not written down in Medieval England, judges and lawyers were forced to rely upon personal recollection and reliable **hearsay,** secondhand testimony or evidence, regarding decisions made before their time. From this practice, the principle of ***stare decisis,*** or **precedent,** developed.

The Latin term *stare decisis* means to stand by that which was decided. In other words, when a court makes a decision based upon the facts of the case before it, that decision is used, unless the decision is subsequently overturned or voided, to provide guidance for other courts facing a later case with similar facts. Common law, during these early times, began to resemble modern-day case law. But it was not until the 1200s that written records of decisions were kept. Obviously, written records provided a more reliable source of earlier decisions than memory. Over time a policy developed that a decision of a court would be binding on that court, as well as other courts of equal or lower status, when confronted with the same or similar issues.

The reason most people readily adopted this policy of relying on precedent is simple: a community or society must have rules of conduct to follow in order to function. People need to know what the rules of conduct are, and once established, the rules will not be easily changed. Common-law courts are so reluctant to interfere with legal precedent that they often uphold prior decisions even though they would decide otherwise if the question before the court were a new one.

Statutory Law

Although common law was the primary source of rules in England, statutory law came to play an increasingly important role. Statutory law is derived from **statutes,** or acts of a legislative body, and is commonly referred to as *legislation*. Statutes are enacted to prescribe conduct, define crimes, appropriate public monies, and in general, promote the public good and welfare. But to the layperson the meaning of *statutes* is often unclear, and it is not always obvious whether a particular statute applies to a given set of facts. So, the courts were given the responsibility of interpreting the statutes and applying them to matters before the court.

The rules governing the early Pilgrims and the various states in which they settled were based upon English common law, statutory law, and the principle of *stare decisis*. These same principles form the backbone of today's U.S. legal system.

Substantive Law

Substantive laws are those laws that create, define, and regulate the rights and duties of individuals, as well as the circumstances under which a court will grant one person the right to sue another. All of the rules and regulations governing our daily lives are examples of substantive laws. These laws are sometimes established by the legislature or may be handed down in decisions by the courts.

Frequently courts are asked to clarify the meaning of substantive laws. In so doing, they may first have to clarify the meaning of a particular statute. If there is no applicable statute, the court then resorts to deciding what the common law rule should be, given the facts of the case. If a rule has been established by precedent *(stare decisis)*, then the court must decide whether the facts of the present case fit the rule. These decisions are reached by examining existing rules of substantive law, by using common sense, and by applying the principles of justice.

Substantive laws often form the basis for a legal **cause of action,** a claim in law or fact sufficient to demand judicial attention. If the **complaint,** the first pleading of the **plaintiff** (the one who initially brings the action) fails to state a proper cause of action, it will be **dismissed** (removed from court or "thrown out").

Procedural Law

Procedural law is quite different from both common law and substantive law. **Procedural law** is the sets of rules that establish the mechanics or steps that people who are involved in a lawsuit or criminal procedure must follow. Procedural law describes the methods used to enforce the rights granted by substantive law. In other words, substantive laws are the rules and procedural laws are the methods of enforcing the rules.

Procedural laws are important because they establish the method by which people are able to access the legal system. Once access to the legal system has been gained, procedural laws spell out the steps to take in preparing for trial, the rules of conduct during the trial, and how to enforce the court's **judgment,** the written version of the judge's decision. For example, if someone owes you money for services that were performed satisfactorily and he or she refuses to pay it, he or she is probably violating a rule of contract law. You may have sufficient cause to sue the debtor. If you live in California and the amount due is $5000 or less, you would file a lawsuit in small claims court. The procedures you would follow would be contained in the procedural laws that govern small claims court cases.

Procedural law also provides the method by which each party presents his or her story to the court and keeps the parties focused on only the relevant issues. In addition, procedural laws provide the means for discovering the other side's position. This prevents either side from having the unfair advantage of the dramatic courtroom surprise so often depicted in television and movie dramas. The goal of procedural law is to bring order to the dispute-settling process so that it will be handled fairly, quickly, and correctly.

Each state has its own set of procedural laws. For example, in California, procedural laws are found in books called the *California Rules of Civil Procedure* and the *California Rules of Criminal Procedure.* Similarly, the procedural rules for federal courts are found in volumes designated as *Federal Rules of Civil Procedure* and *Federal Rules of Criminal Procedure.* Procedural laws change frequently. Since lawyers often rely heavily upon paralegals for their knowledge of procedural law, it is the paralegal's responsibility to stay informed of changes as they occur.

2–3 How Federal Law Is Made

Some laws are easily made and others take more time. In 1914, when the United States Congress designated the second Sunday in May as Mother's Day, there was no debate. Some members of Congress made flowery speeches praising motherhood in general and their mothers in particular. If legislators in either house of Congress felt that mothers did not deserve to have an official day of recognition, they did not say so. The Mother's Day designation is not an enforceable law. You are free to take Mom to dinner or send her flowers and candy, or you can ignore the occasion. The designation of Mother's Day as a piece of legislation required nothing from anyone, and so it was easy to pass.

On the other hand, there is a good possibility that the same members of Congress who read several pages of copy praising mothers into the *Congressional Record* (the printed document containing all Congressional speeches and actions) might strongly work to defeat any bill that is designed to assist mothers. Such bills might be designated to establish federally funded day-care centers for working mothers, increase the income tax deduction for child care, or provide funds to raise the standard of living for single mothers and children living in poverty. Unlike the bill designating Mother's Day, which requires nothing from anyone and is unenforceable, any bill that requires government funding and that would be legally enforced takes a considerable amount of time and effort to become a law.

The Federal Legislative System

The U.S. legislative system is based upon a system of checks and balances that makes it difficult to pass and enforce laws which are likely to seriously change

Figure 2–4 The Government of the United States

THE GOVERNMENT OF THE UNITED STATES

THE CONSTITUTION

LEGISLATIVE BRANCH

THE CONGRESS

Senate **House**

Architect of the Capitol
United States Botanic Garden
General Accounting Office
Government Printing Office
Library of Congress
Office of Technology Assessment
Congressional Budget Office
Copyright Royalty Tribunal
United States Tax Court

EXECUTIVE BRANCH

THE PRESIDENT

Executive Office of the President

White House Office
Office of Management and Budget
Council of Economic Advisers
National Security Council
Office of Policy Development
Office of National Drug Control Policy
National Critical Materials Council
Office of the U.S. Trade Representative
Council on Environmental Quality
Office of Science and Technology Policy
Office of Administration
National Space Council

THE VICE PRESIDENT

JUDICIAL BRANCH

THE SUPREME COURT OF THE UNITED STATES

United States Courts of Appeals
United States District Courts
United States Claims Courts
United States Court of Appeals for the Federal Circuit
United States Court of International Trade
Territorial Courts
United States Court of Military Appeals
United States Court of Veterans Appeals
Administrative Office of the United States Courts
Federal Judical Center

DEPARTMENT OF AGRICULTURE
DEPARTMENT OF COMMERCE
DEPARTMENT OF DEFENSE
DEPARTMENT OF EDUCATION
DEPARTMENT OF ENERGY
DEPARTMENT OF HEALTH AND HUMAN SERVICES
DEPARTMENT OF HOUSING AND URBAN DEVELOPMENT
DEPARTMENT OF THE INTERIOR
DEPARTMENT OF JUSTICE
DEPARTMENT OF LABOR
DEPARTMENT OF STATE
DEPARTMENT OF TRANSPORTATION
DEPARTMENT OF THE TREASURY
DEPARTMENT OF VETERANS AFFAIRS

INDEPENDENT ESTABLISHMENTS AND GOVERNMENT CORPORATIONS

ACTION
Administrative Conference of the U.S.
African Development Foundation
American Battle Monuments Commission
Appalachian Regional Commission
Board for International Broadcasting
Central Intelligence Agency
Commission on the Bicentennial of the United States Constitution
Commission on Civil Rights
Commission of Fine Arts
Commodity Futures Trading Commission
Consumer Product Safety Commission
Environmental Protection Agency
Equal Employment Opportunity Commission
Export-Import Bank of the U.S.
Farm Credit Administration
Federal Communications Commission
Federal Deposit Insurance Corporation
Federal Election Commission
Federal Emergency Management Agency
Federal Home Loan Bank Board
Federal Labor Relations Authority
Federal Maritime Commission
Federal Mediation and Conciliation Service
Federal Mine Safety and Health Review Commission
Federal Reserve System
Board of Governors of the Federal Retirement Thrift Investment Board
Federal Trade Commission
General Services Administration
Inter-American Foundation
Interstate Commerce Commission
Merit Systems Protection Board
National Aeronautics and Space Administration
National Archives and Records Administration
National Capital Planning Commission
National Credit Union Administration
National Foundation on the Arts and the Humanities
National Labor Relations Board
National Mediation Board
National Science Foundation
National Transportation Safety Board
Nuclear Regulatory Commission
Occupational Safety and Health Review Commission
Office of Personnel Management
Office of Special Counsel
Panama Canal Commission
Peace Corps
Pennsylvania Avenue Development Corporation
Pension Benefit Guaranty Corporation
Postal Rate Commission
Railroad Retirement Board
Securities and Exchange Commission
Selective Service System
Small Business Administration
Tennessee Valley Authority
U.S. Arms Control and Disarmament Agency
U.S. Information Agency
U.S. International Development Corporation Agency
U.S. International Trade Commission
U.S. Postal Service

any aspect of our lives. This system of checks and balances in the federal government is composed of three branches: the legislative branch (the House of Representatives and the Senate, collectively called the Congress), the executive branch (the President and members of the Cabinet), and the judicial branch (Federal and Supreme Courts). None of these branches can pass a law without the consent and cooperation of the other two.

The President can and does make program suggestions to Congress, but then both houses of Congress must agree before a law is passed. If the law is challenged the courts will decide if the law is unconstitutional and whether to enforce it. Similarly, a member of Congress can introduce a bill suggesting a program and persuade the other members to pass it. But the President can veto the bill (and Congress, with a two-thirds majority vote, can override the President's veto to pass the bill), or the courts can find it unconstitutional. Although this system greatly slows down the legislative process, it does serve to protect us from overzealous legislators eager to please major election campaign contributors or a President who might be inclined to meddle with your rights and liberties.

The revision of an old law or the passage of a new one can take decades when the three branches of government become embroiled in controversy in the legislative process. Even a relatively simple revision of an existing law that requires funding and enforcement must pass through the Washington equivalent of a mined battlefield in the transformation process from a *bill* (a proposal) to an *act* (passed by Congress) to a *law* (signed by the President or passed by overturning the President's veto).

The purpose of the courts is not to initiate laws but to interpret existing ones. Courts have sometimes interpreted laws in ways that completely change established customs and lifestyles. Integration of public schools and *Roe v. Wade* are examples of Supreme Court decisions that had an impact on nearly every citizen of this country. Sometimes legislators, Presidents, and citizens throughout the country are unenthusiastic about some of the Court's interpretations, but everyone is required to comply with the Court's decisions regardless of personal feelings.

Congress also has the power to provide federal funding for all kinds of programs. State and local governments are not required to accept funds from the federal government for any program, but they rarely decline, even though some states occasionally worry about an infringement of their rights.

Federal Lawmaking in Action

Here is an example of how a bill becomes a law. Congresswoman Votegetter from Big State has been visited by large delegations of working mothers and fathers who feel they need government-supported day-care centers for infants. Large mailbags filled with letters from various groups and individuals arrive daily in the congresswoman's office in support of the day-care center for infants proposal. Congresswoman Votegetter has concluded that introducing a bill to establish federally subsidized day-care centers for very young children in all major cities in the United States would benefit the citizens of her district and help get her reelected.

With the help of her able paralegals, staff researchers, and bill writers, Congresswoman Votegetter introduces her bill, which is assigned number HR (for House of Representatives) 15455. The bill is then assigned to a House committee for hearings. Wanting to get the bill off to a good start, the Congresswoman makes a speech on the floor of the House outlining and emphasizing the need for day-care centers for very young children. Her staff sends a copy of her speech to everyone who has written or called her in support of the bill. Due to the large number of bills that are typically introduced each year, several months will pass before the bill is scheduled for hearing by one of the appropriate House committees.

When the bill finally gets to the Education and Labor Committee it is one of about 500 bills the committee chair must review. The committee chair thinks some of the other bills are more important than this one, but he owes Votegetter some favors. So, he assigns HR 15455 to a subcommittee that will hold hearings on it, probably on the same day the subcommittee is scheduled to hear other bills dealing with day care and related topics.

The subcommittee schedules a hearing on HR 15455. The politically astute congresswoman makes a personal appearance on behalf of her bill and is able to persuade a few of her colleagues to support it. In addition, representatives of various groups who support the bill also appear at the hearing, as well as a representative from a group that says the bill does not go far enough—this group wants night-care centers too, since some parents work at night. A social worker testifies that he can see a real need for day-care centers, and a pediatrician testifies that she believes that some infants might benefit from the day-care experience even if their mothers do not work outside the home.

Those who oppose the bill are also present. Some groups testify that the proposal will be too expensive and will require an increase in taxes. A psychologist testifies that infant children should not be separated from their mothers, and a second pediatrician says that infants do not benefit from day care. In addition, representatives from various groups testify that they feel that a mother's place is in the home, not on the job, and that child care is a personal responsibility, not an obligation of the government or the taxpayers.

The hearing has thoroughly confused most of the committee members and raised more questions. Several of the legislators have now given their research assistants the task of finding answers to some of the questions raised: Do the voters in my district want and need infant day-care centers? How do the various groups who support or oppose my reelection feel about this bill? What do teachers, social workers, and psychologists think the effect of this bill would be? What impact would this bill have on businesses and taxes?

Assuming that enough subcommittee members feel positively toward the bill, it will be recommended to the full Education and Labor Committee, which may or may not set up its own hearings. The full committee could just pass the bill or they might kill it.

If the bill passes the full committee, the next stop is the powerful Rules Committee, which decides whether or not the bill will be placed on the House calendar for the year. If it does not get on the House calendar, the bill is dead for that session. On the other hand, if the bill passes the Rules Committee it is then scheduled to come up for vote. Let's assume that not only is the infant day-care bill scheduled for vote but that the House passes it.

The next step is for Congresswoman Votegetter to make sure that a similar bill is passed in the Senate. Because she is an experienced legislator, Votegetter had one of the two senators from her home state introduce an infant day-care bill in the Senate at the same time that she introduced her proposal in the House.

The Senate bill was assigned a number, SB 1437, and went through the same process as the House bill—assignment to committee, then to subcommittee, and back to full committee with hearings along the way. Finally, SB 1437 ends up before the Senate Rules Committee, which has the power to decide what bills will be placed on the calendar for vote. The infant day-care bill could die in the Senate if the bill does not get placed on the calendar even if the hearing committee voted favorably on it. However, if the bill is not placed on the calendar for vote but has some strong supporters, they may be able to petition it directly onto the Senate floor for a vote. In this imaginary case, not only did Votegetter's bill get scheduled, but when it came up for a vote, the Senate passed it—although in a slightly different version from the one passed by the House. The Senate bill provides funding only if the centers will stay open day and night to accommodate working parents regardless of their hours.

The next step is to organize a committee of members from both the House and the Senate to write a compromise between the two bills they have passed. Then the new, identical bills may be referred back to the committees in the House and Senate where they were first discussed. Or, they may go directly to the floors of each for a vote. Once both the House and the Senate have voted to pass identical bills, now called an *act*, the next stop is the President. If the President has no objections to the bill, the measure will be signed into law.

After the President signs the bill into law, the question of funding is addressed. Originally, the bill called for 50 million dollars in funding, and it passed with that suggested appropriation. However, there is no authorization to make any money available to pay for all those new day-care centers. All this work has been to pass a bill to authorize a program, not to fund it. Another piece of legislation is required to permit the spending of federal funds for Votegetter's infant day-care center program.

The U.S. Constitution provides that all spending proposals must originate in the House and be approved by the House Ways and Means Committee. The chair of this committee, who may well be the second most powerful person in the federal government, is in charge of making recommendations and appropriations. If the Chair of the House Ways and Means Committee does not like the day-care center bill, there is a good chance it will not be funded. Congress frequently authorizes programs and then refuses to allocate funds for them. Or, Congress may decide to allocate some funds, but not the amount specified in the original bill.

Votegetter has two ways of trying to fund her program, which is now law. One way is to initiate a separate appropriations bill. The other way is to attach an amendment to the overall appropriations bill for the Department of Health and Human Services, which will supervise the program, that sets aside 50 million dollars for infant day-care centers. When discussing appropriations, Votegetter herself may oppose the funding of the original bill and instead urge the bill's supporters to settle for 30 million dollars. The reason she might do this is simple: Votegetter is always under pressure to satisfy all her constituents, some of whom are delighted that the infant day-care bill has passed and others who are calling upon her to oppose anything likely to cost tax money. Since she is a particularly astute politician who likes her job, Votegetter knows that if she is not reelected she will not be able to get this program funded and will have no chance to pass any other legislation. So, in order to save the bill and her career, she may be willing to support a compromise funding measure.

Politicians who compromise on some issues are not selling out or being hypocrites. It is sometimes a rational, practical choice if they want to be reelected. No doubt there are some issues on which compromise is not a choice, even if it means the loss of some support and votes. But few issues fall into this category. So politicians routinely make decisions on which issues to compromise and on which to hold firm.

This illustration of the fictitious infant day-care center bill is a relatively simplistic example of how federal law is made. In reality, complex societal issues such as day care or gun control may require decades of discussion and hearings before being resolved.

Constitutional Amendments

As mentioned before in Section 2–1, on rare occasions a bill introduced at the federal level will become a law and a constitutional amendment. One such bill was the Voting Rights Act. In most states a citizen had to be at least 21 years of age in order to vote, but in 1970 both houses of Congress passed bills giving 18-to-21-year-old citizens the right to vote in federal elections. President Nixon signed the bill into law.

The Voting Rights Act sparked heated debates throughout the country, and the discussions continued even after it became law. Several states asked the Supreme Court to declare the new law unconstitutional, stating that though it was legal for the federal government to set up rules on who could and could not vote in federal elections, they could not tell states and local governments how to conduct themselves. This new law, in effect, would create a two-tiered election system and be a costly administrative nightmare, since it granted this group the right to vote in federal elections only.

Within a few months after Congress passed the Voting Rights Act, the United States Supreme Court ruled that according to the Constitution, Congress did not have the right to tell states who could and could not vote in state and local elections. Therefore, in order to ensure that this new group of voters would be permitted to vote in *all* elections, a change in the Constitution was needed.

For a second time, subcommittee hearings were launched to discuss the intent of the law and the administrative problems it would likely cause. Members of the subcommittee concluded that Congress clearly intended for young voters to be able to vote in all elections and that the administrative problems created by dual voting practices would be enormous. The committee recommended that the only expedient way to clear up the legal confusion and problems created by the law was to initiate a federal constitutional amendment in Congress, with the hope that it would pass both houses of Congress and the required number of states in time for the 1972 presidential election.

The Senate and House promptly initiated resolutions and easily received the two-thirds vote of both houses required for adoption of a constitutional amendment. This time the intent of the amendment was clear. Anyone 18 years of age or older would be eligible to vote in any federal, state, or local election. The next step was for three-fourths of the states to approve the amendment in their own legislatures for it to become the Twenty-sixth Amendment to the Constitution of the United States.

Discussions both for and against this amendment to the Constitution were the subject of front-page newspaper articles and filled television and radio airwaves for months. It was apparent that people do not take the task of rewriting the Constitution lightly. Yet their willingness to do so was a reflection of the changing times and an example of how law is to function in and serve a changing society.

Figure 2–5 The Twenty-sixth Amendment to the U.S. Constitution

THE TWENTY-SIXTH AMENDMENT TO THE U.S. CONSTITUTION

The right of citizens of the United States, who are eighteen years of age or older, to vote shall not be denied or abridged by the United States, or by any state on account of age.

Amending the Constitution is a complicated and time-consuming task. Yet in this instance, the task was accomplished in just over three months because of the lobbying efforts of the young voters themselves and some highly effective groups such as Common Cause and the League of Women Voters. Although some legislators feared that their jobs might be in jeopardy whether they were for or against the bill, most were more concerned about the unfair and inequitable image of the country's leaders in asking this particular group of citizens to fight its battles but not take part in the process of electing its leadership.

On June 30, 1971, when the state of Ohio ratified the constitutional amendment, more than 17.5 million citizens became eligible to vote. The bill that made this possible had become a law in less than one year, and the amendment to the United States Constitution was passed in about three months. Passage of this bill and amendment must surely hold the record for speedy, peaceful, revolutionary change in the history of the United States.

2–4 How State Law Is Made

All new laws, whether federal or state, begin with an idea. For example, Jennifer and Jake Citizen are residents of Springfield, Anystate. They are the proud parents of three exceptionally bright children, have a large mortgage on their home, and are not feeling too secure about their jobs. When Jake and Jennifer think about how much it will cost to provide college educations for their three children, ages 10, 12, and 14, they become very concerned.

Anystate, where they live, has a good state university located about 300 miles away in a lovely rural setting. The state legislators voted to locate the university in this remote area about a hundred years ago because the land there was inexpensive. When the Citizens' oldest child is ready for college, she will not be able to commute 600 miles a day to attend classes. So, in addition to tuition, fees, and books there will be the additional costs of housing, food, occasional entertainment, and trips home.

One day Jennifer Citizen has a good idea. If the state university built a branch in Springfield and the other major cities of Anystate, then their children could get a college education at an affordable price and still live at home. Jake is excited to hear Jennifer's idea and they discuss it with their neighbors and coworkers. Several people have the same concerns as Jake and Jennifer, but many are skeptical. "You can't fight city hall" and "Who's going to pay for these branches?" are common reactions. However, there seems to be enough support to prompt Jake and Jennifer to make an appointment with the mayor of Springfield. The mayor is cordial and sympathetic to their concerns and ideas but explains that he cannot help them. Their idea is a state issue, not a local one. He recommends that they make an appointment to see their state representative.

The representative agrees with the Citizens that they have a good idea. He is willing to help them get a law for state university branches passed. He also suggests they see their state senator because their state government works similarly to the federal government. That is, except for the state of Nebraska, all states have two legislative bodies: the House of Representatives or Assembly composed of many members representing smaller districts, and the Senate, with fewer legislators representing larger districts.

Jake, Jennifer, and a few of their neighbors meet with the state senator who represents their district. They find that she agrees that there should be some type of higher education facility in Springfield and the other major cities of

Anystate. However, she thinks a four-year branch of the state university would be too expensive. She suggests and would be willing to sponsor two-year community colleges offering both technical training courses and courses that would transfer to the four-year state university.

The Citizens go back to their representative and tell him about their meeting with the senator. The representative from Springfield likes the senator's community college idea and thinks he will have an easier time getting it passed. So, he drafts a bill providing for the establishment of a two-year community college in every city of the state with a population of more than 75,000. He presents his bill to the clerk of the House of Representatives, who assigns it a number, House Bill (HB) 1275, and refers it to the Joint (House and Senate) Education Committee for hearings, discussions, and recommendations.

In the interim, the state senator has mulled over this matter and she, too, introduces a modified version of the Citizens' idea calling for two-year community colleges to be established in the three largest cities of Anystate. Her bill is numbered Senate Bill (SB) 101, and it, too, is referred to the Joint Education Committee.

The Education Committee schedules a public hearing on these two bills early in the legislative session. The Citizens, their friends, interested organizations and groups, state senators and representatives, all may speak in a public hearing regardless of whether they support or oppose the proposed legislation. Jake and Jennifer have been busy lining up support for their idea. Parents with and without partners are in favor of this proposal, as are both the local and state P.T.A., the League of Women Voters, and the Springfield Garden Club. On hearing day, members of these groups are bussed to Capital City to testify and applaud loudly whenever anyone speaks favorably about HB 1275.

The opposition is in Capital City too. The chair of the committee for legislative programs for the Chamber of Commerce testifies that his organization thinks the community college plan is a good one, but that they have voted to support SB 101 as a more practical and economical alternative. Representatives of the Concerned Taxpayers group and Senior Citizens Against Paying to Educate Other People's Kids testify that the state is spending entirely too much money on education, and they should cut the university budget, forget about branches, and lower taxes. A Major City Homeowners' Association member testifies they are concerned that, if approved, a branch of the university or community college would be built on the vacant land near their neighborhood and having all those hyperactive, radical students nearby would depress real-estate values.

Both the representative and the senator who sponsored the bills appear to give their reasons for favoring the bills and are joined by other senators and representatives who testify both for and against one or both bills. As the late afternoon shadows fall across the hearing-room floor, the chair of the Education Committee declares the open hearing closed and sends everyone home tired but happy, thinking that his or her point of view will prevail.

The next time the Education Committee discusses HB 1275 and SB 101, it is behind closed doors in executive session, with only the committee members present. Now the committee has several options. It can issue a favorable report on both bills, leaving it up to the membership of the house and senate to decide which one should pass; it can issue a favorable report on one of the two bills; it can issue unfavorable reports on both bills; or, it can issue no report on either bill. No report is as bad as an unfavorable report because in either case the bill will not make it to the floor of the house or the senate for discussion. Since most state legislatures receive thousands of bills each session, most of them get no committee report and are never discussed—an occurrence appropriately known as "dying in committee."

But Jake and Jennifer's bill is different. The Education Committee has heard about all the support the community college idea received at the hearing, and they have been swamped with letters, telephone calls, and facsimiles from parents in their districts. Unlike the federal government, most states make sure a bill will be funded before passing it. So, the next step for the community college bill is the Appropriations or Finance Committee. "Money is tight," the Citizens' representative says. "More bills die in appropriations than in any other committee of the legislature, but I'll do my best."

No more testimony is heard by the Appropriations or Finance Committee. Instead, if members have questions they read the transcripts of testimony from the Education Committee. But committee members who hold the state's purse strings tend to pay a great deal of attention to the messages received from their constituents. When there is a huge outpouring of support for a bill, a committee member is likely to think twice before voting against it. On the other hand, if the majority of messages are in opposition to a bill, only a member willing to risk his or her political future would support it.

The Appropriations or Finance Committee is where the legendary wheeling and dealing takes place. Favors get repaid and I.O.U.s are handed out. Although this wheeling and dealing is embarrassing to some people, it is an important part of the American political process and is probably the reason most of the important committee meetings are closed. In any event, it turns out that this is the year for community colleges in Anystate. SB 101 receives a favorable report from the Appropriations Committee, although the amount of money originally requested has been cut in half.

The representative and the state senator who introduced the bills in their respective houses now revise their bills to conform to the version recommended by the Appropriations Committee. Either or both of them could have held fast to their original versions, but doing so would have meant a long and probably useless battle on the floor of either or both houses of the legislature, with the bill not passing before adjournment.

Now the House and Senate bills are the same. They keep their original numbers but probably have added the word *amended* to the title. The bills are scheduled on the calendars of both houses and, after a brief debate open to the public and the press, are passed. Although either or both houses could have rejected the bills at this point, that rarely happens once they have passed the two most important committees with favorable recommendations.

The bill then goes to the Governor, who can either (1) sign the bill, (2) veto the bill, which would send it back to both houses where it would have to repass with a higher majority (usually two-thirds), or (3) allow the bill to become law without the Governor's signature, which happens automatically after it has been sitting on his or her desk for several days or weeks (depending upon the state) without being vetoed.

In this case, however, the Governor signs the bill and presents the pen to Jake and Jennifer Citizen with television and newspaper reporters recording the event for posterity. This event not only enhanced the Governor's political image but provided a direct benefit to the state's First Family. The Governor has three children to educate, too, and one of the locations for a new community college is in Capital City.

The bill is now a law and receives a new name and number, Public Law (PL) or Public Act (PA) 26755—unless you live in California or one of 23 other states that use the petition form of **referendum,** which gives the people the right to vote directly on any proposed legislation. In referendum states, voters can demand that a measure enacted by the legislature and signed by the governor be referred to the voters before going into effect. If the voters turn it down, the process would have to start all over again. Jake and Jennifer Citizen's children might be parents themselves before classes are held in their local community college, but they can be proud of their efforts and hope that their grandchildren will benefit from having a community college nearby.

The majority of laws affecting your life are passed at the state level because the United States Constitution restricts the types of laws that can be passed by federal legislation. In some states, every bill that is introduced must have a committee hearing, no matter how remote the chances are of its passing. For example, for several years the California legislature debated a bill that specified that cows at the state fair had to be placed in stalls with their heads, rather than their behinds, facing people who might be walking through the barns. In Texas, a bill was once introduced prohibiting barbers from discussing subjects on which they were not learned, such as atomic or nuclear energy.

Some states are using computers to process the numbering and recording of bills more quickly. Others have redistricted their two houses, cut the size of their legislatures, or lengthened the time when legislative bodies are in session in attempts to speed up the process. Generally, the result of their efforts has been an increase in the number of bills and issues to debate rather than the expected reduction of both.

2–5 How Local Law Is Made

The Pilgrims barely had time to set up housekeeping before the first town meeting was called to discuss what new laws and regulations should be passed, how they would be enforced, what taxes were needed to run the town, and how they would be collected. Town meetings were the ideal way to get everyone involved in the lawmaking process, and were a far cry from the remote and impersonal government from which these early settlers had fled.

Most of the cities and towns who still use the town meeting form of government are close to their historical roots in New England. They are usually very small towns, and usually found in states such as Connecticut, Vermont, New Hampshire, and Maine. The citizens get together to thrash out issues such as the annual town budget, salaries for employees of the town, the construction of new schools, or the development of property. These meetings often prove to be inconclusive, since even small groups often have difficulty reaching a decision.

Homeowners' Association meetings are remarkably similar in structure and content to town meetings. People who live in condominiums, co-ops, or other types of planned communities get together and decide what assessments are needed to repair and maintain the structure, how those assessments will be collected, what rules and regulations are needed for the owners or occupants, and who will enforce them.

Larger communities have a municipal government that functions similarly to the state and federal systems, with an executive branch (the mayor or first selectman), a legislative branch (a town or city council), and a judiciary branch (magistrate, city, county, or circuit courts).

Cities and towns are usually most concerned with education and budgets, health and housing codes, local taxes and zoning laws. How much they can do in these areas is determined by the state legislature. For example, most cities can set their own tax rates, but they cannot impose new taxes without approval from the state.

The executive branch of local government usually consists of the mayor, his or her appointees, and several boards, all of whom keep the mayor informed on community issues and concerns. Membership on these various boards is by appointment or election, and their power is limited—they usually cannot make any binding decisions. Instead, board proposals dealing with the hiring of more

Figure 2–6 The Long Arm of the Local Law

> Banning loud noise after 11 p.m., restricting the weight of household pets, controlling the color of homes, the size of shrubbery, and the stays of overnight visitors are customary areas in which homeowners' associations feel they have a right to meddle in the private lives of residents. But at least one California homeowners' association went too far and found itself faced with a lawsuit when a 51-year-old female resident was publicly reprimanded after kissing a date goodnight outside her condominium.
>
> "We hear stories all the time about community organizations trying to regulate the behavior of people, but none quite as outrageous as this one," said the Assemblyman representing the district in which the accused resides. Many private homeowners around the country share a governing association that attempts to wield the kind of control over their private lives heretofore unknown and supposedly protected against by the Constitution.
>
> Because of the increasing number of complaints from residents about the overbearing tactics of their homeowners' associations, state legislators are taking a look at the powers given to these local law-enforcement groups and considering bills to rein in that power. Most homeowners will welcome some relief from overzealous associations that go too far in attempting to regulate their private lives.

police or building a new school have to be approved by the city council, or whatever the legislative branch is called in the community.

Many cities today are choosing not to elect a mayor and instead hiring a professional public administrator or city manager for this position. These experts in urban administration supervise the various departments of the city and their directors and deal with the city council, the media, and the citizens in a nonpartisan manner, which is usually more efficient and professional than when a citizen is elected as mayor. City managers are not subject to the same pressures as politicians because they are not elected; but they do sometimes get fired by the city council—either because they are doing a poor job or because the political affiliation of the city council members, who are elected, has changed and they want to hire a more like-minded manager.

Some cities with professional managers have encountered a few problems. One problem has to do with official power. For example, a mayor, as the chief executive officer (CEO) of the community, can veto laws and ordinances passed by the city council. A city manager, on the other hand, is an employee of the city council and has no veto power. This means there is no balance of power between the legislative and executive branches in communities with a council-manager government. However, most cities with a city manager have found that the improvement in efficiency and professionalism more than compensates for any imbalance of power created by this form of government.

Municipal laws and ordinances are limited to the boundaries of the community to which they pertain. Money to pay for community services, which are not paid for by the state or federal government, are raised through real-estate taxes. The percentage of property value to be paid in taxes is usually determined by the city council or by referendum—the twenty-first century's version of the town meeting form of government and one of the best ways to get the most taxpayers involved in the lawmaking process. In most communities the majority of real-estate taxes collected are used for local education programs. The citizens know that when the Board of Education announces that more money will be needed to fund the schools, taxes will be going up. If people believe that a newly passed law or ordinance is illegal, they can apply to the state court for review and interpretation of the legislation.

The American legal system works in much the same way at all levels—federal, state, or local. Although this system of checks and balances is maddeningly slow at times, it does seem to keep us on the track the founders of our country laid down for us and, unlike most other systems in the world, it has survived over several hundred years and served us better than any other.

SUMMARY

2–1

Laws, rules, and rights are parts of the U.S. legal system that most people accept without much thought, yet they are very different in concept and meaning. Laws are the legislative pronouncements of rules that guide the actions of society. Rules are standards, regulations, guidelines, and methods of proceeding, and are enforceable only by the entity that made them. Rights are individual liberties provided by the state and federal constitutions.

Laws, rules, and rights play an important part in shaping the social environment in which we live. Laws settle disputes, which often occur over rules and rights, maintain order in society, provide a structure within which to live, provide the machinery for the government to operate in a balanced fashion, protect the citizens against excessive or unfair government or private power, and help to ensure that people will have the opportunity to enjoy life through the protection of their financial and physical health.

2–2

The U.S. system of jurisprudence is based upon the common law of Medieval England, when judges in small towns resolved disputes by making decisions based upon common sense, fairness, and social custom. Decisions were not yet written down, forcing judges to rely on personal recollection and reliable hearsay regarding decisions made before their time. The principle of *stare decisis*, or precedent, developed from this practice.

Later, when decisions were recorded, judges still relied upon precedent for guidance in decisions. Over time a policy developed that a decision of a court would be binding on that court, as well as on other courts of equal or lower status, when presented with a case having the same or similar issues. Judges today often rely upon precedent when making decisions.

In addition to common law, the courts also rely on statutory laws, commonly referred to as legislation, to settle disputes or maintain order. Statutory laws are enacted to prescribe conduct, define crimes, appropriate public monies, and promote the public good and welfare.

Substantive laws create, define, and regulate the rights and duties of individuals, as well as the circumstances under which a court will grant one person the right to sue another. Procedural laws are the rules that establish the steps which people who are involved in a lawsuit or criminal procedure must follow. Without procedural laws to provide structure and organization, the entire system of jurisprudence would collapse in chaos.

2–3

Some federal laws, such as the designation of Mother's Day, are easy to pass primarily because they require no funding and are unenforceable. Other laws take more time and must wind their way through a complex system of checks and balances.

The federal legislative system comprises three distinct branches of government: the legislative branch, which is composed of the House of Representatives and the Senate and is commonly referred to as the Congress; the executive branch, composed of the President and members of the Presidential Cabinet; and the judicial branch, which includes the Federal and Supreme Courts. On rare occasions, a bill may require an amendment to the Constitution. One example is the Voting Rights Act, which required a constitutional amendment before it could be administered and enforced.

New bills must pass both houses of Congress after hearings by the appropriate subcommittee and committee, before they are given to the President for signature. The President has the right to veto any bill presented for signature, but the bill may still pass into law if two-thirds of the members of each house of Congress vote to pass it. Because the question of funding is addressed after a bill is passed, some bills are never funded and are never enforced.

2–4

The procedure required to pass a state law is identical to the federal legislative process in most states: an idea is presented to a member of the House of Representatives or Assembly and to a Senator; they draft separate bills, which are assigned to committee for discussion; if approved by committee, new identical bills are drafted for approval by both houses; after house approval, the bills are presented to the Governor for signature, veto, or no action. If the Governor vetoes a bill, it may still pass upon a two-thirds vote of each house.

State lawmaking may differ from the federal process in at least two ways: most states address the issue of funding a bill before passing it, and about half the states use the petition form of referendum, which gives the people the right to vote directly on any proposed legislation before it becomes enforceable law.

2–5

Town meetings were used by the Pilgrims to discuss what new laws and regulations should be passed, how they would be enforced, what taxes were needed to run the town, and how they would be collected. Some small New England towns still hold town meetings for this same purpose, but larger cities have a municipal government that functions similarly to the state and federal systems, with an executive branch (the mayor or first selectman), a legislative branch (a town or city council), and a judiciary branch (magistrate, city, county, or circuit courts).

Many cities are choosing to hire a professional public administrator or city manager instead of electing a mayor. City managers are employees of the city council and do not have the mayor's veto power. However, most cities choosing the manager-council form of government operate more efficiently than those with a mayor.

REVIEW

Key Terms

Before proceeding, review the key terms listed below to be sure you understand each one. If necessary, read over the corresponding section of the chapter. When you are ready to test your understanding, answer the Review Questions.

cause of action
common law
complaint
constitution
dismissed
due process
hearsay
judgment
jurisprudence
law
plaintiff
precedent
procedural law
referendum
rights
rules
stare decisis
statutes
substantive law
torts

Questions for Review and Discussion

1. Define the terms *laws, rules,* and *rights.*
2. What are laws supposed to do for people?
3. What do laws not do for people?
4. Briefly outline a history of the U.S. legal system.
5. Describe the common-law system of jurisprudence.
6. How does the principle of *stare decisis* relate to common law?

7. What are the differences between substantive law and procedural law?
8. What are the three branches of the federal legislative system?
9. If you, a citizen, want to get a bill passed through either the federal legislative system or the state legislative system, what steps are involved?
10. What are the differences between a city run by a mayor and one run by a city manager?

Activities

1. Research the various forms of government in your state, county, city, or town. Find out how laws and rules are passed, how they are funded, and how they are enforced. Do the various government agencies or branches employ paralegals and, if so, what tasks do paralegals perform for them? Write a report for extra credit or present your findings to the class.
2. Invite a local elected politician to class to discuss the legislative system.
3. Find out what local elections will be taking place and how you can get involved.
4. Attend a meeting of your city or town council or homeowners' association, observe the process, and report your findings to the class. What suggestions do you have for improving the current system?

CHAPTER 3 Courts

OUTLINE

3–1 Functions and Roles of Courts
- The Court as Dispute Settler
- The Court as Decision Maker
- The Court as Protector

3–2 The Federal Court System
- Jurisdiction of Federal Courts
- Structure of Federal Courts

3–3 The State Court System
- Structure of State Courts
- Court Personnel

3–4 Alternatives to Court
- Arbitration
- Mediation
- Private Judges

3–5 Courts of the Future
- Court Reforms
- Computer-Integrated Courtrooms

COMMENTARY

Mr. Sweeney is as involved with judges, court clerks, and deputy marshals as Mr. Dunn is with the politicians. Perhaps this is because Mr. Sweeney is the partner in charge of litigation and spends a great deal of time in court. Or perhaps it is just the fact that almost everything you have done so far as a legal assistant has involved working with the court system in one way or another. Now that you feel more confident about how laws are made, you decide the next step in your legal assisting education is to learn more about how the courts work.

OBJECTIVES

In Chapter 2 you studied the history of the U.S. legal system and learned how laws are made at the federal, state, and local levels of government. After studying this chapter, you should be able to:

1. Explain the functions and roles of the courts in general.
2. List how the court system is divided and the types of matters heard by each.
3. Describe the two types of federal court jurisdiction.
4. Discuss the structure of the federal court system.
5. Outline the structure of the state court system and its jurisdiction.
6. Describe the job duties of typical court personnel.

7. Discuss some of the alternatives to court as a way to settle disputes.
8. Define *voir dire* and a method for reforming it.
9. Critique the current legal justice system in relation to its overcrowded courts.
10. Describe what is being done to integrate high technology with the courts.

3–1 Functions and Roles of Courts

Laws are needed to maintain order in society and to provide guidelines for settling disputes. Courts are needed to interpret the laws, to resolve disputes in an orderly way, and to ensure that order is maintained in society.

The term **court** has two meanings. One meaning refers to the branch of government that is responsible for the resolution of disputes arising under the laws of the government. But *court* is also frequently used as a substitute for *judge.* For example, you might read that the district court stated in *his* opinion that he disagreed with the circuit court and *its* conclusion. Most people have no trouble in distinguishing between these two meanings for the same term.

The Court as Dispute Settler

Generally, the court system is divided into various parts, each specializing in hearing different types of cases. **Trial courts** are responsible for receiving evidence and determining the application of the law to facts. Some trial courts hear only **criminal cases,** where an action is brought against an individual by either the federal or state government to punish that individual for breaking the law. Other trial courts hear only **civil cases,** actions brought before the court to settle disputes involving individuals, the state or federal government, business entities, individual states, or any combination thereof.

Family court, as the name implies, hears matters involving issues related to a family and its members. Divorce or dissolution, adoptions, custody, and problems of juvenile delinquency are typical family-court issues. Depending upon the state, courts that handle family-related matters are sometimes also called *matrimonial court, domestic relations court,* or *juvenile court.*

Probate court, known in some states as *surrogate court* or *orphan's court,* hears proceedings regarding the estates of deceased or incompetent persons and matters pertaining to guardianship of a minor.

Just as there are 50 different state governments, there are also 50 different state court systems. The names for these courts and the subject matters over which they have **jurisdiction,** the power to hear and determine a case, will vary, but the function of each court varies little from one state to the next.

The Court as Decision Maker

The judge is the chief officer of the court and in this capacity is responsible for settling disputes brought before the court. Unlike the legislative and executive branches of the government, the judicial branch cannot propose or enact laws. The court becomes involved only after someone else has taken action. And even then the court takes no action until both sides in the adversary process have had an opportunity to present their arguments and evidence.

The judge performs two tasks. One task is to determine the facts from the evidence and testimony presented, and the second task is to apply the law to the facts and to determine who should prevail or win. If the parties have requested a trial by jury, the judge instructs the jury as to how the law applies to its findings of fact. The jury then **deliberates,** considers all the evidence and arguments presented, and renders its **verdict,** or opinion, in the matter. Because a verdict is merely the opinion of the jury, it differs from a *judgment,* which is a judicial determination. The jury's verdict may be accepted or rejected by the trial-court judge. If the verdict is rejected, the judge may still use the jury's findings of fact in formulating his or her own judgment.

Once the decision of a judge is reduced to the written document called a *judgment,* which is enforceable by a sheriff or marshal, the dispute usually ends. However, a judge's decision may be overturned on appeal to a higher court if there are sufficient grounds for doing so.

The Court as Protector

As citizens of the United States, we often take for granted our system of jurisprudence with its presumption of innocence until proven guilty, forgetting that the majority of countries in the world follow Roman or civil law, which holds the opposite point of view—you are presumed guilty and must prove you are innocent. Our courts, in their role as protector, ensure that individual citizens are not deprived of their rights and that they will have a fair trial.

In addition, courts work to keep the viewpoints of the majority from infringing upon the rights of the minority. For example, pragmatic lawmakers vote to please the majority of their constituents or they will not be reelected. However, in so doing, they may be infringing upon the rights of those who hold an opposing point of view. The Supreme Court's decisions on desegregation, prayer in school, and abortion came about after certain groups of citizens were unable to persuade their legislators to take action on these matters, which were and still are politically controversial.

It is worth noting that frequently the courts are required to interpret statutes that are unclear. In so doing, on occasion the court takes on yet another role—policy maker.

To summarize, the courts in general serve three functions:

1. To settle disputes through a system of courts divided according to specialization.
2. To make decisions by appointing judges who determine the facts, apply the law to the facts, and decide who should prevail.
3. To protect the rights of the minority from the viewpoints of the majority.

3–2 The Federal Court System

There is little doubt about the far-reaching effects of federal court decisions, yet few people understand how the federal court system works or its jurisdictional authority and limitations. Depending upon your areas of specialization as a paralegal, you may have only infrequent contact with the federal courts or you may deal with them almost exclusively. Knowledge of how the federal court system works will help you feel more comfortable whenever you need to access it.

Jurisdiction of Federal Courts

The jurisdiction of the federal courts is limited by the U.S. Constitution to two general areas. One is cases involving **federal question jurisdiction,** where the meaning or application of something in the Constitution, in a law, or in a **treaty,** an international agreement between two or more countries, is being disputed. Parenthetically, it is important to note that the Constitution gives the President sole power to initiate and make treaties, which must then be approved by the Senate before they become binding on citizens of the U.S. as law. To circumvent the Senate approval process and to facilitate our relationships with other countries, executive agreements, such as trade agreements, are often substituted for a treaty since the President does not need Senate approval to bind the government to an executive agreement.

Federal question jurisdiction extends beyond the areas specifically set forth in the Constitution, such as bankruptcy, patents and copyrights, and interstate commerce, to cases not anticipated by its authors. For example, it is doubtful that even the brilliant authors of the Constitution could have anticipated the modern legal problems involving savings and loans and banking institutions, federal securities law crimes, or violations of federal income tax laws because, in some instances, these institutions did not exist when the Constitution was written. Yet these and other types of cases not anticipated by the Constitution's authors fall into the category of federal question jurisdiction.

Federal question jurisdiction extends to all types of criminal offenses that are against the laws of the United States. Federal crimes are defined by an act of Congress and are listed in the United States Code. Some federal crimes include treason, drug trafficking, and kidnapping. Sometimes a criminal act might violate both a federal and state law. In that event, the offender can be prosecuted in either the state or federal court or both without violating the rule of **double jeopardy,** a provision in the Fifth Amendment to the Constitution that provides that no person shall be tried twice for the same offense.

The other general area of federal court jurisdiction covers cases of **diversity jurisdiction,** where there are controversies between citizens of different U.S. states or between citizens of a U.S. state and a foreign country, its citizens, or subjects. For example, a diversity jurisdiction case might involve disputes between citizens of different states, such as when a resident of New Jersey sues a resident of Illinois, or a dispute between a citizen of the U.S. and a citizen of a foreign country or the country itself. If a business owner in Florida sued her clothing manufacturer in Taiwan for nondelivery of goods and the Taiwan government for interfering with the delivery of merchandise, the federal courts would have jurisdiction. Likewise, cases against the Columbian drug cartel fall under the jurisdiction of the federal courts.

Federal diversity jurisdiction would also include cases in which the citizens of different states sued a foreign state, such as if the citizens of New Hampshire and Maine sued Canada for some reason, or if the states of Colorado and Arizona sued California. No matter who is suing whom, the amount in dispute must be $50,000 or more before legal action can be taken in the federal court.

Each year thousands of cases are filed in the federal courts, requiring the trial courts and the appellate courts to adopt criteria for selecting those cases which they will hear. The *doctrine of judicial self-restraint* requires the federal courts not to accept jurisdiction in disputes where there are no *bona fide* adversaries and where no specific legal remedy can be granted. For instance, let's say you are having a disagreement with your friends who live in another state about whether cats or dogs make the best domestic pets. You have not been able to resolve this dispute yourselves, but you cannot take this dispute to the federal court because you are not true adversaries. There are no legal rights to be enforced, and you would be asking the court to make a value judgment. In addition, for the federal court to accept jurisdiction, the parties bringing the action must have a personal stake in the litigation, and there is none in this example.

When it comes to making value judgments or giving advice, the federal court will not issue advisory opinions on the legality of government actions whether they have already been taken or are being contemplated, nor will it consider hypothetical questions or questions of a political nature that might involve the country's military or political interaction with a foreign country. The purpose of the courts is to determine facts and to make a decision based on their findings of fact, not to impose values or attempt to anticipate the hypothetical.

Structure of Federal Courts

The highest court in the land, the U.S. Supreme Court, was created by Article III of the United States Constitution, which also grants Congress the right to create any lower federal courts as it deems necessary. Many years ago Congress used this congressional power to create two levels of federal courts below the Supreme Court—the United States Court of Appeal and the United States District Courts.

Federal District Courts The United States and its territories—Guam, the Canal Zone, Puerto Rico, and the Virgin Islands—are divided into 94 judicial districts. In addition to federal question cases and civil and criminal cases involving diversity jurisdiction, all bankruptcy cases are filed in the federal district court. Over 400 federal district court judges preside in these various judicial districts, which are established by Congress based largely upon population and caseload. Densely populated districts with large caseloads may have several judges, whereas in less-populated areas one judge may serve several districts.

Figure 3–1 The United States Federal Court System

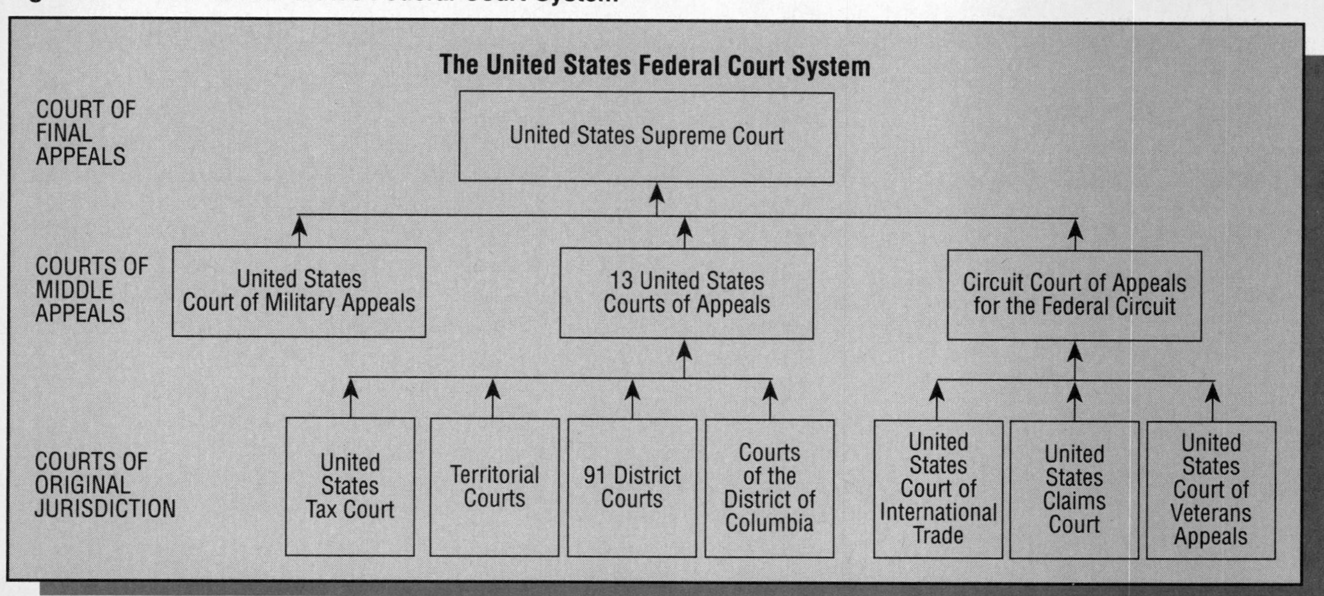

There are two levels of federal courts below the Supreme Court—the Courts of Middle Appeals and the Courts of Original Jurisdiction. *Source*: The United States Government Manual, 1990/91.

Federal court judges are nominated by the President and confirmed by the Senate. As a practical matter, however, candidates for appointment to the district court bench are usually brought to the attention of the President by a U.S. Senator from the state in which the judge will be appointed. Once confirmed, federal court judges may serve, conditionally upon good behavior, for life, and are not subject to a mandatory retirement age. **Impeachment,** the process of charging a public official with wrongdoing such as treason, bribery, or other high crimes while in office, is the only way a federal court judge can be removed from the **bench,** another synonym commonly used to refer to the court.

You will recall that at the time the federal court system was established by the Constitution, there were few qualifications for judges other than good moral character and competency to make decisions. (Refer to the discussion in Chapter 1 on the qualifications to be a judge.) To this day the law does not require federal judges to be lawyers, but the constitutional requirement for competency to serve implies that only lawyers will be considered for the position. The American Bar

Figure 3–2 The Thirteen Federal Judicial Districts

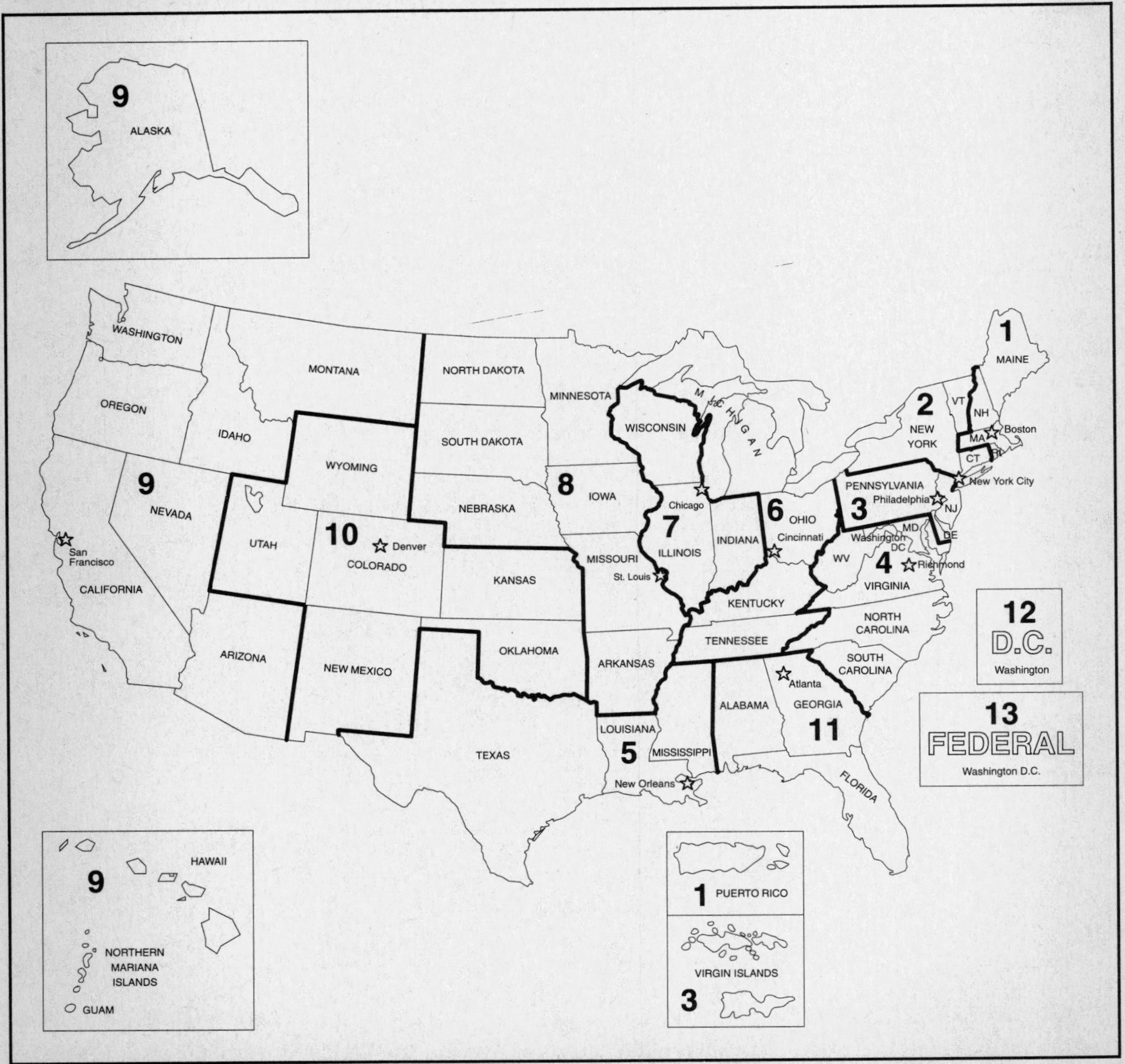

The United States and its territories are divided into thirteen Federal District Courts.

Association, the U.S. Department of Justice, and several prominent legal organizations have established a screening process for candidates to ensure that only qualified individuals will be appointed to the federal bench.

U.S. Courts of Appeal For the purpose of hearing appeals from decisions made in the federal district courts, the continental U.S. and its territories are divided into 11 geographic regions known as circuits with larger territorial boundaries than the district courts. In addition to these 11 circuits, illustrated in Figure 3–2, there are two additional circuit courts for a total of 13—the District of Columbia Circuit, which hears appeals cases only for the District of Columbia, and the Court of Appeals for the Federal Circuit, which hears appeals in certain types of patent and copyright cases and matters involving international trade.

Each court of appeals has jurisdiction over appeals from the federal district courts and federal administrative agencies operating within its circuit. Cases brought before this court are usually heard by a panel of not less than two, nor more than three, of the approximately 200 judges who serve the appeals court throughout its various circuits. When a case is heard by a panel, at least two of the judges must agree before there is a binding decision.

Cases brought before the U.S. Court of Appeals include appeals from civil and criminal cases decided by the federal district courts, as well as appeals from such courts as the Territorial Courts or the U.S. Tax Court. All decisions of the U.S. Court of Appeals must be in writing, stating its findings of fact and conclusions of law. The courts of appeals, in making decisions, are required to follow the majority opinions of the U.S. Supreme Court.

United States Supreme Court The U.S. Supreme Court, sometimes referred to as the court of last resort, may be the final destination of some legal journeys. Presiding over this august body is the Chief Justice. The Chief Justice and the eight Associate Justices are appointed by the President of the United States with the advice and consent of the majority members of the Senate. Supreme Court Justices are also appointed, conditionally, for life, or until they voluntarily retire.

Six Justices are required to constitute a quorum, and the majority of Justices must be in agreement before a Supreme Court decision becomes official. The Supreme Court session begins the first Monday in October and continues until the end of June, except for the rare occasion when it might be necessary to convene during the summer to hear an important case, such as the Nixon tapes case pertaining to Watergate.

In addition to presiding over the sessions and deliberations of the Supreme Court, the Chief Justice chairs both the Federal Judicial Center, the research and development branch of the federal judiciary responsible for training new federal judges, and the Judicial Conference of the United States, a representative group of the more than 600 federal judges that considers proposed legislation in new areas of law and how to increase the efficiency of the federal courts.

The Supreme Court has **appellate jurisdiction,** the ability to review decisions of the state and federal courts of appeal, and it may, in limited circumstances, hear cases on appeal directly from the federal district courts. Additionally, the Constitution gives the U.S. Supreme Court **original jurisdiction.** This is the ability to hear and decide all issues of fact and law in the same way a trial court would, when a case involves an ambassador or other public minister or consul, and also cases in which a U.S. state is involved. For example, if an American bank brought suit against a foreign dignitary for breach of contract, or the State of New York filed a suit against Canada over the boundary of Niagara Falls, these lawsuits would originate in the Supreme Court.

Figure 3–3 Current U.S. Supreme Court Justices

Top row (L-R) Associate Justices David Souter, Antonin Scalia, Anthony Kennedy and Clarence Thomas. Bottom row (L-R) Associate Justices John Paul Stevens and Byron White, Chief Justice William Rehnquist, Associate Justices Harry Blackmun and Sandra Day O'Connor. *Source*: Reuters/Bettman.

To summarize the federal court system in general, it is limited by the Constitution to two areas of jurisdiction:

1. Federal question jurisdiction
2. Diversity jurisdiction

It is composed of three levels of courts, each of which has additional limits of jurisdiction:

1. The federal district courts, which hear criminal and civil federal question, diversity, and bankruptcy cases;
2. The U.S. Courts of Appeal, which hear appeals from federal district courts and federal administrative agencies;
3. The U.S. Supreme Court, which may review decisions of any state or federal court and which has original jurisdiction when an ambassador or other public minister or foreign country is involved in a lawsuit.

3–3 The State Court System

Unlike the federal court system, which operates from one basic structure and one set of procedural rules, regardless of the geographic location of its various districts and circuits, each of the 50 states has its own state court system. Figures 3–4 through 3–8 illustrate the court systems in five states: California, Florida, Illinois, New York, and Texas. These figures will give you an idea of how diverse individual state court systems can be.

Obviously, discussing each state system at length is beyond the scope of this text. Therefore, during the discussion that follows, please refer to Figure 3–9, showing the American Bar Association's illustration of typical state court systems and nomenclature.

Structure of State Courts

In order to keep the state courts functioning as efficiently as possible, most states, particularly those with dense populations, use multitiered systems (see Figure 3–9).

Justice or Magistrate Courts In those states that have them, justice or magistrate courts are the foundation courts in the judicial hierarchy. Their primary function is to provide the local population, which is sometimes isolated in rural areas, with access to the legal system. Justice courts have limited jurisdiction in both civil and criminal cases, and many do not have their own full-time judges or staff. Instead, clerks and judges from other nearby courts are often assigned to take care of administrative duties and to hear cases on certain days of the month. In some states, these lower court judges are not required to be attorneys. Those who are lawyers can maintain a private practice, but they may not appear before justice courts in their own county.

Municipal or County Courts The municipal court or county court is the trial court one tier above the justice courts and one tier below the superior court, circuit court, or its equivalent. In some states, the civil and criminal jurisdiction of the municipal and justice courts are the same. The difference between a municipal court and a justice court is usually based entirely upon the population of the particular judicial district. For example, a state may determine that when the population of a district exceeds a certain number—say, 40,000 people—a municipal court is automatically established.

Municipal courts and their equivalents have limited jurisdiction in both civil and criminal cases. Jurisdiction in civil and criminal cases is often determined by the dollar amount in controversy or the severity of the crime. Some states, for example, limit municipal court jurisdiction to civil cases involving $25,000 or less, and to criminal misdemeanor and infraction cases. Residency of the parties to the action is a factor in determining geographic jurisdiction, since most states have established branch courts in various counties within the state.

Small Claims Courts Small claims courts, or "people's courts," are also under the jurisdiction of the municipal courts or county courts. The amount in controversy to qualify for small claims jurisdiction and the procedures vary by state, but in those states that have small claims courts, the cases are heard under simplified procedures and without attorneys. Some states are raising the ceiling on the amount in controversy to be heard in small claims court as another way to reduce the caseloads of higher courts.

Figure 3–4

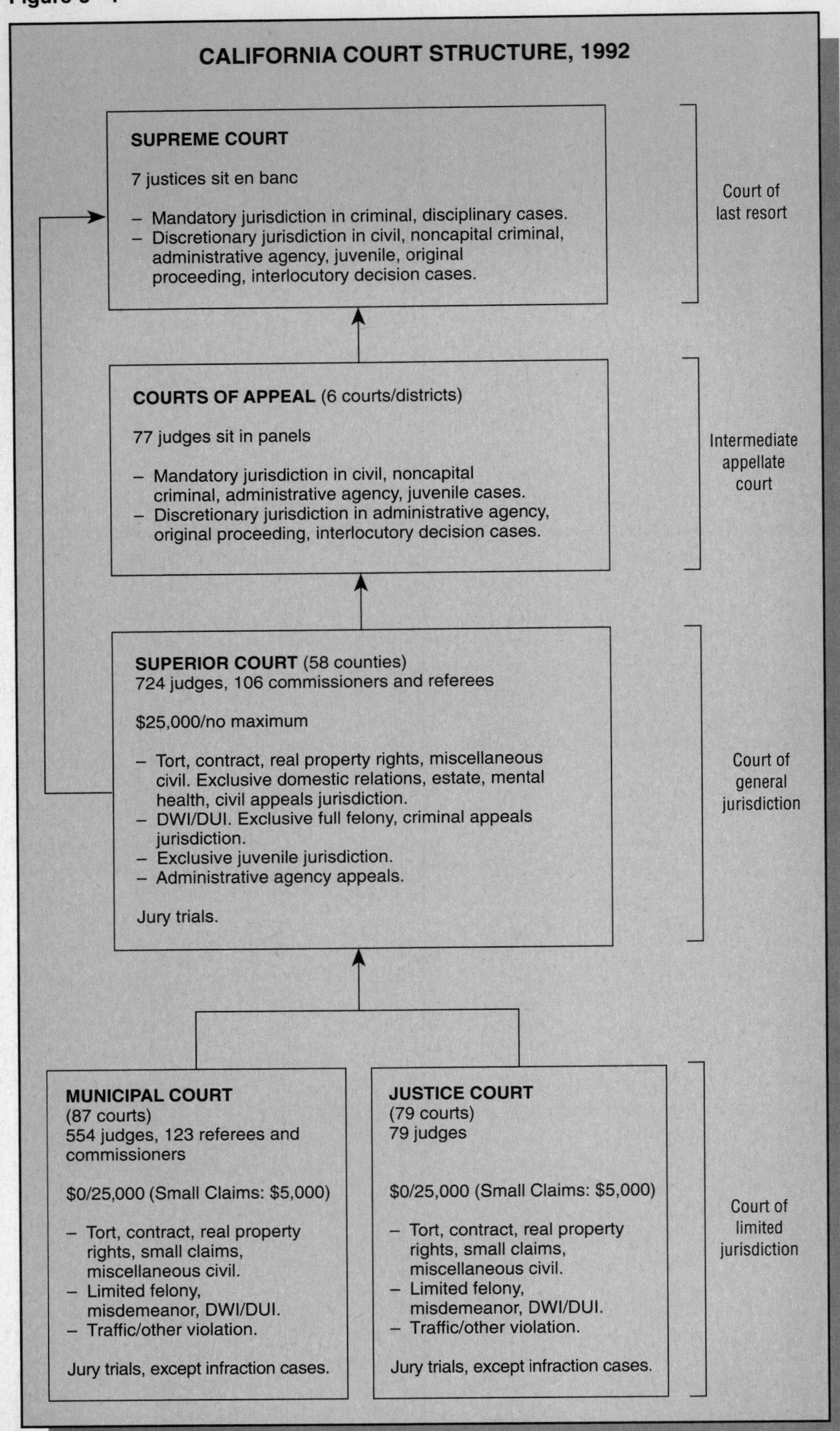

CALIFORNIA COURT STRUCTURE, 1992
SUPREME COURT
7 justices sit en banc
– Mandatory jurisdiction in criminal, disciplinary cases.
– Discretionary jurisdiction in civil, noncapital criminal, administrative agency, juvenile, original proceeding, interlocutory decision cases.
Court of last resort
COURTS OF APPEAL (6 courts/districts)
77 judges sit in panels
– Mandatory jurisdiction in civil, noncapital criminal, administrative agency, juvenile cases.
– Discretionary jurisdiction in administrative agency, original proceeding, interlocutory decision cases.
Intermediate appellate court
SUPERIOR COURT (58 counties)
724 judges, 106 commissioners and referees
$25,000/no maximum
– Tort, contract, real property rights, miscellaneous civil. Exclusive domestic relations, estate, mental health, civil appeals jurisdiction.
– DWI/DUI. Exclusive full felony, criminal appeals jurisdiction.
– Exclusive juvenile jurisdiction.
– Administrative agency appeals.
Jury trials.
Court of general jurisdiction
MUNICIPAL COURT
(87 courts)
554 judges, 123 referees and commissioners
$0/25,000 (Small Claims: $5,000)
– Tort, contract, real property rights, small claims, miscellaneous civil.
– Limited felony, misdemeanor, DWI/DUI.
– Traffic/other violation.
Jury trials, except infraction cases.
JUSTICE COURT
(79 courts)
79 judges
$0/25,000 (Small Claims: $5,000)
– Tort, contract, real property rights, small claims, miscellaneous civil.
– Limited felony, misdemeanor, DWI/DUI.
– Traffic/other violation.
Jury trials, except infraction cases.
Court of limited jurisdiction

The California Court Structure, 1992. *Source*: West's Legal Desk Reference. Reprinted with permission.

Figure 3–5

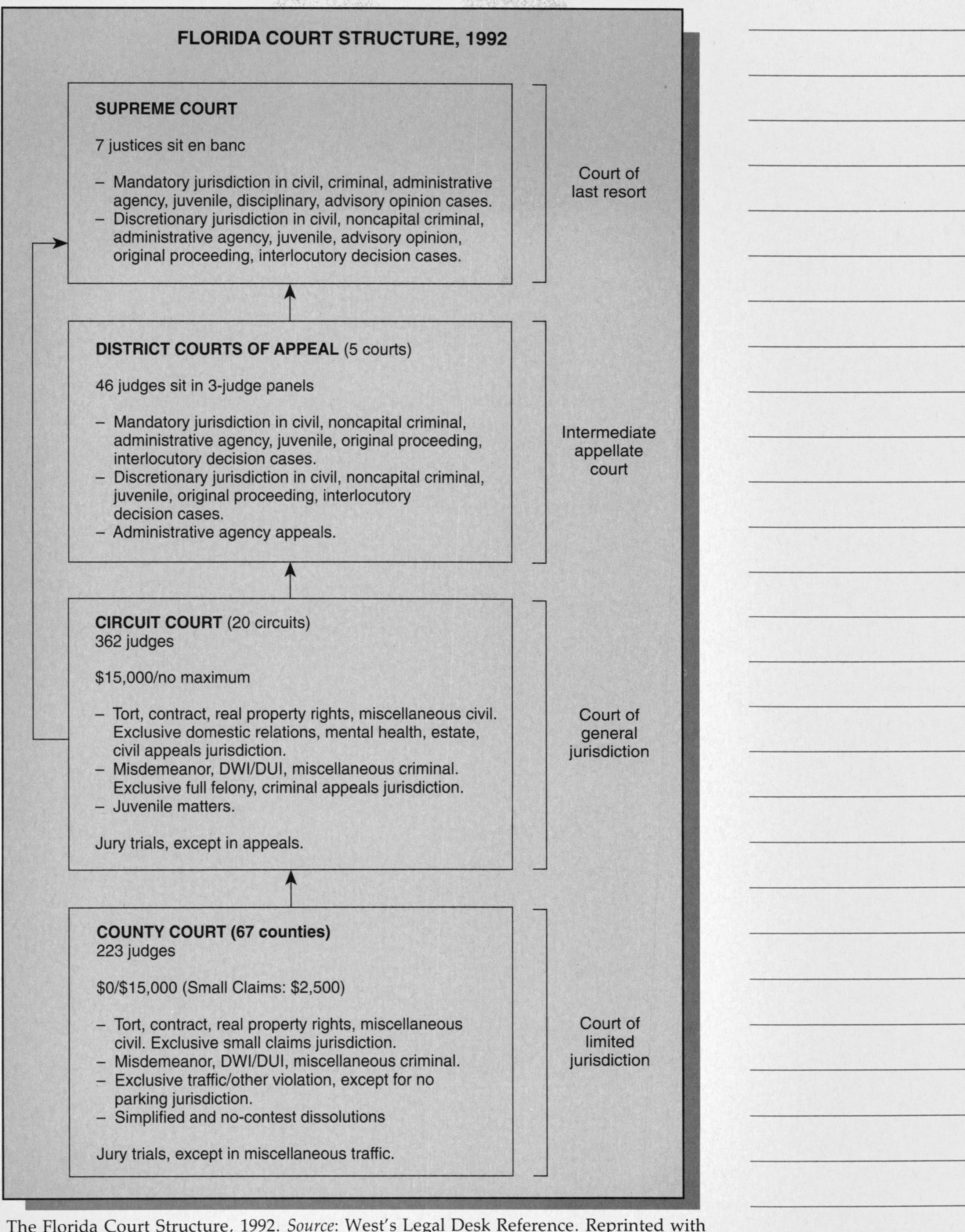

FLORIDA COURT STRUCTURE, 1992
SUPREME COURT
7 justices sit en banc
– Mandatory jurisdiction in civil, criminal, administrative agency, juvenile, disciplinary, advisory opinion cases.
– Discretionary jurisdiction in civil, noncapital criminal, administrative agency, juvenile, advisory opinion, original proceeding, interlocutory decision cases.
Court of last resort
DISTRICT COURTS OF APPEAL (5 courts)
46 judges sit in 3-judge panels
– Mandatory jurisdiction in civil, noncapital criminal, administrative agency, juvenile, original proceeding, interlocutory decision cases.
– Discretionary jurisdiction in civil, noncapital criminal, juvenile, original proceeding, interlocutory decision cases.
– Administrative agency appeals.
Intermediate appellate court
CIRCUIT COURT (20 circuits)
362 judges
$15,000/no maximum
– Tort, contract, real property rights, miscellaneous civil. Exclusive domestic relations, mental health, estate, civil appeals jurisdiction.
– Misdemeanor, DWI/DUI, miscellaneous criminal. Exclusive full felony, criminal appeals jurisdiction.
– Juvenile matters.
Jury trials, except in appeals.
Court of general jurisdiction
COUNTY COURT (67 counties)
223 judges
$0/$15,000 (Small Claims: $2,500)
– Tort, contract, real property rights, miscellaneous civil. Exclusive small claims jurisdiction.
– Misdemeanor, DWI/DUI, miscellaneous criminal.
– Exclusive traffic/other violation, except for no parking jurisdiction.
– Simplified and no-contest dissolutions
Jury trials, except in miscellaneous traffic.
Court of limited jurisdiction

The Florida Court Structure, 1992. *Source*: West's Legal Desk Reference. Reprinted with permission.

Figure 3–6

ILLINOIS COURT STRUCTURE, 1992
SUPREME COURT
7 justices sit en banc
– Mandatory jurisdiction in civil, criminal, administrative agency, juvenile, lawyer disciplinary, original proceeding, interlocutory decision cases.
– Discretionary jurisdiction in civil, noncapital criminal, administrative agency, juvenile, certified questions from the federal courts, original proceeding, interlocutory decision cases.
Court of last resort
APPELLATE COURT (5 courts/districts)
34 authorized judges sit in panels, plus 9 supplemental judges
$15,000/no maximum
– Mandatory jurisdiction in civil, noncapital criminal, administrative agency, juvenile, original proceeding, interlocutory decision cases.
– Discretionary jurisdiction in civil, interlocutory decision cases.
– Administrative agency appeals.
Intermediate appellate court
CIRCUIT COURTS (21 circuits)
780 authorized circuit and associate circuit judges
$0/$15,000 (Small Claims: $2,500)
– Exclusive civil jurisdiction (including administrative agency appeals).
– Exclusive criminal jurisdiction.
– Exclusive traffic/other violation jurisdiction.
– Exclusive juvenile jurisdiction.
– Jury trials in most cases.
Court of general jurisdiction

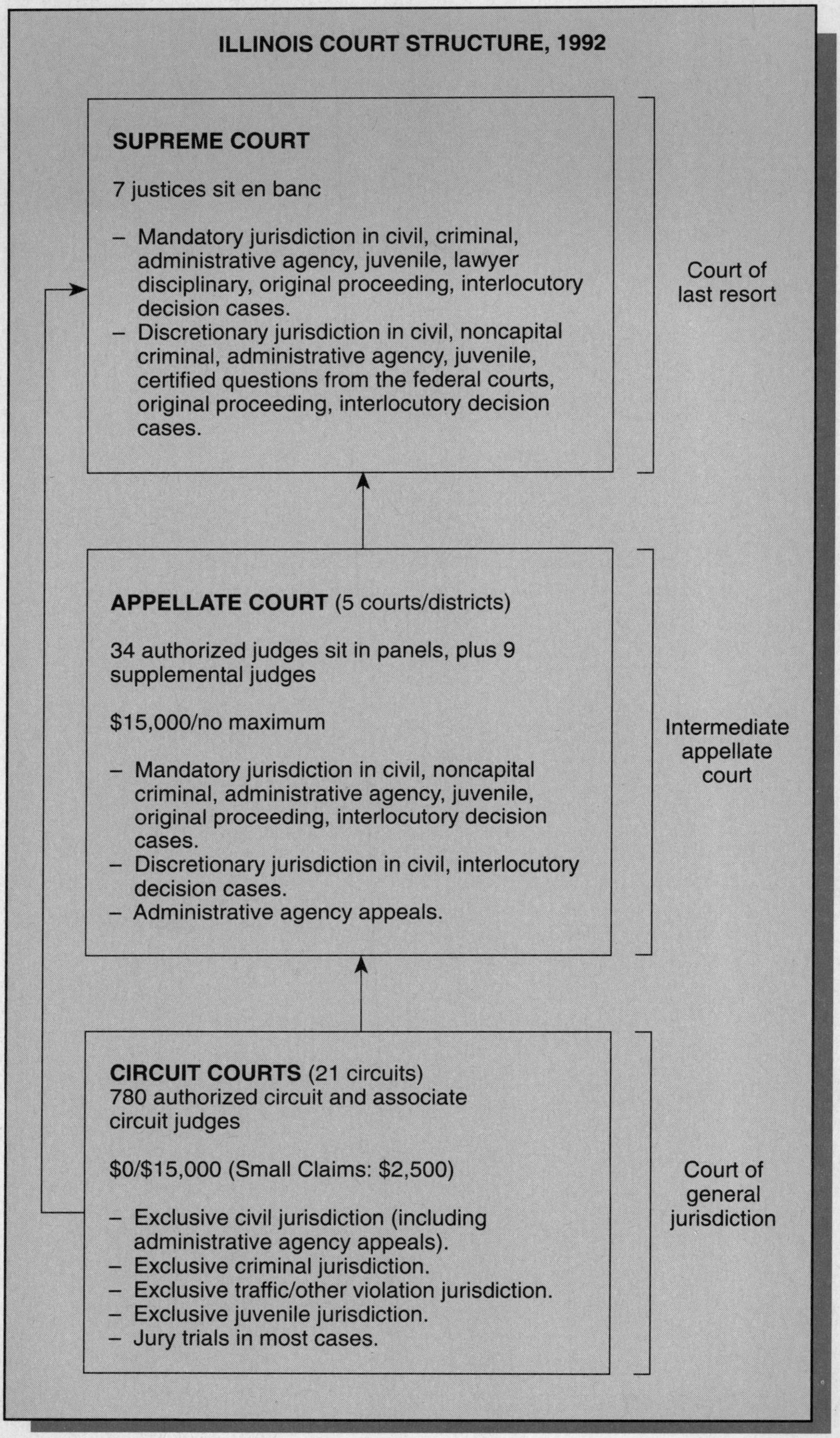

The Illinois Court Structure, 1992. *Source*: West's Legal Desk Reference. Reprinted with permission.

Figure 3–7

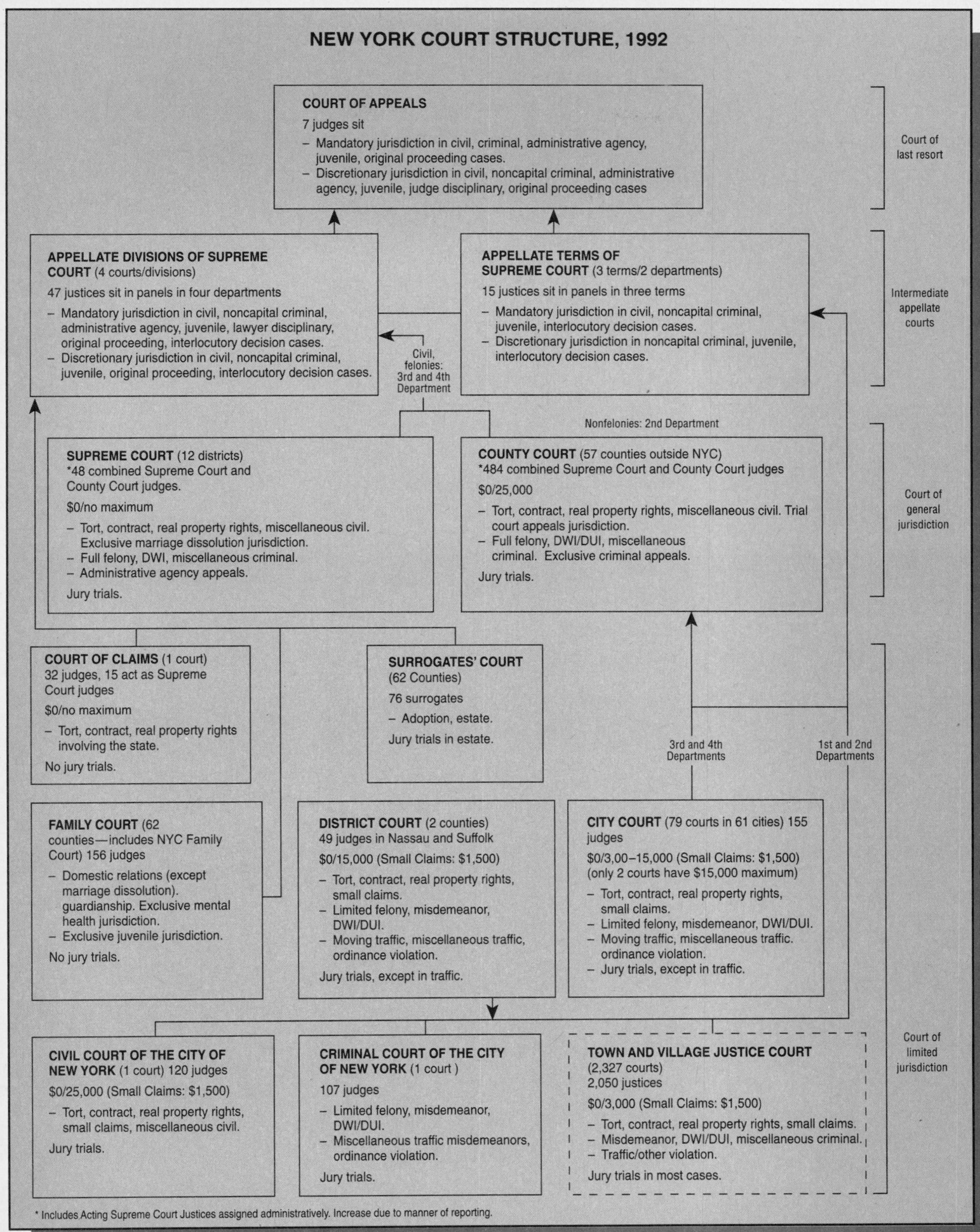

NEW YORK COURT STRUCTURE, 1992
COURT OF APPEALS
7 judges sit
– Mandatory jurisdiction in civil, criminal, administrative agency, juvenile, original proceeding cases.
– Discretionary jurisdiction in civil, noncapital criminal, administrative agency, juvenile, judge disciplinary, original proceeding cases
Court of last resort
APPELLATE DIVISIONS OF SUPREME COURT (4 courts/divisions)
47 justices sit in panels in four departments
– Mandatory jurisdiction in civil, noncapital criminal, administrative agency, juvenile, lawyer disciplinary, original proceeding, interlocutory decision cases.
– Discretionary jurisdiction in civil, noncapital criminal, juvenile, original proceeding, interlocutory decision cases.
Civil, felonies: 3rd and 4th Department
APPELLATE TERMS OF SUPREME COURT (3 terms/2 departments)
15 justices sit in panels in three terms
– Mandatory jurisdiction in civil, noncapital criminal, juvenile, interlocutory decision cases.
– Discretionary jurisdiction in noncapital criminal, juvenile, interlocutory decision cases.
Intermediate appellate courts
Nonfelonies: 2nd Department
SUPREME COURT (12 districts)
*48 combined Supreme Court and County Court judges.
$0/no maximum
– Tort, contract, real property rights, miscellaneous civil. Exclusive marriage dissolution jurisdiction.
– Full felony, DWI, miscellaneous criminal.
– Administrative agency appeals.
Jury trials.
COUNTY COURT (57 counties outside NYC)
*484 combined Supreme Court and County Court judges
$0/25,000
– Tort, contract, real property rights, miscellaneous civil. Trial court appeals jurisdiction.
– Full felony, DWI/DUI, miscellaneous criminal. Exclusive criminal appeals.
Jury trials.
Court of general jurisdiction
COURT OF CLAIMS (1 court)
32 judges, 15 act as Supreme Court judges
$0/no maximum
– Tort, contract, real property rights involving the state.
No jury trials.
SURROGATES' COURT (62 Counties)
76 surrogates
– Adoption, estate.
Jury trials in estate.
3rd and 4th Departments
1st and 2nd Departments
FAMILY COURT (62 counties—includes NYC Family Court) 156 judges
– Domestic relations (except marriage dissolution). guardianship. Exclusive mental health jurisdiction.
– Exclusive juvenile jurisdiction.
No jury trials.
DISTRICT COURT (2 counties)
49 judges in Nassau and Suffolk
$0/15,000 (Small Claims: $1,500)
– Tort, contract, real property rights, small claims.
– Limited felony, misdemeanor, DWI/DUI.
– Moving traffic, miscellaneous traffic, ordinance violation.
Jury trials, except in traffic.
CITY COURT (79 courts in 61 cities) 155 judges
$0/3,00–15,000 (Small Claims: $1,500) (only 2 courts have $15,000 maximum)
– Tort, contract, real property rights, small claims.
– Limited felony, misdemeanor, DWI/DUI.
– Moving traffic, miscellaneous traffic. ordinance violation.
– Jury trials, except in traffic.
CIVIL COURT OF THE CITY OF NEW YORK (1 court) 120 judges
$0/25,000 (Small Claims: $1,500)
– Tort, contract, real property rights, small claims, miscellaneous civil.
Jury trials.
CRIMINAL COURT OF THE CITY OF NEW YORK (1 court)
107 judges
– Limited felony, misdemeanor, DWI/DUI.
– Miscellaneous traffic misdemeanors, ordinance violation.
Jury trials.
TOWN AND VILLAGE JUSTICE COURT (2,327 courts)
2,050 justices
$0/3,000 (Small Claims: $1,500)
– Tort, contract, real property rights, small claims.
– Misdemeanor, DWI/DUI, miscellaneous criminal.
– Traffic/other violation.
Jury trials in most cases.
Court of limited jurisdiction
* Includes Acting Supreme Court Justices assigned administratively. Increase due to manner of reporting.

The New York Court Structure, 1992. *Source*: West's Legal Desk Reference. Reprinted with permission.

Figure 3–8

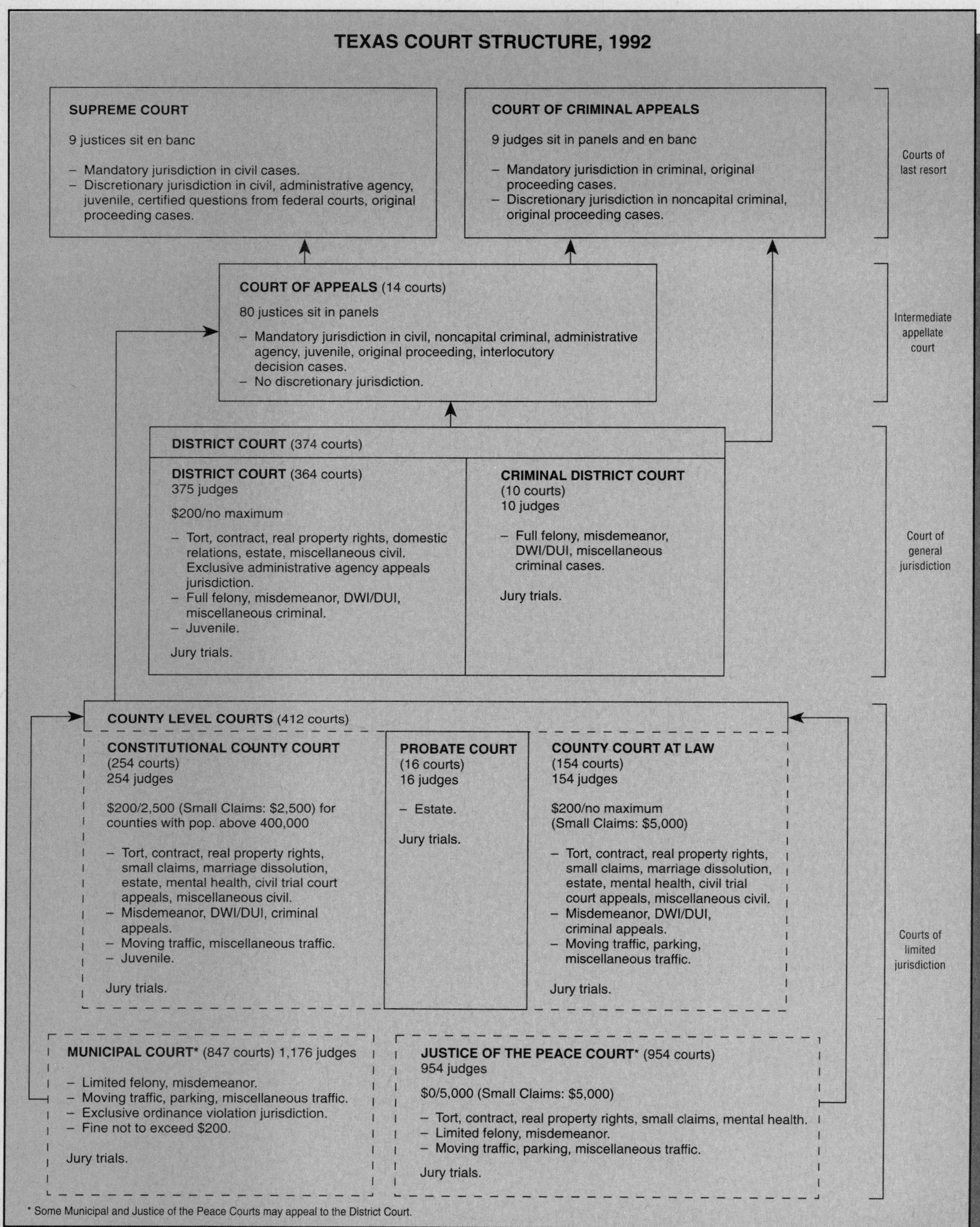

TEXAS COURT STRUCTURE, 1992
SUPREME COURT
9 justices sit en banc
– Mandatory jurisdiction in civil cases.
– Discretionary jurisdiction in civil, administrative agency, juvenile, certified questions from federal courts, original proceeding cases.
COURT OF CRIMINAL APPEALS
9 judges sit in panels and en banc
– Mandatory jurisdiction in criminal, original proceeding cases.
– Discretionary jurisdiction in noncapital criminal, original proceeding cases.
Courts of last resort
COURT OF APPEALS (14 courts)
80 justices sit in panels
– Mandatory jurisdiction in civil, noncapital criminal, administrative agency, juvenile, original proceeding, interlocutory decision cases.
– No discretionary jurisdiction.
Intermediate appellate court
DISTRICT COURT (374 courts)
DISTRICT COURT (364 courts)
375 judges
$200/no maximum
– Tort, contract, real property rights, domestic relations, estate, miscellaneous civil. Exclusive administrative agency appeals jurisdiction.
– Full felony, misdemeanor, DWI/DUI, miscellaneous criminal.
– Juvenile.
Jury trials.
CRIMINAL DISTRICT COURT
(10 courts)
10 judges
– Full felony, misdemeanor, DWI/DUI, miscellaneous criminal cases.
Jury trials.
Court of general jurisdiction
COUNTY LEVEL COURTS (412 courts)
CONSTITUTIONAL COUNTY COURT
(254 courts)
254 judges
$200/2,500 (Small Claims: $2,500) for counties with pop. above 400,000
– Tort, contract, real property rights, small claims, marriage dissolution, estate, mental health, civil trial court appeals, miscellaneous civil.
– Misdemeanor, DWI/DUI, criminal appeals.
– Moving traffic, miscellaneous traffic.
– Juvenile.
Jury trials.
PROBATE COURT
(16 courts)
16 judges
– Estate.
Jury trials.
COUNTY COURT AT LAW
(154 courts)
154 judges
$200/no maximum
(Small Claims: $5,000)
– Tort, contract, real property rights, small claims, marriage dissolution, estate, mental health, civil trial court appeals, miscellaneous civil.
– Misdemeanor, DWI/DUI, criminal appeals.
– Moving traffic, parking, miscellaneous traffic.
Jury trials.
Courts of limited jurisdiction
MUNICIPAL COURT* (847 courts) 1,176 judges
– Limited felony, misdemeanor.
– Moving traffic, parking, miscellaneous traffic.
– Exclusive ordinance violation jurisdiction.
– Fine not to exceed $200.
Jury trials.
JUSTICE OF THE PEACE COURT* (954 courts)
954 judges
$0/5,000 (Small Claims: $5,000)
– Tort, contract, real property rights, small claims, mental health.
– Limited felony, misdemeanor.
– Moving traffic, parking, miscellaneous traffic.
Jury trials.
* Some Municipal and Justice of the Peace Courts may appeal to the District Court.

The Texas Court Structure, 1992. *Source*: West's Legal Desk Reference. Reprinted with permission.

Figure 3–9 An Illustration of a State and Local Judicial System

State Supreme Court

(Court of final resort. Some states call it Court of Appeals, Supreme Judicial Court, or Supreme Court of Appeals.)

Intermediate Appellate Courts

(Only 23 of the 50 states have intermediate appellate courts, which are an intermediate appellate tribunal between the trial court and the court of final resort. A majority of cases are decided finally by these appellate courts.)

Superior Court

(Highest trial court with general jurisdiction. Some states call it Circuit Court, District Court, Court of Common Pleas, and in New York, Supreme Court.)

Probate Court*

(Some states call it Surrogate Court or Orphan's Court (Pa.). It is a special court that handles wills, administration of estates, guardianship of minors and incompetents.)

County Court*

(These courts, sometimes called Common Pleas or District Courts, have limited jurisdiction in both civil and criminal cases.)

Municipal Court*

(In some cities, it is customary to have less important cases tried by municipal justices or municipal magistrates.)

Justice of the Peace and Police Magistrate**

(Lowest courts in judicial hierarchy. Limited in jurisdiction in both civil and criminal cases.)

Domestic Relations Court

(Also called Family Court or Juvenile Court.)

* Courts of special jurisdiction, such as Probate, Family, or Juvenile, and the so-called inferior courts, such as Common Pleas or Municipal courts, may be separate courts or may be part of the trial court of general jurisdiction.

** Justices of the Peace do not exist in all states.Their jurisdictions vary greatly from state to state where they do exist.

Source: American Bar Association, Law and the Courts, 20, (1974). Reprinted with permission.

Superior or Circuit Courts Often, the superior court is a trial court with general or residual jurisdiction. In other words, depending upon the state, the superior court might accept all cases that are not given by statute to any other trial court. In some states, the probate court, juvenile court, family law court, and conciliation court are all a part of the superior court system, which has jurisdiction regardless of the amount of money involved or type of crime committed.

Jurisdiction of the superior court extends to all felony cases and all civil cases above the jurisdictional limits of the lower courts. In addition, superior courts hear appeals from decisions of municipal and justice courts.

Intermediate Appellate Courts Not all states have an intermediate appellate court. In those states that do, the appellate court is the court of review for the superior court and often has original jurisdiction in proceedings requiring the issuance of a **writ,** which is a written order issued by the court with directions as to what is to be done. For example, when in a criminal proceeding the court issues a writ of ***habeas corpus,*** a Latin phrase meaning *you should have the body,* the purpose is to determine whether the petitioner is being legally confined. In a civil action, a writ of *habeas corpus* might be used to challenge the validity of child custody, a deportation, or commitment to a mental institution.

Another type of writ commonly issued by an appellate court at its discretion is a writ of ***certiorari,*** a Latin word (pronounced sir-she-rare-ree) referring to a means of gaining appellate review. In some states, a similar writ is called a *certification.* This writ is issued by any higher court to a lower one for the purpose of inspecting and reviewing the lower court's proceeding for any irregularities. For instance, a writ of *certiorari* may be issued by the U.S. Supreme Court to any federal or state court to review a *federal question* if at least four of the nine justices vote to hear the case. In recent history, this was the means by which *Roe v. Wade,* originally a state court case, became a federal court matter.

The appellate court might also issue a writ of ***mandamus,*** Latin for *we command,* which requires a public servant or official to perform a ministerial act that the law considers an absolute duty. For example, the sheriff of Yourtown, U.S.A. has an opening for a sergeant's position. After going through the proper procedures to find a qualified applicant, the position remains unfilled because the sheriff and the mayor are engaged in a personal vendetta. The top qualified candidate for the position petitions the court to issue a writ of *mandamus* forcing the sheriff to fill the vacant position. It should be noted that a writ of *mandamus* is used infrequently, and only when any other judicial remedies have failed or are inadequate.

Supreme Court The highest court in the state is the state supreme court. Some states call this court the court of appeals, the supreme judicial court, or the supreme court of appeals. Justices of this high court review decisions of the state's appellate court, but they also have original jurisdiction in *habeas corpus, certiorari,* and *mandamus* proceedings. In some states, the supreme court automatically reviews all cases in which the death penalty has been pronounced by the trial court.

Decisions of the state supreme court are regularly published in each state and are binding on all other courts in the state.

In summary, the structure of the multitiered state court systems varies by state, but generally is categorized as follows:

1. Justice or magistrate courts have limited jurisdiction in civil and criminal cases.

2. Municipal or county courts have jurisdiction in civil cases limited to a certain dollar amount, such as $25,000 or less; jurisdiction in criminal matters is limited to misdemeanor and infraction cases. Small claims courts are part of this level of the state court system.
3. Superior or circuit courts are trial courts that accept all cases not assigned by statute to any other trial court and which may hear cases on appeal from the municipal and justice courts.
4. Intermediate appellate courts may issue special writs such as writs of *habeas corpus,* writs of *certiorari,* and writs of *mandamus,* as well as hear cases on appeal from the superior court.
5. State supreme court reviews decisions of the appellate court and also may issue writs.

Court Personnel

Whether you are working in the federal courts or the state courts, court personnel are generally the same and perform similar tasks. It can be an advantage for you to become personally acquainted with the people in the various courts with whom you need to interact on a regular basis.

Judges As discussed earlier in this chapter, judges in the federal court system are appointed by the President with advice and consent from the Senate. By contrast, in some states, state court judges are appointed initially by the Governor but subsequently must be elected on a nonpartisan ballot by the voters who reside in their judicial district in order to retain their positions. State supreme court judges are typically appointed to serve longer terms than the other state court judges (usually twelve years), but they, too, must receive voter affirmation on a statewide basis at the first gubernatorial election following the appointment in order to continue in office.

In particularly overcrowded lower state courts, attorneys are often asked to fulfill the role of judge ***pro tempore,*** or *pro tem,* a Latin phrase meaning *for the time being.* Attorneys are selected by the presiding judge of the court to serve in this capacity. With the exception of some justice courts and magistrate courts, full-time judges are not allowed to maintain a private law practice.

Law Clerks Law clerks are employed by judges to perform a wide range of duties. They are usually third-year law students or recently graduated lawyers. Often the law clerk's duties are focused in three areas: researching motions, writing memorandum opinions, and preparing jury instructions.

Frequently, a law clerk may be asked to study a **motion,** which is a request submitted by attorneys to the court for a ruling on a pending action or point of law, and the adverse party's response to it. Then the law clerk will research the applicable law and write a memorandum to the judge, who may then rule on the motion or request counsel to appear for oral argument. If the case is particularly complex or involves an important legal question, the judge may ask the law clerk to prepare a written **memorandum opinion,** a document in which the judge's decision and the law on which he or she relied is set down in detail.

Law clerks may also help judges prepare written **jury instructions,** which set forth the questions of fact that the jury must decide. Paralegals who work for trial attorneys sometimes also assist in preparing jury instructions. Whoever prepares jury instructions must be completely familiar with the facts of the case and have a thorough understanding of the applicable law. For example, in a recent case before a California jury, one fact to be decided was not whether the defendant was guilty of holding sex parties in his home but whether he was running a business in a residential neighborhood, because he was charging people a fee to attend these weekend orgies.

Some law clerks perform administrative functions for the judges, such as keeping the **docket,** a list of cases on the court's calendar, and serving as liaison with the attorneys to help them settle any disputes that may arise in preparing for trial. Regardless of the tasks performed by law clerks, they are bound by the same high code of ethics as the judges and other court personnel. At times they are required to walk a fine line between being helpful and courteous yet not succumbing to efforts by some lawyers to gain an unfair advantage or a particular favor.

Secretary The judge's secretary performs traditional secretarial duties, such as typing legal documents, memoranda, and correspondence for the judge and the law clerks. In addition, the secretary may keep track of the docket and schedule trials and conferences, in courtrooms where the deputy does not perform these administrative functions. Judges' secretaries are assuming more responsibility and a wider variety of duties in today's overcrowded courtrooms, where several hundred cases may be pending at any one time.

Figure 3–10 A Typical Legal Office Activity

A judge and law clerk confer on a case file while the secretary takes notes of the meeting. *Source*: Bob Mullenix.

Court Reporter It is the court reporter's job to record all proceedings verbatim, either by shorthand or by using a machine designed for this purpose. He or she then transcribes the recorded proceedings if requested by the judge or one of the parties to the action. In some courtrooms, the court reporter is responsible for keeping exhibits introduced during the trial. Most courtroom reporters are salaried. However, some are self-employed or work through a court-reporting service. Court reporters charge an additional fee for preparing a transcript of a proceeding.

Courtroom Deputy The traditional functions of the courtroom deputy, sometimes called a *bailiff,* include recording the minutes of courtroom proceedings, marking and keeping exhibits, administering oaths, receiving jury verdicts, and in some cases preparing appropriate judgments. In today's court, however, the courtroom deputy might also be responsible for some of the administrative and management details, such as calendaring dates and times for status conferences and motion hearings.

Court Clerk The clerk's office is the center of the record-keeping and service functions of the court where pleadings are filed and official records are maintained. Depending upon the volume of litigation and the size of the court's district, the clerk's staff may consist of many or just one or two deputy clerks. It is the deputy clerk's responsibility to set up new files, accept and file pleadings, record pleadings on central docket sheets, mail out orders, and prepare statistical information.

In addition, deputy clerks are responsible for summoning a jury and administering the jury program. The objective of a jury program is to make the best use of jurors' time and yet have a jury available when needed. Since cases often settle at the last minute, it is difficult to predict just when they might be needed. For instance, while deputy clerks are in the final stages of **impaneling** a jury, the process by which jurors are selected and sworn in, the attorneys might be settling the case on the courthouse steps. Instead of sending the jurors home, the deputy clerk might refer them to another judge who is about to begin jury selection on a different case. Deputy clerks try to work closely with the judges' staffs to make good use of time for both jurors and judges.

United States Marshal Although the U.S. Marshal's office works closely with the courts, it is not part of the judicial branch of government. The marshal's office reports to the Attorney General of the United States and is a part of the executive branch.

Sometimes referred to as the courtroom police, the marshals are responsible for providing security in the courtroom and for serving all pleadings that are required by law to be served by the marshal. In some states, private process servers have taken over the function of serving routine legal documents requiring personal service, but marshals are still required to serve writs and perform other types of services.

For example, the marshal's office is responsible for transporting and retaining custody of defendants in criminal cases who need to appear in court. In addition, once a jury has been selected and sworn in, the marshal takes charge of the jury and is the only officer of the court who may communicate with the jury outside the courtroom. Since they perform a variety of duties, several marshals may be in the courtroom during a criminal trial, depending on the case before the court. At the very least there will be one marshal in charge of the jury,

Figure 3–11 Courtroom Scene

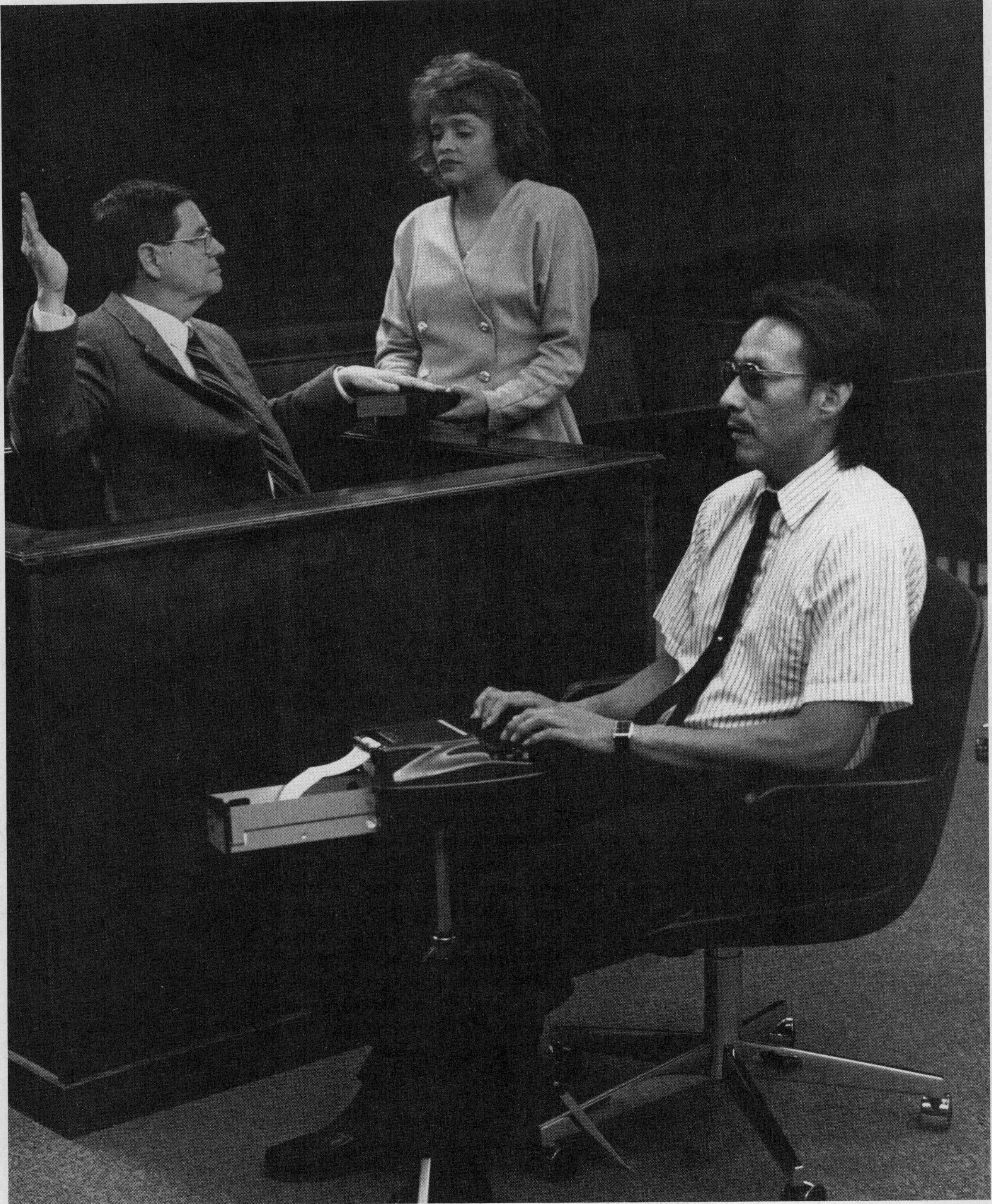

A court reporter will record a witness's oath as it is administered by a courtroom deputy. *Source*: Bob Mullenix.

Figure 3–12 A Court Clerk's Office.

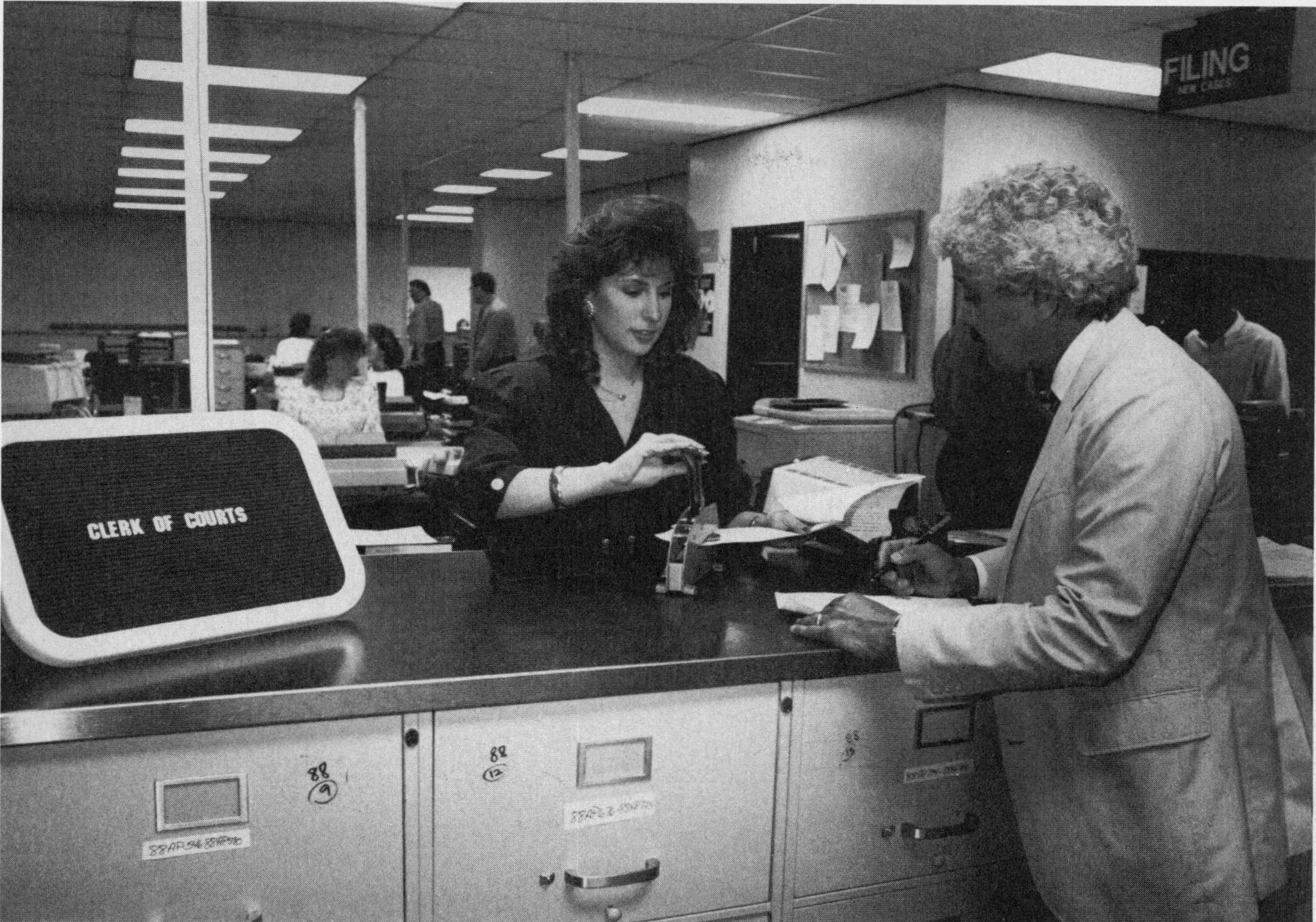

Pleadings are accepted at the filing window of a court clerk's office. *Source*: Bob Mullenix.

one to watch the defendant, and another to maintain security in the remainder of the courtroom.

If the trial has received unusual publicity or is controversial, several more marshals will be called upon to protect the safety of the judges and their staff, as well as to help maintain order and security. It is not uncommon for judges' lives to be threatened, and it is becoming increasingly common for concealed weapons to be carried into the courtroom and fired in anger or despair.

In summary, you can expect to find the following personnel associated with the typical court:

1. The judge
2. One or more law clerks
3. The judge's secretary
4. The court reporter
5. A courtroom deputy
6. The court clerk and deputy clerks
7. Several U.S. marshals

Figure 3–13 A Criminal Proceeding

A Marshall is always present in the courtroom during a criminal proceeding. *Source*: James H. Pickerell/Stock Boston.

3–4 Alternatives to Court

Most of our court systems are overcrowded to the point where four- and five-year delays before a case comes to trial are common. There are just too many cases and not enough judges or courtrooms to handle them, regardless of which branch of the court system is examined. For example, consider the caseload facing judges in Orange County, California, which has a population of about 2.5 million people. During the year 1989–90 the four justices sitting in Division 3 of the 4th District Court of Appeals disposed of an average of 378 cases each for a total of 1511 cases, or about 1.7 cases per day. During the same period, the Orange County Superior Court clerk's office had 11,749 new motor vehicle accident filings.

But the judges of the Orange County Municipal Court are among the busiest of that state's court personnel. Excluding parking cases, these 56 justices disposed of 830,926 civil and criminal cases during the year 1989–90 for an average of 14,838 cases per judge, or about 67.5 cases per day. By comparison, the Los Angeles Municipal Court, with 111 judicial officers, disposed of 1,147,944 cases, or 10,342 per judge, 47 cases per day. With these kinds of caseloads, the obvious question is: Is enough time and attention being given to these legal matters, which may have a profound and lasting effect on the lives of the people involved?

Several theories have been advanced to explain the events that are contributing to the overloaded court system. Some of the theories are: an ill-designed judicial system unable to cope with the caseload presented to it; a society that increasingly looks to the court to right its wrongs, whether real or imagined; too many lawyers filing frivolous lawsuits; and an increase in criminal activity that challenges the constitutional guarantee of the right to a speedy trial. To ensure speedy trials, the U.S. Supreme Court ruled in May 1991 that any person picked up by police without a warrant is entitled to a hearing within 48 hours to ensure that the arrest is justified. This ruling means that authorities may no longer hold arrested people in jail over weekends and holidays simply because the courthouse is closed; judges must now be available on weekends and holidays for hearings in criminal matters.

It is safe to assume that for whatever reasons most court systems are currently facing unprecedented numbers of case filings without adequate courtrooms or personnel to dispose of the cases in a quick and cost-effective manner. Because of the long delays now associated with litigation, a revolution of sorts is taking place in several areas across the country to help speed up the dispute-resolution process.

Arbitration

There are three ways to settle a dispute in the legal world that do not involve going to court: arbitration, mediation, and private judges. **Arbitration** is the dispute-settling process in which the parties agree that an impartial third party, called the *arbitrator,* will act as a judge and make the decision.

Arbitration has been the primary means used to settle labor disputes for several years now, not only with organized labor unions but with disputes involving police officers' and firefighters' contracts. Arbitration is so commonplace among these groups that some labor organizations have a staff of permanent arbitrators exclusively for the purpose of resolving disputes between labor and management.

Already fairly common in commercial disputes and labor management relations, arbitration is now required by some states in uninsured motorist and no-fault insurance plans and by some health-care providers. Smaller service businesses and an increasing number of doctors, lawyers, and lending institutions are putting a provision for arbitration in their standard contracts. The agreement usually specifies how the arbitrator will be selected and other mechanics of the process, such as whether the decision of the arbitrator may be appealed. Normally, the agreements provide that the decision of the arbitrator is final and binding; rules of evidence are informal; and that the parties will split the costs of arbitration.

The American Arbitration Association estimates that they handle approximately 64,000 cases nationwide each year, usually lasting one to three days in length. The costs associated with arbitration begin at $300 for commercial and construction cases involving up to $10,000 in claims. If the claim exceeds $10,000 or falls outside the commercial and construction areas, the arbitration fee is based on a sliding scale that varies depending upon the amount of the claim.

Mediation

Mediation is a different process from arbitration. A **mediation,** unlike arbitration, is merely advisory in nature and is nonbinding. Instead of making a decision for the parties, the mediator attempts to facilitate an agreeable resolution of the controversy. Common users of this type of advisory dispute resolution are labor unions, homeowners' associations, cities, counties, and other governmental entities. Families experiencing various types of problems including disputes over custody and visitation also use the services of mediators.

Mediation is particularly helpful in cases where the basic issue is something more than how much money the defendant will be required to pay to the plaintiff. For example, where there is an ongoing business or personal relationship, mediation is a useful way to resolve differences and maintain the relationship.

The mediation is conducted in a manner determined by the mediator. Statements and explanations may be presented and attorneys are sometimes present, but the hearing resembles a discussion in a conversational setting rather than an interrogation on the witness stand. The parties may consider the effect of the proposed agreement on each of them, unlike courts where the personal effect the decision may have on the parties is not usually considered as part of the decision-making process.

When an agreement is reached, a settlement agreement may be drafted. Or mediation may result in an agreement to apologize, an offer of future business, or in the claimant's agreement to accept services instead of money. If the dispute cannot be resolved in mediation, the parties may then turn to arbitration or litigation.

Arbitration and mediation services are offered by nonprofit organizations such as the American Arbitration Association and various mediation service centers, some of which are run by the courts, as well as by privately owned, for-profit businesses such as Judicate, a Philadelphia-based company with offices nationwide, and the California-based Judicial Arbitration and Mediation Services (JAMS).

Private Judges

In addition to arbitration and mediation, for-profit dispute resolution businesses offer another way to settle differences—private judging services by retired justices. The parties in a pending civil lawsuit may enter into a stipulation agreeing to a trial by a **private judge** of their own choosing. If the parties are unable to agree upon which private judge they want to hear their case, the court may appoint one.

Since this proceeding originates by court order, it is a formal one and follows the rules of procedure and evidence (unless the parties agree otherwise) and results in findings that stand as the decision of the court. The decision of the judge is enforceable and may be appealed, as with a regular trial court judgment.

Some advantages to hiring a private judge are obvious: the parties select their own judge in whom they all have confidence, which results in fewer time-wasting motions and appeals; the case is prepared for trial only once, since cases are heard on the date selected by the parties; there is no jury, so the parties may agree on any set of rules for presentation of the case that is mutually acceptable; the judge is worried only about the case before him or her; and, the judge's decision is rendered promptly.

In addition, the cost of litigation is greatly reduced with a private judge. Typically, each party to the lawsuit would pay about $175 an hour, plus a nominal processing fee, for the services of a private judge. The average case before a private judge takes about six hours and costs about $1000 for each party.

By contrast, the average deposition costs about $2000, and that is only one of many expenses before a case goes to trial.

If using the services of a mediator, arbitrator, or private judge to settle legal disputes has a down side, it is a difficult one to imagine. The primary criticism has been that the status of the office may be somewhat diminished when retired justices join the rent-a-judge ranks. Another criticism is that these alternatives to dispute resolution favor the rich. That is, justice is expedited for those who can afford to hire arbitrators, mediators, or private judges, whereas those without funds must wait for their day in court.

The American Bar Association estimated in 1990 that there were more than 410 dispute resolution centers in the U.S., processing more than two million cases each year. With two million fewer cases winding their way through the courts, even the harshest critics find it difficult to argue against alternatives to dispute resolution that have a positive impact on both an overburdened system and the parties in dispute. Without these alternatives, the wait would be even longer for those who choose to or must use the courts.

In summary, some alternative methods of resolving disputes include:

1. Arbitration,
2. Mediation, and
3. Private judges.

3–5 Courts of the Future

Although no one can accurately predict how the courts of the future will look or operate, it is safe to predict that with the steps currently being taken, courts in the twenty-first century will be remarkably different from those of today. The areas in which to expect major differences are in procedure and automation.

Court Reforms

Courts of the future may themselves be able to offer more arbitration and mediation services, as well as devise other ways to resolve disputes. But citizens will always demand the option of trial by jury, which will, of necessity, take place in the traditional courtroom environment. But courts around the country are actively seeking ways to streamline operations, from offering 24-hour, 7-day-a-week services and reforming current procedures to computerizing the courtroom.

Voir Dire One of the hottest court reforms to hit some states recently is ***voir dire.*** *Voir dire* is the examination of prospective jurors by the court and attorneys for the plaintiff and the defendant to determine whether an individual exhibits an attitude that would keep her or him from being able to serve as a fair and impartial juror in the case before the court.

Under some of the new state courts' *voir dire* reform rules, only the trial judge initially examines the prospective jurors. When the judge has completed his or her examination, counsel for each party then have the right to examine any of the prospective jurors, but they must adhere to a time limit set by the trial judge. In many instances, after the judge's examination, counsel and the judge are in agreement on whether to keep or discharge a prospective juror.

Why are these new *voir dire* rules important in court reform? Under the former rules of procedure, selecting a jury could take weeks or months, particularly if the case had been highly publicized. The new *voir dire* rules, recently enacted in some states and being discussed in others, mimic the federal laws pertaining to jury selection by giving the judge more control of the process. In addition, under the new rules lawyers may seek the court's permission to submit written questionnaires to prospective jurors, the contents of which are determined by the court.

Written questions have two distinct advantages in jury selection. One is that with written responses the lawyers can look up a juror's response to a certain question instead of having to rely on memory, thus reducing the possibility that someone might be accepted as a juror whom the attorney wished to have excused. For instance, when a jury is being impaneled, 100 or more people may be called for *voir dire*. It is impossible for the court or the attorneys to remember the answer given to a particular question by Prospective Juror No. 26, who was asked to remain as a possible juror, when they are now questioning No. 67.

The second advantage to written questionnaires is that jurors find answering difficult routine questions—such as, Have you or any member of your family taken drugs or been convicted of a felony?—easier than if asked to do so in public. Often they do not answer these questions truthfully in public, but are more likely to do so in writing. The new *voir dire* rules can reduce the time required to impanel a jury from several weeks to a few days in many cases.

As in all court reform debates, there is a good deal of political and judicial philosophy surrounding the changes in *voir dire*. Some attorneys and judges think that extensive, searching *voir dire* conducted by the court and counsel together is necessary not only to pick impartial juries, but also to legitimately allow the lawyers to present themselves and their cases to the jurors in the best light. Others are most willing to let the judges take a more leading role in selecting a jury. All agree, however, that something must be done to speed up the process.

Fast Track In 1988, the State of California introduced a pilot program commonly known as *fast track* in an attempt to relieve the congestion in its overcrowded courts. Nine counties were selected for a three-year test of the fast track program. The goal of the program is to dispose of civil actions by settlement, trial, or other means within 36 months or less from the date the complaint is filed.

Superior court judges in the counties with the fast track program have considerable freedom to develop local rules, including policies, procedures, and forms to achieve the goal. By putting judges in charge of managing the cases instead of allowing lawyers to dictate the flow of litigation, unnecessary court proceedings and filings have been eliminated, trials begin on schedule, and cases are regularly monitored by court personnel to ensure that they are moving through the system in a timely manner.

At the end of its first three years in operation, the conclusions are that the California fast track program is exceeding expectations in keeping civil cases moving through the nine pilot courts, and more counties are now implementing the program. In the typical fast track court, the majority of civil cases are being disposed of within two years of filing, half of the jury trials are being completed within one week, and the backlog of pending cases is being decreased on average to less than two years.

The main problem casting a shadow over cases on the fast track is the growing number of criminal cases, which take precedence over civil cases, thereby frequently derailing the cases on the fast track.

Computer-Integrated Courtrooms

Beginning in 1983, when the National Shorthand Reporters Association (NSRA) modified stenographic equipment to translate machine shorthand within seconds and display the real-time translation on courtroom video screens at the judge's bench, counsel tables, and in the witness box when needed, the application of high technology to the court system became one of the fastest-growing phenomena to have a resounding impact on the legal profession.

NSRA's system has evolved to where judges and lawyers can now display transcripts of depositions or testimony from an earlier trial on their computer screens. In addition to following testimony on their computer terminals, they can go to another screen and retrieve other transcript material relating to the topic being discussed by doing a key-word search. With access to databases such as LEXIS® and WESTLAW®, lawyers can also do research while in the courtroom. Systems with these capabilities have been operating in some district courts in Dallas and Phoenix for several years and have received an enthusiastic response from most of the judges and lawyers.

Networking databases is another use of computer technology being used on an experimental basis in a few judicial systems. In the Eighth Judicial Circuit of Florida, the clerks' offices, sheriff's office, judges' chambers, state attorney's office, and public defender's office are all connected to each other by one integrated computer network. When the system is statewide, law enforcement agencies, prosecutors' offices, correctional institutions, and the court will be linked together to access information. For example, using the integrated computer network, a defense attorney in a criminal action could easily make inquiries about a client's prior criminal activity in another county.

Another type of integrated network system has moved beyond the experimental stages in the State of Washington. There attorneys now have access to docket information by dialing an 800 number that connects the attorney's personal computer to the court's computer for 80 percent of the state courts, including the supreme court, superior courts, municipal courts, and juvenile courts.

As the price of technology falls, courts across the nation are expected to move quickly to optical imaging, a method used to store huge numbers of documents, exhibits, photographs, and fingerprints on laser disks. With the addition of split-screen capability, you could be looking at a file docket on one side of the screen and simultaneously pull up a specific document listed on the docket on the other side of the screen.

Some courts, such as the traffic division of the Los Angeles Municipal Court, no longer keep hard copies of traffic tickets. Instead, all tickets are stored in the computer using the imaging process. When someone comes in to pay a ticket, the name is keyed in and the ticket appears on the computer screen.

Videoconferencing technology is at the top of the wish list for many state and federal courts. In predominantly rural states, such as Utah, Montana, and Wyoming, just about everyone involved with the judicial process could benefit from a videoconferencing system. For example, instead of everyone having to travel to the courthouse, often over long distances and at great expense, a judge would be able to go to a specially equipped courtroom, the attorney and client would go to a local videoconferencing center, and the hearing would be conducted on the video screen using computers and telephone hook-ups. In the federal courts, videoconferencing would be especially helpful when a party lives out of state, is out of the country, or is physically unable to appear in the courtroom.

Most of the current computer technology is being used primarily in state court systems because they tend to be smaller in size than the federal system, and much of the technology is still in the experimental stages. However, because the cost of the technology is coming down and training programs are widely available, it is reasonable to expect that the phenomenon known as the Computer Integrated Courtroom (CIC) will continue to expand in both the state and federal courts nationwide.

SUMMARY

3–1

The court performs three functions—dispute settler, decision maker, and protector—and the term *court* has two meanings: the branch of government responsible for settling disputes, and as a substitute for judge. The court in its role as dispute settler is typically divided into various parts: trial courts for criminal cases and civil cases; family courts for dissolutions, adoptions, and custody matters; and probate courts for proceedings regarding deceased or incompetent persons and guardianship matters. The court, unlike the legislative and executive branches of government, can only become involved in the dispute resolution process after someone else initiates action. In this role as decision maker, the judge performs two tasks: determining facts from the evidence and testimony and applying the law to the facts to determine which party should prevail. The high court protects the viewpoint of the majority from infringing upon the rights of the minority by having the power to review the decisions of the lower courts.

3–2

The jurisdiction of the federal courts is divided by the U.S. Constitution into two general areas: cases involving federal questions, such as where the application of the Constitution, the law, or a treaty is being disputed, and those involving diversity jurisdiction, such as when controversies arise between citizens of different states or between citizens of the U.S. and a foreign country. At the foundation of the federal court system are the 94 judicial districts, each with one or more federal district courts, which are courts of original jurisdiction for federal question cases, diversity jurisdiction cases, and bankruptcy cases. At the next level are the U.S. Courts of Appeal, which hear appeals from criminal, civil, and tax court cases and federal administrative agencies. The U.S. Supreme Court, the highest court in the country, has appellate jurisdiction over any state and federal court decision, as well as original jurisdiction in cases where an ambassador or other public minister is involved or where the United States is involved. Federal court judges are appointed by the President to serve, conditionally, for life after confirmation by a majority of the members of the U.S. Senate.

3–3

There are as many types of state court systems as there are states. However, the typical state court system is multitiered. The foundation courts are the justice or magistrate courts, followed by the municipal or county courts, then the superior or circuit courts, the appellate courts, and at the highest level, the state supreme court. Typical court personnel include the judge and his or her staff of law clerks and secretaries; the court reporter; the courtroom deputy; the court clerk; and the U.S. marshals who are charged with keeping the courtroom secure and maintaining order.

3–4

Because of the overcrowded condition of most state courts, people are seeking other ways to resolve their disputes. Arbitration, when money is involved, and mediation, when relationships are also important, are two types of dispute-resolution alternatives to going to court. Parties to a civil lawsuit may also agree to retain the services of a private judge, whose decision has the same force and effect as that given by a judge in a courtroom. All these alternatives have the advantage of taking less time and money than the usual resolution process of the traditional court.

3–5

Courts themselves are looking for ways to streamline procedures and speed up the trial process. Among the procedures being reformed in many states include *voir dire,* the examination of prospective jurors, in which the judge is being given a bigger role, and a program known as *fast track* in which the goal is to dispose of civil actions within three years or less after the complaint is filed. In addition to reforming procedures, many courts are in the process of being fully computerized and integrated with various types of databases to provide a wide range of information at the fingertips of judges and counsel in the courtroom. As courts experience success with reformed procedures and the price of technology falls, the courts of the future are expected not only to look different but to operate more efficiently as well.

REVIEW

Key Terms

Before proceeding, review the key terms listed below to be sure you understand each one. If necessary, read over the corresponding section of the chapter. When you are ready to test your understanding, answer the Review Questions.

appellate jurisdiction
arbitration
bench
certiorari
civil cases
court
criminal cases
deliberates
diversity jurisdiction
docket
double jeopardy
family court
federal question jurisdiction
habeas corpus
impaneling
impeachment
jurisdiction
jury instructions
mandamus
mediation
memorandum opinion
motion
original jurisdiction
private judge
pro tempore
probate court
treaty
trial courts
verdict
voir dire
writ

Questions for Review and Discussion

1. How would you describe the general functions and roles of the courts?
2. Because of the diversity and complexity of cases brought to the court, most court systems, particularly the state courts, are divided by areas of specialization. How is the court system divided and what types of cases are heard by each?
3. The federal courts have jurisdiction over two general types of cases. What are they?
4. How is the federal court system structured?
5. Outline the typical state court system and its jurisdiction.
6. The personnel in most state and federal court systems are the same. What are the job titles and functions of the usual court personnel?
7. What are some of the alternatives to going to court as a way to settle a dispute?
8. Define *voir dire* and a method currently being used to shorten it.
9. Critique the current legal justice system in relation to the overcrowded courts.
10. Describe what is being done to integrate high technology with the courts.

Activities

1. Arrange a tour of the nearest state and federal court facilities. Ask the clerk to describe the clerk's job and to explain what happens to legal documents after the paralegal prepares and files them.

2. Go to the nearest court and witness a trial or hearing. Compare and discuss what you see taking place in the courtroom with what is portrayed on television and in the movies. What is the same and what is different?
3. Illustrate your state court system, its various divisions, the names of each, and the jurisdiction of each.
4. Write a paper discussing your suggestions for reforming the current state or federal judicial system.

CHAPTER 4 Criminal Law

OUTLINE

4–1 Introduction to the Criminal Justice System
- A History of Lawlessness
- A Tradition of Common Law
- Overview of the U.S. Criminal Justice System

4–2 The Accused
- Fourth Amendment Protections
- Fifth Amendment Protections
- Sixth Amendment Protections
- Eighth Amendment Protections

4–3 The Lawyers
- The Prosecution
- The Defense

4–4 The Trial
- Investigation
- Arrest
- Bail
- Indictment
- Arraignment
- Plea Bargaining
- Pretrial Motions
- Trial
- Sentencing

4–5 A Day in the Criminal Court
- Kellie's Shopping Trip
- Michael's Mishap

COMMENTARY

Mr. Dunn's close friend and client, the president of Your Town's Largest Company and pillar of the community, has been arrested for allegedly failing to pay taxes and engaging in fraudulent business practices. His one phone call from jail is to Mr. Dunn who is on vacation. The call is put through to you, Mr. Dunn's legal assistant. When you came to work at Dunn & Sweeney, a law firm whose clients are primarily businesspeople, you never thought you would have to deal with the criminal justice system. Now you are expected to know enough to help a client and, at the same time, not jeopardize your career. With trepidation, you answer the call and begin yet another odyssey of learning in your legal career.

OBJECTIVES

In Chapter 3 you learned about the structure, jurisdiction, organization, and personnel of both the federal and state court systems. After studying this chapter, you should be able to:

1. Contrast the U.S. criminal justice system with the Roman civil law system.
2. Discuss the U.S. criminal justice system and its two categories of criminal behavior.
3. List the rights guaranteed by the Fourth, Fifth, Sixth, and Eighth Amendments to the U.S. Constitution.
4. Discuss the role of the prosecutor.
5. Contrast the role of the defense counsel with that of the prosecutor.
6. List the steps in the criminal trial process.
7. Explain how bail is determined.
8. Describe the role of the grand jury.
9. Discuss the reasons for the most common pretrial motions.
10. Describe the sentencing stage of the criminal trial process.

4–1 Introduction to the Criminal Justice System

In the fall of 1990, the National Center for Health Statistics released figures indicating that the homicide death rate for men between the ages of 18 and 24 in the United States is 70 times higher than Austria's, 73 times higher than Japan's, 22 times that of Western Germany, and 12 times that of 24 other countries. Among African-American males between the ages of 18 and 24, homicide is the leading cause of death.

A History of Lawlessness

Although most of us consider ourselves to be law-abiding citizens, limiting our crime sprees to infrequent traffic law infractions, the history of our country is filled with stories of crime and violence.

The 13 original colonies were settled by as many (if not more) criminals swept from the English jails as by upstanding citizens of good character who were fleeing religious or political persecution. Whereas it is common knowledge that Great Britain colonized Australia by transporting undesirables from London's slums, and ridding its jails of convicted murderers and thieves, it is less well known that the American colonies were also subjected to a deluge of the worst elements from British society. During the 40-year period from about 1660 to 1700, more than 4500 convicts were sent to America's colonies; 8846 more were sent to Annapolis, Maryland between 1745 and 1775.

These were not the hard-working, industrious colonials memorialized in the history books. They were thieves, rapists, and murderers. No doubt a great many of these transported convicts took advantage of the opportunities offered by the promised land and built a new crime-free life for themselves upon arrival. But there is also no doubt that the more hardened criminals reverted to or continued with the only lifestyle they knew. It was this latter group who introduced a tradition of crime and violence to the new colonies. How to deal with it has been a continuing problem plaguing the country since its infancy.

A Tradition of Common Law

The U.S. system for dealing with crimes and criminals appears, at times, to be both harsh and ineffective. Perhaps this is due in part to the adversarial nature of our courts and our tradition of common law. Almost all European countries and nearly all Third World countries with a European cultural heritage, have legal systems based on the so-called inquisitorial method, which has its roots in the 2000-year-old civil or Roman law. The exceptions are Great Britain and Ireland. Note that here *civil law* refers to the traditional criminal justice system of most Western European countries, and is not to be confused with the more commonly known definition of civil law, which refers to noncriminal matters.

Charles Maechling, Jr., former professor of law at the University of Virginia and former member of the law faculty of Cambridge University, gives this view of the U.S. criminal justice system (*ABA Journal*, January 1991):

> Only the Anglo-Saxon countries cling to a judicial parody of the medieval tournament—lawyers for the state and the defense fight for the body of the accused before a judge as umpire and a jury carefully selected for its ignorance of the personalities and issues before it.
>
> The narrow focus on the accused, coupled with the disproportionate power and authority of the state, necessitates a bristling array of constitutional safeguards and procedural rules to level the jousting field and protect the defendant's rights. The tournament, or trial, is the supreme event: Nothing in the prior stages of the criminal justice process has any validity until proved to the satisfaction of the jury in open court.
>
> Anglo-American trial procedure has a limited purpose—to enforce the tournament rules. As every first-year law student learns, the function of the trial is not to establish the truth: It is to convince the jury beyond a reasonable doubt that the accused is guilty of the crime he is charged with, and nothing else.

The process of proving guilt is carried out in the most awkward way possible, with innumerable obstacles to overcome along the way. Then, the jury is asked to determine guilt or innocence on the narrowest grounds. The choice before the jury is not "What, if anything, did the defendant do that was against the law?" but "Did the defendant do exactly what the prosecution alleges?" Under the tournament rules of the adversarial process, you can see how some of the guilty may go free, whereas the innocent may become victims of the system.

By contrast, the rules of the civil law or inquisitorial process are based on the notion that justice can be served by objective methods of inquiry rather than by pitbull confrontations in a judicial arena. The inquisitorial process—note the derivation of the term *inquisitorial* is from *inquiry*, not *inquisition*—does not make the trial the main event in the way the accusatory process does. In the civil law process, the trial is just the public finale of an ongoing investigation, with every bit of relevant information about the case going into the file. Then the collected material is examined, weighed for its value, and a judgment is made as to whether or not it all adds up to a solid case against the suspect. The emphasis is on building a case that will hang together based on all the information available after accumulating corroborative evidence, examining possible witnesses and taking supportive statements, and resolving any ambiguities and uncertainties. Only then, under the civil law process, is the decision made to bring a suspect to formal trial. At this point, the burden of proving innocence shifts to the accused because, under this system, the defendant would not reach the trial stage at all without a strong case against him or her.

Professor John Merryman of Stanford University, a leading comparative-law scholar, notes that if innocent, he would prefer to be tried by a civil-law court, but if he were guilty, he would prefer to be tried by a common-law court. Even though judges, lawyers, and citizens alike are actively seeking answers to the question of what's wrong with the system, it is unlikely that reforms would lead to adopting the civil law method in this country. We

4–2 The Accused

Although it is true that some courts do not respond as quickly and efficiently as they would like to and that justice is not always fair and impartial, a large part of the inherent tension in the criminal justice system is due to conflicting ideologies. Everyone wants justice administered faster and with greater efficiency, but most of us also want to make sure that all the rights of the accused are protected. The result of these conflicts is that there is a correlation between the number of laws designed to protect the rights of the accused and the amount of time required to dispose of a case before the court.

Protection for the rights of the accused stems from the Supreme Court's interpretations of the first ten amendments to the U.S. Constitution, the Bill of Rights. Although the provisions of the Bill of Rights were originally intended to apply only to matters involving the federal government, the provisions were subsequently extended to all the states with the adoption of the Fourteenth Amendment, which provides for due process and equal protection of the laws. Individual states may determine what is a crime and create their own court system and procedure for handling criminals, but in so doing they cannot go beyond the limits established by the Bill of Rights.

Let's take a look at four of the amendments and the rights and privileges granted by them to everyone residing in the U.S., whether a citizen or not. The rights and privileges granted by the Bill of Rights are referred to collectively as **procedural due process.**

Fourth Amendment Protections

It was not uncommon during the early days in our country's history for citizens to hide soldiers, weapons, and various types of confidential information in their homes. It was also common for members of the militia or other peacekeeping officers to invade private homes without provocation, often leaving behind death and destruction. These actions were reminiscent of the tyranny from which many colonists had fled and they were unacceptable. The Fourth Amendment was therefore included in the Bill of Rights to counter the abuses from searches conducted without warrants and was designed to safeguard the public's legitimate or reasonable expectation of privacy.

The Supreme Court has interpreted this amendment to mean that no person's home, automobile, place of business, or other property may be searched unless the police have probable cause to believe that smuggled goods are on the premises or that there is evidence of a crime at the place to be searched. In the event evidence is illegally obtained—that is, obtained without a warrant—it must be barred at trial under a rule known as the **exclusionary rule.** Under the protections afforded by the Fourth Amendment, some courts have also excluded evidence obtained

Figure 4–2 The Fourth Amendment

THE FOURTH AMENDMENT

The right of the people to be secure in their persons, houses, papers and effects, against unreasonable searches and seizures, shall not be violated, and no Warrants shall issue, but upon probable cause, supported by Oath or affirmation, and particularly describing the place to be searched, and the persons or things to be seized.

by invasions of a person's body, such as by compulsory vaccinations, blood tests, body cavity searches, or the surgical removal of a bullet.

The exclusionary rule is just one of the tensions existing between law enforcement officers and the criminal justice system. It would seem that, though there is an increasing demand from the public to take criminals off the streets, the police are hampered in doing so by the equally increasing demand for protection against illegal searches.

Fifth Amendment Protections

The Fifth Amendment provides that a person shall not be required to answer for a federal felony unless **indicted,** or accused, by a **grand jury.** Since the states are not constitutionally required to have grand juries, only about half of them do. A grand jury is a group of people, usually about 23 in number, drawn, summoned, and selected according to law to investigate and inform a court of criminal jurisdiction on crimes committed within its jurisdiction and to indict persons for crimes when it has discovered sufficient evidence to hold a person for trial. The purpose for a grand jury is to protect the accused by placing a barrier between the state's law enforcement agencies and the individual.

The protections of this amendment include that no person shall be placed in double jeopardy, or tried twice for the same offense, and that no person shall be compelled to be a witness against him- or herself in a criminal case, the **privilege against self-incrimination** commonly known as "taking the Fifth." When invoking the privilege against self-incrimination, the accused does not have to prove that he or she is innocent, nor is he or she obligated to take the witness stand or even to talk about the incident. Instead, it is up to the prosecutor to prove the defendant is guilty.

Because of the *Miranda v. Arizona* case, 384 U.S. 436 (1966), the United States Supreme Court extended the application of this privilege against self-incrimination to cover preliminary and routine questioning by police officers. The rights established by that case are called the **Miranda warnings.** Prior to questioning by the police, everyone must be warned that they have the right to remain silent, that any statement they make may be used against them, that they have the right to have an attorney present, and that if they cannot afford an attorney, one will be appointed by the government. As with evidence obtained in violation of the Fourth Amendment, any evidence obtained in violation of *Miranda* cannot be presented in court under the exclusionary rule.

Figure 4–3 The Fifth Amendment

THE FIFTH AMENDMENT

No person shall be held to answer for a capital, or otherwise infamous crime, unless on a presentment or indictment of a Grand Jury, except in cases arising in the land or naval forces, or in the Militia, when in actual service in time of War or public danger; nor shall any person be subject for the same offense to be twice put in jeopardy of life or limb, nor shall be compelled in any criminal case to be a witness against himself, nor be deprived of life, liberty, or property, without due process of law; nor shall private property be taken for public use without just compensation.

Figure 4–4 The Sixth Amendment

THE SIXTH AMENDMENT

In all criminal prosecutions, the accused shall enjoy the right to a speedy and public trial, by an impartial jury of the State and district wherein the crime shall have been committed; which district shall have previously ascertained by law, and to be informed of the nature and cause of the accusation; to be confronted with the witnesses against him; to have compulsory process of obtaining witnesses in his favor, and to have the assistance of counsel for his defense.

Sixth Amendment Protections

The term *speedy,* as used in the Sixth Amendment, has been widely interpreted. For instance, some states, such as New York and Alaska, require that a person picked up by the police without a warrant is entitled to a hearing within 24 hours. Other states require hearings within 36 hours; still others take as long as a week. To ensure protection under the Sixth Amendment, in 1991 the U.S. Supreme Court ruled that a person who is picked up by the police without a warrant is entitled to a hearing within 48 hours to ensure that the arrest is justified, regardless of whether the time period falls within a weekend or on a holiday. Many lower courts are now open for extended hours seven days a week because of this ruling and the increasing number of arrests. The strain put upon the courts in terms of personnel requirements and money to fund the additional hours is creating even more tension in the entire system.

The right to be confronted with adverse witnesses gives the defendant the right to be present in the courtroom at every stage in the trial. But transporting defendants back and forth from jail to the courtroom is also time-consuming and expensive, creating additional tensions within the system.

The right to have the assistance of defense counsel is the result of the Supreme Court's realization that without an attorney the defendant's chances of a fair trial are greatly diminished. If the accused cannot afford to hire an attorney, then one will be appointed by the court. But the Supreme Court also realized that some attorneys are better than others, and ruled further that if the defense attorney's failures or omissions on behalf of the defendant are outstandingly bad and the defendant is convicted because of the attorney's ineptness, the conviction is not valid. This right to representation by counsel is not limited to serious offenses, but extends to any offense for which a person might possibly go to jail—even for one day. However, if the offense is punishable by a fine only, the accused does not have a right to a court-appointed attorney.

Eighth Amendment Protections

The term *cruel and unusual punishment* is also subject to disparity in interpretation. It has come to mean punishment that is characterized by the unnecessary infliction of pain, which is out of proportion to the crime. For example, the Supreme Court ruled in *Coker v. Georgia,* 433 U.S. 584 (1977) that when no life has been taken, the death penalty is out of proportion to the crime of rape.

However, with the proliferation of jailhouse lawyers, inmates of prisons around the country are filing class-action lawsuits charging the system with, among other things, cruel and unusual punishment because of overcrowded

Figure 4–5 The Eighth Amendment

THE EIGHTH AMENDMENT
Excessive bail shall not be required, nor excessive fines imposed, nor cruel and unusual punishments inflicted.

living conditions in the prisons. One such lawsuit was recently filed in Orange County, California, when the sheriff announced that beginning in January 1992 there would be no smoking allowed anywhere in the jail. Prisoners who are heavy smokers are charging that denying them their right to smoke is cruel and unusual punishment, whereas those who are nonsmokers are charging that subjecting them to secondhand smoke from the smokers is cruel and unusual punishment. The county is offering all prisoners who smoke the opportunity to kick the habit by participating in a treatment program provided by the county.

It is readily apparent that there are many conflicts inherent with the current system of criminal justice, which was designed to protect citizens against the power of the government. However, the protection afforded by the constitutional rules may, in fact, impede prosecution.

4–3 The Lawyers

Lawyers and paralegals play important roles in criminal law regardless of whether they work for the prosecution or the defense, but the roles of each side are very different.

The Prosecution

The **prosecutor** is a person who pursues a lawsuit or criminal trial of persons accused of crime. The prosecutor is usually a public official such as a district attorney, county prosecutor, or the U.S. Attorney, if the crime is a federal offense. However, in some instances involving minor offenses, the prosecutor may be the complainant or a private attorney designated by the court to act on the complainant's behalf. In certain other cases, the legislature may appoint a *special prosecutor* to conduct a limited investigation and prosecution, such as in the Iran-Contra investigation and the savings and loan scandals.

In carrying out the duties of the office a public prosecutor has a great deal of discretion in deciding whom and when to prosecute. Prosecutors will not take a case to trial unless they genuinely believe that the accused is guilty, because they cannot afford to lose a case. If a prosecutor loses a case, it usually cannot be appealed as it can by the defense. So, in deciding which cases to take to trial, the prosecutor's office will conduct a thorough investigation and amass a great deal of evidence before going forward with a case. In most instances, only the strongest cases will be prosecuted. However, if there is reason to believe that someone is guilty of previous crimes and is likely to commit future ones, the prosecutor may decide to accept the challenge of taking a weaker case to trial in an attempt to reduce the number of offenders on the streets.

The American Bar Association's *Minimum Standards Relating to the Prosecution Function and the Defense Function* states that the prosecutor's basic role is to seek justice, not merely convictions, because of the prosecutor's special duty as a public official. The minimum standards call for the prosecutor to use restraint in the discretionary use of governmental powers, such as in deciding which cases to take to trial. Further, as a public official, during the trial the prosecutor may make decisions that are normally made by an individual client but which may affect the general public. Finally, our system of criminal justice requires that the accused is to be given the benefit of reasonable doubt.

As you might imagine, giving prosecutors the discretion to choose which cases will be prosecuted is subject to regular and lengthy debate from those critics who contend that the prosecutors may be substituting their personal values for the community's values in making their decisions. For example, when two individuals commit the same crime, one may be prosecuted and the other may not; the decision would likely be based on a number of factors. Likewise, some crimes are prosecuted and others are not. Because most prosecutors are overworked and understaffed, it is virtually impossible to take all cases to trial. Some decisions to prosecute are no doubt political, particularly in those states where the prosecutors are elected. For instance, it is unlikely that cases against community leaders, their children, business associates, or close friends will be heard in the courtroom in a community where the prosecutor is elected to office.

Federal prosecutors, on the other hand, are relatively immune to political pressures because U.S. Attorneys are appointed by the President with approval by the Senate. Personal motives are extremely important to a prosecuting attorney, whether state elected or federally appointed, because motives can create ethical dilemmas for the attorney. Consider, for example, the ethical conflict created if the prosecutor has a vendetta against a certain defendant or is interested in furthering his or her career by taking on a particular case that will be widely publicized. There is likely to be an ethical conflict between convicting an individual and seeking justice for a crime.

The Defense

Contrary to the fantasy depicted on television, only a small percentage of attorneys specialize in criminal defense cases; most attorneys specialize in business matters and civil litigation cases. Any lawyer may be called upon, however, to handle an occasional criminal case, if only when one of his or her business clients runs into trouble of a criminal nature or when appointed by the court to represent someone without the means to hire his or her own counsel.

Unlike the prosecutor, whose ethical obligations are centered on seeking justice, the defense attorney's ethical obligations are focused on the accused's constitutional rights to representation by counsel, to protection against self-incrimination, to presumption of innocence, and to attorney-client confidentiality.

The first question a criminal defense lawyer must ask herself or himself is whether to agree to represent a particular client. On this subject, the American Bar Association says that a lawyer is under no obligation to represent every person who wants to become a client, but that neither should a lawyer lightly decline to accept employment, since it is the objective of the bar to make legal services available to all who request them. Occasionally, in fulfilling this objective a lawyer might be required to accept employment that may be unattractive. However, the ABA clearly states that if the intensity of the lawyer's personal feelings are such that they may impair the effective representation of a prospective client, then the lawyer should decline employment.

If a lawyer is appointed by the court to represent an indigent client, the American Bar Association says that the lawyer may only decline representation for compelling reasons. Compelling reasons do not include such factors as repugnance of the subject matter of the proceeding, the identity or position of a person involved in the case, or the belief of the lawyer that the defendant is guilty.

In most cases, the defense lawyer is not permitted to withdraw from a case if he or she discovers the client is guilty. In the adversarial system of criminal justice the defendant is entitled to have representation in court just as the victim—the government and society—is represented by the prosecutor. It is the duty of defense counsel to present the best defense possible that is in the best interests of the client. In some cases the defense may present nothing. Instead, an attempt is made to cast doubt on the prosecutor's case, since the prosecutor has the obligation to present witnesses and evidence and to prove that the defendant is guilty.

Unfortunately, many people tend to associate the lawyer with the crime he or she is defending, forgetting that the defense lawyer is merely an officer of the court and the agent for the accused. Thus, when defending an unpopular client or one charged with a heinous crime, the public's view of the lawyer is often the exact opposite of the ABA's Model Rules of Professional Conduct, which states that a lawyer's representation of a client, including representation by appointment, does not constitute an endorsement of the client's political, economic, social, or moral views or activities. Rather, the client's right to representation by a lawyer is guaranteed by the Sixth Amendment, and the lawyer is merely fulfilling that obligation to represent the client to the best of his or her ability.

Some states have a system of public defenders who represent the indigent. But most public defenders routinely face a barrage of criticism from the police, citizens, and the clients they are representing. The main complaint seems to center around the number of cases—between 80 and 90 percent—in which the defendants **plea bargain** instead of going to trial. *Plea bargaining* is the process whereby the accused and the prosecutor negotiate a mutually satisfactory disposition of the case. In the minds of some people, plea bargaining is tantamount to getting off without punishment. Additionally, some defendants mistakenly think the public defenders are merely the powerless servants of a system that is against them, and that they are the pawns. However, public defenders do enjoy at least one indisputable advantage: they know better than any outsider how the system works. Most people would prefer to be represented by someone who knows the system, and is known by others in it, rather than by someone with little experience in the criminal court.

4–4 The Trial

The number of people who are actually brought to trial on criminal charges is small compared to the number who are accused of committing a crime. Imagine the entire criminal justice process as a pyramid. On the bottom of the pyramid are all the individuals who are arrested. In the middle are those who are actually charged with having committed a criminal offense. At the top of the pyramid are those who go to trial; some of them will be convicted, some will not. But before an accused person can be put on trial all the *pretrial* processes must be completed.

Figure 4–6

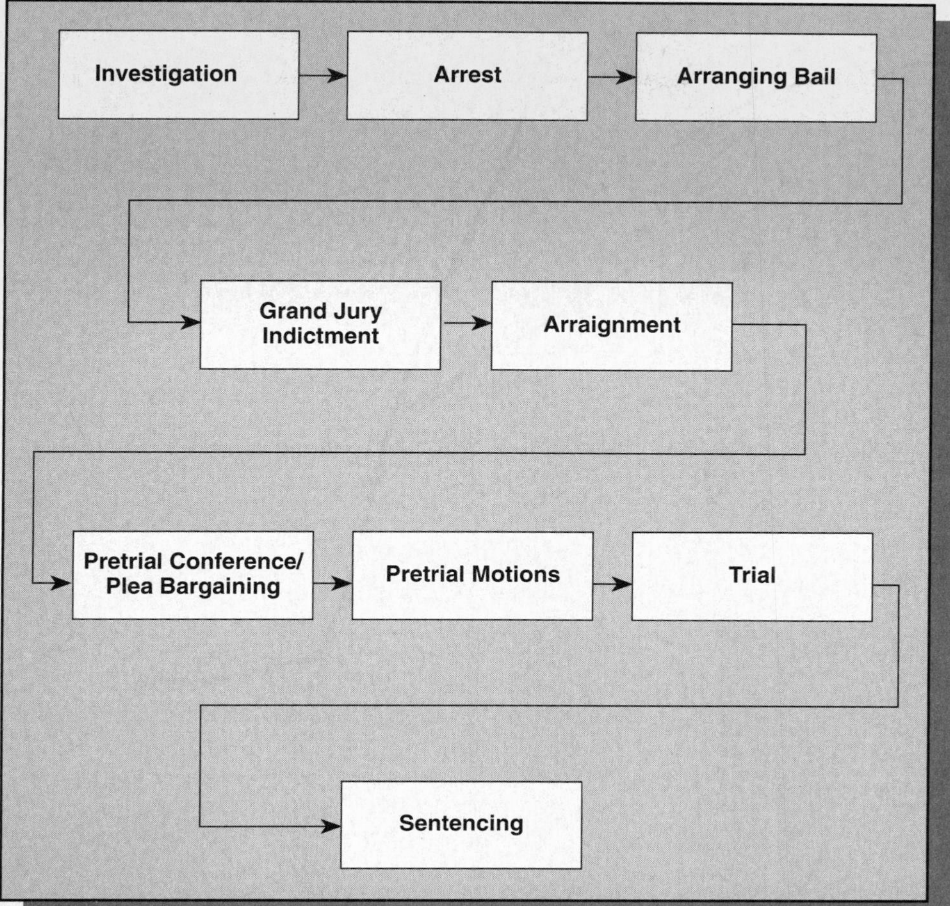

The Criminal Justice Process.

Investigation

The criminal justice process begins with an investigation. When the police, the district attorney's office, the Internal Revenue Service, or the Federal Bureau of Investigation have reason to believe that a crime has been, or is being, committed, they commence an investigation.

Some investigations are initiated because a person or persons have been observed acting suspiciously. Others are triggered by reports from victims or third parties. Still other investigations come about as the result of a general crackdown on certain criminal activity, such as drug trafficking.

The techniques employed in most investigations include: collecting information from a variety of sources; watching and ultimately questioning those who are acting suspiciously; locating and questioning possible witnesses; examining physical evidence; and searching individuals, vehicles, or premises after a warrant has been obtained. Some investigations may include surveillance, undercover activities, videotaping, and electronic eavesdropping.

Legal assistants who work for private law firms, insurance companies, and state or federal government agencies often take an active part in conducting

Figure 4–7 Fingerprinting

As part of the booking procedure, the accused will be fingerprinted. *Source*: Bob Mullenix.

routine investigations that may lead to the next stage in the criminal justice process: the arrest.

Arrest

After investigation, if there is enough evidence to indicate there is probable cause that a crime has been committed, an individual may be **arrested,** or taken into custody. The individual is then transported to the police station for **booking,** where the accused is photographed, fingerprinted, and charged with committing a crime. With the help of computers, suspects' fingerprints are now routinely checked against those on file with other law-enforcement agencies throughout the country to determine whether the person in custody is wanted elsewhere.

Most arrests rely heavily upon the investigation process, and many are made without a warrant but with probable cause. That is, in making an arrest without a warrant, the police may rely on personal observation of a crime being committed, reports from victims or third parties, or upon probable cause when a person is acting suspiciously.

As discussed previously, any suspect who is arrested must be given the *Miranda* warnings of the right to remain silent and the right to have an attorney. Interestingly, the protection offered by *Miranda* often creates its own problem: The police in many multicultural cities around the country are experiencing problems in making legal arrests of people who speak English as a second language (ESL) or who do not speak or understand English at all. If no translator is present, people with limited English language ability may inadvertently waive their *Miranda* rights. Also, since the laws of the countries from which many of these people come presume the accused is guilty, immigrants from those countries are often not aware that in this country they have certain legal rights that are protected by the Constitution.

Bail

Since the primary objective of any person who has been arrested is to be set free, the next step in the process is to arrange for **bail,** the posting of cash or other form of security such as equity in real property, given to ensure that the suspect will appear in court as required. A **bail bond,** sometimes also known as an *appearance bond* when a minor offense is involved, is the document **executed,** or signed, in order to secure the release of an individual in custody. If the defendant does not have enough cash to post bail, a **surety** may be called upon

Figure 4–8

PARTIAL BAIL SCHEDULE FOR STATE OF CALIFORNIA
(Effective January 1, 1990)

FELONY PENAL CODE		**MISDEMEANOR PENAL CODE**	
Gross Vehicular Manslaughter (intoxication)	$25,000	Assault and Battery	500
Mayhem	25,000	Prostitution—first offense	1000
Mayhem—life imprisonment	50,000	Possession of a Concealed Weapon	1000
Kidnapping	50,000	Annoying Children	1000
Kidnapping for Extortion	250,000	**VEHICLE CODE**	
Kidnapping for Robbery	100,000	Auto Theft	10,000
Assault with intent to Rape	25,000	Felony Hit and Run	10,000
Assault with weapon—intent to Rape	50,000	Felony Drunk Driving	10,000
Assault with deadly weapon	10,000	**HEALTH AND SAFETY CODE**	
Rape	50,000	Narcotics possession (other than marijuana)	5000
Spousal Rape	10,000	Possession for sale of narcotics (less than 1 oz.)	25,000
Child Abuse/Endangerment	10,000	Possession for Sale of Cocaine (1 kilo or more)	200,000
Burglary—residential	25,000	Sale of Narcotics (less than 1 oz.)	25,000
Petty Theft with Prior	10,000	Sale of Narcotics (1 kilo or more)	250,000
Possession of a Deadly Weapon	10,000	Inducing minor to violate narcotics law	25,000
		Manufacturing controlled substances	100,000

Partial bail schedule for the State of California.

Figure 4–9

In the Central Orange County (California) Judicial District, nearly 48% of the people arrested and released on bail during the first five months of 1991 failed to appear for their trials. Here is a breakdown of bail jumpers by category of crime:

Type of Offense	Number Released on Bail	Number of No-Shows	Percentage Who Failed to Show
Drug offenses*	856	374	48
Larceny	71	46	65
Weapons violations	17	7	41
Fraud	33	21	64
Assault	28	17	61
Sex crimes	31	10	32
Property crimes	49	31	63
Personal crimes**	26	15	58
Vehicular offenses	158	82	52
Disorderly conduct	14	7	50
Miscellaneous	4	4	100
Total	**1287**	**614**	**48**

*Includes driving under the influence of drugs, including alcohol.
**Includes cruelty to children, failing to provide for a child, and injuring a spouse.

Bail jumpers statistics.

to bail out the defendant. The surety may be a friend, family member, or bail bondsman who posts bail for the accused. If the accused fails to appear as required for court dates, the surety may lose the money or other security posted. On the other hand, if the accused appears in court on the day or days required, the surety's obligation is satisfied and the money or security posted is returned.

The amount of bail, whether for a felony or misdemeanor, is usually set in the arrest warrant or fixed according to a county or state schedule. A legal assistant should have a current bail schedule for the county in which he or she is working. They are available from the clerk's office in the criminal court, the local bar association, or a bail bondsman.

In some cases, bail is based upon the defendant's prior record and the seriousness of the crime. However, for some crimes, such as first-degree murder, no bail is set; the accused must be incarcerated until the trial. If the court believes the defendant is not likely to appear in court as required or if the crime is a felony offense, the amount of bail may be set at several hundred thousand dollars. On the other hand, if the defendant has a job, a family, and is a resident of the community with no prior convictions, the court may decide to release the defendant on his or her **own recognizance (o.r.).** This means that the defendant has agreed to appear in court as required without posting bail.

Indictment

After bail has been set, evidence held by the police is given to the prosecuting attorney, who must determine whether to bring formal charges against the suspect. If the prosecutor is persuaded by the evidence that there is probable cause that a crime was committed and that it was committed by the accused, the prosecutor may seek an **indictment,** a formal written accusation charging a person with a crime, from a grand jury.

Typically, grand jury proceedings are held privately, without the presence of the accused or defense counsel. Members of the jury may question the prosecutor, and they may subpoena witnesses for questioning. The jury may decide to issue an indictment as requested by the prosecutor on the charge presented or on some other charge, or they may decide not to indict at all. However, in most cases, the grand jury follows the prosecutor's request. Indictments must clearly state the offense with which the accused is charged so that an adequate defense may be prepared. Once an indictment is filed, the case is passed on to the court with a request for a trial date. At that point the prosecutor must proceed to trial unless the court has reason to dismiss the case.

Only about half the states have a grand jury system. In those states without a grand jury or in cases where the prosecutor does not ask for a grand jury indictment, the prosecutor may prepare accusatory pleading documents known as an *information* or a *complaint.* After the indictment, complaint, or information is filed, if the accused is not already in custody, a **bench warrant,** an order from the court empowering the proper legal authorities to seize a person, is issued for his or her arrest.

Arraignment

Next, the defendant is brought before a **magistrate,** or officer of the court, and is formally charged with having committed an offense. In most jurisdictions, this appearance or proceeding is called an **arraignment.**

At the arraignment the defendant is informed of his or her constitutional rights to plead not guilty, to have a trial by jury, to confront and cross-examine witnesses, and to be represented by counsel. After the charges are read, the defendant is asked to enter a plea. The plea choices are: guilty, not guilty, or ***nolo contendere,*** a Latin phrase meaning "I do not wish to contest it." A plea of *nolo contendere* is not an admission of either guilt or innocence, and may not be used in any other case against the defendant as proof of guilt. However, a *nolo contendere* plea is treated, in all other respects, the same as an admission of guilt. The defendant may include an explanation for his or her acts, such as being insane at the time of committing the act or that the act was committed to prevent a greater harm from occurring.

If the defendant enters a guilty plea, the magistrate must determine whether the plea is entered voluntarily, whether the defendant understands the consequences of his or her decision, and whether the defendant is mentally competent. If the guilty plea is accepted, the next step is sentencing. There is no trial. In many states, the court cannot accept a plea of guilty unless the crime is a felony not punishable by death and unless the defendant is represented by counsel.

Plea Bargaining

Some courts schedule a pretrial conference specifically for the purpose of trying to resolve the case without having to go to trial. At such a conference, or during any stage of the process prior to completion of trial, most jurisdictions will permit the defense attorney and the prosecutor to engage in **plea bargaining.**

Plea-bargaining negotiations can result in the defendant pleading guilty to a lesser offense or to only one or some of the counts in a multicount indictment. In return for pleading guilty, the prosecution agrees to obtain concessions as to the type and length of the sentence or a reduction of the number of counts. The judge is not usually involved in the plea-bargaining process, but he or she has the right to decide whether to accept or reject the plea and its attendant bargain once it is disclosed to the court and is placed upon the record. Once a plea bargain is accepted, the state must honor the terms of the bargain.

Plea bargaining is entered into for several reasons: If the defense counsel believes that the jury will return an adverse verdict, he or she may decide a guilty plea to a lesser charge is in the client's best interest. Many defense attorneys believe that a defendant may be more injured by failing to plead guilty than by pleading guilty because there is no way to predict what a jury will decide. Prosecutors have too many cases to try, so they are usually interested in negotiating plea bargains. Defendants are usually interested in plea bargaining because if they plead guilty, they are usually free until the day of sentencing. Since jails are notoriously unpleasant places to be, the prospect of being set free, if only briefly, is appealing to most who are being detained—particularly those who cannot make bail. Finally, plea bargaining saves time and money. Without it, not only would the entire judicial system get hopelessly behind, but the court system would have to be greatly expanded, at taxpayer expense, or cases would simply not get heard.

The plea-bargaining process is not without its critics. But the right to plea bargain was approved by the U.S. Supreme Court (*Santobello v. New York,* 404 U.S. 257 [1971]), and that recognition led to the American Bar Association's setting standards for the conduct of negotiations. Despite the critics, increasing the number of plea-bargained cases is another way to speed up the criminal justice process and free up the courtrooms for civil trials.

Pretrial Motions

In criminal cases there are a number of **motions** that can be made before the trial begins. For instance, a motion can be made to dismiss the case, to move it to another jurisdiction for trial, or to compel the prosecutor to produce certain evidence for examination by defense counsel prior to commencement of trial. Some common pretrial motions include the following.

Motion for Change of Venue Generally, the defendant is tried where the crime was allegedly committed. However, if it appears that the defendant would not be able to get a fair and impartial trial in that jurisdiction, the court may grant a Motion for Change of **Venue,** the geographic location where the case is to be tried. These motions are common in cases involving a high-visibility individual, a heinous crime, or where there has been a great deal of publicity about the case. Even then, the court considers a motion for change of venue carefully because of all the resulting operational and administrative ramifications of deciding to change venues.

Motion to Suppress Evidence One of the most frequently used motions is the Motion to Suppress Evidence. The theory behind this motion is that evidence the prosecution intends to use at trial was illegally obtained and in violation of the defendant's Fourth Amendment rights. If the court finds from the facts presented in the motion that the evidence was illegally seized, it must **suppress the evidence,** not allowing it to be introduced at the trial. In some instances, if the evidence was crucial to the prosecution's case, the prosecutor may decide to drop the case if the Motion to Suppress is granted.

Motion to Dismiss The Constitution requires that the indictment, information, or complaint set forth the exact nature of the charges against the defendant. Defense counsel may file a Motion to Dismiss on the grounds that the charges are not specifically stated and that the defendant is therefore prevented from preparing an adequate defense. More often, Motions to Dismiss are filed on the grounds that a police officer did not have probable cause to arrest and search an individual or his or her property. If the court finds that the police officer did in fact violate the defendant's constitutional rights in making the arrest or in conducting a search, the Motion to Dismiss will be granted.

Motion for Discovery and Inspection The pretrial procedure by which one party gains information, facts, and documents held by another party is known as **discovery.** Under the Federal Rules of Criminal Procedure, not only is the scope of material available for discovery quite broad, but any state discovery procedure must be reciprocal to be constitutional. In other words, neither the defense counsel nor the prosecution may withhold from one another information that is relevant to the case being tried. A Motion for Discovery and Inspection may be filed if there is reason to believe that pertinent information is being withheld by either side.

Motion to Sever Occasionally there is more than one defendant on trial for the same crime, such as when members of a gang are brought to trial for drug trafficking or when two members of a family allegedly conspired to murder their parents. If one of the defendants thinks that the bad reputation or confession of a codefendant will create prejudice against him or her, a Motion to Sever may be filed with the court asking for separate trials.

Critics of the system often complain that many criminals go free because of a minor legal technicality. But, in criticizing the system, there is a tendency to forget about or to overlook the constitutional rights that are at stake. Although it is true that occasionally a criminal might go free because a police officer did not have probable cause to conduct a search or to arrest, the situation would be worse if the police had the right to search or arrest anyone at will.

Trial

If the case is not dismissed in the pretrial motion stage and if the defendant continues to maintain that he or she is not guilty, then the case will go to trial. In all cases where the defendant may go to prison, the Sixth Amendment guarantees the right to trial by jury unless the defendant waives the right. In the event the defendant waives the right to trial by jury, the case will be heard by a judge.

Jury Selection The next step in the trial process is for the court to notify about 60 people who meet the state's residency requirements and who are over the age of 18, in good mental and physical health, with sufficient knowledge of the English language to appear at the courthouse to begin the *voir dire* examination process. The number of people summoned for jury duty depends upon how difficult it might be to *impanel,* or seat, a jury. If the case is likely to last several months or years, or if the jury is to be **sequestered,** separated from others until the trial is over, several hundred people may have to be summoned before a jury is impaneled.

Figure 4–10 A Typical Jury

A jury will listen carefully to the lawyer as she or he presents the facts during a trial by jury. *Source*: Jim Pickerell/Stock Boston.

The jury selection process varies from state to state and from state court to federal court, as well as from one judge to the next. In some courts, the judge takes a leading role in questioning prospective jurors, whereas in others the attorneys conduct the examination. Prospective jurors may be excused from jury duty for a number of reasons. For instance, attorneys on either side may ask that a prospective juror be excused if he or she does not meet the state statute requirements for jurors or if during *voir dire* the juror indicates he or she may be prejudiced in any way toward the defendant. A request to excuse a juror under these circumstances is called a **challenge for cause.** Other prospective jurors may be excused using a **peremptory challenge,** which doesn't require that a specific reason be given for not selecting them. Both sides are entitled to a certain number of peremptory challenges, the number of which is prescribed by state statute or court rule. Other jurors may be excused for financial hardship reasons, because they are single heads of households, or because they own and operate a small business.

When it comes to picking a jury, the prosecution generally tends to select individuals with strong ties to the community. Whereas, the defense counsel looks for people who may be able to identify with the defendant's circumstances. Even though the purpose of *voir dire* is to select a jury that will be impartial and thus give the defendant a fair trial, it is no secret that some trials are more fair than others. This happens because juries, like any individuals, have their own personalities. For example, defendants who are from a minority group, who are physically unattractive, or have a homosexual lifestyle may fare less well with a jury, than say, beautiful people, war heroes, or celebrities. Because of this phenomenon, an attorney who is representing a physically unattractive, homosexual, or minority client may advise him or her to waive the jury and let the judge decide his or her fate.

Furthermore, getting a trial by jury of your peers is becoming increasingly difficult because of the method by which prospective jurors are summoned in the first place. Most often jurors are selected from voter registration lists, and since many people, especially young people and poor people, tend not to vote, they are automatically excluded from being called for jury duty. In addition, professional people such as doctors, lawyers, teachers, and paralegals are usually excused from jury duty. The result is that most juries tend to be middle-class and middle-aged, not representative of a cross-section of the community, and certainly, in most cases, not a jury of one's peers. However, until someone comes up with a better way to do it, we are stuck with the present jury-selection system.

The Trial After the jury has been impaneled and the oath has been administered to them by the court, the defense counsel and the prosecutor each make his or her opening statements to the jury, summarizing for them what they think the evidence will show.

The prosecution then begins the presentation of its case by calling its witnesses. Each witness is first examined by the prosecuting attorney in a process called **direct examination.** Questions are usually phrased in such a way as to make the answers of benefit to the party doing the questioning. Any documents or other items pertaining to the testimony being given are presented as evidence and marked as exhibits. Once the prosecuting attorney has completed interrogating a witness, the defense attorney has an opportunity to question the same witness in a process called **cross-examination.** After the prosecution has called all of its witnesses, the case for the defense is presented in the same procedural way.

During the trial objections may be raised by either side to questions being asked of witnesses. Some objections will be **overruled** by the judge, or not allowed, and the witness is required to answer the question. Others will be **sustained,** or approved, and the witness is not allowed to answer. After all witnesses have been called and all evidence has been presented, the attorneys make their closing arguments to the jury. The jury is then instructed by the court on the issues it must decide and *retires,* leaves the courtroom for the jury room, to *deliberate,* or consider all the evidence and arguments presented. Most states require that the verdict in most criminal cases be unanimous, but sometimes a jury cannot agree even after spending a great deal of time deliberating. A **hung jury** is one whose members cannot reach a verdict by whatever degree of agreement is required. When this happens the prosecutor may decide to retry the case with a new jury or, if the jury was hung because the majority of the jurors thought the defendant was innocent, the judge may decide to dismiss the case in the furtherance of justice.

The trial itself is similar to a stage performance, with the script being written while it is being performed by the lawyers, the judge, and the witnesses. The stage props include the judge's bench, which is usually in the front of the courtroom and elevated for visibility. The prosecutor's table is placed closest to the jury box, and the person primarily responsible for investigating the case will sit at the prosecutor's table along with the prosecutor. The defense counsel and the defendant are at the table farthest away from the jury. A paralegal or investigator working for the defense might also sit at the defense counsel's table.

The spectators sit on benches behind the bar, which separates them from the main characters of the courtroom drama.

Even though the courtroom is open to the public and people may come and go as they wish, the general atmosphere of the courtroom is quite formal, and appropriate dress is required from everyone in attendance. When the judge enters or leaves the courtroom, usually everyone must rise. The judge is respectfully addressed as "Your Honor," and anyone addressing the judge is required to stand unless they are physically unable to do so.

Trial lawyers try to create an atmosphere of high drama for maximum impact on the jury. Doing so requires a special talent and a great deal of skill. Some of today's best trial lawyers hone their courtroom skills by taking acting classes especially designed for trial lawyers. It is important to remember, however, that the purpose of a trial is not to provide a stage to showcase a lawyer's acting abilities but to prove guilt beyond a reasonable doubt. But sometimes using a few theatrical techniques may contribute toward reaching the desired outcome.

Sentencing

The trial is over. The judge or the jury has reached a verdict. Now it is time for the judge to deliver the **sentence,** the punishment ordered by the court to be inflicted upon the person found guilty of a crime. Sentences are either *noncustodial,* such as probation and/or a fine, or *custodial,* requiring a term in prison or the county jail, or a combination of the two, known as a **split sentence.** A **suspended sentence** places the defendant on a fixed term of probation without having to serve any time in prison. When a person is convicted of more than one crime, a sentence will be imposed for each crime. Sentences for multiple crimes can be served *concurrently,* at the same time, or *consecutively,* one after the other.

In some courts, the judge will instruct the jury to sentence the defendant. In other state and federal courts, the judge alone is responsible for sentencing. In either situation, the burden of determining an appropriate sentence is a heavy one. The primary question to be answered by those asked to sentence the guilty is: What are we trying to accomplish with the sentence? Rehabilitation, deterrence, and protection of the public are possible answers. If the crime was a violent one, protection of the public against future crimes will be of great concern, and imprisonment is likely. On the other hand, if deterrence is the objective, consideration must be given not only to what type of punishment will best prevent others from committing the same type of crime but also to how that sentence will be communicated to the public. Rehabilitation as an objective is often difficult to accomplish, since even expert penologists (criminologists who study prisons and offenders) cannot agree on who is and who is not capable of being rehabilitated.

In determining a sentence to fit the crime, some judges, prior to sentencing, will ask the probation department to compile a *presentence report* on the guilty party. Most presentence reports contain both the defendant's and the official version of what happened, as well as a personal, family, and financial profile of the defendant including his or her employment, military, and health records, and any other information that may help in making the appropriate sentencing decision. The probation officer usually includes his or her recommendation for sentencing, but the judge is under no obligation to follow the probation officer's recommendation. In most cases, a copy of the presentence report is given to defense counsel for review with the defendant prior to sentencing.

The sentence may include the payment of a monetary fine, which goes to the government body instituting the action, or payment of money to the victim as restitution, often a condition for probation. If the defendant is placed on probation, that probation is conditional: the defendant is usually confined to the state or sometimes to a local area; he or she must be continuously employed; and report according to schedule to a probation officer. Probation violators rarely get a second chance; after a probation revocation hearing, they are usually sent to prison.

Our current system of criminal justice is not without its faults and its critics. Overcrowded prisons not only reflect the faults of society itself but also raise the question of whether the system is doing what it is supposed to do. Some people think that the purpose of prison is only to get the criminals off the streets, or protect the public. Others think that people in prison should be educated, trained for productive work on the outside, or otherwise rehabilitated. Still others believe that the problems are deeply rooted in the family, community, and culture and should be addressed at that level as a way to prevent crimes in the future. The one thing everyone can agree upon is that our criminal justice system is close to being out of control and may be headed for disaster.

Everyone associated with the criminal justice system, but particularly the accused, relies heavily upon the attorneys who are involved at every stage of the process. For that reason, paralegals and others who work for defense lawyers and prosecuting attorneys need to be aware of the various steps in the process and the procedures for each step.

4–5 A Day in the Criminal Court

It is sometimes difficult to understand how the criminal justice system works without having experienced it. To illustrate, let's take a look at what happened to a couple of young people who ran into conflict with the law.

Kellie's Shopping Trip

Kellie is a 13-year-old girl who lives in a suburb of a major city in Texas. She is a good student, has working parents who are active in the community, and has never been in any kind of trouble. Kellie was in a department store doing some shopping for herself and looking for a birthday gift for one of her friends. She found a CD that she knew her friend would like, unthinkingly slipped it into her shopping bag, and walked toward the front door. Before she was out the door, she was stopped by the store's security officer, who escorted her to the manager's office and called the police. When the police arrived, they searched Kellie's shopping bag, found the CD, and took her to the police station, where they called her parents.

While they were in the manager's office, Kellie was told of her *Miranda* rights, but since she had never been in any trouble before she was traumatized by the entire event and did not clearly understand what was going on. When the police officer asked her if she wanted a lawyer to be present during questioning, Kellie thought that saying yes was the same as admitting she was guilty. So, she said no.

At the police station, when the officer questioned her about the CD in the shopping bag, Kellie told him that she was on her way to get a birthday card to include with the gift for her friend and that she was going to pay for the CD and the card together. The officer pointed out that the greeting card counter was not located near the front door. Kellie became confused and contradicted herself.

(The greeting cards had been near the front door until two weeks prior to this event, but no one mentioned this during the questioning.)

Kellie's distraught parents arrived and were told there was probable cause to believe that Kellie had committed a crime. She was subsequently arrested and charged with the crime of shoplifting. Because Kellie was only 13, her case would be heard in Juvenile Court, a branch of the family court system where the hearings are closed to the public and the press and there is no jury. Kellie's parents were told that they could hire a lawyer to represent Kellie, but they were given the impression that since the charge was a minor one and Kellie had no prior record, it was unnecessary to bring a lawyer into this case.

The decision Kellie's parents made about hiring a lawyer could change her entire life. If she were an adult and found guilty, she would be facing misdemeanor charges; since she had no prior record, Kellie would probably be let off with a warning and a fine. However, Kellie was not an adult, and charges of juvenile delinquency could put her in a reform school or other institutional program for children designed to rehabilitate delinquents. Most judges have not been inside one of these juvenile detention facilities and are not familiar with the kinds of lessons that are taught there. Suffice it to say that most people would be willing to forgo the opportunity to learn the lessons of life taught in these facilities.

Kellie maintained that she was innocent; that she was going to pay for the CD along with the birthday card. Her parents believed her and decided to hire a lawyer. At the hearing, the store's security officer testified that he saw Kellie pick up the CD and walk toward the front door. Under cross-examination, however, Kellie's lawyer found that she was stopped before she left the store, that the greeting card department had been recently moved, and that she might indeed have thought she was heading for the greeting cards rather than trying to skip out with stolen goods.

Then the police officer was questioned about searching Kellie's shopping bag. He did not have a search warrant, but since Kellie had given him permission to look inside the bag the judge found the search to be a legal one. On the witness stand, Kellie said that she didn't request an attorney immediately because she was frightened and confused and thought that by doing so she would be admitting guilt, and that she was not guilty.

The judge was doubtful about the entire incident and decided to dismiss the charges against Kellie. He warned her to be more careful when shopping in the future.

Had Kellie's parents not believed her or felt that she needed to be taught a lesson, this unfortunate situation could have turned out much differently. If they had not hired a lawyer to cross-examine the store's security officer and the police officer, she would probably have been found guilty. The court's probation officer might have put together a glowing report on Kellie, and she might have been placed on probation. Then she would have had to report regularly to a probation officer and live under certain restrictions imposed by the court—and she would have a police record. Police records on juveniles are sealed and confidential, but they nevertheless sometimes surface later in life, creating problems in applications for college and employment.

On the other hand, if the probation officer's report contained even the slightest amount of unfavorable information, Kellie might have been sent to a juvenile detention and reform institution for a period of time left to the discretion of the judge—or until she was deemed "rehabilitated."

The point of Kellie's story is this: even a relatively minor oversight can lead to major trouble with the law, and, when in trouble with the law, always insist on having a lawyer. Everyone, including a child, is entitled to be represented by legal counsel.

Kellie's brush with the law had a happy ending, although she will no doubt have to deal with some long-term emotional scars. But, many more people have a different experience with the criminal justice system. Michael is one of those.

Michael's Mishap

Michael is 19 years old and living in a rented room in New York City. He came alone to the Big Apple from his family home in Virginia with a dream of making his fortune on Broadway. He has no relatives nearby and only a few friends, with whom he occasionally uses drugs on a social basis. Michael is currently looking for work. One Saturday night while high on drugs and flat broke, he tried to snatch a purse from a fragile-looking woman on the street. Michael picked the wrong woman. His intended victim was a judo instructor, and she knocked him to the ground with a few fast blows to his head and body. She then called the police and waited with Michael until they arrived. He was arrested on the spot; no warrant is needed when someone is caught in the act of committing a crime. He was searched—police may search a person caught in the act as part of a legal arrest—handcuffed, and taken off to the nearest police station.

Michael was in big trouble. The arresting officer found a knife, some cocaine, and a couple dozen unidentified pills on him. So, in addition to the attempted purse-snatching charge, there were charges of carrying a concealed weapon and possession of illegal drugs. Michael was booked on all these charges, fingerprinted, photographed, and locked up overnight until he could be further questioned in the morning. When read his *Miranda* rights, Michael requested that an attorney from the public defender's office be appointed to represent him.

The next morning Michael was brought to the magistrate's court, where sufficient cause to ask for an indictment on all charges was established. His lawyer requested that Michael be released on his own recognizance, but the judge did not agree that he should be allowed free without bail. With no job and no family ties to the city, the judge believed Michael would skip. Bail was set at $10,000. Since Michael had no money or friends to bail him out, he went to jail to await trial.

The New York City jail where Michael and others are held pending hearings or trials is aptly called The Tombs. The jail is dirty, crowded, noisy, frightening, and infested with vermin. Since all detainees are innocent until proven guilty, it may seem unfair to lock them up in such a terrible place. However, for obvious reasons judges are worried about letting indicted people who cannot raise bail go free until their trial. On the other hand, those people who have money or property or can pay a bail bondsman rarely go to jail until they have been convicted. So, unfortunately, in this not-quite-perfect system only people like Michael go to jail before having been found guilty.

Next, Michael's case was presented to a grand jury. After deliberating for about five minutes the grand jury decided there was enough reason to issue an indictment. While Michael was languishing in The Tombs, his court-appointed defender was busy at the prosecuting attorney's office trying to find out what evidence the state had against Michael. When confronted with the sworn statement of the victimized judo instructor, the arresting officer's report, and the physical evidence—fingerprints on the victim's purse, the knife, and the drugs—Michael's attorney quickly concluded that the state had a good case against his client and would most likely be able to prove that Michael was guilty as charged.

The lawyer suggested to Michael that he plead guilty to one of the minor charges against him in return for the prosecutor's promise to drop the rest of the charges. So, when Michael appeared before the judge he pled guilty to purse snatching. Because he did not have a prior record and the probation report was not derogatory, the judge sentenced him to six months in prison and three years' probation. Michael cannot appeal the verdict, since he entered a plea of guilty, unless he wishes to accuse his attorney of unduly influencing him to enter a guilty plea. Had Michael decided to plead innocent of all charges, he would have had a jury trial, with witnesses. If he had been found guilty by a jury, the judge would have passed sentence. Michael could have appealed the verdict to a higher court if the trial court had erred in some way during the trial. Cases cannot be appealed simply because the defendant does not like the outcome; there must be an error in the trial court proceedings to warrant an appeal.

However, Michael thought he got off lucky this time and vowed never to run afoul of the law again as he was escorted back to his cell in The Tombs to contemplate the rest of his life.

As these cases against Kellie and Michael illustrate, there are checks and balances built into the system that attempt to make it as fair as possible. Sometimes injustices do occur, as with any system. However, the American criminal justice system, with all its imperfections, is based upon the principle that the accused is innocent until proven guilty. This system is vastly different from most countries in the world, where the defendant is presumed to be guilty and must prove innocence. Under which system would you rather live?

SUMMARY

4–1

Many convicts from the jails of Great Britain were sent to settle the 13 original colonies of the U.S.; although some, no doubt, changed their lives, others did not. The U.S. way of dealing with criminal activity is based in common law, unlike many other countries in the world, which use the older Roman or civil law. The primary difference between the two has to do with the presumption of guilt or innocence. In the common law system the accused is presumed innocent until proven guilty. In the civil law system the accused is presumed guilty and must prove innocence. There are two categories of criminal behavior: misdemeanors, which are considered less serious crimes and which carry less severe punishment; and felonies, which are considered serious crimes and are punishable by forfeiting certain rights such as freedom.

4–2

Anyone accused of a crime in the U.S. is protected by certain rights guaranteed by the first ten amendments to the Constitution. The Fourth Amendment protects people from unreasonable searches and seizures without probable cause. The Fifth Amendment places a barrier between the state's law enforcement agencies and individuals by requiring a grand jury indictment for a felony crime. Further protections include that no person shall be tried twice for the same offense and that no person is compelled to be a witness against her- or himself. The application of the privilege against self-incrimination was extended by the *Miranda* warnings, which require that the arresting officers inform accused persons of their rights under the Constitution. The Sixth Amendment provides for a speedy trial and the right to assistance by counsel. The protections of the Eighth Amendment include not imposing excessive bail or fines nor subjecting the accused to cruel and unusual punishment.

4–3

The prosecutor is usually a public official such as a district attorney, often elected, who brings a lawsuit on behalf of the government against a person accused of committing a crime. The prosecutor's role is to seek justice, not merely convictions. In seeking justice, the prosecutor will bring to trial only those cases which he or she is most likely to win. The defense attorney's role is to focus on protecting the defendant's constitutional rights regardless of how counsel might personally feel about the crime or the criminal.

4–4

The criminal justice process begins with an investigation, which proceeds to an arrest, arrangement for bail in most cases, the grand jury indictment, an arraignment, plea bargaining, pretrial motions, and then the trial itself. After the verdict is rendered, the defendant is sentenced by the judge. Some cases may be appealed if the trial court erred in some way during the trial.

4–5

Even a minor oversight, such as unintentional shoplifting, can lead to major trouble with the law. When charged with a crime, everyone should always insist on being represented by an attorney. The criminal justice system is not perfect, tending to favor people who have money or property. People lacking the financial means to post bail are often kept in jail until their hearing or trial. In other words, they are in effect presumed to be guilty.

REVIEW

Key Terms

Before proceeding, review the key terms listed below to be sure you understand each one. If necessary, read over the corresponding section of the chapter. When you are ready to test your understanding, answer the Review Questions.

arraignment
arrested
bail
bail bond
bench warrant
booking
challenge for cause
courts of record
crime
criminal justice system
cross-examination
de novo
direct examination
discovery
double jeopardy
exclusionary rule
executed
felony
grand jury
hung jury
indicted
indictment
magistrate
mayhem
Miranda warnings
misdemeanor
motions
nolo contendere
overruled
own recognizance
peremptory challenge
plea bargain
privilege against self-incrimination
procedural due process
prosecutor
sentence
sequestered
split sentence
suppress the evidence
surety
suspended sentence
sustained
venue

Questions for Review and Discussion

1. How is the U.S. criminal justice system different from the Roman civil law system?
2. To what does the term *criminal justice system* refer? Define the two categories of criminal behavior.
3. What rights are guaranteed by the Fourth, Fifth, Sixth, and Eighth Amendments to the U.S. Constitution?
4. What is the role of the prosecutor?
5. How does the role of the defense counsel differ from that of the prosecutor?
6. List the steps in the criminal trial process.
7. How is bail determined?
8. What is the purpose of the grand jury?
9. Discuss the most common pretrial motions and the reasons for them.
10. Describe the sentencing stage of the criminal trial process.

Activities

1. Show the videotape *The Constitution: That Delicate Balance,* Episode 4: "Criminal Justice and a Defendant's Right to a Fair Trial," produced by Media and Society Seminars in association with WNET/Thirteen, New York, and WTTW, Chicago, distributed by Films Incorporated, 5547 N. Ravenswood Ave., Chicago, IL 60640-1199. (Thirteen episodes, 60 minutes each. Available at many public libraries.)
2. Have students write a paper about the ethics, procedures, and problems of the criminal justice system as portrayed in the movie *And Justice for All,* available from video rental stores.
3. Invite a public defender and prosecuting attorney to speak to the class about their roles in the criminal justice system.
4. Plan a field trip to witness a day in criminal court.

NOTES

CHAPTER 5 Civil Law

OUTLINE

5–1 Introduction to Civil Law
5–2 Torts
  Intentional Torts Against a Person
  Intentional Torts Against Property
  Unintentional Torts
  Defenses to Negligence
  Strict Liability Torts
  Business-Related Torts
5–3 Contracts
  Elements of a Contract
  Types of Contracts
5–4 Civil Procedure
  Commencing the Lawsuit
  Discovery
  Trial
  Appeal

COMMENTARY

Every day at Dunn & Sweeney brings new opportunities. Just yesterday, it seems, you were spending your time talking to bail bondsmen, private investigators, revenue agents, and character witnesses, trying to build a case in support of Mr. Dunn's client who found himself in a very embarrassing criminal law situation. Today Mr. Sweeney has asked you to be a part of his litigation group and to work on a few civil cases. You are excited about this opportunity to learn another aspect of the law. Although you have a general understanding of what a contract is, your knowledge of torts is limited to the kind you eat. Can civil law be that different from criminal law? Law is law . . . isn't it?

OBJECTIVES

Chapter 4 provided you with an overview of the criminal justice system. After studying this chapter, you should be able to:

1. Contrast criminal law and civil law.
2. Define the term *tort*.
3. Compare and contrast intentional torts against persons with intentional torts against property.
4. Discuss business-related torts.
5. List the elements of an unintentional tort.
6. Identify common defenses to negligence.
7. List the four elements of a contract.

8. Discuss the most common types of contracts.
9. Outline the steps in a civil lawsuit.
10. Explain the appeals process and how it differs from the trial process.

5–1 Introduction to Civil Law

There is another legal system, known as civil law, that parallels the criminal justice system but deals with different types of issues and has different procedures and objectives. Instead of being concerned with acts against society for which punishment is sought, **civil law** is concerned with acts against individuals for which compensation or other relief is sought.

Civil law is created by statute and by common law. For the most part, civil laws are those that establish the acceptable day-to-day standards of behavior for our society. In addition, statutory civil law and common law define the rules by which liability is determined in the majority of civil lawsuits. That is, civil laws not only tell us that it is wrong to destroy the property of others, but also provide guidelines for establishing who is liable for any wrong inflicted upon individuals or their property.

Unlike criminal law, where the state is a party to the lawsuit, in civil cases the state's involvement is limited to providing a place and a person to assist the disputing parties in settling their differences. No one goes to jail or pays a fine in a civil case. But the **defendant,** the person being sued, may be ordered to pay damages to the plaintiff, the person who initiates the lawsuit.

Civil cases arise because one person believes that he or she has been wronged by another individual, institution, or organization. For instance, the man who owns the house next to yours shoveled the snow from his walks after the last snowstorm, but failed to put sand on the ice remaining on the sidewalk. As you walked by you slipped on the ice in front of his house and fractured your wrist. Depending on how you feel about your neighbor, you might decide to file a lawsuit against him for leaving the sidewalk in an unreasonably dangerous condition. If you win the lawsuit, your neighbor or his insurance company may be required to pay your medical expenses and perhaps to reimburse you for lost wages and compensate you for the pain you experienced. The state has no interest in your lawsuit against your neighbor; the state simply provides the arena in which you and your neighbor can settle your differences.

Civil cases also result when one person fails to live up to the terms of an agreement with another person or organization. For example, when your house needed painting you contracted with an experienced housepainter to paint the house white and the trim blue. The contract called for the painter to use a good quality paint and for the work to be done in a professional manner. Not only did the painter do a terrible job—blue paint was smeared onto the white areas in many places—but following the first rain, the new paint started to peel. You had given the painter $500 toward the total amount of $1500, but when he came by to collect the balance due you asked him to either repaint the house or refund your $500. The painter refused to repaint the house or to refund the $500 and instead sued you for the balance due of $1000. You, of course, countersue the painter for return of the $500.

The state has no interest in this lawsuit either, except to help you and the painter determine whether you were parties to a legal contract and whether the terms of that contract were properly carried out. However, if it turns out that the painter had intentionally misrepresented himself to be a professional painter

Figure 5–1

A carelessly painted house. *Source*: Dennis Zimmermen.

when, in fact, the last time he used paint was in kindergarten, and that instead of using first-quality paint he used paint purchased at a government surplus auction, he might also be accused of fraud, which is a crime against the state and for which he might be arrested and tried separately.

The subject matter of civil lawsuits is myriad and complex, ranging from the loss of life to nuisance complaints about barking dogs. This chapter, which is merely an introduction and overview of civil law, is limited, therefore, to just two essential areas—torts and contracts—since to understand the fundamental principles of tort law and contract law is to understand the fundamentals of civil law and civil litigation.

5–2 Torts

A **tort** is the wrongful conduct of one person that causes injury to another; it is a French word of Latin derivation meaning *wrong*. The person committing the tort is called a **tortfeasor.** Tort law covers a wide variety of wrongful conduct, ranging from acts that threaten your personal safety and property to acts that invade your privacy or impugn your reputation.

Tort law is one area of common law that is always changing to meet the needs of a constantly changing society. For example, prior to the last decade most employees never considered filing a lawsuit against a former employer who gave them a poor recommendation. Likewise, until recently one spouse could physically and emotionally injure the other spouse or their children without fear

Figure 5–2

CRIMINAL LAW		CIVIL LAW
State or federal government on behalf of the people	Action initiated by	Plaintiff or petitioner
To punish, deter, or rehabilitate	Purpose	To compensate for wrongful act and/or deter others
Beyond a reasonable doubt	Proof required	Preponderance of evidence
Fines, imprisonment, death	Sanctions available	Monetary damages, injunction, specific performance
Conviction or acquittal	Outcome of trial	Judgment or dismissal
Felony: homicide, manslaughter, robbery, burglary, grand larceny, bribery, arson Misdemeanor: public intoxication, vagrancy, prostitution, disturbing the peace, assault	Examples of offense	Tort: assault, battery, false imprisonment, defamation, invasion of privacy, trespass, negligence, strict liability Breach of Contract: insurance, real estate, sales, services

This chart contrasts criminal law and civil law.

of being charged with committing a tort. But now the courts are viewing differently the rights of employers and employees, spouses, and minor children. These are just two examples of how tort law continually evolves to meet the changing needs of the society it protects.

Tort law and criminal law are similar in some ways, yet different in others. Both involve wrongs committed against others. Most crimes involve torts. But a tort is not always a crime. A crime is such a reprehensible act that it is considered not only a wrong against an individual, but a wrong against the state and society as a whole, for which the punishment is usually the deprivation of some right. Therefore, the state—or the people of the state—brings the lawsuit against a criminal. A tort, by contrast, is a civil action in which one individual brings a lawsuit against another and for which the punishment is usually the payment of monetary compensation, or **damages.** However, in an assault, for example, there could be both a criminal act that would be prosecuted by the state and a tort which would be the basis for a civil action.

The purpose of tort law is to provide a remedy to the injured party; to determine under what circumstances and to what extent the victim may be responsible for his or her loss; or, to determine when someone else may be entirely responsible for the victim's loss.

Tort law is divided into three categories: (1) intentional torts; (2) negligence; and, (3) strict liability. The typical tort lawsuit, however, involves the intentional or negligent act of one person against another resulting in personal or property damage.

Intentional Torts Against a Person

As the term implies, an **intentional tort** is an act that the tortfeasor made a conscious decision to perform with the expectation that the intended victim would in some way be harmed or otherwise injured. It is the *intent* to bring about injury or harm that is important in determining a tort action; the nature of the damage is irrelevant in determining whether there was intent. For instance, if Jason intentionally shoves George with enough force to knock George to the ground and George breaks his arm, it does not matter that Jason did not want to break George's arm. Jason did intend to bring about harmful or offensive contact to George, and he is liable for the consequences of his actions including the injury to George's arm.

The concept of intent is *subjective*, that is, based on individual feelings, but the law generally assumes that the tortfeasor is aware of the normal consequences of his or her actions and intends for those consequences to result. When Jason shoved George, he expected George to go flying and thus committed an intentional tort. On the other hand, a playful poke or pat on the shoulder is not an intentional tort even if the person touched suddenly pulls away and in so doing is injured.

Assault Any word or action that is intended to cause the person to whom it is directed to fear or have apprehension of immediate physical harm or any offensive touching is an **assault.** For example, if your client brings a gun to a

Figure 5–3

Jason has committed an intentional tort. *Source*: Dennis Zimmermen

meeting in your office there is no assault unless she removes it from her purse and points it at you. Whether it is loaded or not is irrelevant because you fear immediate physical harm. If she shoots the gun to your side to scare you or shoots directly at you with a blank gun, that also is an assault. On the other hand, if she hits you with a bullet, that is a *battery*.

However, a coworker who threatens the forceful delivery of an unwanted kiss may be guilty of assaulting the receptionist. Tort law protects your freedom from fear of harmful or offensive contact from others.

Battery Unconsensual, harmful, or offensive physical contact intentionally performed is a **battery.** If Jason had shoved George with the intent of breaking his arm, his action would clearly have been a battery. However, a battery can occur without physical injury; the contact need only be harmful or offensive. Whether the contact, which can be to any part of the body or anything attached to it, is offensive or not is determined by the **reasonable person standard.** That is, would a reasonable person have reacted the same way under the circumstances?

The contact can be made by the tortfeasor or by some force that he or she sets in motion, such as throwing a rock or poisoning food. Malice does not need to be shown for a battery to occur; the motive does not matter. Only the intent to bring harmful or offensive contact, even if it occurred as a joke or during play, is important in determining whether the victim is to be compensated. Damages can be for emotional harm or loss of reputation as well as for physical harm in a battery case.

Tort law protects your right to personal security and safety, such as in the case of the secretary who receives an unwelcome kiss on the back of her neck while her arms are pinned to her side by a certain supervisor whenever he requests her to complete a routine typing assignment. The supervisor's actions are intentional, offensive, and fail the reasonable person standard.

A defendant who is sued for assault or battery can raise a number of legally recognized defenses. The most common ones follow. (1) *Consent.* When you sign a consent form allowing your child to play football knowing that there is a good possibility that the child may get hurt, the court may find there is no liability for any injuries suffered by the child. (2) *Self-defense.* You may use reasonable force to protect yourself from real or apparent danger. (3) *Defense of others.* You may take reasonable action to protect others from real or apparent danger. (4) *Defense of property.* You may use reasonable force to protect your property, but recognize that the law values life more than property. For example, using force that is likely to cause death or serious injury to protect your property may not be considered reasonable by the court. Rigging a booby trap to trigger a gun that will kill anyone who might attempt to break into your empty house would probably be considered excessive, impermissible force.

False Imprisonment Commonly called *false arrest*, **false imprisonment** is the unjustified, intentional confinement, restraint, or detention of another person without that person's consent. The restraint must be total, so that it amounts to an imprisonment—that is, employing the use of physical barriers, physical restraint, or threats of physical force directed toward the victim, the victim's immediate family, or the victim's property. However, merely obstructing another person's movement, stopping them, or locking someone out of a room is not enough to constitute false imprisonment. Neither is applying moral pressure or future threats.

No physical force need be used to imprison someone falsely, so long as the victim reasonably believes that he or she is being restrained for any appreciable duration against his or her will. Remember Kellie and her alleged shoplifting incident in Chapter 4? Had the store's security officer locked Kellie in the manager's office for twenty or thirty minutes while he went off to find the store manager, then the owner of the store, the manager, and the security officer might all have been sued for false imprisonment if Kellie's lawyer could prove that the detention was totally unreasonable and unnecessary. Shoplifting losses cost businesses an estimated 18 billion dollars a year. Yet it is not unusual for a business owner to be confronted with a false imprisonment lawsuit after attempting to confine a suspected shoplifter for questioning. This is true despite the fact that most states have adopted some type of merchant-protection legislation allowing merchants to detain a suspected shoplifter for probable cause for a reasonable period of time and in a reasonable manner. Furthermore, in false imprisonment cases, the law believes that the mental distress and the potential harm to the detainee's reputation is so great that damages are presumed and need not be proved.

Infliction of Emotional Distress The intentional infliction of emotional or mental distress has been viewed as a tort more recently by some courts where there is a recognized interest in protecting freedom from mental distress as well as physical security. **Infliction of emotional distress** is defined as an intentional act of such extreme and outrageous conduct that it goes beyond the bounds of human decency and causes another to experience severe emotional distress. For example, if you are forced to witness harm being done to your child by another person, or if a prankster telephones you with the news that your spouse has been in a terrible accident, this conduct is considered to be extreme and outrageous beyond the bounds of human decency. You could take legal action for your resulting mental pain and anxiety if you knew the identity of the perpetrator.

Attempting to preclude the filing of frivolous lawsuits by people who cannot deal with the everyday stresses of life, the law scrutinizes the nature of the acts that fall under this tort. Therefore, offensive or insulting language is not usually sufficient to support a lawsuit for emotional distress; neither is suffering some indignity or annoyance. However, repeated annoyances with threats may be enough. For example, a bill collector who uses extreme methods to collect an outstanding debt may intentionally inflict enough emotional distress on the debtor to support a tort action. In most cases, emotional distress must be evidenced by physical illness before the court will award damages.

Defamation The torts of assault, battery, and false imprisonment protect your body. The tort of **defamation** of character protects your good reputation. *Defamation* is the publication or oral communication of a statement that is injurious to the name or reputation of another. A general duty is imposed by law on everyone to refrain from making false, defamatory statements about other people. Breaching this duty in writing or in print is called **libel;** breaching this duty orally involves the tort of **slander.**

Publication, or making defamatory statements to or within the hearing of a third party, is the key element for the defamation tort. If you write a private letter to your employer accusing her of embezzling funds, that action is not libelous. When she calls you into her office and you tell her that she is dishonest, incompetent, and a discredit to the profession, you are not engaging in slander. However, if you dictated the letter to a secretary or if another person was present in your employer's office and overhead your remarks, the court may very well conclude that your defamatory statements were published. It is important to note that any person who republishes or repeats defamatory statements about another can be held liable even if that person reveals the original source of the statements.

There are four types of false statements that the law considers slanderous *per se*, or on their face, and which do not require proof of damages before being actionable: (1) a statement that another person has a loathsome communicable disease; (2) a statement that another person has committed improprieties while engaging in a profession or trade; (3) a statement that another person has committed or has been imprisoned for a serious crime; (4) a statement that an unmarried woman is unchaste.

The truth is usually an absolute defense against a defamation charge when the entire statement at issue is true, not just a part of it, and when the truth applies specifically to the charges being made, not to some other similar but different charges. For example, if the accusation is that your boss has embezzled money from the firm, it is not sufficient to show that she is known to be of bad character or that she once took money belonging to her sister. On the other hand, if the statement is substantially true there is no need to prove every detail. If you are accusing her of embezzling $50,000 and the actual amount is only $35,000, the accusation is justified.

Another defense against a defamation tort may be privilege or immunity. Judges and attorneys often make statements during a trial that are considered privileged and cannot be the basis for a defamation charge. Likewise, members of Congress and legislators are immune from liability for any false statements they may make during a debate even when they know the statements are untrue and may be malicious. In fact, most of the false and defamatory statements that concern public figures, those people who knowingly place themselves in controversial public situations, and which are published by the media are considered to be privileged if the statements are made without malice.

The law recognizes two types of privileged communications: *absolute privilege*, such as in the above examples of judicial proceedings and legislative hearings, and *qualified privilege*, which is based on the common-law concept that the right to know or speak is equally important as the right not to be defamed. Letters of recommendation and employee evaluations are examples of qualified privileged communications, which make allowances for making mistakes in the communication without liability for defamation. In general, if the statements were made in good faith and were published only to those with a legitimate interest, the communication falls within the qualified privilege.

To prove malice, the plaintiff must show that the defendant knew the statements were false or acted with reckless disregard of the truth. There is often a fine line between freedom of speech and the torts of libel and slander.

Slander of Title, Disparagement of Goods, and Defamation by Computer

There are three business-related torts involving defamation. False statements made about a person's business, product, or title to property is called *disparagement of goods* or *slander of title*, depending upon the case. *Defamation by computer* occurs when false or erroneous information about a person's credit standing or business reputation is obtained by computer and that information prevents the person from obtaining further credit. Recently, a record number of lawsuits have been filed against credit-reporting agencies because of the false and erroneous information supplied to lenders that prevented many people from being considered for a home mortgage.

Invasion of Privacy The invasion of privacy tort protects your right to solitude and freedom from the prying eyes of the public. There are four different acts that qualify as an invasion of privacy: (1) the use of a person's name, picture, or other likeness for commercial purposes without their permission; (2) intrusion upon a person's affairs or seclusion, such as invading a person's home, illegally searching a handbag or briefcase, eavesdropping by wiretap, unauthorized scanning of a bank account, window peeping, and compulsory blood testing; (3) publication of information that places a person in a false light, which might also be a defamation tort; and (4) public disclosure about private facts that an ordinary person would find objectionable, such as a newspaper story about a private citizen's sex life.

Misrepresentation The tort of misrepresentation for purposes of fraud and deceit for personal gain includes five elements: (1) The facts or conditions were misrepresented with the knowledge that they are false or with reckless disregard for the truth; (2) there was an intent to induce the other person to rely on the misrepresented facts; (3) the deceived party justifiably relied on the misrepresented facts; (4) the deceived party suffered damages as a result of the reliance; (5) there is a causal connection between the misrepresentation and the injury suffered.

Reliance must be upon a statement of fact, not opinion, unless the person offering the opinion, such as a lawyer, is known to have a superior knowledge of the subject matter. Relying on a lawyer's opinion would be regarded the same as relying upon a statement of fact.

Fraud occurs only when a person represents a statement of fact to be true when he or she knows it is false. For example, it is fraudulent to claim to prospective buyers of your house that the roof does not leak when you know it does. On the other hand, when you claim to be the best bankruptcy paralegal in the county, you are engaging in *puffing*, or *seller's talk*, not fraudulent or deceitful misrepresentation, because "best" is a subjective term, not an objective statement of fact.

Intentional Torts Against Property

The law separates property into two categories: real property, which is land and things permanently attached to it, such as a house and the lot on which it sits, and personal property, those things that can be moved, such as the furniture and furnishings inside the house, jewelry, money, and stocks and bonds.

Torts against property, which are actually wrongs against the person who has legal rights to the property, include (1) trespass, (2) conversion, and (3) nuisance.

Trespass **Trespass** occurs whenever a person enters onto or causes anything to enter onto land owned by another, or remains on or permits anything to remain on the land without permission from the owner. The purpose of the tort of trespass is to protect the rights of an owner to exclusive possession of property; it does not require that any harm be done to the land.

Originally, legal rights to real property gave the owner exclusive possession not only of the land itself but also to the space from the center of the earth beneath the property to the heavens above it. However, that rule has been relaxed in modern times primarily because of the need for aircraft to fly over privately owned land.

Some common examples of trespassing include walking or driving on land posted with "no trespass" signs; shooting across the land with a gun or a bow and arrow, or throwing rocks at a building owned by another; damming a river that causes water to back up on another's property; or extending your house onto a neighbor's property. A guest in your home is not trespassing unless you ask the guest to leave and he or she refuses to go. But any person who enters your property to commit a crime, such as stealing, is considered to be a trespasser whether or not the property is posted.

Trespassers are liable for any damage they cause to the property. But only under certain circumstances will the owner of the property be held liable for any injuries the trespassers might sustain while on the property. For instance, property owners cannot set traps intending to injure trespassers, and owners must warn others of any dangers on the property, such as posting "guard dog" signs on the premises. However, owners may use reasonable force to remove trespassers from the property without being liable for assault and battery. Likewise, owners may remove a trespasser's personal property from the premises as long as they do so with reasonable care.

Trespass to Personal Property Similar to the tort of trespass to land, trespass to personal property occurs when another person interferes with your right to exclusive possession and enjoyment of your personal property or causes harm to your personal property. For example, if one of your fellow students takes your *Introduction to Legal Assisting* book and hides it so that you cannot find it for several days prior to the final exam, your practical-joking friend is guilty of trespass to personal property.

Conversion The tort of **conversion** occurs when someone takes personal property owned by another and places it into service or otherwise deprives the owner of its use. For instance, in stealing merchandise from a store the thief not only commits a crime but the tort of conversion as well. Similarly, when the taking of property is unlawful, trespass occurs; keeping the property is conversion. Even if the property was taken with the permission of the owner, if the borrower fails to return it, conversion may have occurred.

For example, Don, your brother-in-law, borrowed a couple of your power tools with your permission. After using them, Don loaned the tools to his neighbor, Jack. Jack did not finish his project and put the tools in his garage overnight. During the night a thief broke into Jack's garage and stole a bicycle and your power tools. Don is guilty of conversion. He is liable for the reasonable value of replacing your tools because, although Don did not intend for the tools to be stolen, he did intentionally and knowingly lend them to Jack, and in so doing converted the property.

Likewise, when someone buys stolen goods he or she is guilty of conversion even if the buyer was unaware that the goods were stolen because, under the law, the intent to exercise control over property is necessary for conversion to exist, not the intent to engage in wrongdoing. If the rightful owner of the stolen property brings a tort action against the buyer, the buyer must pay the owner even though money has already been paid to the thief.

Nuisance In tort law, a **nuisance** is a wrong arising from an unreasonable or unlawful use of property to the discomfort, annoyance, inconvenience, or damage of another. Nuisances can be either public or private wrongs. For example, the smoke from burning garbage, which pollutes the entire neighborhood, is a public nuisance, whereas garbage piled up next to a neighbor's property, which not only smells bad but attracts rats, is a private nuisance.

Indecent, improper, or unlawful personal conduct might also fall into the nuisance category, but the definition of nuisance when applied to personal conduct is highly subjective. Similar to other torts, a nuisance may also involve a crime, but many times the dividing line is a fine one, such as in cases of indecent exposure and sexual harassment. Damages may be awarded to the person who suffers as the result of a nuisance, but in many instances an injunction to stop the nuisance is an equally appropriate remedy.

In summary, the law recognizes the following as intentional torts:

1. Assault
2. Battery
3. False imprisonment
4. Infliction of emotional distress
5. Defamation, including libel and slander
6. Slander of title, disparagement of goods, and defamation by computer
7. Invasion of privacy
8. Misrepresentation, including fraud and deceit
9. Trespass to real and personal property
10. Conversion
11. Nuisance, public and private

Paralegals, particularly those who work in a general practice, will find themselves frequently interviewing clients who think they are being intentionally wronged by others and from whom they are seeking some remedy. Often these clients pursue legal action based on principle rather than on actual damages.

Unintentional Torts

The prior discussion of intentional torts focuses on those acts where there is intent to cause harmful consequences. But the law also recognizes the unintentional tort of negligence, where there is neither the intent to cause harmful consequences nor the belief that any harm will occur.

Negligence is the failure to exercise the degree of care that a reasonable person would exercise under the same circumstances. Stated another way, any conduct that falls below the standard established by law for the protection of others against unreasonable risk of harm is considered to be negligent conduct. Not only is negligence established by tort law, but so, too, is the degree of negligence. The law categorizes negligence as: (1) *slight negligence,* the failure to use great care; (2) *ordinary negligence,* the failure to use ordinary care; and (3) *gross negligence,* the failure to use even slight care.

Some of the previous illustrations of intentional torts may instead have been negligent torts if they were done carelessly, without intent, such as Jason carelessly bumping into George, who falls and breaks his arm, or the neighbor who carelessly fails to remove all the snow and ice from his sidewalks. In determining negligence, you need to examine the manner in which the tort was committed and be certain that the following four elements are present:

1. That the defendant owed a *duty of care* to the plaintiff.
2. That the defendant *breached the duty of care.*
3. That the plaintiff suffered an *injury* recognized by law.
4. That the plaintiff's injury was a direct effect of the defendant's breach of the duty of care.

Duty of Care The underlying concept of duty of care is that everyone is free to act as they please so long as their actions do not infringe upon the rights and interests of others. Tort law uses the reasonable person standard to measure whether a breach of duty of care has occurred. The reasonable person standard, which is a legal concept subject to exhaustive discussion and debate, does not refer to how a particular person *would* act, but how society as a whole thinks a person *should* act in the same circumstance.

If the hypothetical reasonable person actually existed, society assumes that he or she would always be conscientious, careful, even-tempered, and honest. An even higher standard of care is applied to individuals who possess intelligence, knowledge, and skills greater than those of the ordinary person. Thus, paralegals and lawyers, doctors, psychiatrists, architects, engineers, and other professionals are required to have a higher minimum duty of care standard under tort law for actions involving their professions, and these professionals are held accountable for performing to this higher standard. In other words, the duty of care standard might vary from one individual to the next, based on a number of factors.

Breach of Duty of Care In determining whether the duty of care standard has been breached, the law considers several factors. One such factor is whether the failure to live up to the reasonable person standard of care was an *act,* such as driving through a red light, or an *omission,* e.g., failing to pay attention to traffic conditions while behind the wheel of a car. Driving through a red light may have been an intentional act, a careless act, or a carefully performed but nevertheless dangerous act. If that act results in a legally recognized injury, then negligence has occurred. On the other hand, if the driver was simply not paying attention when he ran the red light and no one was injured, the duty of care standard breached was an omission and does not qualify as a negligent tort.

Injury The primary purpose of tort law is to compensate the victims for legally recognized injuries that result from wrongful acts, not to punish the wrongdoers—although in some torts the injured party may be awarded punitive damages in an effort to discourage others from performing the same acts. Therefore, some type of loss, harm, or wrong must have occurred as a result of breaching the duty of care standard in order for the victim to receive compensation.

Cause The fourth element in the negligence tort equation addresses the relationship between cause and effect, or the resulting injury. Questions the court asks to assist in determining cause include: Was the plaintiff's injury the result of the defendant's act? Or would the injury have occurred anyway? If the plaintiff's injury would not have occurred without the defendant's act, then there is **causation in fact.** For example, when Ralph went through a red light his car struck Sally's, and she sustained injuries that would not otherwise have occurred. But, in addition, suppose that while Ralph and Sally were waiting for the paramedics to arrive, another car came through the same intersection and slammed into Sally's car, which was already in the intersection. The question to be answered now is one of **proximate cause,** a legal term used to establish the extent of liability due to the defendant's conduct. In other words, is the connection between Ralph's driving into the intersection against a red light and Sally's resulting damages strong enough to justify imposing all liability on Ralph alone? Proximate cause is not strictly a question of fact but one of law and policy.

If you were to summarize and present the four elements of the unintentional tort of negligence as an equation to help in remembering them, it might look like this:

Negligence = duty of care + breach of duty + cause and effect + injury

Defenses to Negligence

Assumption of risk, contributory negligence, comparative negligence, and the last-clear-chance doctrine are common defenses in negligence cases. In those states that have not abolished the **assumption of risk** defense, it applies when a plaintiff voluntarily enters into a risky situation knowing the risk involved. For example, if you decide to bungee jump from a hot air balloon, you know there is a risk of being killed or injured. The risk you are assuming is the risk of death or injury from jumping out of the balloon while tied to a bungee cord, but not any risk that might normally be attributed to hot air ballooning, such as the risk of injury should the balloon suddenly fall from the sky because of some mechanical failure in the apparatus.

The **contributory negligence** defense, on the other hand, is common where both parties have been negligent and their combined negligence caused the injury. When Sally sued Ralph for damages as a result of their unplanned meeting in an intersection, Ralph claimed that Sally was contributorily negligent because her car was already in the intersection when Ralph entered against a just-turned red light. But sometimes raising the contributory negligence defense can backfire; the court may decide that both parties were at fault and deny damages to either of them.

However, rather than allowing contributory negligence to completely negate a cause of action, many states are allowing recovery based on **comparative negligence.** Under this concept both Sally and Ralph are assigned a percentage of negligence representing the degree to which each was at fault. If the court finds that Ralph is more negligent than Sally, Sally will be able to recover the percentage of damages that was caused by Ralph's negligence. On the other hand, if Sally's negligence is found to be higher than Ralph's, she may receive nothing and instead find herself the defending party in a counterclaim in which Ralph is seeking damages against her.

Finally, the **last-clear-chance** defense allows the plaintiff to recover full damages despite the plaintiff's failure to exercise care in the face of certain danger. For example, if Sally saw that Ralph was not going to stop when the light turned red and she made no attempt to get out of his way, under the last-clear-chance doctrine Ralph is not permitted to use Sally's negligence as a defense if the court finds that Ralph had the last clear chance to stop his vehicle but failed to do so, thus hitting Sally. As you can imagine, this defense is not easy to apply, and in those jurisdictions where the comparative negligence rule has been adopted, the last-clear-chance defense is no longer being used.

Strict Liability Torts

Both intentional and negligence torts are the result of failing to apply a reasonable standard of care and thereby causing an injury. The category of torts known as **strict liability,** or liability without fault, uses reasons other than fault in determining liability for injury, and is most often applied to abnormally dangerous activities.

Figure 5–4

Assumption of risk. *Source*: Adventure Photo.

The law defines an abnormally dangerous activity as one that: (1) involves potentially serious harm to individuals or to property, for instance, storing or using explosives in a densely populated area; (2) involves a high degree of risk that being reasonably careful will not completely guard against, such as keeping wild animals as pets; and (3) is not commonly performed in the community, for example, storing hazardous waste materials in or near commercial or residential areas. Although the activity is performed with reasonable care, there is still the risk of injury. Under these circumstances, the court considers it fair to ask the individual engaging in the activity to pay for any injury caused by the activity.

Other applications of the strict liability principle have been in the area of workers' compensation acts and product liability. Liability in this type of case is considered to be a matter of social policy and is based on two factors: (1) the employer's or the manufacturer's ability to bear the cost of the injury better than the injured party by spreading the cost out to members of society in general through an increase in the cost of services provided or goods produced; and (2) the fact that the employer or the manufacturer stand to make a profit from the activities that resulted in the injury and should therefore bear the cost of injury as an operating expense.

Do not conclude from this brief discussion of the strict liability principle that there are no legitimate defenses to this type of tort action. But, as a practical matter, businesses rely on insurance coverage to assist them in paying for damages that may result from a strict liability tort action.

Business-Related Torts

Defined as the wrongful interference with another's business rights, **business tort** law is a result of our free-enterprise economic system. Although nearly everyone agrees that unrestricted competition leads to a healthy economy, some overly zealous competitive endeavors might lead to intentional torts and crimes. The law allows businesses to engage in reasonable activities to obtain a fair share of the market or to recapture business that has been lost to a competitor, but the law does not allow businesses to engage in activities that are designed to eliminate the competition completely.

Although business tort law is extensive and varied, the most common torts of a business nature fall into these general categories: (1) wrongful interference with a contractual relationship; (2) wrongful interference with a business relationship; (3) wrongfully entering into business; and (4) infringement of trademarks, trade names, patents, and copyrights.

Wrongful Interference with a Contractual Relationship This business tort requires three elements: (1) the existence of a valid, enforceable contract between two parties; (2) a third party who knows this contract exists; and (3) this third party must cause either of the two parties to the contract to break the contract for the purpose of advancing the financial gain of the third party.

Any lawful contract can be the basis for this type of tort whether the contract is between a firm and its employees, a firm and its customers, or between individuals. For example, a top-producing sales representative has an enforceable employment contract with her current employer. Yet she is being actively courted by her company's largest competitor to come to work for them, despite the fact that the competitor is aware of her existing employment contract. If the competitor is successful in its courtship, and her current employer can show that without the third party's interference the contract would not have been broken, damages may be awarded to the current employer, should the current employer decide to commence a tort action against the competitor.

Wrongful Interference with a Business Relationship This tort distinguishes between competitive behavior and predatory behavior, and in so doing relies upon whether a business is attempting to attract customers in general or whether it is soliciting only those customers who have already shown an interest in the product or service being offered.

For example, Company A's salesperson cannot follow Company B's salesperson through his territory for the purpose of soliciting the same customers, even if the customer did not purchase anything from Company B. Likewise, a clerk from one department store in a mall cannot stand in the doorway of another store in the same mall attempting to divert customers to his or her store.

Not only will the court issue an injunction to stop predatory behavior, but it will also award damages to the business alleging interference when it can prove it suffered a monetary loss.

Wrongfully Entering into Business There are two types of business situations to which the general idea of a freely competitive society does not apply. One is when entering into the business is a violation of the law, such as starting a beauty salon or massage parlor without the required license in a state that requires licensing of these businesses, or starting a radio station without being licensed by the Federal Communications Commission (FCC).

The second type of business situation where the idea of free competition does not apply involves competitive behavior that is predatory in nature, such as starting a business for the sole intended purpose of driving another firm out of business. Although it is often difficult for the court to determine where the normal desire to compete and earn a profit ends and a tort action begins, it is the emphasis on bad motives that helps the court decide.

For example, you are the owner of an established temporary-help agency with an outstanding reputation and an enviable list of satisfied accounts. A former employee, whom you discharged for lacking integrity and engaging in dishonest practices, decides to open a competing business in the same community. This former employee contacts all of your former accounts, as well as the people who worked temporary assignments for your agency, and says false, malicious things about you. Not only was false information given, but customers were promised tremendous discounts and other incentives to switch their business to the new agency. As a result, before you could control the damage, you lost so many accounts and workers that you had to close down your business. If you file a tort action and can prove that the defendant's sole purpose in opening the business was to injure you and destroy your business, you will likely be awarded damages.

Infringement of Trademarks, Trade Names, Patents, and Copyrights When an individual or a company falsely induces buyers to believe that one product is another, the practice is known as *passing off*. Watches, clothing, handbags, and luggage are just a few examples of the estimated $10 billion worth of goods that are passed off each year, sometimes through reputable merchants.

When a tort action is filed, the court must decide whether a typical customer paying ordinary attention would be deceived when presented with one product that looks like the other. If so, the court will find there has been an infringement of a trademark, trade name, patent, or copyright.

A **trademark** is any word, name, symbol, emblem, motto, or device used by a manufacturer or merchant to distinguish its goods or products from those produced by another. The commonly used symbol ® indicates that the trademark is protected by law. Similarly, a **service mark,** denoted by the letter *S* within the circle, is used to distinguish the services of one person or company from those of another. Airlines and television characters such as well-known cartoon characters are often registered as service marks.

A **trade name** distinguishes a company, business, or partnership, rather than a product or service. There are no clear guidelines to determine when the name of a corporation can also be regarded as a trade name. In particular, trade names such as Coca-Cola, Xerox, Kleenex, and Scotch Tape have acquired secondary meanings and are often used generically. Nevertheless, the courts will not allow another company to use those names in any way that might deceive the public.

A **patent** is a grant from the government that allows an inventor who has satisfactorily demonstrated to the patent office that the invention is genuine and novel the exclusive right to make, use, and sell the invention for a period of 17 years. The patent holder uses the word *Patent* or *Pat.* followed by the patent number to notify everyone that the invention is patented and that any manufacturing, using, or selling of the invention without the patent holder's permission constitutes an infringement of the patent and is subject to legal action.

A **copyright,** commonly indicated by the symbol © (no longer required for protection against infringement) is a statutory right now granted for life plus 50 years to authors, originators of artistic productions, and developers of computer programs. It is important to note that an *idea* cannot be copyrighted, but the way in which an idea is *expressed* can be. Reproduction of copyrighted material is permitted under Section 107 of the Copyright Act without the payment of royalties under certain circumstances including "for purposes such as criticism, comment, news reporting, teaching (including multiple copies for classroom use), scholarship, or research . . ." All other uses of copyrighted material may be an infringement of copyright for which penalties or legal remedies may be imposed.

In addition, the law recognizes there are some processes or information that cannot be patented, trademarked, or otherwise protected. Businesses, therefore, sometimes protect their *trade secrets* by having their employees sign a contract agreeing never to divulge such information or processes. Likewise, using a person's name or likeness without that person's permission is subject to the tort action of *appropriation.* The law maintains that a person's right to privacy includes the right to the exclusive use of his or her identity.

5–3 Contracts

With an understanding of contract law, you will possess another key to the U.S. legal system. Not only is it the foundation upon which many other specialized areas of the law are built, but contracts are also the foundation for all commercial transactions and most everyday activities. Unlike tort law, which is based upon society's expectations regarding interpersonal conduct, contract law is based upon a promise and an agreement between individuals. Contracts, then, are as varied as the types of agreements into which individuals might agree to enter.

A **contract** may be defined as a legally enforceable promise or set of promises. A **promise** is a declaration to do something or to refrain from doing something in the future. So, if two people promise each other they will perform some specific act in the future, or they promise each other to refrain from doing a specific act, they may be creating a contract. If either of them does not fulfill his or her contractual obligation, a **breach of contract** will occur. The party who does not keep the promise may be subject to legal sanctions such as the payment of money to the other party for *failure to perform,* or the law may require the breaching party to fulfill the promise, a legal concept known as *specific performance.*

Elements of a Contract

Regardless of the subject matter of the promises, there are four elements necessary for a contract to exist: (1) agreement; (2) consideration; (3) capacity; and (4) legality.

Agreement For the parties to reach agreement, there must be an *offer* and an *acceptance.* An offer is nothing more than one party communicating to another what he or she is willing to do. When one party consents to the other party's offer, there is acceptance of the offer, and the parties are in agreement. The party making the offer must intend to enter into an immediate contract: "I will sell you my family law textbook for $25," not merely set forth the terms for future negotiation: "I usually sell my used textbooks at half price."

An offer remains open until it (1) expires: "You have until 9 a.m. tomorrow to let me know if you want to buy my book"; (2) is withdrawn: "I've decided to keep my book, so I am withdrawing my offer to sell it to you"; (3) is rejected: "No, thanks, I prefer a new book"; or (4) is accepted: "It's a deal. Here's $25."

Consideration Any *inducement*—motive, cause, reason, or price—to a contract qualifies as consideration. Without consideration there is no contract. Consideration must be legal and given in exchange for the promise or performance of the other party. In the preceding example, monetary consideration of $25 was exchanged for a used textbook. But consideration does not need to be monetary. For example, when both parties agree to enter into a marital settlement agreement, merely signing the agreement constitutes legal consideration.

Capacity The parties to a contract must be of legal age and mentally competent. Thus, a contract entered into with a minor, a mentally incompetent person, or an individual so intoxicated that he or she did not understand what the agreement was about would not be a legal contract.

Legality The contract must be for a legal purpose and not against public policy. In other words, legal contracts must not involve criminal activities such as drug dealing, gambling, and murder for hire, or involve leases of property that violate health and building codes, or in which exorbitant interest rates are charged.

To summarize, a contract must

1. Contain an offer and acceptance.
2. Include consideration.
3. Be between competent parties of legal age.
4. Be for some lawful purpose.

Figure 5–5

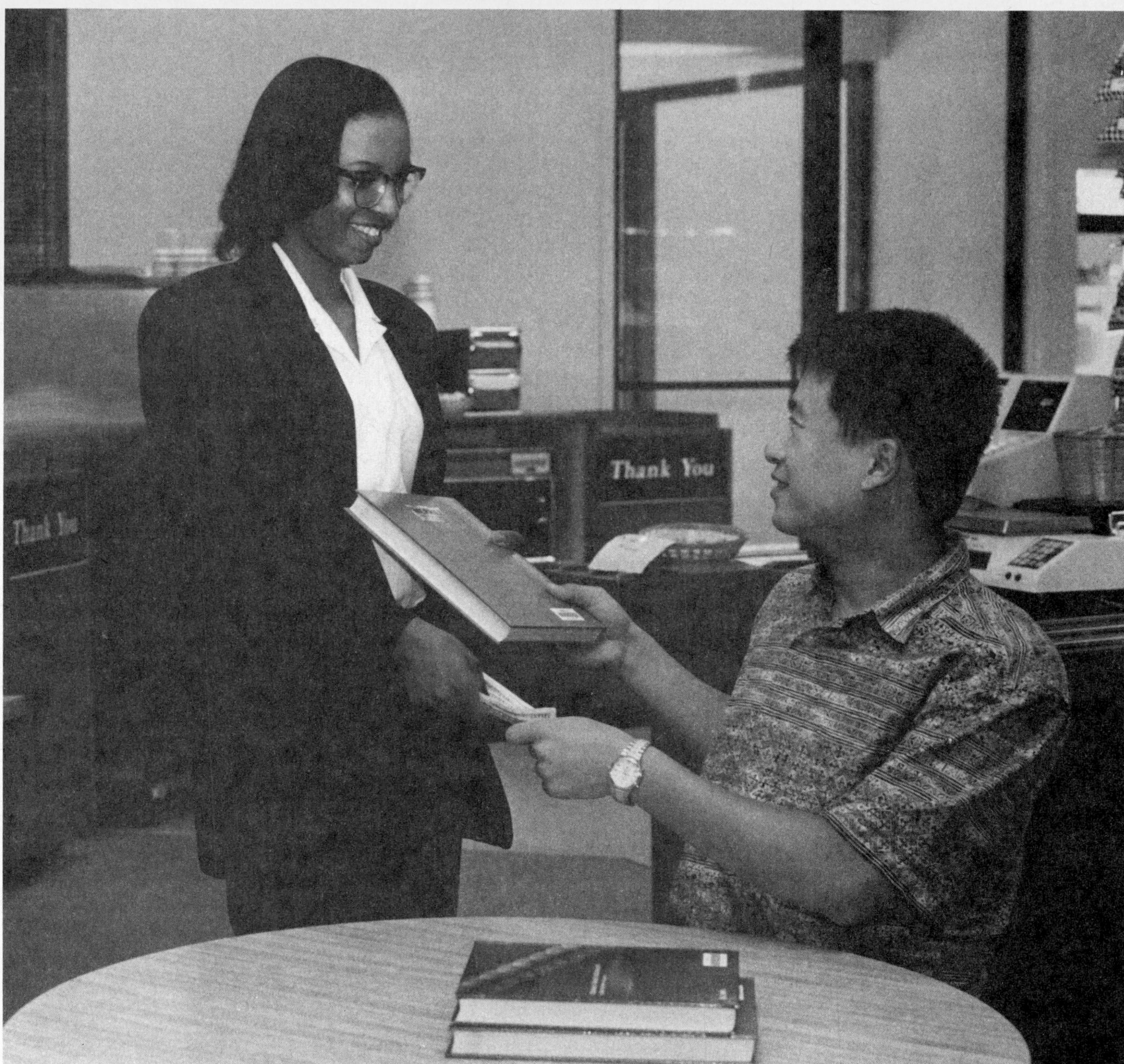

College students contracting to buy books. *Source:* Doug Martin.

Types of Contracts

In addition to the four elements just discussed, every contract has two parties: the *offerer*, who makes the offer, and the *offeree*, the person to whom the offer is made. In addition, most agreements fall into one or more of three broad categories—bilateral or unilateral contracts, express or implied contracts, and formal or informal contracts.

Bilateral or Unilateral Contracts Simply stated, a **bilateral contract** is a promise for a promise. Using the used-textbook sale example, a bilateral contract might be: "I promise to buy your business law textbook for $25 if you will promise to bring it to my house tonight." A **unilateral contract,** on the other hand, is a promise for an act. For example, "I promise to buy your textbook for $25 if you will bring it to my house tonight."

What happens in a unilateral contract if the offerer changes his or her mind after the offeree has begun performance but not completed it? Let's say another student, who really needs the money, has offered to sell you his used business law text for $25. When you call your buddy attempting to revoke the unilateral contract, you find that he has already left home and is on his way over to your house to deliver the book. The traditional view of law is that acceptance occurred only on full performance. That is, until the book is delivered and paid for there is no full performance and therefore no acceptance of the offer. The modern view, however, is that the offer becomes irrevocable once performance has begun. This view does not mean that there is acceptance, but does prohibit the offerer from revoking the offer for a reasonable period of time. So, according to the modern legal viewpoint, you are probably obligated to buy the book from your buddy once he gets to your house—unless you can renegotiate the agreement.

Another classic law-school illustration of a unilateral contract is Scott saying to Nancy, "If you walk across the Brooklyn Bridge, I'll give you $10." Scott is promising to pay only when Nancy has walked the entire length of the Brooklyn Bridge. According to the law of contracts, acceptance of Scott's offer occurs only when Nancy has completed crossing the bridge. If Nancy decides not to walk the bridge, there are no legal consequences.

To summarize, the difference between a unilateral and a bilateral contract is this: in a unilateral contract only one party, the offerer, is obligated to perform because the offeree has already performed his or her part of the deal, or the contract would not exist; in a bilateral contract both parties are obligated to perform because the contract reflects only their promises to do so.

Express or Implied Contracts In an **express contract,** all the terms and conditions of the agreement are fully and explicitly stated, either orally or in writing. Agreements to buy or sell real estate and automobiles are common examples of express written contracts. When your classmate offered to sell you his used textbook for $25, an express oral contract was made.

However, contracts may also be **implied-in-fact,** such as when the conduct of the parties indicates that they intended to form a contract and that conduct creates and defines the terms of the contract. For example, when you go to the doctor you usually do not agree beforehand that you will pay the doctor a certain fee in exchange for his or her performance of certain acts. Rather, it is implied that the doctor will use his or her best efforts to take care of your medical problems and that you will pay a reasonable fee for this service.

Three elements are necessary for an implied-in-fact contract to exist: (1) some service or property was furnished; (2) the person expected to be paid for that service or property and the receiving party knew or should have known that payment for the service or property was expected; and (3) the receiving party had an opportunity to reject the service or the property and did not do so.

A contract may also be **implied by law.** In these types of contracts the law imposes requirements on the parties even when the parties have not entered into a contractual obligation. Implied-by-law contracts attempt to impose a quasi-contract on the parties in order to prevent one party from being unjustly enriched by the actions of another without having to pay for that benefit. For example, a doctor comes upon the scene of an accident and performs medical services on the unconscious victim but is unsuccessful in saving the victim's life.

Even though the unconscious victim could not have expressly or by implication from his conduct entered into a contract to pay for the doctor's services, the court would likely permit the doctor to recover the reasonable value for her services from the decedent's estate.

Formal and Informal Contracts Contracts that require a special form or method of creation to be enforceable are called **formal contracts.** These types of contracts would include: (1) contracts under seal, that is, a contract on which a waxed seal is placed or that simply uses the word *seal* at the end of the document; (2) recognizances, such as the criminal recognizance bond; (3) negotiable instruments, including checks, notes, and certificates of deposit; and (4) letters of credit, a promise by a bank to honor on behalf of its customer a demand for payment by a foreign supplier of goods.

All other types of contracts except those that must be in writing, such as for the purchase of real estate, are said to be **informal contracts,** since the contracts are based on substance rather than on their form.

Attorneys and paralegals frequently work with clients who have problems resulting from a contractual obligation. The preceding discussion is merely an overview of contract law for the purpose of familiarizing you with the terminology and some of the legal concepts of civil law. Courses in business law and civil litigation will provide you with more knowledge and skills in these specialized areas.

5–4 Civil Procedure

All civil lawsuits follow the same basic steps, but actual procedure will vary by state and by county. Generally, civil lawsuits follow three stages. First, there is the commencement of the lawsuit, followed by the discovery phase, leading to settlement or trial. Occasionally, there is a fourth stage if the decision of the trial court is appealed. Not only are paralegals involved at each step of the process, but attorneys and court personnel rely upon them to keep the lawsuit moving through the various stages to its completion.

To illustrate the various steps in a typical civil tort action, let's use the Sally and Ralph situation discussed previously, where Ralph failed to stop for a red light and ran into Sally's car in the intersection.

Commencing the Lawsuit

After being hit by Ralph's car, there was about $10,000 worth of damages to Sally's new car. Sally, even though she was wearing a seatbelt, also had a cut across her forehead resulting from where her head hit the windshield. She had bruises on her chest, face, arms, and legs. Her entire body was stiff and sore. An ambulance took Sally to the local trauma center where she was X-rayed and examined by a physician. The doctor told her to get bed rest for a few days and to come back in a week for another examination.

Ralph, too, had some damages to his car and some stiffness in his upper body for a few days following the accident. However, the damages Ralph sustained amounted to only about $5000.

Several weeks later Sally asks Mr. Dunn, of Dunn & Sweeney, where you work as a litigation paralegal, to represent her interests in this matter. After a brief interview with Sally, Mr. Dunn agrees to represent her on a **contingency fee** basis; that is, the firm will receive a percentage of the amount it is able to recover for Sally as its fee. If the firm is not able to recover damages for Sally, then the firm will receive no fee. Mr. Dunn has now turned the file and the client over to you to proceed.

You lead Sally into your office, offer her some coffee or a cold drink, and ask her to relate in detail the facts of the accident while you take copious notes. Because of the amount of damage to Sally's vehicle and her continuing, ongoing medical bills, now amounting to over $25,000, you determine that the superior court has jurisdiction over this lawsuit. Further, the accident occurred nearly four months ago, but the **statute of limitations,** the time fixed by law within which to bring legal action, has not yet expired. Sally has brought with her a copy of the police report of the accident, letters from her insurance company and Ralph's insurance company each pointing the finger of liability at the other, and copies of her medical bills, which are growing larger with each passing month.

After Sally leaves your office, you begin drafting the complaint, which is the plaintiff's first **pleading.** All the formal papers filed with the court by the parties in a lawsuit containing their positions on the issues in dispute are called *pleadings*. The original complaint, which states the facts on which Sally's *cause of action* against Ralph is based, is signed by the attorney and usually *verified* under oath by the client as to its factual content. Some courts request that you complete and submit other types of forms, designed primarily to gather statistics, simultaneously with the complaint.

In addition to preparing the complaint, you also prepare the **summons,** which is the notice to Ralph that a civil action has been filed in which he has been named a defendant and that he has a certain time specified by law in which to file his response, or **answer,** to the complaint or he will lose the case by default. The original summons and complaint, together with several copies of each, and a check to pay the court's filing fee are then taken to the courthouse.

Next, the court clerk *issues* the original summons, that is, the clerk affixes the official seal of the court on the summons, inserts the date, and signs it. The original summons is then returned to you, but the original complaint is *filed* with the court, or placed in the court's file. After all the defendants have been served, you will then file the original summons with the court. The clerk then *conforms* the copies of the summons and complaint by placing a filing stamp on each document indicating the date on which the original complaint was filed. A conformed copy of the summons and complaint is placed in the client's file in your office, and another copy is *served* on the defendant.

For the summons and complaint to be legally served, in most instances it must be handed to the defendant personally by someone who is not a party to the lawsuit. However, in special circumstances, such as when a defendant is avoiding service or cannot be located, legal service may also be made in other ways, such as by substitution, that is, by leaving papers with another adult at the premises, or by certified mail with a return receipt, or by placing a notice in the newspaper. Usually a U.S. Marshal or a professional process server is used to serve legal documents, but sometimes a paralegal or legal secretary might be asked to serve papers on the defendant. The person who serves the summons and complaint then completes an Affidavit of Service, which is also filed with the court, swearing under oath or penalty of perjury that legal service has been made.

The next step is up to the defendant, Ralph, who may file his answer to the complaint, or a **demurrer,** a statement that does not dispute the facts but asserts that the plaintiff failed to state a sufficient cause of action on which to base a claim against the defendant. But Ralph may also decide to file a **counterclaim** against Sally, alleging that he has a cause of action against her. In the event a demurrer is filed, a court hearing will be scheduled to let a judge determine whether the demurrer is valid; if the demurrer is *sustained,* or determined to be valid, the court will in all likelihood allow Sally's attorney to file an *amended complaint,* following the same procedural steps for service as for the original complaint. If Ralph's attorney files a counterclaim against Sally, the two lawsuits run concurrently through the remainder of the judicial process.

Ralph might choose, instead, to ignore the summons and complaint, which is a bad idea. Doing so would likely result in a *default judgment* being entered against him ordering him to pay Sally the amount of damages she has claimed.

Once an answer is filed, the case is said to be *at issue,* and the appropriate document may be filed by either party requesting the court to set a date for trial. Even though there is still a great deal of work to be done prior to a trial, it is often appropriate to request a trial date as soon as possible, because in some of the more crowded courts civil trials are being scheduled two or three years in advance.

Discovery

Once the initial pleadings have been filed and served, the next step in the civil litigation process is to begin the discovery phase. Discovery procedures allow all the parties to the lawsuit to obtain facts from each other in order to better prepare for trial. Since paralegals play an important part in discovery proceedings, Mr. Dunn has asked you to prepare a set of **interrogatories** and serve them by mail on Ralph's attorney. Interrogatories are written questions addressed to a party in the lawsuit asking for answers pertaining to the subject of the litigation. A **bill of particulars** is another type of legal document designed to elicit even greater factual details, and may be used instead of or in addition to the interrogatories. For example, in answering the interrogatories Ralph may give some information on which you wish to have clarification or greater detail.

Figure 5–6

SAMPLE OF INTERROGATORIES IN A CIVIL LAWSUIT

9. State the name and address for each person for whom you are claiming damages for personal injuries.
10. Describe in detail for each person listed in your response to Interrogatory No. 9 all injuries and symptoms, whether physical, mental, or emotional, experienced since the occurrence which is the subject of this lawsuit and which are claimed to have been caused, aggravated by, or otherwise contributed to by said occurrence.
11. For each medical practitioner who has examined or treated any of the persons named in your answer to Interrogatory No. 9 for any injuries or symptoms described in Interrogatory No. 10, state:
    a. The name, address, and specialty of each medical practitioner.
    b. The date of each examination or treatment.
    c. The physical, mental, or emotional condition for which examination or treatment was sought or performed.
12. Has any individual listed in your answer to Interrogatory No. 9 been hospitalized as a result of the occurrence? If so, please state:
    a. The name and location of each hospital.
    b. The dates of each hospitalization.
    c. The conditions treated during each hospitalization.
    d. The nature of the treatment rendered during each hospitalization.

Samples of interrogatories.

In that instance, a follow-up question in a bill of particulars would be appropriate.

Preparing, serving, and obtaining a response to interrogatories and a bill of particulars are relatively inexpensive discovery methods, but they take a great deal of time. A more expensive but also more efficient method of obtaining the facts is to schedule a **deposition,** which is an in-person question-and-answer session conducted under oath and recorded by a court reporter or on videotape during which counsel for both sides are present and have the opportunity to question the individual being deposed. Depositions may be taken of parties to the lawsuit or witnesses. Just as the paralegal is routinely involved in preparing interrogatories and in assisting the client in preparing his or her answers to interrogatories, the paralegal may also be involved in preparing the client for a deposition.

Other discovery documents a legal assistant may prepare include a **request for admissions,** a document in which the other side is asked to admit that certain facts are true so that they do not have to be proven at trial, thus saving valuable court time, and a **request for the production of documents and things,** which allows the other side to review and inspect before trial any documents or other evidence expected to be presented at trial. The defendant may also file a *request for physical or mental examination* of the plaintiff; this is the only discovery procedure that requires court approval.

During the discovery stage, either side may make a number of motions requesting a particular order or ruling by the court. The most common is a **Motion for Summary Judgment,** which is a request that the court end the case without a full trial. The Motion for Summary Judgment states to the court that if it looks at the facts of the case and the evidence presented to date, the court would surely find that the other side could not possibly win and there is no need for a trial.

Usually at various times during the discovery phase of the litigation, the parties attempt to negotiate a settlement. In fact, settling a lawsuit out of court is the primary objective of most attorneys, because going to trial is the most lengthy and costly way to end a dispute. However, it is not always possible to settle out of court, and when settlement is not possible going to trial is the next step in the civil litigation process.

Trial

Before trial begins a pretrial conference is held before a judge, often in the judge's private office or chambers. During this conference the attorneys present a general outline of the trial, identifying the major issues that will be presented, and give a report on the status of their discovery proceedings. The judge usually urges counsel once again to try diligently to settle the case or to consider arbitration.

If all attempts at settlement fail, the case will go to trial. If a jury is requested, *voir dire* commences. Paralegals are often in attendance during the *voir dire* examination, contributing their impressions of prospective jurors and developing questions for the jurors to answer. Throughout the trial, the paralegal may be asked to perform additional research and to keep track of exhibits being placed into evidence, as well as to provide emotional support to the attorney and the client.

Once the trial is completed and a decision has been made, the judge signs the judgment and the clerk files the document and sends endorsed copies to counsel for plaintiff and defendant. After the judgment has been filed and copies have been served on all parties, the defendant has a number of days, usually 30, in which to decide whether to appeal the court's decision.

Appeal

It is important to note that the defendant may not file an appeal merely because he or she is unhappy with the outcome of the trial. Appeals are limited primarily to questions of law, such as whether, during the trial the judge erred in applying the law or in conducting the trial, or whether the trial court had jurisdiction to try the case.

If the case is heard on appeal, it is not retried. Rather, the attorney for the **appellant,** the party bringing the appeal, files an appellant's brief that summarizes what took place at the trial, states the errors that the attorney thinks the trial judge made, gives a legal analysis of the errors, and asks the appeals court to reach another conclusion. Then the **appellee,** the person against whom the appeal is brought, files his or her brief. Sometimes the appellant might file a brief in response to the appellee's brief. However, neither party can raise any legal arguments on appeal that were not raised at the trial, nor may they bring up any new causes of action or new theories. Paralegals are used extensively to perform research and draft appeals briefs.

After the briefs have been filed, a limited amount of time is scheduled for the attorneys to present oral arguments before the justices of the appeals court, who may interrupt the attorneys during their presentations to ask questions. When the justices have heard the arguments of counsel, they deliberate in private on the case and take a vote. The majority rules. The justices then write and publish their opinion.

If no appeal is filed, the case is closed and the losing party pays the amount of the judgment awarded to the prevailing party. Once the judgment has been paid, a *satisfaction of judgment* is prepared and filed, documents are returned to the client, and the office file is purged and closed.

Even the simplest and most routine civil litigation cases, such as the one briefly described here, will take several months or several years to resolve. The litigation paralegal is an integral part of the process from beginning to end, serving in many capacities, not the least of which is the primary liaison between the client and the attorney, the court, and opposing counsel. For this reason alone, law firms depend upon their litigation paralegals and place a great deal of responsibility on their skills and sound judgment.

SUMMARY

5–1

The civil justice system is concerned with acts against individuals for which compensation or other relief is sought. Created by statute and by common law, civil laws establish the everyday standards for behavior in society and define the rules by which liability is determined in the majority of lawsuits. Unlike criminal law, the state's involvement in civil lawsuits is limited to providing the forum in which the disputes are settled.

5–2

Tort law is concerned with the wrongful conduct of one person that causes injury to another, and includes acts that threaten your personal safety and property as well as acts that invade your privacy or impugn your reputation. Tort law falls into three categories: intentional torts, which are conscious acts performed with the expectation that the intended victim will be harmed in some way; negligence, or unintentional acts that result from the failure to exercise that degree of care which a reasonable person would exercise in the same circumstances; and strict liability torts, which are most often applied to abnormally dangerous activities.

5–3

Contract law forms the foundation for all commercial transactions and for most everyday activities. A legal contract contains four elements: agreement between the parties; some form of consideration or an inducement to enter into the agreement; the legal and mentally competent capacity to enter into a contract; and a lawful purpose for the contract. Contracts may be expressed orally or in writing, or they may be implied by the conduct of the parties. Breaching a contract may result in legal sanctions, such as the payment of money for failure to perform or specific performance, the requirement that the breaching party fulfill the terms of the contract.

5–4

Although actual procedure will vary by county and state, all civil lawsuits nevertheless follow the same general steps. The plaintiff must first file a complaint against a defendant, who must be legally served with the pleadings and must file a response or have a default judgment taken for failure to respond to the complaint. Once the defendant's answer has been filed, the discovery process begins, which may include interrogatories, bills of particulars, depositions, requests for admissions, and motions. If the parties are unable to settle their dispute, the case will go to trial before a judge and/or a jury. Once a decision has been made and the trial is concluded, the case may be appealed if the court erred in some way during the trial proceedings. Attorneys have an ethical responsibility to their clients to make every effort to settle a case before it goes to trial.

REVIEW

Key Terms

Before proceeding, review the key terms listed below to be sure you understand each one. If necessary, read over the corresponding section of the chapter. When you are ready to test your understanding, answer the Review Questions.

answer
appellant
appellee
assault
assumption of risk
battery

bilateral contract
bill of particulars
breach of contract
business tort
causation in fact
civil law
comparative negligence
contingency fee
contract
contributory negligence
conversion
copyright
counterclaim
damages
defamation
defendant
demurrer
deposition
express contract
false imprisonment
formal contracts
implied-by-law
implied-in-fact
infliction of emotional distress
informal contracts
intentional tort
interrogatories
last-clear-chance
libel
Motion for Summary Judgment
negligence
nuisance
patent
pleading
promise
proximate cause
reasonable person standard
request for admissions
request for the production of documents and things
service mark
slander
statute of limitations
strict liability
summons
tort
tortfeasor
trademark
trade name
trespass
unilateral contract

Questions for Review and Discussion

1. What are some of the differences between criminal law and civil law?
2. Define the term *tort*.
3. Compare and contrast intentional torts against persons with intentional torts against property.
4. What are the most common types of business-related torts?
5. List the four elements of negligence, an unintentional tort.
6. What are some of the most common defenses to a negligence lawsuit?
7. To be legal, a contract requires four elements. What are they?
8. List and define the most common types of contracts.
9. Outline the steps in a civil lawsuit.
10. On what general grounds can the trial court's decision be appealed?

Activities

1. To increase comprehension of terminology, make and use flash cards. For extra credit, develop a crossword puzzle using the terms in this and previous chapters.
2. Invite a litigation paralegal to speak to the class on a typical day in a civil litigation practice.
3. Assemble the forms used in your court for civil cases. Go step by step through the procedures to make sure you understand each one.
4. Plan a field trip to the courthouse to see firsthand the filing of pleadings from the clerk's point of view.
5. Attend a civil trial and write a report contrasting your expectations prior to attending the trial with what actually took place.

PART TWO

CLIENT SERVICES

NOTES

CHAPTER 6 Interviewing and Investigation Skills

OUTLINE

6–1 Preparing Yourself for the Interview
- Interviewing Techniques
- Develop a Goal and a Plan
- Prepare an Outline
- Professionalism

6–2 Preparing the Environment
- Use Space to Build Rapport
- Control Interruptions
- Make the Client Comfortable

6–3 Preparing the Client
- Reveal Your Agenda
- Clarify Your Status
- Confidentiality
- Note Taking
- Taping the Interview
- Handling Distractions

6–4 Preparing the File Memorandum
- Caption
- Body
- Action Steps

6–5 Conducting an Investigation
- Purpose for Investigation
- Investigation Resources
- Computer-Aided Investigation

6–6 Interviewing Witnesses
- Attitude of Interviewee
- Be Prepared
- Use a Checklist
- Understand the Law
- Handling the Hostile Witness
- Preparing the Witness Statement

COMMENTARY

Your knowledge and skills as a paralegal are expanding rapidly. So are your functions and responsibilities. Mr. Sweeney called you from court a few minutes ago, explaining that he has been detained. He asks you to interview a new client who has retained the firm to represent her in what may be a sexual harassment or job discrimination matter. The charges involve the partner at another prominent law firm, but Mr. Sweeney says he is confident that you have just the right attributes to make the client comfortable and to build rapport. Not wanting to disappoint Mr. Sweeney and confident in your ability to tackle any problem, you decide not to tell him that you have never conducted a client interview before. Instead, you seek out the advice of someone with experience in interviewing and find out what steps to take.

OBJECTIVES

After studying this chapter, you should be able to:

1. Compare and contrast the terms *interview* and *interrogation.*
2. Apply good listening skills to build rapport and gather information.
3. Prepare an outline for a client or witness interview.
4. Discuss the part professionalism plays in conducting an interview.
5. Prepare the environment appropriately to establish rapport, privacy, trust, and professionalism during an interview.
6. Discuss the various elements of the interview process to make the interviewee more comfortable.
7. Compose a file memorandum of the interview.
8. Define the term *investigation.*
9. List common sources of information used during an investigation.
10. Compare and contrast a client interview and a witness interview.

6–1 Preparing Yourself for the Interview

Recall the last time you were interviewed. The interview may have been for a job or when you entered this program or when you applied for a student loan or bank financing for your car. Maybe the last time you were interviewed occurred the other day when you met someone for the first time and exchanged information about your families, communities, or occupations. Regardless of the circumstances, the interview occurred for one specific reason—to gather information.

The purpose for conducting an **interview** is to gather information about the case in a face-to-face meeting. Although, on occasion, conducting an interview over the telephone might be necessary, you will lose the opportunity to observe body language as well as the chance to establish rapport. For these reasons, in-person interviews are preferred. During the interview you should refrain from commenting on, criticizing, or offering an opinion on the content of the information. Stated another way, the focus of an interview should be on gathering information, not on evaluating it. Evaluation should be saved for later, after you have had time to think about the interview in its entirety.

Start by keeping an open mind and concentrate on building rapport. For example, if you begin the interview with the belief that the person you are interviewing is hostile or uncooperative, you are more likely to direct the interview to prove your assessment is correct, rather than building trust. In doing so, you might overlook some important information. It is better to be free of preconceived biases so that you can concentrate on listening to what the client is saying and shift direction as necessary to follow the client's thought patterns. Changing direction to follow the flow of information as it is presented is what makes the exchange an interview instead of an interrogation.

An **interrogation** is another way to gather information by only asking questions. Usually the questions in an interrogation are closed, requiring only a "yes" or "no" answer. By contrast, an interview is an exchange of ideas and information based on open-ended and follow-up questions. In an interrogation

Figure 6–1

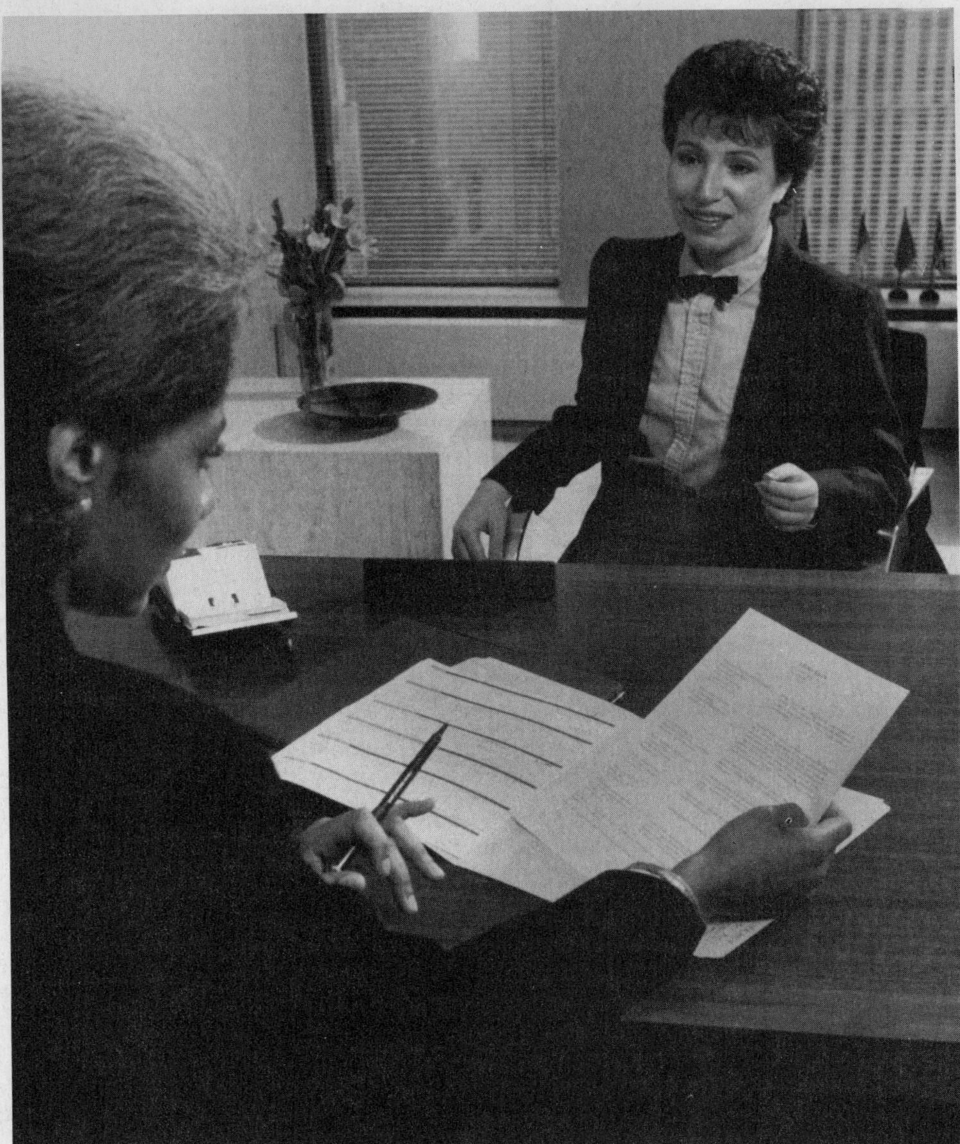

The focus of an inteview is to gather information about the prospective job candidate. *Source*: Richard Hackett.

the person who is asking the questions directs and controls the content of the information, but in an interview the content and flow of information may go in any number of directions, if the interviewer so desires.

An interrogation is a procedure used to verify known facts; an interview is a process used to discover new information. The interrogator often knows the answer to the question before it is asked, whereas the interviewer does not. Since interrogations tend to be intimidating, they are more appropriate for the witness stand than for eliciting voluntary information. For these reasons, when you are preparing to interview for the purpose of gathering facts and information, it is important to recognize the differences between conducting an interview and an interrogation.

For example, in Figure 6–2 compare the style of one legal assistant using an interrogator's approach to getting information from a client with that of another who is using the interview technique. Which one is likely to get more information? Which style is more rapport-building?

Interviewing Techniques

Good interviewers know what kinds of questions to ask and when to ask them. Generally speaking, there are two types of questions: open questions, which encourage the speaker to respond with more than one or two words, and closed questions, which usually require only a short response.

Even the most skilled interviewers have difficulty getting some people to

Figure 6–2 Example of Style Differences Between an Interrogation and an Interview

INTERROGATION

LA: State your name and current address.
Client: Connie Munson. 210 East Winslow, Tempe, Arizona.
LA: Are you still employed by Timble & Turner?
Client: No.
LA: When did you leave Timble & Turner?
Client: On February 12.
LA: Why did you leave?
Client: I felt uncomfortable.
LA: When?
Client: When people would not talk to me and they stopped giving me cases to work on.

INTERVIEW

LA: Ms. Munson, I need to check the personal data in the file for accuracy. Please tell me your full legal name and your current address.

Client: I usually go by Connie Munson but sometimes I use my married name, Connie Munson-Baker. We've lived at 210 East Winslow for about two years but we are hoping to be able to buy a house before the end of the year.

LA: Have you been married long?

Client: About three years. My husband, Charles Baker, is a land developer. We want to get a house of our own so we can start a family. But, now that I'm unemployed it looks like it's going to take longer than we had planned.

LA: Tell me why you are no longer working at Timble & Turner.

Client: After word got around that I had filed a sexual harassment complaint with the personnel department against Mr. Turner, I really got the cold shoulder from everyone. Nearly everyone stopped talking to me, except for Cindy who knew what was going on and has been very supportive. I probably could have put up with the silent treatment, but when I ran out of work and asked for more no one would give me a new case file to work on. They either said they didn't have any work to give me or that everything was covered. I knew that wasn't true because we had several new cases come into the office recently and everyone was complaining about the work load. I could see how things were going and just decided to leave. That was at the end of the second day after I filed the complaint in personnel.

open up. However, questions beginning with the words "what," "why," and "how" will nearly always result in an extended response. By contrast, questions beginning with "are," "who," "when," "which," and "do" will most likely result in a "yes" or "no" answer or a very short response. But one of the most effective interviewing techniques is to say to the client, "Tell me about . . . ." When you compare the responses in Figure 6–2 you will notice that there is a significant difference in the amount of information gathered when the interviewer asked open questions. Although not all of the information may be pertinent to the case, giving the client the opportunity to choose the amount and content of the information presented is one way of establishing rapport and making him or her feel you are interviewing, not interrogating.

Learn to Listen Listening is a skill that can be developed. The main reason why most people are not good listeners is that they are not paying attention to what the speaker is saying. Instead, the listener is formulating a response for when it is his or her turn to speak. Many times the response is inappropriate. The tendency is to offer advice, "You should . . . ,"or to be sympathetic, "You poor thing," or to state your opinion, "I think you were treated unfairly."

Although these types of responses may be appropriate for personal conversations, they are not appropriate in an interview. Rather than build rapport, offering personal comments or your own point of view can set up false hopes and expectations that may present problems later on. It is best to remember that you are performing in a professional capacity, not a personal one, regardless of how much you may like the person you are interviewing or how much empathy you feel for him or her.

When you are interviewing a client you might think of yourself in the role of a counselor, not a problem solver. Solving the client's problems is what you do once you have gathered enough information to determine the problems. Your job during the interview is to gather information, not to come up with solutions. That means you must get the client to talk more while you talk less. Good listeners are able to keep the information flowing without offering advice, giving an opinion, or judging the content. In other words, avoid making statements such as, "I think you should start divorce proceedings immediately," or "You should have gone directly to the police," or "Don't you think you handled that situation badly?" Comments of this nature will likely be interpreted as an attack, to which the typical response is defensiveness or intimidation.

What responses are appropriate in your role as information gatherer? Here are some examples.

1. When you want more information or need to clarify facts, ask the client: "Can you explain that another way?" Or, "Do you mean that . . . ?"
2. If you want the client to consider other aspects of the problem, you could say: "As I understand it, you have decided to . . . and the reasons are . . . ."
3. Discussing feelings builds rapport, shows empathy, and might lead to more information. "How did you feel when that happened?" Or a reflective comment such as "You must feel you weren't treated fairly" will usually encourage further details.
4. Summarize the client's problems and direct his or her thinking toward a solution by using statements and questions similiar to these. "As I understand it, these are the key issues as you see them" (then list the issues). "What would you like to see happen now?" "Is there anything else I should know?"
5. To encourage the person to continue talking and to show that you are listening, you need only periodically interject, "I see," or "That's

interesting," or "Then what happened?" Referring back to something that was said earlier is another way to indicate you are paying attention. For example, "Earlier you indicated that . . . " or "During our last meeting you seemed concerned about . . . . Is that still a concern?"

These listening techniques are easy to remember and to use. Furthermore, they are nonthreatening and do not invade the person's privacy, yet they encourage the sharing of even the most intimate information and help to build a trusting relationship between you and the client.

Develop a Goal and a Plan

A good interview requires advance preparation. Some people make the mistake of thinking that since the interview process involves two skills they already possess—talking and listening—nothing more is required. The truth is that most of us are not very good at either talking or listening. Too often the mouth is engaged before the brain, resulting in an unclear message. Most people talk more than they listen.

To overcome these communication shortcomings, good interviewers prepare in advance and have an established goal. That is, you should know what result you want before you set up the meeting. Perhaps the purpose of the initial interview is to establish rapport and a working relationship. If so, the communication would be focused on providing personal and professional information and looking for common interests and shared experiences. Your questions would be of a more general nature: "Where do you live? What schools do your children attend? Where did you go to school? How do you spend your free time?" In this type of interview, you would respond with some personal information of your own.

In most instances, the purpose for the interview is to get enough information from the client so your attorney can make an evaluation of the merits of the case. For that reason questions of a personal nature would be limited, whereas emphasis would be placed on the specifics—unless, of course, the nature of the case requires that you focus on personal information, such as in a family-law matter. When the purpose for the interview is strictly business, then the tone you set should be professional and businesslike instead of conversational. Whatever the reason for the interview, there are always time constraints. Therefore, you need simultaneously to control the interview and put the client at ease. Advance preparation is the key to conducting a good interview.

Prepare an Outline

Once you know the purpose or the goal for the interview, the next step is to prepare a brief outline of the points you want to cover. An interview rarely flows along a logical sequence; rather, it often wanders from one point to another. Without an outline, you will find that you have used up all your time without finding out anything of substance.

List the important points you want to cover on a legal pad. Put only two or three points on a page, leaving ample space after each one to record the client's response and to make notes for follow-up questions. As each point is covered to your satisfaction, check it off. You might want to use colored pens to differentiate those items requiring research from those you want to follow up on with an individual. One advantage to using colored pens to record information during the interview is that later it is easier to flip through your notes and find what you are looking for instead of having to read through each page.

Some law firms will have interview forms for you to follow. These forms are helpful in providing guidelines, but you should never come to rely exclusively on any form, thinking that its existence relieves you of the obligation to properly prepare for the interview. Cases are not identical and neither are client interviews.

Vital Statistics Without exception, you will always want to ascertain a client's **vital statistics,** or certain routine personal data. A client's vital statistics would include the client's name, address, daytime and evening telephone numbers, and place of employment. Make a note of where and when are the best times to reach the client. Ask if you may contact the person at work. Some firms also require the client's date of birth, Social Security number, and driver's license number. This information is often needed to obtain copies of records or reports from hospitals, police departments, and insurance companies. Similar information about a married client's spouse might also be required, whether or not the spouse is a party to the lawsuit.

Since obtaining this information can take several minutes, some law firms ask new clients to complete a printed form with this information prior to the interview. Doing so might create feelings of impersonality rather than involvement. Before taking this approach, the savings in time should be weighed against any possible negative impression the client is likely to hold of the value the firm places on its clients.

Five Ws and an H Following the vital statistics information in your outline will be the who, what, when, where, why, and how questions. Even though you might list the questions on your legal pad in this information-gathering style favored by journalists, if you ask them in the same style, your interview will take on the characteristics of an interrogation. Consider using the "Tell me about . . ." approach mentioned earlier and make notes, checking off each category as the client covers it in his or her narrative of events. By giving the client some latitude in the breadth and depth of information he or she is being asked to share with you, you may be surprised to learn some important and interesting facts that would not have been revealed if you were following your own script.

Follow-up As the story unfolds, you will be making notes on those areas requiring research and investigation. Avoid interrupting the client's story, since you may force the storyteller off track. In addition, most clients want to please you. When you interrupt them too often you risk sending the message that you are not hearing the right information. The result could be that the client reveals only the information that he or she thinks you want to hear. The more the client monitors the information, the less likely you are to get the whole story.

For this reason, a free-flowing, stream-of-consciousness recollection of events can be more informative and productive than directed questioning. You do not want to be in a position where several months into a lawsuit you find that a client withheld important information simply because they did not think it was relevant. Or, worse, the information was withheld because you did not ask the right question.

Results What does the client want? What results does he or she expect? Although the true answer to these questions cannot be determined until the attorney has had an opportunity to evaluate the merits of the client's case, it is nevertheless always a good idea to find out what the client expects. It is not your job, however, to comment one way or the other on the client's expectations or chances of success in pursuing a legal claim. In fact, to do so is unethical. Should the client ask for your opinion about the chances for success or the worth of the case, you must tell the client that is a matter to be discussed only with the attorney.

Release Forms It is important that you have the client sign all appropriate release forms so that the firm can obtain any medical, employment, or other documents and records required for the case. Some of the forms can be completed, but several blank forms should also be signed by the client to be kept in the file and used as needed.

If you fail to get the release forms signed by the client, it will only delay your investigation. Most agencies will not release any information without the individual's written consent.

Retainer Agreements It is unethical for a legal assistant to set fees, but frequently it is part of the legal assistant's role to explain to the client the terms of the **retainer agreement,** a contract for fees and costs, as well as the firm's billing procedure. Although discussing payment for services may be uncomfortable, it is a subject that must nevertheless be addressed. Prior to meeting with the client you should be informed of the content of any discussions the attorney has had with the client on this subject.

Nearly every state now requires that there be a signed retainer agreement between the law firm and the client. If your state is one that does not automatically require retainer agreements, sound business practices and professionalism do require that there be a written agreement in the client's file.

Professionalism

Regardless of the subject matter or the content of the interview, you must remain professional at all times. You are not required to, nor should you comment on or judge the information as it is presented. Focus on gathering the facts. Do not get caught up in emotions. Never say anything derogatory about the opposing party or anyone connected with the case. You never know when an offhand remark or expression will come back to haunt you.

Professionalism also includes the way you dress for the interview, the tidiness of the location where the interview is held, and your manners. Do not smoke, chew gum, play with paper clips or your pens. Clean off your desk, put away any files you are working on to preserve the confidentiality of other clients. When clients see a disorganized desk, they also see a disorganized paralegal. Clutter not only produces stress, it also calls into question your competence.

6–2 Preparing the Environment

It is equally important for you to give some thought to where the interview is going to take place. Sometimes there is no choice, such as when the client is in jail. However, in many instances, you may select from a variety of alternatives:

your office, the client's home or place of business, a restaurant, or even a golf course or health club.

Regardless of the location there are several factors, in general, that you will want to keep in mind and control to the extent possible.

Use Space to Build Rapport

The use of space is one of several elements that make up the **subtext** of all communications. Julius Fast, author of *Subtext: Making Body Language Work in the Workplace* (New York: Penguin Group, 1991) defines *subtext* as "a kind of covert language that may add to the spoken text, reinforcing it and strengthening it; or may contradict the text, canceling out any promises or agreements." Other elements in addition to use of space that are part of the subtext of any communication include facial expression, gestures, eye contact, touch, appearance, posture, and movement. Together these elements are more commonly known as **body language.**

Whether in your office, the client's home, or a restaurant, the seating arrangement will influence the tone of the interview. For example, if your office is arranged in a typical fashion it will no doubt resemble a typical office arrangement as illustrated by Figure 6–3.

If you choose to sit behind the desk with the client sitting in front of it, the desk not only acts as a barrier between the two of you—keeping the client at a distance—but it also sends a signal of power. The subtext of this seating arrangement is the message that you are in charge; that you have more power

Figure 6–3 A Typical Office Arrangement

Source: Dennis Zimmerman.

and authority than the client. If you are attempting to establish rapport, trust, and a sense of equality, do not distance yourself by sitting behind a desk.

Feelings of distance and formality can be reduced by placing the client's chair at the side of your desk as illustrated in Figure 6–4. Now only the corner of the desk is between the two of you. This arrangement is generally more comfortable, particularly if you are going to be reviewing photographs and documents with the client, and it infers a certain degree of intimacy.

Getting away from the desk altogether is the best way to achieve informality and equality. Many offices and conference rooms are now furnished with a conversation grouping including a couch, low coffee table, and visitor chairs. A subtext of relaxed informality and equality is signaled by this type of furniture arrangement, and it is usually more conducive to keeping the communication channels open than sitting behind a desk as illustrated in Figure 6–5.

The typical paralegal office is not usually spacious enough to accommodate a conversation grouping, requiring some creative improvising in order to achieve the desired result. If it is possible to borrow the office of someone who does have an informal seating corner, this might be your first choice. Or the conference room might work better than your office. At the very least, if your office furniture and space are restricted to the minimum, consider placing the client chairs in the corner with a small, low table or plant between them, as illustrated in Figure 6–6.

Whether the meeting takes place in the client's home or in an office, you will undoubtedly have a choice of where you want to sit. If you have an established goal for the meeting, that should help you in making your decision. Regardless of where you choose to sit, a subtext of interest and involvement is communicated when you lean forward toward the client. Leaning back or away indicates disbelief and boredom—a subtext not likely to make the client talkative.

Figure 6–4 An Informal and More Comfortable Office Arrangement

Source: Dennis Zimmerman.

Figure 6–5 A Conversation Grouping for a Conference Room

Source: Dennis Zimmerman.

Control Interruptions

In order for both you and the client to keep focused on the interview, you must attempt to control any interruptions or distractions. Ask the receptionist to hold your calls and/or turn off the bell on your phone. If you have an answering device on your telephone, turn it on and return any calls after the interview has been concluded.

To keep coworkers from knocking on your door, place a "do not disturb" sign on your door or use some other type of signalling device indicating that you are conducting an interview and do not wish to be interrupted.

Make the Client Comfortable

When possible, adjust the room temperature so that it is not too hot or too cold. Either condition will make the client uncomfortable and want to terminate the interview as quickly as possible. If you cannot control the room temperature, you should warn the client when making the appointment that your office tends to be unusually cool or warm so that he or she may dress appropriately.

Figure 6–6 A Conversation Corner in a Small Office

Source: Dennis Zimmerman.

Make sure that you have an ample supply of tissues near the client's chair, as well as a notepad and a pen so that the client may also make notes if required. Fresh water and clean glasses are also a good idea. Of course, you will offer coffee, tea, or a soft drink.

Depending upon the complexity of the case and the emotional state of the client, an initial interview may take from 45 minutes up to two hours or more to get the details and information you need. If the interview is an extended one, suggest taking a break after every 50 minutes or so to give both of you an opportunity to refresh yourselves and pull your thoughts together.

6–3 Preparing the Client

Equally important to preparing yourself and the environment for the interview is the preparation of the client. Unless the client is habitually litigious, he or she has probably had little contact with the legal system and its procedures. Clients usually do not know what to expect and they are often intimidated by the entire process. After all, you are a stranger asking another stranger to bare some of the most intimate details of his or her life to you. You need only put yourself in a similar situation to be able to imagine how the client must feel and why he or she is reluctant to tell everything, particularly in the first meeting.

Reveal Your Agenda

When you make the appointment with the client reveal your **agenda,** the list of things to be done during the meeting, including how much time you are allowing for the interview, and any documents or other items the client should bring to the meeting.

At the beginning of the interview, state your agenda again: "We have 45 minutes to discuss . . . ." Presenting an agenda at the beginning of the interview helps to keep both you and the client focused on the purpose for the meeting.

Clarify Your Status

Before you commence the interview, remind the client that you are a paralegal, not a lawyer, and that you cannot give legal advice. Since some people will not understand the nature of the paralegal function, you might take this opportunity to explain the differences between a paralegal and a lawyer. You will want to emphasize that you work under the supervision of a lawyer and that he or she will be kept informed of every aspect of the case.

Assure the client that he or she will be seeing the attorney, if he or she has not already done so, and say when that meeting is likely to take place. Be sure to explain that all decisions will be made by the lawyer but that you can be considered the primary liaison between the client and the attorney. If the client expresses disappointment that the attorney is not present or refuses to proceed with the interview, you have several options: You can ask the attorney to come into the meeting to reassure the client; if the attorney is not available, you can ask for the client's cooperation in answering just a few preliminary questions with the hope that once the interview begins the client will feel more comfortable with you; or you can terminate the interview and reschedule for a time when the attorney is available. Your professionalism in handling this situation may be the final persuasive factor in securing your status as an integral part of the client's legal team.

Confidentiality

To put the client at ease, emphasize that the attorney-client privilege extends to you. This means that any information given to you is done so in confidence and will be shared only with the attorney handling the case.

Ask the client to let you know if there is any information that should not be included in the file. Sometimes it is necessary for a client to reveal sensitive information that might prove embarrassing if it were to become public, such as giving birth to an illegitimate child who was put up for adoption when the client was a teenager. If at any time you feel it is necessary for you to reveal the information to the attorney and the attorney determines that the information is important to the client's case, then assure the client that he or she will be contacted before any action is taken.

Note Taking

Unfortunately, it is impossible to take notes and maintain eye contact with the client. Yet taking notes is an important part of the interview process. Because lack of eye contact may send a message of disinterest, it is important for you to tell the client that you will be taking notes and that doing so is not a sign that you are not paying attention. On the contrary, taking notes during an interview indicates that you are very interested in what the client is saying.

Transcribe your notes as soon as possible after the interview. You will be working on several files simultaneously. The longer the amount of time between the interview and the transcription of your notes, the greater the likelihood of error. Few people are blessed with an infallible memory. You do not want to be in the embarrassing position of having to ask the client to come back for another interview because you cannot read your notes.

Taping the Interview

Although taping the interview might make you feel more comfortable, it often has the opposite effect on the client. Some people feel very self-conscious when a tape recorder is placed in front of them. If you think it is important to get the interview on tape, you must first discuss it with the client and get his or her consent. Once the interview has begun and the tape is recording, you should begin by stating that the interview is being recorded and ask for the client's consent.

For example, you could begin by stating: "Today is April 20, 19XX, and this is the first interview with Connie Munson, taking place in the office of paralegal Kelsey Smith with the law firm of Dunn & Sweeney. This interview is being recorded with the permission of Ms. Munson. Is that correct, Ms. Munson?" This same information should be restated at the end of the tape for purposes of identification and as a precautionary measure in the event it was not recorded at the beginning of the tape. It is important that the client be heard on tape giving permission to record the interview.

Videotaping interviews may become more commonplace in the future as more people become comfortable with the technology and with being seen and heard on videotape. Conducting an interview on videotape provides everyone with the opportunity to study the client's or witness's body language and to see how the person is likely to appear if called to give testimony in court. Obviously, having knowledge of the individual's ability to be credible and handle him- or herself in stressful circumstances would be invaluable to attorneys working on the case. If the client gives permission to videotape the interview, you would begin in the same way as you would if you were audiotaping. That is, state your name and the date, and ask the client's permission to videotape while the tape is running. Then repeat the opening remarks at the end of the tape. If more than one tape is used, number and identify subsequent tapes at the beginning and the end of each.

Taping the interview does not relieve you from the responsibility of taking notes. There is no other way to be sure that you cover all the areas on your outline and to be able to follow up on information as the interview progresses from one topic to another. Tapes are very helpful in refreshing your memory or clarifying a point when you are writing your memorandum for the file, and they can be invaluable later on when you are preparing for trial. But relying on tapes alone could result in disaster, particularly if the tapes are lost, stolen, or misplaced.

Handling Distractions

If the interview is taking place in your office, you can control some of the distractions by having your telephone calls held and closing the office door.

However, if the interview is in the client's home, you should ask the client to arrange for someone to take care of any children who might be present and to take precautionary steps to keep neighbors or other unexpected visitors from the home during the interview.

Do not permit friends or relatives to be present during the interview. If you need to talk with these people, you can do so at a later time and alone. The presence of other people will inhibit the flow of information, particularly if it is sensitive or embarrassing to the client.

From time to time, you may find yourself in the position of facing the reluctant interviewee. Even though you are using your best interviewing and listening skills and have taken extra effort to control the environment, the client is answering in monosyllables or giving no information at all. When it is obvious that your valiant efforts are producing few results, it is best for you to terminate the interview and ask someone else in the office to take over the case. Nothing you can do will overcome negative chemistry. Staying on the case will only make matters worse and could lose the client to another firm. It is important that you understand that getting along with everyone is not possible and that some personalities just do not click. It is better for you to remove yourself from any case where, for whatever reason, you will not be able to produce maximum results rather than place your credibility and professionalism at risk.

6–4 Preparing the File Memorandum

At the conclusion of the interview and before your notes are stale and your memory dimmed, the next step in the interview process is the preparation of a written memorandum for the file.

Many law firms have a standard format for you to follow for file memoranda, but others will expect you to know how to write a memorandum without a form. In either event, all file memoranda should contain information similar to the following example.

Caption

The caption contains all the identification information for the memorandum, as shown in Figure 6–7. The caption includes the name of the person to whom the memorandum is directed, the name of the person who conducted the interview and is writing the memorandum, the date of writing, the name of the client's file and the file number, and the subject matter of the memorandum.

Some law firms may include more information, such as the vital statistics, in

Figure 6–7 A Sample File Memorandum

FILE MEMORANDUM

TO:	Name of Supervising Attorney	DATE: Date memo prepared
FROM:	Your Name	FILE NO.: Client file number
FILE NAME:	Name of client file	
RE:	Subject of memorandum, such as Initial Interview with Connie Munson.	

an interview memorandum, but few will ask for less than that shown in Figure 6–7.

Body

Following the caption is the body of the memorandum, which usually begins with an opening sentence stating the reason for the memorandum. As you write the memorandum keep in mind that the reader was not present during the interview.

Begin by telling the reader when and where the interview took place, who was present, and any other pertinent information about the interview. Then continue with a narrative of the events as told to you by the client. Do not use a question and answer format like that illustrated in the interrogation section of Figure 6–1 unless you are specifically asked to do so.

Memoranda, in general, are written in a prose style and are organized in a logical sequence of factual events. Even though the interview itself may have wandered from one point to another, your job is to organize the information logically and present it to the reader in a way that is easy to understand.

You should attempt to anticipate any questions the reader might have and answer them. Nothing frustrates an attorney more than reading a file memorandum late at night and finding there are questions left unanswered. When this happens you are likely to be given back the file with a request to rewrite the memo.

As you compose the memorandum, you may find that you neglected to ask the client an important question or two. When that happens, contact the client by phone and ask for the information or clarification before you prepare your final draft to submit to your supervisor. It is unlikely, regardless of how skilled you become at interviewing, that you will think to ask all the pertinent questions during an interview. On the other hand, if you have to call the client more than once to get information that was overlooked during the interview, you need to spend more time preparing for the interview.

Figure 6–8 is one example of how to begin the body of your file memorandum.

Figure 6–8 Body of the Interview Memorandum

The following is a memorandum of the initial client interview with Connie Munson, which took place in my office on April 20, 19XX. The interview was taped with the permission of Ms. Munson and the original tape is in the firm's safe marked with the client's file number.

CHRONOLOGY OF EVENTS

Ms. Munson began by stating that she is no longer employed by Timble & Turner. She left the firm voluntarily on February 12, 19XX, because of the circumstances that occurred after she filed a sexual harassment complaint against Mr. Turner on February 10, 19XX.

The following is a chronology of the events that led up to Ms. Munson filing the complaint with the firm's Administrator, Helen Montgomery . . .

PERSONAL DATA

Ms. Munson has been married for about three years to land developer Charles Baker. The couple has been renting a home for the past two years at 210 East Winslow in Tempe. The Bakers do not have any children and are planning to buy their own house in the next year . . .

Since interviews differ slightly in content and length, you will have to decide what information to include and how to identify your title heads. Whatever you decide, place yourself in the reader's position and use headings that are appropriate for the telling of the client's story. For example, in Figure 6–8, the Chronology of Events might have been called Background Information or Client History. If the memorandum pertains to an auto accident you would want to have headings for Location of Accident, Witnesses, Insurance Coverage, and Injuries.

There is flexibility in preparing memoranda, but remember that the purpose of headings is not only to organize the information but also to keep the reader from guessing what information is coming next. Headings also save time. When anyone needs to refer to the memorandum for a specific piece of information the headings should be able to direct them to it.

The body of the memorandum is used to set forth all the pertinent information revealed in the interview. Using this information, the attorney can evaluate the case and decide how to proceed. Court pleadings may be drafted using the data you have collected and research projects may be assigned.

Action Steps

The final section of the memorandum should indicate the next steps to be taken. Perhaps you have arranged another appointment with the client for a second interview or asked the client to provide you with some documents or other information. It could be that you want to interview a witness or obtain police reports. Or maybe you have a question about a point of law that needs to be answered by the attorney or researched in the library.

The action steps section could be viewed as your "to do" list or research and investigation guide. Regardless of what you call it, this section gives the attorney an indication of what you consider to be the areas requiring further investigation or research. In most instances, you would not take action on any item included in this section without first discussing it with your supervising attorney and receiving approval to proceed.

One last comment about interviews: do not throw away your handwritten notes after you prepare the file memorandum. Most law firms have a rule about keeping everything until a case is concluded. You never know when you might be called upon to refresh your memory about a certain point and may need to refer back to your old notes. It is not unusual to identify one file specifically for the purpose of keeping all handwritten notes for each complex case. In some instances, you just put your entire legal pad or steno pad into the expanded file and use it for all interviews and notetaking as the case progresses.

6–5 Conducting an Investigation

The next steps section of the client interview memorandum will often suggest the areas requiring investigation. For example, there may be witnesses to locate and interview or individuals and corporations to be served with pleadings. If the case progresses to a jury trial, you may be asked to locate personal information on prospective jurors.

In most states, paralegals who are employees of a law firm are usually exempt from the licensing requirements of the state's Private Investigator Act or its equivalent. However, freelance paralegals or other individuals who are hired as independent contractors on a case-by-case basis might be required to have a private investigator's license if they intend to engage in any investigatory practices as part of their assignments. You should familiarize yourself with the requirements in your state before accepting an investigation assignment or hiring someone outside the firm for this purpose.

John J. Horgan, author of *Criminal Investigation* (Glencoe/Macmillan McGraw-Hill, 2d ed.) defines **investigation** as an observation or inquiry into allegations, circumstances, or relationships in order to obtain factual information. Most legal assistants are called upon to perform many investigations as a routine function of their position. Horgan has identified several desirable attributes for anyone who is charged with carrying out the duties and responsibilities of an investigator. Among these attributes are the following.

1. *Suspicion and curiosity.* Do not take anything for granted and develop a habit of being inquisitive. Wondering about how people are dressed, the type of car they drive, their quickness to produce identification or an alibi may lead you to other pertinent information. Do not hesitate to ask questions. A desire to learn the truth is satisfied only through questioning and probing for understanding.
2. *Observation and memory.* Use your five senses to observe and remember anything unusual about a person's posture, movement, appearance, mannerisms, or speech. Understanding how to interpret body language will provide additional clues to an individual's reliability and honesty.
3. *Lack of bias.* Prejudgment often results in incorrect conclusions and unfair treatment. Working to keep yourself from being biased toward anyone connected with the case or their position in the lawsuit will help you to form a more complete picture of all the events and circumstances surrounding the case.
4. *Patience, understanding, courtesy.* Always use self-control, tact, and respect in your role as an investigator regardless of whom you are investigating or interviewing. Do not become impatient with people who are unable to recall dates, places, and events or provide you with other data. Maintaining professionalism at all times is extremely important to your success in being able to obtain the information and cooperation needed to properly represent a client.

Purpose for Investigation

Aside from the obvious reason to conduct an investigation—to obtain factual information—the results of an investigation can mean the success or failure of a legal action. For example, a thorough investigation not only helps you and the attorney determine the direction of legal research but also provides insight and awareness of the opposing side's case. If the investigator has been successful in putting biases aside and keeping prejudgments to a minimum, he or she will have been able to look at the issues from all sides. This total perspective is required not only to fully represent the client but to keep any surprises from surfacing during a trial or settlement negotiations.

The investigator's report will reveal a number of things including the proper parties to the action and where to locate them for service of pleadings, the identity of witnesses and the ones to call to give testimony, the identity and credibility of witnesses for the opposition, the cooperativeness or hostility of witnesses, and what questions to ask of each witness. The investigation should also result in identifying any tangible or physical evidence that will be introduced by either side. In addition to providing a wealth of information, perhaps the most important result of a thorough investigation is that it will help the attorney to determine the best course of action to take for the client.

Investigation Resources

It is easy to understand the value of a thorough investigation. But how does someone who is not a professional private investigator begin and where do you turn for information? Fortunately—or perhaps unfortunately, depending upon your point of view on privacy—there are many sources of information available to anyone who wants to access them.

File Documents You would, of course, begin any investigation by reading the client file. Understanding the facts of the case is critical to knowing what questions to ask and of whom to ask them. If the file contains discovery documents such as depositions, interrogatories, requests for admission statements, and memoranda of interviews and conversations, you will want to read and understand all of these.

You might want to check with the county clerk's Register of Actions to find out whether the individual under investigation has been or is currently involved in any other lawsuits. Once a legal action is filed with the county clerk's office, the file is a matter of public record. That means that access to the file and its contents is available to anyone who has the case number. The case number can be found in a book called the Register of Actions at the county clerk's office. Actions are listed in the register alphabetically by name as well as chronologically by case number.

In addition to the file contents, locate, study, and photocopy any newspaper or magazine articles about the case or related to it. Your local public library and newspaper office have back issues of newspapers and periodicals for reference purposes.

Individuals It is important that you establish a network of contacts in the community to provide additional sources of information or leads. Professional organizations such as your local paralegal association are essential for this purpose. The more community resources you have to call upon, the more likely you are to be successful in locating the information you want.

In addition to your personal network, Figure 6–9 shows a partial list of categories of people who could be sources of information for any given investigation you might be conducting. This listing is far from all-inclusive. Its

Figure 6–9 Possible Sources of Information

Possible Sources of Information	
Apartment house manager	Condominium association board member
Bank employees	Barbers and beauty shop operators
Bartenders	Building security staff
Elevator operators	Building door openers
Garage and parking lot employees	Janitors and maids
Hotel and motel employees	Pawnshop employees
Gas and electric company employees	Neighbors
Teachers	Police department employees
Firefighters	School crossing guards
Truck drivers	Restaurant employees
Gas-station attendants	Grocery store clerks
Gardeners	Delivery services

purpose is to raise your awareness that, depending on the information you are seeking, nearly everyone could be a potential source. Inquisitive investigators may need to interview many people before locating the right source.

Police Records If a report was filed with the police involving your client, you will be able to obtain a copy of that report and any other police records on the client with the client's written permission. Additionally, because of your employment with a law firm, you might also be allowed access to other records and reports maintained by the police department, including individual arrest records, photo albums, traffic and accident reports, and wanted bulletins. Some police departments are more cooperative than others in providing information. Your courtesy, professionalism, and trustworthiness will no doubt be considered before any information will be provided.

City and County Agencies Information on individuals, businesses, and corporations may be found in several public-record sources compiled and maintained by city and county officials. Figure 6–10 is a partial listing of various city and county resources and examples of information available for reference purposes. Information maintained by each agency will vary by city,

Figure 6–10 City and County Public Record Information Sources

City and County Public Record Information Sources	
Assessor's Office	Real and personal property tax records, deeds, transfers, mortgages.
Building Department	Building permits, blueprints, construction details, inspection records.
Civil Service Commission	Employment records, personnel histories, liens filed against employees, other personal data.
Coroner's Office	Autopsy and inquest reports, names and description of deceased persons, names of witnesses, property found on deceased and disposition of it.
County Clerk's Office	Marriage licenses, adoptions, fictitious business names, naturalization applicants, information on civil lawsuits including divorce proceedings. Criminal Division has information on criminal actions heard in superior court.
County Recorder's Office	Judgments; trust deeds; mortgages; notice of mechanic's liens; abstracts of judgment; wills admitted to probate; records of marriages, births, and deaths.
County Treasurer's Office	Information on tax levies on land, improvements, and personal property; collection of taxes; and payments to county employees, welfare recipients, school teachers, and other types of district employees including retired employees.
Fire Marshal	Building and premise inspections.
License Bureau	Business licenses and permits issued in the city.
Sanitation Department	Garbage and trash subscribers.
Street Department	Maps of city, correct street numbers, alleyways, easements, and former street names.
Voter Registration	Roster of registered voters including name, address, occupation, place of birth or naturalization, political party affiliation, handwriting specimens, and nomination papers of candidates for county offices.
Welfare Office	Background and social history information on persons receiving public assistance.

county, and state. This listing is a representative sample only and should not be relied upon as the only information resource for every state. Part of your job as a legal assistant is to be familiar with the public-record information agencies in your geographic location and the information available from each.

State Agencies In addition to the numerous city and county agencies that maintain records and provide information, there are also various administrative agencies at the state level that are sources of information. Among these are the secretary of state's office and the state's sales tax collection agency, both of whom maintain records regarding businesses and corporations. The office of the state treasurer, auditor, or controller can provide information about property ownership and payment of taxes.

Other state agencies that provide information to investigators and law firms may include the department of motor vehicles, parole boards, department of fish and game, alcohol beverage licensing boards, health departments, labor boards, and the state attorney general's office.

Federal Sources of Information The United States Post Office maintains a national change-of-address system with about 90 million up-to-date addresses that are available if you have a prior address for anyone you are trying to locate.

The U.S. Army, Air Force, Navy, Marine Corps, Coast Guard, Merchant Marine, Merchant Seamen, and National Guard maintain records on all active-duty and retired personnel. Records for each branch of the armed forces are maintained in separate locations scattered throughout the country, but a telephone call to your local armed-forces recruiting office will provide you with information on where to write for the information you are seeking. The Veterans Administration also maintains records on both active and inactive personnel that can be accessed through either their local office or the national records-processing center in St. Louis, Missouri.

In addition, you can sometimes obtain information from the Department of Justice, the Federal Bureau of Investigation, the Drug Enforcement Agency, and the Immigration and Naturalization Service.

Local and Private Sources Do not overlook telephone directories and city directories for information. Although these sources of information may seem obvious, it is the obvious that is most often overlooked. Public libraries usually keep local telephone directories for a year or two, and many have directories for several cities throughout the country.

Most public libraries also have city directories or Criss-Cross® directories that list all streets alphabetically and give street numbers and telephone numbers. For verifying both current and old addresses and an individual's occupation, these directories are invaluable. You need only the person's name, address, or telephone number to locate this information in a city or Criss-Cross® Directory. These directories, which are published and updated annually by private companies, also provide information on the neighbors of the person under investigation. Interviewing the neighbors can often provide you with information you would not be able to get anywhere else.

The Better Business Bureau and the Chamber of Commerce maintain records on local businesses, rackets, and confidence-game operators. Chambers of Commerce often have back issues of city directories and telephone directories, as well as information on businesses that are members of the Chamber.

You may purchase information from Dun & Bradstreet on businesses, including financial and credit data, who owns the business, and whether the business is organized as a corporation, partnership, or sole proprietorship.

For a fee, credit-reporting agencies may also provide information on people who have applied for credit or may have used credit in transacting business. These credit reports include the person's current and former addresses, sources of income, occupation, places of employment, bank accounts, assets, references, and brief personal history.

Who's Who directories provide biographical data on men and women in the country who have achieved distinction in their professions, careers, or colleges. The data often include educational information, organizational memberships, religious and political affiliations, marital status, family, and spouse information. The directories are often available at public libraries and college or university libraries.

Medical directories, trade associations, professional organizations, moving companies, and utility companies are other sources of information that the investigator might wish to pursue.

Computer-Aided Investigation

Several software packages are now available to make conducting an investigation easier and less time-consuming. Law firms that routinely need to have certain information available are finding the purchase of investigative software to be an efficient and cost-effective alternative to hiring outside private investigators. For example, most of the commercially available software can provide a paralegal with around-the-clock access, using a desktop computer and telephone line, to criminal records, department of motor vehicle records, civil filings, consumer reports, business records, Uniform Commercial Code filings, real property searches, outstanding judgments, bankruptcy filings, tax information, and the legal status of corporations, including the names and addresses of the board of directors. Software packages are available for either nationwide searches or statewide only.

6–6 Interviewing Witnesses

Once you have interviewed the client and completed your preliminary investigation, you will no doubt find there are witnesses or others with information who need to be contacted and interviewed. Although there are many similarities in conducting any kind of interview, such as having a goal and being prepared, there are also some differences.

Attitude of Interviewee

The primary difference between the client interview and the witness interview is the interviewee's attitude. The client voluntarily came to your law firm for help, but the witness or other person with information you seek did not. Some people want to do everything they can to be helpful. Others are willing to provide help so long as it is not personally inconvenient for them or is not likely to result in any extended involvement with the case. Still others will be totally uncooperative.

Since these information resources have no monetary interest in the outcome of the case, you must rely upon their desire to be helpful. You should be willing to inconvenience yourself for their convenience and treat each one with respect even if it is not reciprocated. For this reason, most witness interviews are conducted outside your office, often with someone else present. Although it is preferable to conduct a one-on-one interview, it is not always possible to do so with a witness or a neighbor. To insist upon privacy would probably create suspicion and animosity, neither of which is helpful in getting the person's cooperation.

Be Prepared

Do not make an appointment to interview anyone without being familiar with the facts of the case. If you do, the interview will be a waste of time and the interviewee will resent you for imposing. Although you may not know all the facts of the case—if you did, you would not need to conduct the interview—you should at least have a general understanding of the events leading up to the lawsuit.

Before the interview, read and understand all the pleadings filed by any of the parties in the lawsuit. Likewise, read and be familiar with all the file memoranda including attorney notes, the contents of police reports, doctor's statements, photographs, interviews with the client or other people, and any other file documents.

Use a Checklist

Follow the same procedure in preparing an outline for a witness interview as you would for a client interview. Start with the vital statistics and work your way through the who, what, when, where, why, and how questions.

Questioning a witness usually calls for more directed questions than with a client because you want to keep the witness focused on the event as he or she saw it. That does not mean that you should not give the witness some latitude in the telling of the story, but you do need to keep in mind that the witness's time has value and that you are an intrusion. If the interview is allowed to take too much time, you might find yourself on the doorstep without the information you came to get and unable to schedule another appointment.

With witnesses you are usually well advised to concentrate on the job you came to do instead of building rapport. The witness will never be your best friend, but he or she could be the client's ally in court. Your respect for their time and cooperation will be appreciated.

Understand the Law

It is not enough to be familiar with the contents of the file. Before you begin an interview you should also understand the law involved. If you do not have a general understanding of the law, you will find it more difficult to formulate appropriate questions, and you might overlook an important piece of information.

For example, suppose that your law firm is representing a client whose neck had been broken when her car was hit in the driver's side by another driver who lost control of his car on a curve. The hospital bills for your client, who is a single mother, are staggering. She will not be able to return to work for at least a year and will be required to continue physical therapy for an extended period of time. Full recovery is doubtful.

Unfortunately, the driver of the other car, a 22-year-old single bookkeeper, died in the accident. During an interview with the bookkeeper's parents about insurance coverage you were told that their son carried only the minimum coverage, that he had no assets, and that he lived at home. Even after an hour of questioning, it seemed that your client was not going to receive any financial help from the person who caused the accident—that is, until the mother said, as you were about to leave, that none of this would have happened if her son had not been delivering accounting reports to a client on his way home at the request of his supervisor.

Because you have an understanding of some basic legal concepts, including agency relationships and employer liability, this statement would indicate that further questioning is appropriate about the employer-employee relationship and the nature of the errand that created the opportunity for the accident. Financial assistance—from the employer—might be a possibility for your client after all.

Nothing in the file would have prepared you to respond to the witness's offhand remark about the errand. Only an understanding of legal theory and concepts would tell you that this is an area requiring further inquiry.

Handling the Hostile Witness

Uncooperative witnesses will challenge your tact and diplomacy skills. If you start with the nonthreatening vital statistics questions and work up to the more important ones, you will have an opportunity to show some empathy for the position the witness is in and to exhibit your appreciation for his or her time and willingness to talk to you. Usually a witness will begin to relax when you tell the individual that you are there only to get the facts, not to influence his or her point of view or to get him or her to commit to one side or the other.

However, if your professionalism and charm are not working, it may be necessary for you to resort to more devious tactics to gain cooperation from a hostile witness, such as catching him or her off guard. Think of different angles from which you might approach the subject matter instead of asking straight-on questions. For example, look for and talk about interests you have in common, such as basketball, saving the environment, or seeing that justice is served. The more the witness feels at ease with you, the more likely he or she will eventually open up and tell you the information you came to get.

Once you have opened the door to information, use restraint. If you go rushing in, the result could be off-putting to the very person you are trying to win over. With some witnesses you may have to go back several times before you get the information you want. You can never have too much patience and preseverance when you are dealing with an uncooperative or hostile witness.

Finally, if your best diplomacy skills do not work, you can always use the word *subpoena* to get a hostile witness's attention. Nearly everyone knows what a *subpoena* is and most people will do whatever is necessary to avoid being served with one. As a last resort, you can give the witness the choice of being cooperative and giving you a statement or being served with a *subpoena* and ordered to appear in court. Faced with that choice, witnesses usually choose to cooperate.

Preparing the Witness Statement

An appropriate goal for nearly every witness interview is to leave the interview with a written and signed statement of what the person witnessed. If that is your goal, be prepared with a pad of paper and a pen. After you have talked to the witness, you will need to take a few minutes to write down the witness's statement before you end the interview. If you wait to get a signed statement until after you have had an opportunity to transcribe and type up your notes, you may find that the witness is no longer willing to cooperate.

The statement does not need to be a formal legal document. After all, it is going to be handwritten. It should, however, be legible, since the document may be introduced in court as evidence. Ask the witness to read over the statement and correct any mistakes by drawing a line through the entry and

Figure 6–11 Witness Statement

WITNESS STATEMENT

Taken by: ______________________ Date: __________

Taken at: ______________________ Time: __________

Date of Accident/Incident/Occurrence: ______________________

Location: ______________________

Case Name: ______________ vs. ______________

File No.: ______________________

WITNESS INFORMATION

Witness Name: ______________________ Date of Birth: ______

Home Address: ______________________

Place of Employment: ______________________

Employer's Address: ______________________

Telephone Numbers: Home ________ Work ________ Message ________

Occupation: ______________ Social Security Number ________

Witness Statement:

____

____

____

____

____

____

____

____

____

Page Number ___1___ ______________________

Signature

initialing the correction. In addition, number each page of the statement and have the witness initial or sign each page at the bottom.

At the end of the document, include a statement such as the following: "I, the undersigned, do hereby declare under penalty of perjury that I have read the foregoing statement consisting of (*insert number*) pages and I do hereby certify that it is true and correct to the best of my knowledge and belief. Executed on (*month, date, and year*) at (*city and state*)." Then, have the witness sign his or her name following the preceding declaration. Make a photocopy of the statement when you get to the office and send it to the witness with a letter of thanks for cooperating. Figure 6–11 is an example of a form to follow in preparing a witness statement.

Taping the Witness Interview The same principles apply to taping a witness interview as to taping a client interview. Some witnesses will be intimidated and reluctant to be candid, since they are not sure how the information will be used. If the witness does consent to taping, be sure to get permission on tape at the beginning of the interview and again at the end.

In some instances, such as when interviewing a child or a minor, taping is a very good idea. Why? One reason is because a witness statement from a child should not sound like it was prepared by a paralegal. Another reason is to ensure privacy and cooperation. For example, if you need to interview an adolescent accused of sexual or substance abuse charges and neither of you wants a parent or school administration official present, you should insist on taping the interview. In these types of situations, the witness is more likely to be cooperative with his or her privacy assured. Additionally, taping an interview with a minor is protection for you. If you are ever called upon to explain or defend the way the interview was conducted, the interview will be on tape.

In a recent survey conducted by the National Association of Legal Assistants (NALA), 59 percent of the respondents indicated that conducting client and witness interviews is a routine function of their legal assistant job. Thirteen percent held interviews daily, 24 percent weekly, and 22 percent at least once a month. It is essential for your success that you develop this vital paralegal skill.

SUMMARY

6–1

An interview is conducted for the purpose of gathering information in a face-to-face meeting and is usually most productive when the interviewer uses open questions and allows the interviewee wide latitude in how to provide the information. An interrogation is another means of gathering information that relies on closed questions and the interviewer being in complete control. Both forms of information gathering require advance preparation, including developing a goal for the interview and using a written outline to ensure the appropriate questions are asked to achieve the goal. Good interviewing and listening techniques are essential for success as an interviewer, as is being able to maintain your professionalism in stressful situations.

6–2

Proper planning and advance preparation of the environment where the interview will be conducted is an equally important component of the process. The arrangement of furniture in the room where the interview will be conducted can help establish rapport and trust or set up barriers between you and the interviewee. Interruptions and distractions should be minimized, with steps taken to ensure the interviewee's privacy, confidentiality, and comfort.

6–3

The client should be informed of the agenda for the interview at the time the appointment is made, including how much time is being scheduled for the interview, the nature of the topics to be discussed, and what documents to bring. Prior to commencing the interview itself the paralegal should clarify his or her status for the client and emphasize that the attorney-client confidentiality privilege extends to the paralegal. The decision to tape the interview is the client's choice and can be done only with the client's permission. Note taking is essential whether or not the interview is taped.

6–4

No interview is complete until the file memorandum has been prepared. The file memorandum is used by the attorney to evaluate the case, the client's chances for success, and the direction in which to proceed. While preparing the file memorandum the paralegal should keep in mind the reader, who most likely was not present during the interview, and anticipate questions the reader is likely to want answered. All pertinent information is organized under descriptive headings in the body of the memorandum. The last section of the memorandum suggests areas requiring follow-up, such as researching points of law, investigating facts, locating and conducting witness interviews, and gathering supporting documents.

6–5

The purpose for conducting an investigation is to observe or inquire into allegations, circumstances, or relationships in order to obtain facts. The investigation process is greatly facilitated when the investigator is suspicious and curious, uses the five senses in observing and remembering the unusual, maintains a lack of bias, and exhibits patience, understanding, and courtesy at all times. Many information resources are available to the general public, including file documents located in the county clerk's office, individuals who may have had contact with the person under investigation, police records, and various federal, state, city, and county agencies. To save time in conducting an investigation, many law firms have purchased or subscribe to computer-aided investigation software packages, allowing around-the-clock access to information on individuals and businesses.

6–6

The primary difference between a client interview and a witness interview is the interviewee's attitude. A client who has willingly retained the services of a law firm and its staff is likely to be more cooperative than a witness, who may be reluctant to become involved in a legal matter in which there is no financial stake. To prepare for a witness interview, the paralegal needs to understand not only the facts of the case but also basic legal concepts. Without an understanding of legal concepts, pertinent information may be overlooked and questions may remain unanswered. The statements of witnesses need to be memorialized in writing or on tape. Since witnesses may later decide to be uncooperative or disappear, it is preferable to take a written statement at the interview and have the witness sign it under penalty of perjury.

REVIEW

Key Terms

Before proceeding, review the key terms listed below to be sure you understand each one. If necessary, read over the corresponding section of the chapter. When you are ready to test your understanding, answer the Review Questions.

agenda
body language
interrogation
interview
investigation
retainer agreement
subtext
vital statistics

Questions for Review and Discussion

1. Compare and contrast the terms *interview* and *interrogation.*
2. Describe how good listening skills can be used to build rapport and gather information.
3. What are the key elements in preparing an outline for an interview?
4. What part does professionalism play in conducting an interview?
5. What steps can you take to establish rapport, privacy, trust, and professionalism in the interview environment?
6. Discuss the steps you would take to prepare the client for the interview.
7. What are the components of a written file memorandum of the interview?
8. Define the term *investigation.*
9. What are some of the most common sources of information used during an investigation?
10. Compare and contrast a client interview and a witness interview.

Activities

1. Prepare for and conduct a client interview with a classmate. Pretend that the interviewee is seeking a divorce from a spouse who is having an affair and may be involved in drug dealing. There are minor children from the marriage, which has lasted for twelve years. During the marriage only one spouse was regularly working outside the home for money. After the interview is completed, prepare a written file memorandum of the interview.
2. Prepare for and conduct a client interview with a classmate. Pretend that the interviewee was involved in an automobile accident involving injuries to drivers and passengers of both vehicles. After the interview is completed, prepare a written file memorandum of the interview.
3. Locate and ascertain the rules and requirements to become a licensed private investigator in your state.
4. Locate the public information re-

sources for your state and local area. Compile a list with name of agency, street and mailing address, phone number, name of contact person, type of information provided, and cost of obtaining that information. Provide copies of the compiled list to your classmates.

5. Role-play a witness interview with a classmate based on the facts obtained in Activity No. 1 or Activity No. 2. Prepare a witness statement.
6. Pretend you are investigating yourself or a close relative. Contact the sources of information generally available and share with the class how much information is available on the person you investigated.

CHAPTER 7 Introduction to Legal Analysis, Research, and Writing

NOTES

OUTLINE

COMMENTARY

Interviews and investigations often result in gathering more information, which leads to more work—library work. There are questions of law to be answered or issues of law to be applied. Understanding the law as it applies to the client's problem is the first step in being able to find a solution. If finding the appropriate source of information was difficult when you were doing the field investigation work, then finding the applicable law in the law library may prove just as challenging. However, one thing you have learned to count on is that most functions of your job as a paralegal involve a system—a logical, pragmatic system to help you perform the task efficiently and accurately. Legal research is no different. Once you know the system, you will be able to do the job. For a start, you have the facts concerning the client's problem and a note from the attorney telling you to prepare a written evaluation of the situation for a scheduled meeting with the client in two days. What you don't have is a clue about how to proceed with this task.

OBJECTIVES

After studying this chapter, you should be able to:

1. Define the term *legal analysis* and explain its importance.
2. List the five steps in the legal analysis process.

3. Use the "5Ws and an H" journalism technique to raise legal analysis questions.
4. Categorize facts into legal issues.
5. Analyze a legal problem.
6. Locate and apply the law to a legal problem.
7. Decipher case citations.
8. Update case citations.
9. Discuss computer-aided legal research programs.
10. Outline a legal research memorandum.

7–1 Legal Analysis

All paralegals must develop the fundamental skills of analyzing facts, identifying the legal issues raised by the facts, researching the applicable law, and reporting the results by writing a legal research memorandum. It is through these processes that the information obtained in the client interview and subsequent investigation of documents, records, and witnesses that the lawyer is able to properly assess and prepare the client's case. Based upon the information that you have provided, the lawyer will then be able to sit down with the client to evaluate the merits of the case and make important decisions, such as whether to settle out of court, enter a plea bargain, or take the case to trial before a judge or a jury.

Legal Analysis Format When Violated Rule Is Known

How do you know whether a valid legal claim exists? You don't know until you have analyzed the facts and issues in question. The process of applying rules of law or statutes to the given facts of a case is called **legal analysis.** The purpose of legal analysis is to compare the relationship of a certain rule or statute to the facts of a particular case in order to determine the strengths and weaknesses of that case.

Although there are several approaches to analyzing a case, one of the best ways, when you know the rule or statute the client is alleged to have violated, is to organize the pertinent information in this manner:

1. Locate and quote the rule or statute.
2. State the relevant facts and circumstances of the case being analyzed.
3. Raise questions or issues.
4. Analyze the key elements of the rule or statute against the facts of the case.
5. State your conclusion.

The following fictionalized version of an actual case will illustrate how to use this format in performing a case analysis when you know which rule the client is accused of violating.

Joseph M. Montgomery, 45, is a resident of Shady Oaks Glen, an upscale suburban neighborhood located in an unincorporated area of an affluent city. A majority of the residents are largely white-collar professionals. After several complaints from Montgomery's neighbors about an increase in traffic and the number of cars parked on the streets on weekend nights, the sheriff's department assigned an officer to investigate. Preliminary investigation revealed that Montgomery might be operating an adult entertainment business from his residence. At the D.A.'s insistence, the sheriff assigned an undercover vice officer to investigate. After the vice officer was able to get invited to one of the weekend parties at Montgomery's house, he reported seeing topless dancing and sexual activities. Furthermore, the officer reported that Montgomery's house had been renovated specifically for the purpose of making it into an adult party house. Bedrooms had been partitioned into small carpeted areas where couples paired off, and the garage had been converted into a bar with a dance floor. The vice officer also reported that he was charged $20 for attending the party and was invited to join "The Club" for a fee of $50.

The district attorney brought charges against Montgomery, accusing him of operating an adult entertainment business from his residence in violation of County Code Sec. 7-9-146.2. The complaint alleged, among other things, that Montgomery was operating a business called "The Club" and he placed ads in local publications and sent out newsletters to attract couples to his home on weekend nights. Couples were allegedly charged $50 to join "The Club" and $40 to attend a party.

Using the legal analysis format shown, this is how you would analyze the Montgomery case.

Step 1: Quote the Rule or Statute In some instances such as this one, you already know the rule to be analyzed against the facts of Montgomery's case because it was provided in the district attorney's complaint—County Code Sec. 7-9-146.2. Your first step is to locate the rule in the County Code books and to quote it verbatim at the top of a clean sheet of paper on your writing pad. If the rule is a long one, you need only quote the relevant portions. However, care must be taken not to omit any portion that might at first seem irrelevant but which is, in fact, essential to the analysis. You do not want to waste time by having to go back and look up the statute again because your later research has led you to reconsider whether you left out a relevant portion of the rule. To prevent this from happening, experienced paralegals usually make a couple of photocopies of the entire rule or statute, inserting one complete copy in the client's file and highlighting on the second copy only those portions that appear to apply to the facts being analyzed.

The County Code section that Montgomery is accused of violating is a long one. Following is the quoted portion that is relevant to this example.

> (b) *Definitions:* For the purposes of this section, the term "adult entertainment business" is defined to include each and every one of the following described uses: . . .
> *Adult business:* Either: (1) any business which is conducted exclusively for the patronage of adults, and as to which minors are specifically excluded from patronage thereat . . . ; or (2) any business . . . where employees or patrons expose "specified anatomical areas" or engage in "specified sexual activities"; or (3) any other business or establishment which offers its patrons services or entertainment characterized by an emphasis on matter depicting, exposing, describing, or discussing or relating to "specified sexual activities" or "specified anatomical areas."

Step 2: State the Relevant Facts This is your client's version of the facts in this case.

Joseph M. Montgomery is a 45-year-old, single computer programmer who owns and resides in the 5000-sq. ft. home on 1.5 acres at 4765 Shady Oaks Glen. He has lived at this address for eight years, from which he operates his successful computer-consulting business. Montgomery frequently invites business acquaintances, friends, and others to his home on weekends to network, socialize, use the pool and spa, and enjoy the gardens. He claims that his parties have grown in attendance and frequency primarily due to word of mouth, but that they do not create any unusual traffic or parking problems in the neighborhood.

He does run advertisements in local newspapers, and he has started sending out a newsletter as a means of gaining attention for his computer-consulting business. Last year he did remodel his home and added several smaller work-space areas to accommodate the new computer equipment and other machines he purchased for his expanding consulting business. At that time he decided to add a bar and dance floor in the garage in an attempt to keep his guests away from the area where his computers are located.

Occasionally, Montgomery "passes the hat" at a party to help cover the cost of the refreshments. Contributions are voluntary, but he estimates that most of his guests put in about $20 each. Montgomery is not aware of any sexual activities taking place during these parties but admits that he does not watch his guests every minute and does not consider himself responsible for their behavior.

Step 3: Raise the Questions or Issues What questions or issues about this case are suggested from a reading of the rule and the facts? The questions or issues are often more easily identified if you follow the "5Ws and an H" journalism technique: who, what, when, where, why, and how. The ultimate question to be answered is: Is Montgomery likely to be convicted of violating Sec. 7-9-146.2? Arrange the facts that determine the answer to this question.

Who: Montgomery and guests in his home
What: Conduct of Montgomery and guests led to accusation of operating an adult entertainment business from a residence
When: Most weekends during the past year
Where: From Montgomery's home at 4765 Shady Oaks Glen, an unincorporated area in the county
Why: Neighbors complained of increased traffic and parking problems
How: Undercover vice officer reported seeing topless dancing and sexual activities at a party and was charged $20 for attending the party
Query: Is Montgomery operating an adult entertainment business from his home? What is the likelihood that Montgomery will be convicted?

Step 4: Analyze Key Elements and Facts The next step is to break down the rule into its separate ingredients or factors, called key elements, each of which must be proven by the district attorney in order for Montgomery to be found guilty of violating the rule.

To complete this step, go back to the relevant parts of the rule quoted in Step 1. Read the rule again. Then, on separate pages of your note pad, list and number the key elements, leaving a couple of inches of space beneath each one.

Next, go back and read the facts of the case applying to each key element. Mr. Montgomery has provided you with many facts that are not applicable or relevant at this point. Notice that you are more focused now on only the essential elements of the rule and the facts that apply to those elements. Part of your analysis is to determine the likelihood of each element being proved, as well as to suggest any research or investigation to be done.

Following are the key elements of the rule and an analysis of the facts in the Montgomery case.

Key Element #1: "business conducted exclusively for the patronage of adults" Debatable. Not clearly established that Montgomery is operating an adult entertainment business. Clearly established that he operates a computer-consulting business from his home, but this does not violate any County Code. Check contents of ads and newsletter. Find out if children ever attend these parties. Are they specifically excluded?

Key Element #2: "where patrons expose specified anatomical areas" Debatable. What body parts constitute "specified anatomical areas"? What does "expose" mean? Does wearing a thong-style bathing suit, opaque attire, or a low-cut, diaphanous dress to a pool party at a private residence qualify?
Key Element #3: "where patrons engage in specified sexual activities" Debatable. What is the definition of "specified sexual activities"? Would it include dancing the lambada? Playful touching in the pool?
Key Element #4: "entertainment characterized by depicting, exposing, describing, or discussing or relating to specified sexual activities or specified anatomical areas" Debatable. Does this rule mean that when a group of people get together at a party in a private residence they cannot tell jokes or stories with a sexual connotation or innuendo? Do guests dancing alone or with each other qualify as entertainment? Client not aware of movies, videotapes, or other forms of pornography being shown or displayed.
Summary: The district attorney argues that Montgomery is operating an adult entertainment business from his residence; that guests are charged a fee to attend parties nearly every weekend for the purpose of engaging in sexual activities. Montgomery admits that he operates a computer-consulting business from his residence and that he frequently invites guests to parties in his home on weekends; that these guests might voluntarily contribute money to offset the expense of the food and drink; and that he does not police the activities of his guests and is not aware of any sexual activities taking place during the parties.

Step 5: Conclusion Finally, draw a brief conclusion based upon the facts and the rule. In some instances, you may be able to conclude there is little or no basis for the legal action, given the rule and the facts. However, in other situations, your conclusion may be that further research is necessary before a definitive conclusion can be drawn. Your conclusion in this case might be:

Whether Montgomery is likely to be convicted of violating County Code Section 7-9-146.2 depends upon (1) whether the district attorney can produce enough evidence in addition to the vice officer's report to convince a jury that Montgomery is operating an adult entertainment business from his home; (2) the credibility of the vice officer who claims to have witnessed certain sexual acts taking place during one weekend party, which Montgomery does not deny but rather claims no knowledge of; (3) Montgomery's credibility as a witness and his personal and professional reputation; (4) the evidence of his legitimate computer-consulting business; (5) the testimony of other witnesses on his behalf.

It would appear that the D.A. has a weak case, but further research is suggested in the definitions of key elements of the rule. It might also be prudent to talk to Montgomery again to be sure that he has not overlooked any possibly damaging facts or witnesses that the district attorney's office may have uncovered in its investigation.

This case did go to trial before a jury. The defendant was acquitted after the jury failed to reach a verdict, and the district attorney decided not to retry the case.

7–2 Legal Research

If you are a fan of mystery stories and like to piece together jigsaw puzzles, you will find many similarities between those forms of entertainment and performing legal research. For example, in the Joseph Montgomery legal analysis problem, you were given the equivalent of a picture of the finished puzzle—the particular code section that the client was accused of violating. That information will always be provided in criminal law matters. Your job is to take the various pieces of the puzzle and see if they are all there to complete the D.A.'s picture.

However, in civil law cases, it is often left up to the paralegal to follow a trail of facts, forming the various pieces of the puzzle along the way and then fitting them together to complete a picture. Sometimes, even when all the pieces are in place, the picture is still unfocused, calling for the logic of a Jessica Fletcher or Perry Mason. Frequently, though, when all the pieces are in place, you know exactly in which direction to go.

The questions are: when you are not provided with a specific rule to quote and analyze, but just a problem, how do you proceed? How do you determine which facts are relevant to the research problem? Where do you look for the law that might apply?

It is appropriate at this point to clarify a few things about legal research in general. If you are feeling slightly overwhelmed about now, you share similar feelings with about 99 percent of your classmates. After all, a great deal of new information is being thrown at you in this introductory course. Rest assured that with more coursework in legal research and more time spent in the law library you will gain confidence in being able to zero in on the basic facts and key legal elements of any problem that may cross your desk. Soon you will be able to *tentatively* recognize the areas of law that might be applicable to the relevant facts of a client's problem. Just as doctors and nurses often make a tentative diagnosis of a patient's illness before performing further research in the laboratory, lawyers and paralegals usually form a tentative point of view of a client's problem before heading off to do research in the law library. Sometimes a preliminary examination proves to be sufficient, but often it is only through the process of trial and error that conclusive results are obtained.

Problem Analysis Format

If you are not provided with a particular rule or statute to research, as in the Montgomery example, how do you proceed without this information? Where do you begin?

Two leading publishers of law books suggest that you start with a problem analysis and categorize the facts into possible legal issues. West Publishing Company suggests organizing issues this way:

1. PARTIES involved in the case
2. PLACES where the facts arose; THINGS involved
3. BASIS of action; or ISSUE involved
4. DEFENSES to the action or issue
5. RELIEF SOUGHT (what does the client want?)

Lawyers Cooperative Publishing Company suggests a similar format categorized along these lines:

1. THINGS involved in the case
2. ACTS that took place
3. PERSONS involved
4. PLACES where the acts involved arose

As you can see, there is more than one way to perform this routine procedure. Either of these suggested formats will lead you through the steps of identifying the facts and then the applicable law; your instructor or supervising attorney may also have their own way of organizing this material. In any event, the point is to be able to take the facts of a problem and organize them to find a solution.

Problem Analysis When Rule Violated Is Unknown

The following legal problem, which surfaced during a conversation with a part-time employee in a law firm, can be used to illustrate how to categorize facts for problem analysis using the West Publishing Company guidelines.

> Polly Sanchez-Smith and her husband signed a one-year lease on an apartment in Springfield, Illinois that is close to her part-time job in your law firm and to the campus where she is completing her legal assistant certificate program. Within a few weeks after moving in, Polly found the apartment was so badly infested with cockroaches that she and her husband could not tolerate living there. They are staying in a nearby motel while contemplating their next step. What legal issues are raised by Polly's plight?

In organizing the fact lists, the object is to identify as many facts for each category as possible, whether or not they were provided by the client. Common sense and life experiences will provide you with helpful information and insight in problem analysis. Brainstorming with other students or coworkers can be helpful in identifying the maximum number of possibilities. Eventually some elements will be eliminated, but others will offer important clues and suggest areas for further investigation. For example, given the facts of Polly's problem, the category lists might contain the following items:

PARTIES/PEOPLE/STATUS	Tenant-landlord Property manager-agent Husband-wife Interracial marriage
PLACES/THINGS	Apartment building Rural area under development City of Springfield County of Sangamon State of Illinois Cockroaches, insects, vermin Sanitation Healthful environment Health hazard
BASIS OF ACTION	Breach of contract Violation of health and safety codes Failure to provide habitable apartment
DEFENSES	Food left out Apartment not kept clean City landfill area close by Construction nearby
RELIEF SOUGHT	Extermination Withhold or prorate rent payments Cancel lease agreement Reimbursement for motel expenses

Parties/People/Status In this category you are attempting to identify the relationships of the parties involved and/or their status. In this example, there are several relationships: landlord-tenant, property manager-agent, and husband-wife. However, relationships could also be, politician-constituent, parent-child, employer-employee, and buyer-seller. Status categories could include minors, minorities, illegal aliens, and incompetents. You will want to research cases and statutes involving people in similar relationships or having similar status.

Places/Things Place refers to the specific location where the event took place, including whether in a rural or urban area and the geographic region. These are all important in determining which court has jurisdiction and for guiding you to the proper research references. For example, cockroaches in Polly's apartment is a state law problem, not a federal one. Common sense would tell you to concentrate your research on Illinois state law, in general, and the health and safety codes for the County of Sangamon and the City of Springfield, specifically.

Under the category of things you listed cockroaches, of course, since these are the creatures creating Polly's problem. However, life experience tells you that the most obvious solution is frequently not the right one. In this case, the category of cockroaches might be too narrow in which to find any relevant case law. If you expand the category to include insects and other vermin you will likewise expand your opportunities to find some applicable case law.

Unfortunately, case law rarely falls into neat, specific categories. Remember that the problem here is that Polly's apartment is uninhabitable because of the cockroaches. If you do not find anything pertaining specifically to cockroaches, insects, or vermin in apartment buildings, you will need to go back to the drawing boards and come up with another strategy. One logical extension of legal analysis in this case would be to question what conditions contribute to the presence of cockroaches. Lack of cleanliness? Sanitation? Location?

You might also expand your research opportunities by moving from specifics—cockroaches—to generalities, such as those things that, in general, would cause an apartment to be uninhabitable—lack of heating, too much noise, no electricity, improper sanitation. In other words, when analyzing facts you can use analogies of things that may have similar legal consequences if specific case law is not available.

Basis of the Action Because Polly and her husband signed a one-year lease for the apartment, there is a contract between them and the landlord. Assuming that the contract required the landlord to provide a habitable apartment, since the landlord failed to provide such apartment, the contract has been breached. However, the landlord may also be violating certain health and safety codes, which should be researched.

Defenses to the Action Lawyers and paralegals must always be able to argue both sides of any dispute in order to be adequately prepared to represent the client. Defenses to the action provide you with the opportunity to analyze the case from the other point of view. In other words, you must think about what defenses the landlord is likely to raise to defeat Polly's claim. Was Polly a poor housekeeper who left food lying about, which attracted the roaches? Did she fail to keep the apartment clean, creating a haven for insects and other vermin, that, in turn, attracted the cockroaches? Or is the problem an environmental one caused by being located too close to a landfill area or garbage dump? Is any construction taking place in the neighborhood that might increase the presence of roaches and insects?

Relief Sought What does Polly want? This category is a reflection of the client's preferences and the type of claim or injury suffered. Polly might be satisfied to have the place exterminated and made livable. Perhaps she feels it appropriate to withhold payment of rent or to prorate the rent until she can safely return to the apartment. She might also want to be reimbursed for any expenses she incurred because she had to move into a motel until the cockroach problem is solved. Or, she might just want to cancel the lease agreement and quickly move from the apartment, asking the landlord to pay her moving expenses and to refund her deposits.

Until you become more familiar with legal rules, concepts, and terminology you may experience some difficulty in identifying words and phrases for the basis of the case, defenses, and relief-sought categories. Consequently, do not be concerned at this stage if you have trouble with these categories. Instead, concentrate on words for the other categories relating to people, places, and things. This will be sufficient to get you going on your research and with each assignment you will learn more about the process.

Identifying and Organizing the Legal Issues

Categorizing the facts is a tremendous help in sorting out the various legal issues in question and identifying those that require research. For example, the fact analysis of Polly's cockroach problem indicates there are at least three areas that require research:

1. Does a landlord in the City of Springfield, County of Sangamon, State of Illinois have an obligation to provide a habitable rental unit?
2. If so, is a cockroach infestation a breach of that obligation?
3. What remedies are available to the tenant if the landlord has breached the obligation to provide a habitable rental unit?

The above questions are the initial ones that your research will attempt to answer. Do not be surprised if new issues present themselves once your research is under way. Often, as you begin to read the codes and case books, more questions come to mind. You may find yourself reevaluating the information you have and going back to the client with additional questions. Such is the nature of legal research—there are always more questions than answers.

Your research efforts will be greatly facilitated if you attempt to organize the issues in some logical fashion. This is particularly important when you are researching a complex case with many interrelated issues. But the wisdom of organizing the issues is readily apparent in this single-issue case. For instance, if you did not organize the issues, you might squander a number of billable hours if you were to research the remedies available to Polly before you discovered the extent of her landlord's obligations and liability.

Having categorized, identified, and organized the issues, you are now ready to take your legal pad of notes into the library and open the books.

Locating the Law

For the average paralegal student, initial encounters with the law library are awesome. Rather than overwhelm you with a comprehensive guide to legal research, this text is limited to an introduction and overview of some of the basic tools you can expect to find in a typical law library.

As you recall, the U.S. legal system was designed to be flexible in order to meet the changing needs of the society it serves. This flexibility, however, creates some inherent problems for the legal researcher, not the least of which is that when stated in print the law is often imprecise. Laws are a collection of ideas formulated in the minds of people who then attempt to set these ideas down on paper. But these ideas are not always fully formed when they are written, and people frequently disagree over their content and meaning. Do not be discouraged when you find that others do not agree with the findings of your research or your conclusion. Rather, it is important that you be open to the ideas and opinions of others because it is from these exchanges with other legal scholars that you will learn more about the law. Take comfort from the fact that even the Supreme Court Justices do not always agree with each other.

U.S. law is divided into two categories known as primary authority and secondary authority, and within these categories there is an established hierarchy. Sources of primary and secondary authority are given in Figure 7–1 and listed in order of their importance in legal research.

Primary authorities are frequently referred to as *the law*. It is mandatory that you cite the highest relevant primary authority that is applicable to the facts you are researching. Constitutional law, federal and state, is the supreme law, followed in importance by federal and state statutes. Next in importance are statute-authorized administrative regulations, such as state and local codes. The final category of primary authority is reports of cases from a higher court within the same jurisdiction. In other words, if the problem you are researching concerns the right for a private citizen to own a weapon, you would find ample support for your position on this topic in all of the primary authority categories. But ultimately, constitutional law will prevail since the right to bear arms is guaranteed by the U.S. Constitution.

In reading the list of secondary authorities, it is apparent that arranging primary authority in a hierarchy is an easier task than it is for secondary authority. To some lawyers and judges, thoughtful, logical secondary authority that is presented in a scholarly and persuasive manner is considered to be almost at the level of primary authority. But the fact is that most secondary authority is merely descriptive and serves best as a way to find primary authority.

Do you need to look in each and every resource to adequately research a legal question? The answer, in most cases, is no. If the problem is a procedural one, you will refer to the code books on civil or criminal procedure for your state; if the problem is a federal one, use the federal procedure codes.

But if the question is not procedural, in most cases you will start your legal research in the statute or code books for the jurisdiction in which the legal

Figure 7–1 Legal Authorities

Primary Authorities

Constitutions.
Statutes.
Administrative rules and codes authorized by statute and adopted according to statute.
Cases from a higher court within the same jurisdiction.

Secondary Authorities

Cases from outside the jurisdiction, or a lower court within the jurisdiction, or a coequal court within the jurisdiction.
Annotations in statute books.
Case headnotes, reporter's additions, editorial additions.
Legal textbooks, legal treatises.
Law reviews, bar journals.
Law dictionaries.
Form books.
Attorney General opinions.
Legal encyclopedias.
Digests.
Citators.

problem occurred, such as in the cases of Joseph Montgomery and Polly Sanchez-Smith. However, if the legal problem is more broad in scope and complexity, you will want to expand your research to include information from other courts in your jurisdiction and outside it.

The *American Law Reports Digest (A.L.R.)* published by The Lawyers CoOperative Publishing Co. is a good place to begin because it is a collection of recent cases from various state and federal courts, regularly updated with the use of cumulative pocket parts. Another frequently used digest is published by West Publishing Co. In general, all digests are collections of **headnotes,** usually one-sentence summaries of a particular point of law in a precedent-setting case. Headnotes are not the law, but they will lead you to the law. The digests are arranged alphabetically by key words; see, for example, the cover page from Volume 9 of the *A.L.R. Digest* and the cover page from Volume 47 of the *West's California Digest* in Figure 7–2.

The primary purpose of any legal digest is to pull together all the references to precedent-setting cases for easy access to the legal researcher. Some digests are prepared for a single state, such as *West's California Digest;* others, such as West Publishing Company's *Reporter System* are prepared for groups of neighboring states. For example, the *North Eastern Reporter, Second Series* (N.E. 2d) reports case decisions from Illinois, Indiana, Massachusetts, New York, and Ohio.

Still other digests are prepared for a single court, such as the United States Supreme Court, or for a certain period of time, such as the *American Digest System,* which abstracts and organizes reports of cases from 1658 to date, and the *Decennial Digests,* which report cases in ten-year intervals from 1896 to the present.

Researching the Law Using Lawyers Co-Op Materials Suppose you want to find out what qualifies as a "bludgeon instrument" within the meaning of criminal law. One key word from your problem analysis would no doubt be *weapon.* First, you would find the appropriate A.L.R. volume containing words beginning with *W.* In this case it is Volume 9, shown in Figure 7–2. By turning to the index for this volume, you will find that a discussion of weapons begins on page 662. For the novice legal researcher, it is unusual to be this lucky with your first key word selection. More likely, you would have to select several key words from your problem analysis, locate these words in the digest's index, and then consult each section of the statutes to which the index refers before you find the information you are researching.

If you do not find any of your key words in the index, this is a signal for you to go back to the facts of the case and reevaluate the issues in question or gather more facts, since you have obviously overlooked something. But, for purposes of this example, let's assume that you not only had the good sense to equate bludgeon with weapon, but you also had the good fortune of finding an appropriate annotation under the topic of weapons in the *A.L.R. Digest.* See Figure 7–5.

Case Citations

Before you can proceed with your research, you must first understand the **cryptography,** or code, of the legal profession. Whether citing a directive from one of the legal encyclopedias, such as the *A.L.R. Digest,* or citing a specific case, all legal citations are read the same. The series of letters and numbers that make up the code that refers to court decisions is called the **citation.** Its purpose is to

Figure 7–2a Cover page from ALR Digest

AMERICAN LAW REPORTS

ALR

DIGEST

OF

DECISIONS AND ANNOTATIONS

WITH RELATED

TOTAL CLIENT-SERVICE LIBRARY®

REFERENCES

ALR 3d, ALR 4th, ALR Fed

VOLUME

9

SUNDAY

TO

ZONING AND LAND CONTROLS

Source: The Lawyers Cooperative Publishing, a division of Thomson Legal Publishing Inc. Reprinted with permission.

Figure 7–2b Cover page from West's California Digest

WEST'S

CALIFORNIA DIGEST 2d

Volume 47

DESCRIPTIVE-WORD INDEX
P—Z

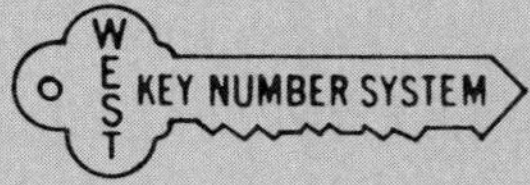

ST. PAUL, MINN.

WEST PUBLISHING CO.

Source: Bancroft-Whitney. Reprinted with permission.

Figure 7–3 National Reporter System

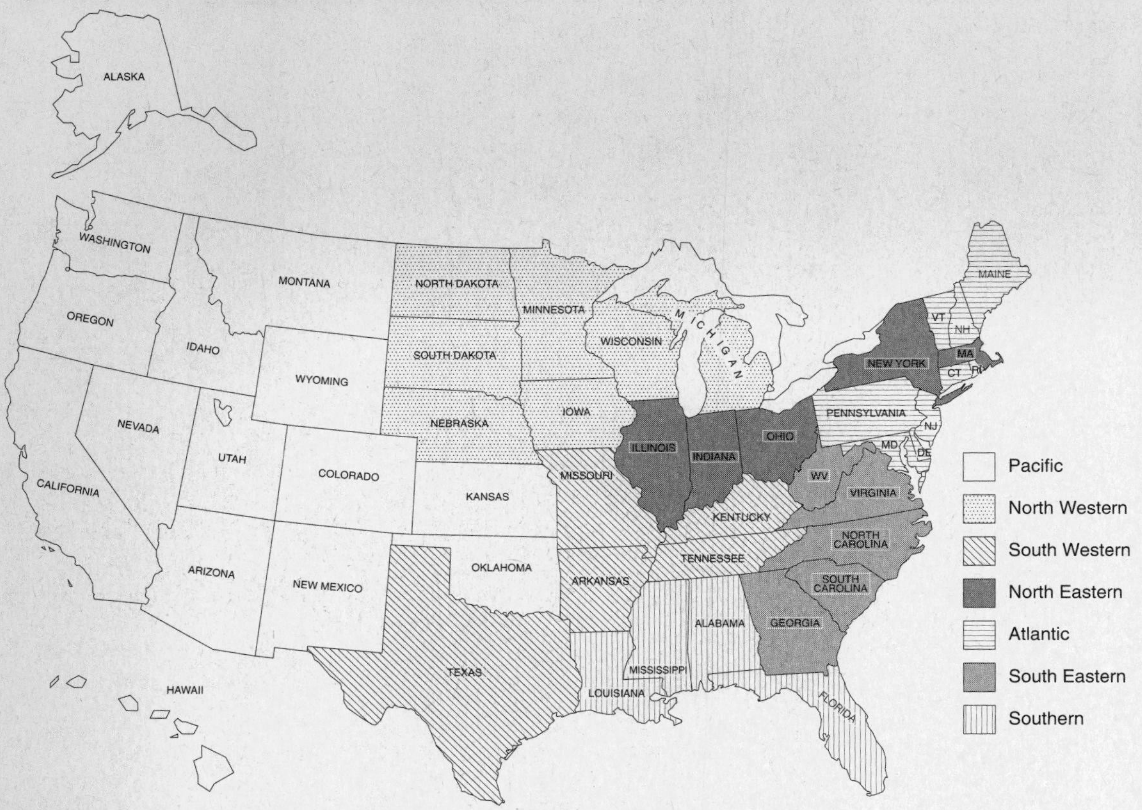

Source: West's Legal Desk Reference. Reprinted with permission.

help the researcher locate the court's written decisions. Using Figure 7–5 as an example, the first reference under the annotation, or summary, section reads:

> What constitutes a "bludgeon," "blackjack," or "billy" within meaning of criminal possession statute, 11 ALR4th 1272

This appears to be exactly the information you are seeking. The citation tells us that if you look in Volume 11 of *American Law Reports (A.L.R.)*, 4th Series, you will find an extensive discussion of the term *bludgeon* as it applies to criminal matters on page 1272. If you were to turn to page 1272 in Volume 11 of *A.L.R.*, you will find the beginning of an extensive discussion on the subject of the meaning of *bludgeon* with references to specific cases, which you may want to read and cite in the written memorandum of your research findings that you will be required to prepare for the client's file.

For example, the discussion on this page cites two cases: *People v. Grubb* (1965) 63 Cal 2d 614, 47 Cal Rptr 772, 408 P2d 100; and *People v. Canales* (1936) 12 Cal App 2d 215, 55 P2d 289, cited in the footnote, which you should always read and consider in legal research.

Case citations always contain the following five elements.

1. An abbreviated version of the case name, for instance, *People v. Grubb* (not *The People of the State of California v. Michael Raymond Grubb*). Anywhere the case name is cited, such as in a legal brief or memorandum, the name of the case, including the *v.*, which is an abbreviation for the word *versus*, is always italic (or underlined). Example: *People v. Grubb*, 63 Cal 2d 614 (1965).

Figure 7–4 Outline of the Law

OUTLINE OF THE LAW

Digest Topics arranged for your convenience by Seven Main Divisions of Law
For complete alphabetical list of Digest Topics, see Page XI

1. PERSONS
2. PROPERTY
3. CONTRACTS
4. TORTS
5. CRIMES
6. REMEDIES
7. GOVERNMENT

1. PERSONS

RELATING TO NATURAL PERSONS IN GENERAL

Civil Rights
Dead Bodies
Death
Domicile
Drugs and Narcotics
Food
Health and Environment
Holidays
Intoxicating Liquors
Names
Poisons
Seals
Signatures
Sunday
Time
Weapons

PARTICULAR CLASSES OF NATURAL PERSONS

Absentees
Aliens
Chemical Dependents
Citizens
Convicts
Illegitimate Children
Indians
Infants
Mental Health
Paupers
Slaves
Spendthrifts

PERSONAL RELATIONS

Adoption
Attorney and Client
Employers' Liability
Executors and Administrators
Guardian and Ward
Husband and Wife
Labor Relations
Marriage
Master and Servant
Parent and Child
Principal and Agent
Workers' Compensation

ASSOCIATED AND ARTIFICIAL PERSONS

Associations
Beneficial Associations
Building and Loan Associations
Clubs
Colleges and Universities
Corporations
Exchanges
Joint-Stock Companies and Business Trusts
Partnership
Religious Societies

PARTICULAR OCCUPATIONS

Accountants
Agriculture
Auctions and Auctioneers
Aviation
Banks and Banking
Bridges

V 1—1

OUTLINE OF THE LAW

1. PERSONS—Cont'd

PARTICULAR OCCUPATIONS —Cont'd

Brokers
Canals
Carriers
Commerce
Consumer Credit
Consumer Protection
Credit Reporting Agencies
Detectives
Electricity
Explosives
Factors
Ferries
Gas
Hawkers and Peddlers
Innkeepers
Insurance
Licenses
Manufacturers
Monopolies
Physicians and Surgeons
Pilots
Railroads
Seamen
Shipping
Steam
Telecommunications
Theaters and Shows
Towage
Turnpikes and Toll Roads
Urban Railroads
Warehousemen
Wharves

2. PROPERTY

NATURE, SUBJECTS, AND INCIDENTS OF OWNERSHIP IN GENERAL

Abandoned and Lost Property
Accession
Adjoining Landowners
Confusion of Goods
Improvements
Property

PARTICULAR SUBJECTS AND INCIDENTS OF OWNERSHIP

Animals
Annuities
Automobiles
Boundaries
Cemeteries
Common Lands
Copyrights and Intellectual Property
Crops
Fences
Fish
Fixtures
Franchises
Game
Good Will
Logs and Logging
Mines and Minerals
Navigable Waters
Party Walls
Patents
Public Lands
Trade Regulation
Waters and Water Courses
Woods and Forests

PARTICULAR CLASSES OF ESTATES OR INTERESTS IN PROPERTY

Charities
Condominium
Dower and Curtesy
Easements
Estates in Property
Joint Tenancy
Landlord and Tenant
Life Estates
Perpetuities
Powers
Remainders
Reversions
Tenancy in Common
Trusts

VI 1—2

OUTLINE OF THE LAW

2. PROPERTY—Cont'd

PARTICULAR MODES OF ACQUIRING OR TRANSFERRING PROPERTY

Abstracts of Title
Adverse Possession
Alteration of Instruments
Assignments
Chattel Mortgages
Conversion
Dedication
Deeds
Descent and Distribution
Escheat
Fraudulent Conveyances
Gifts
Lost Instruments
Mortgages
Pledges
Secured Transactions
Wills

3. CONTRACTS

NATURE, REQUISITES, AND INCIDENTS OF AGREEMENTS IN GENERAL

Contracts
Customs and Usages
Frauds, Statute of
Interest
Usury

PARTICULAR CLASSES OF AGREEMENTS

Bailment
Bills and Notes
Bonds
Breach of Marriage Promise
Champerty and Maintenance
Compromise and Settlement
Covenants
Deposits and Escrows
Exchange of Property
Gaming
Guaranty
Implied and Constructive Contracts
Indemnity
Joint Adventures
Lotteries
Principal and Surety
Rewards
Sales
Subscriptions
Vendor and Purchaser

PARTICULAR CLASSES OF IMPLIED OR CONSTRUCTIVE CONTRACTS OF QUASI CONTRACTS

Account Stated
Contribution

PARTICULAR MODES OF DISCHARGING CONTRACTS

Novation
Payment
Release
Subrogation
Tender

4. TORTS

Assault and Battery
Collision
Conspiracy
False Imprisonment
Forcible Entry and Detainer
Fraud
Libel and Slander
Malicious Prosecution
Negligence
Nuisance
Products Liability
Seduction
Torts
Trespass
Trover and Conversion
Waste

VII 1—3

OUTLINE OF THE LAW

5. CRIMES

Abduction
Abortion and Birth Control
Adulteration
Adultery
Affray
Arson
Bigamy
Blasphemy
Breach of the Peace
Bribery
Burglary
Common Scold
Compounding Offenses
Counterfeiting
Criminal Law
Disorderly Conduct
Disorderly House
Disturbance of Public Assemblage
Dueling
Embezzlement
Embracery
Escape
Extortion and Threats
False Personation
False Pretenses
Fires
Forgery
Fornication
Homicide
Incest
Insurrection and Sedition
Kidnapping
Larceny
Lewdness
Malicious Mischief
Mayhem
Miscegenation
Neutrality Laws
Obscenity
Obstructing Justice
Perjury
Piracy
Prize Fighting
Prostitution
Rape
Receiving Stolen Goods
Rescue
Riot
Robbery
Sodomy
Suicide
Treason
Unlawful Assembly
Vagrancy

6. REMEDIES

REMEDIES BY ACT OR AGREEMENT OF PARTIES

Accord and Satisfaction
Arbitration
Submission of Controversy

REMEDIES BY POSSESSION OR NOTICE

Liens
Lis Pendens
Maritime Liens
Mechanics' Liens
Notice
Salvage

MEANS AND METHODS OF PROOF

Acknowledgment
Affidavits
Estoppel
Evidence
Oath
Records
Witnesses

CIVIL ACTIONS IN GENERAL

Action
Declaratory Judgment
Election of Remedies
Limitation of Actions
Parties
Set-Off and Counterclaim
Venue

VIII I—4

OUTLINE OF THE LAW

6. REMEDIES—Cont'd

PARTICULAR PROCEEDINGS IN CIVIL ACTIONS

Abatement and Revival
Appearance
Costs
Damages
Execution
Exemptions
Homestead
Judgment
Jury
Motions
Pleading
Process
Reference
Stipulations
Trial

PARTICULAR REMEDIES INCIDENT TO CIVIL ACTIONS

Arrest
Assistance, Writ of
Attachment
Bail
Deposits in Court
Garnishment
Injunction
Judicial Sales
Ne Exeat
Pretrial Procedure
Receivers
Recognizances
Sequestration
Undertakings

PARTICULAR MODES OF REVIEW IN CIVIL ACTIONS

Appeal and Error
Audita Querela
Certiorari
Exceptions, Bill of
New Trial
Review

ACTIONS TO ESTABLISH OWNERSHIP OR RECOVER POSSESSION OF SPECIFIC PROPERTY

Detinue
Ejectment
Entry, Writ of
Interpleader
Possessory Warrant
Quieting Title
Real Actions
Replevin
Trespass to Try Title

FORMS OF ACTIONS FOR DEBTS OR DAMAGES

Account, Action on
Action on the Case
Assumpsit, Action of
Covenant, Action of
Debt, Action of

ACTIONS FOR PARTICULAR FORMS OR SPECIAL RELIEF

Account
Cancellation of Instruments
Debtor and Creditor
Divorce
Partition
Reformation of Instruments
Specific Performance

CIVIL PROCEEDINGS OTHER THAN ACTIONS

Habeas Corpus
Mandamus
Prohibition
Quo Warranto
Scire Facias
Supersedeas

IX 1—5

OUTLINE OF THE LAW

6. REMEDIES—Cont'd

SPECIAL CIVIL JURISDICTIONS AND PROCEDURE THEREIN

Admiralty
Bankruptcy
Equity
Federal Civil Procedure

PROCEEDINGS PECULIAR TO CRIMINAL CASES

Extradition and Detainers
Fines
Forfeitures
Grand Jury
Indictment and Information
Pardon and Parole
Penalties
Searches and Seizures

7. GOVERNMENT

POLITICAL BODIES AND DIVISIONS

Counties
District of Columbia
Municipal Corporations
States
Territories
Towns
United States

SYSTEMS AND SOURCES OF LAW

Administrative Law and Procedure
Common Law
Constitutional Law
International Law
Parliamentary Law
Statutes
Treaties

LEGISLATIVE AND EXECUTIVE POWERS AND FUNCTIONS

Bounties
Census
Customs Duties
Drains
Eminent Domain
Highways
Inspection
Internal Revenue
Levees and Flood Control
Pensions
Post Office
Private Roads
Public Contracts
Public Service Commissions
Schools
Securities Regulation
Social Security and Public Welfare
Taxation
Weights and Measures
Zoning and Planning

JUDICIAL POWERS AND FUNCTIONS, AND COURTS AND THEIR OFFICERS

Amicus Curiae
Clerks of Courts
Contempt
Court Commissioners
Courts
Federal Courts
Judges
Justices of the Peace
Removal of Cases
Reports
United States Magistrates

CIVIL SERVICE, OFFICERS, AND INSTITUTIONS

Ambassadors and Consuls
Asylums
Attorney General
Coroners
District and Prosecuting Attorneys
Elections
Hospitals
Newspapers
Notaries
Officers and Public Employees
Prisons
Reformatories
Registers of Deeds
Sheriffs and Constables
United States Marshals

MILITARY AND NAVAL SERVICE AND WAR

Armed Services
Military Justice
Militia
War and National Emergency

X 1—6

Source: West Publishing Co. 1982. Reprinted with permission.

Figure 7–5 ALR Digest

§ 93 WATERS

Consult other ALR Digests for earlier cases

prohibited the discharge of treated effluent at a location, proposed by a local sanitary sewer district, 1.1 miles below the main Minneapolis water intake, but were valid for all other purposes, where, although malfunctions or sabotage of the sewage treatment and water purification plants combined with certain river conditions could lead to a danger to public health if the district were allowed to proceed as proposed, such combined contingencies were so extremely unlikely to occur that they were counterbalanced by other considerations, including the urgency of new sewage disposal requirements, and by the high cost and undesirable effects of alternative arrangements. *North Suburban Sanitary Sewer Dist. v Water Pollution Control Com. (1968) 281 Minn 524, 162 NW2d 249, 32 ALR3d 199.*

[Annotated]

§ 94 Liability of supplier of water

Text References:

78 Am Jur 2d, Waters §§ 11, 12, 26, 27, 211-220; 78 Am Jur 2d, Waterworks and Water Companies §§ 47, 58, 67

Practice References:

18 Am Jur Pl & Pr Forms (Rev), Municipal Tort Liability, Forms 154-156, 161-162; 18 Am Jur Pl & Pr Forms (Rev), Negligence, Forms 311-314; 24 Am Jur Pl & Pr Forms (Rev), Water, Forms 371-383; 25 Am Jur Pl & Pr Forms (Rev), Waterworks, Forms 4, 14, 21-29

25 Am Jur Proof of Facts 233, Water Pollution—Sewage and Industrial Wastes; 8 Am Jur Proof of Facts 2d 101, Municipality's Failure to Maintain Sewers Properly

2 Am Jur Trials 293, Locating Scientific and Technical Experts; 6 Am Jur Trials 555, Use of Engineers as Experts; 18 Am Jur Trials 495, Subterranean Water Pollution

US L Ed Digest, Waters §§ 67, 68

Annotations:

Liability for overflow of water confined or diverted for water power purposes, 91 ALR3d 186

Liability of water supplier for damages resulting from furnishing impure water, 54 ALR3d 936

Liability of water distributor for damage caused by water escaping from main, 20 ALR3d 1294

Water distributor's liability for injury due to condition of service lines, meters, and the like, which serve individual consumer, 20 ALR3d 1363

The rule of absolute liability for damage by the release of collected waters is limited to those situations where the water escapes from a primary reservoir, or a main so related to it as to call for application of the same principle, and does not extend to an escape of water from a line placed in a public street to carry water from a main to the premises of the user. *Quigley v Hibbing (1964) 268 Minn 541, 129 NW2d 765, 20 ALR3d 1353.*

[Annotated]

A statute providing that all persons selling water to the public for drinking and household purposes shall take every reasonable precaution to protect the water from contamination is a public health protection measure and is not applicable to the determination of the rights and duties of parties in an action by a laundry company against a municipal corporation for damages allegedly caused by impurities in the water furnished. *Coast Laundry, Inc. v Lincoln City (1972) 9 Or App 521, 497 P2d 1224, 10 UCCRS 1379, 54 ALR3d 930.*

A municipal corporation furnishing a supply of water for its inhabitants for compensation is not an insurer or a guarantor of the quality of the water it furnishes to its customers and cannot be held liable for damages caused by impurities in the water furnished unless it knew or ought to have known of the impurities; there is no express or implied warranty of merchantability or fitness for a particular purpose in connection with the sale and supply of water. *Coast Laundry, Inc. v Lincoln City (1972) 9 Or App 521, 497 P2d 1224, 10 UCCRS 1379, 54 ALR3d 930.*

[Annotated]

WEAPONS

Scope of Topic: This topic covers the carrying or possession of weapons, either openly or under concealment; including the right to bear arms generally; regulations and offenses connected with the carrying and possession of weapons; licenses and permits; and penalties and forfeitures.

Treated elsewhere are matters arising under the laws governing the militia (see MILITIA) or under the game laws (see GAME AND GAME LAWS); the use of weapons in the commission of certain specific injuries or crimes (see such topics as ASSAULT AND BATTERY; HOMICIDE; ROBBERY; etc.); and the possession of burglar's tools (see BURGLARY).

662

WEAPONS § 1

Consult pocket part for later cases

§ 1 Generally
§ 1.3 Manner of carrying or concealment
§ 1.5 Place where defendant was at time of carrying
§ 2 Who may carry
§ 3 What weapons may be carried
§ 4 Requiring license or permit
§ 5 Justification or excuse
§ 6 Penalty or forfeiture
§ 7 Federal legislation

§ 1 Generally

Text References:

6 Am Jur 2d, Assault and Battery § 54; 31 Am Jur 2d, Explosions and Explosives §§ 2, 123, 127, 128; 79 Am Jur 2d, Weapons and Firearms, §§ 2-5, 7-28, 32, 33

Practice References:

7 Federal Procedural Forms L Ed, Criminal Procedure §§ 20:1 et seq.

25 Am Jur Pl & Pr Forms (Rev), Weapons and Firearms, Forms 1 et seq.

20 Am Jur Legal Forms 2d, Weapons and Firearms §§ 262:1-262:6

29 Am Jur Proof of Facts 65, Firearms Identification

USCS, Constitution, 2nd, 5th and 6th Amendments; 18 USCS §§ 922, 922(a)(6), 922(m), 923(d)(1)(C), 923(g), 924; 18 USCS Appx § 1202

US L Ed Digest, Carrying Weapons § 1; US L Ed Digest, Constitutional Law §§ 346, 854; US L Ed Digest, Criminal Law § 46.6

Annotations:

What constitutes a "bludgeon," "blackjack," or "billy" within meaning of criminal possession statute, 11 ALR4th 1272

Walking cane as deadly or dangerous weapon for purpose of statutes aggravating offenses such as assault and robbery, 8 ALR4th 842

Parts of the human body, other than feet, as deadly or dangerous weapons for purposes of statutes aggravating offenses such as assault and robbery, 8 ALR4th 1268.

Dog as deadly or dangerous weapon for purposes of statutes aggravating offenses such as assault and robbery, 7 ALR4th 607

What constitutes "dangerous weapon" under statutes prohibiting the carrying of dangerous weapons in motor vehicles, 2 ALR4th 1342

Pocket or clasp knife as deadly or dangerous weapon for purposes of statute aggravating offenses such as assault, robbery, or homicide, 100 ALR3d 287

Automobile as dangerous or deadly weapon within meaning of assault or battery statute, 89 ALR3d 1026

Burden of proof as to lack of license in criminal prosecution for carrying or possession of weapon without license, 69 ALR3d 1027

Burden of proof as to lack of license in criminal prosecution for carrying or possession of weapon without license, 69 ALR3d 1054

Application of statute or regulation dealing with registration or carrying of weapons to transient nonresident, 68 ALR3d 1253

Scope and effect of exception, in statute forbidding carrying of weapons, as to person on his own premises or at his place of business, 57 ALR3d 938

Who is entitled to permit to carry concealed weapons, 51 ALR3d 504

Possession of bomb, Molotov cocktail, or similar device as criminal offense, 42 ALR3D 1230

Kicking as aggravated assault, or assault with dangerous or deadly weapon, 33 ALR3d 925

Validity and construction of regulations governing carrying, possession, or use of tear gas or similar chemical weapons, 30 ALR3d 1416

Validity and construction of gun control laws, 28 ALR3d 845

Judicial review, under 18 USCS § 923(f)(3), of revocation or denial of application for license to import, manufacture, or deal in firearms or ammunition, 61 ALR Fed 511

When has applicant for license under Gun Control Act of 1968 "willfully" violated statute or regulations within meaning of 18 USCS § 923(d)(1)(C), 59 ALR Fed 254

Seizure and forfeiture of firearms or ammunition under 18 USCS § 924(d), 57 ALR Fed 234

Meaning of "engage in business" under 18 USCS § 923(a) providing that no person shall engage in business as a firearms or ammunition importer, manufacturer, or dealer without a federal license, 53 ALR Fed 932

State pardon as affecting "convicted" status of one accused of violation of Gun Control Act of 1968 (18 USCS §§ 921 et seq.), 44 ALR Fed 692

Validity, construction, and application of 18 USCS § 922(a)(6), making it unlawful to knowingly make any false or fictitious oral or written statement in connection with the acquisition or attempted acquisition of any firearm or ammunition, 43 ALR Fed 338

Federal constitutional right to bear arms, 37 ALR Fed 696

Lawfulness of sale or other disposition of firearms or ammunition under 18 USCS § 922(d), 34 ALR Fed 430

Validity, construction, and application of provisions of Gun Control Act of 1968 (18 USCS §§ 922(m) and 923(g) and implementing regulations relating to firearms registration and recording requirements imposed upon federally licensed firearms dealers, 33 ALR Fed 824

What constitutes unlawful "dealing in fire-

663

Source: The Lawyers Cooperative Publishing, a division of Thomson Legal Publishing Inc. Reprinted with permission.

Figure 7–6 Page from 11 ALR 4th 1272.

11 ALR4th CRIMINAL POSSESSION OF "BLUDGEON"

11 ALR4th 1272

What constitutes a "bludgeon," "blackjack," or "billy" within meaning of criminal possession statute

---

This annotation is intended to collect and discuss state and federal[1] cases dealing with the question whether particular instruments fit the definition of a "bludgeon," "billy," or "blackjack" within the meaning of criminal statutes prohibiting the possession or carrying of such weapons, expressly.

It is not intended to state or discuss herein any relevant statutory or regulatory provisions except insofar as they are reflected by reported cases within the scope of this annotation, and the reader is therefore advised to consult the current enactments of any jurisdiction of interest.

◆

In the determination whether instruments in question in fact constituted illegal weapons, the major difficulties appear to have been the defining of similar weapons precisely and the distinguishing of such weapons from legitimate instruments.

When the question revolves around the nature of the particular weapon—for example, whether the object is more accurately described as a blackjack or bludgeon—the cases reveal an awareness of the basic similarities among the weapons described and show the flexible attitude of the courts in not requiring narrow specificity so long as the object can be described as a weapon generally of the kind proscribed by the statute.[2] In turn, the status of the object as a proscribed weapon seems to turn on its similarity to legitimate instruments and on the modification, if any, of the instrument from its original state. A baseball bat or set of karate sticks, for example, has a legal, commonly accepted use generally falling outside the statutes. However, modifications rendering these objects roughly similar to weapons seem to raise a risk of criminal liability for the possessor.

◆

In the following cases the courts held that the instruments in question were or could be found to be a billy, bludgeon, or blackjack for purposes of particular state statutes prohibiting possession of such weapons.

A baseball bat 20 inches long, broken a few inches from the bottom of the handle, taped at the smaller end, and heavier at the unaltered end was held to be a billy in People v Grubb (1965) 63 **Cal** 2d 614, 47 Cal Rptr 772, 408 P2d 100. The police found the bat during a routine search of the defendant's car, and the defendant admitted that he owned the bat, that he had possessed it for approximately 2 years, that he carried it in his other automobiles for use in self-defense, and that he had struck people with it on at least two occasions. Also, he called the bat a "billy." These

---

1. No federal cases were found.

2. See People v Canales (1936) 12 **Cal** App 2d 215, 55 P2d 289, infra, in which the court held that an indictment charging possession of a blackjack, or billy in the alternative, was not improper, noting that the statute defined the prohibited instruments or weapons not in specific terms, but as being of a kind commonly known as a blackjack or billy. The court concluded that the trial court did not err in overruling the defendant's demurrer, since the statutory language forbade ownership of any weapon of the class represented by blackjacks and billies.

1273

Source: The Lawyers Cooperative Publishing, a division of Thomson Legal Publishing Inc. Reprinted with permission.

2. The volume number of the series in which the case is reported, in this case Volume 63.
3. The abbreviated name of the reporter series, which tells you the state in which the decision was made as well as the court; in this example, Cal 2d contains the reports of California Supreme Court decisions, second series.
4. The page number where the case begins, page 614.
5. The year of decision in parentheses. If the year of the decision was 1943, for instance, the signal to the researcher is that the case holding has been a principle of law in existence for a long time and the issue may be considered firmly settled. On the other hand, a 1990 cite indicates that the case is fresh and may suggest a new trend in the law on the subject.

A Uniform System of Citation, a handbook published by The Harvard Law Review Association and the leading authority for proper citation of cases, recommends one set of rules for published cases and another for use in typewritten documents. This handbook recommends that whenever cases are published in law books or law-review articles the date be placed directly after the case name, which is not underlined. But in typewritten documents such as legal briefs or memoranda that are prepared by paralegals and lawyers, the date is placed at the end of the citation and the name of the case is underlined. Also note that in published cases the period is dropped after the *v* in the case name, but included when citing the case name in a typewritten document. All legal researchers should have their personal paperback copy of this handbook.

Most state cases must be cited to at least two reporters. In the above example, the cite to 47 Cal Rptr 772 is the official state reporter, and the third citation, 408 P2d 100, is to the unofficial West Publishing Company regional reporter. To locate this case in any of these reporters, you would follow the same procedure just outlined. That is, the first number refers to the volume of the series in which the case is reported, followed by the page number in the volume. If you turn to page 772 in Volume 47 of the *California Reporter* (Cal. Rptr.) series, or to page 100 in Volume 408 of the *Pacific Reporter, Second Series* (P2d) you will find the case of *People v. Grubb.*

As you can see, there is a great deal of information contained in a case citation in code form: the case name, the state where the case was filed, the date of the decision, the court making the decision, and the volume, page number, and name of the reporter series in which the case is reported. For this reason, it is extremely important that citations be proofread several times to make sure they do not contain any errors or transpositions. Attorneys and judges rely upon the accuracy of your legal research. Nothing angers any researcher more than to attempt to look up a cited case and not be able to find it because a number has been transposed. It is your responsibility to check the keyboarding work of others as well as your own work to ensure complete accuracy in citing cases.

Supplemental Pocket Parts

Because the law is always changing, it is extremely important that you check the supplemental pocket parts that are found in the back of the law books for any changes which might have occurred since the book was published. These advance sheets, which are similar to small paperback books, are prepared every few weeks and automatically shipped to purchasers of the books that they update. Since the information contained in the advance sheets is cumulative, the old pocket parts should be discarded and replaced with the new ones immediately upon arrival. In law firms without a librarian, the paralegal is usually expected to perform this task.

Turning to the supplement for 11 A.L.R.4th 1272, you will find the most

Figure 7–7 Supplement for 11 ALR 4th 1272

11 ALR4th 1245–1250 ALR4th

For latest cases, call the toll free number appearing on the cover of this supplement.

ing by defendants in view of defendant's belated claim that quality of residue originally furnished by plaintiffs was inadequate, and where need for additional sample was not supported by reasonably specific factual justification; however, in view of limited quantity of residue available for destructive testing, plaintiffs would be required to furnish to defendant any reports pertaining to scientific testing of residue undertaken on plaintiffs' behalf, redacted to exclude opinions of plaintiffs' experts. Castro v Alden Leeds, Inc. (1986, 2d Dept) 116 App Div 2d 549, 497 **NYS**2d 402.

11 ALR 4th 1261–1267

Excessiveness or inadequacy of punitive damages awarded in personal injury or death cases. 35 ALR4th 441.

Excessiveness or inadequacy of punitive damages in cases not involving personal injury or death. 35 ALR4th 538.

Punitive damages: power of equity court to award. 58 ALR4th 844.

Bad faith tort remedy for breach of contract. 34 Am Jur Trials 343.

VERALEX®: Cases and annotations referred to herein can be further researched through the VERALEX electronic retrieval system's two services, **Auto-Cite®** and **SHOWME®.** Use Auto-Cite to check citations for form, parallel references, prior and later history, and annotation references. Use SHOWME to display the full text of cases and annotations.

Also holding or recognizing that in products liability cases successive awards of punitive damages to separate plaintiffs bringing successive actions against single defendant are permissible.

Colo— Palmer v A.H. Robins Co. (1984, Colo) 684 P2d 187, UCCRS 1150.

Miss— Jackson v Johns-Manville Sales Corp. (1986, CA5 Miss) 781 F2d 394, CCH Prod Liab Rep ¶ 10893, cert den (US) 92 L Ed 2d 743, 106 S Ct 3339 (applying Miss law).

Tex— Hansen v Johns-Manville Products Corp. (1984, CA5 Tex) 734 F2d 1036, 15 Fed Rules Evid Serv 1807, reh den (CA5 Tex) 744 F2d 94 and cert den (US) 84 L Ed 2d 814, 105 S Ct 1739, 105 S Ct 1750 (applying Tex law).

In action brought by manufacturer of intrauterine device seeking class certification for numerous parties claiming to be injured by said device, court noted, in support of requested certification for class action, that defendant had due process right to be protected against unlimited multiple punishment for same course of conduct, and protection against multiple awards of punitive damages justified request for class certification. Re Northern Dist. of California "Dalkon Shield" IUD Products Liability Litigation (1981, ND Cal) 526 **F** Supp 887, 33 FR Serv 2d 624, vacated on other grounds Re Northern Dist. of California, Dalkon Shield IUD Products Liability Litigation (1982, CA9 Cal) 693 F2d 847, 34 FR Serv 2d 646, cert den A.H. Robins Co. v Abed (1983) 459 US 1171, 74 L Ed 2d 1015, 103 S Ct 817, later proceeding Re A.H. Robins Co., "Dalkon Shield" IUD Products Liability Litigation (1983, Jud Pan Mult Lit) 570 F Supp 1480, later proceeding Kontoulas v A.H. Robins Co. (1984, CA4 Md) F2d 312.

Punitive damages was available since "overkill doctrine," which provided that successive compensatory awards are sufficient to achieve exemplary and punitive purposes so that allowing successive punitive awards only creates overkill and threatens recovery of any award by subsequent plaintiffs, was not applicable under Tennessee law. Dykes v Raymark Industries, Inc. (1986, CA6 Tenn) 801 F2d 810, 21 Fed Rules Evid Serv 953, ceret den (US) 55 USLW 3746 (applying **Tenn** law).

64

For latest cases, call the toll free number appearing on the cover of this supplement.

11 ALR4th 1272–1277

Validity of state statute proscribing possession or carrying of knife. 47 ALR4th 651.

VERALEX®: Cases and annotations referred to herein can be further researched through the VERALEX electronic retrieval system's two services, **Auto-Cite®** and **SHOWME®.** Use Auto-Cite to check citations for form, parallel references, prior and later history, and annotation references. Use SHOWME to display the full text of cases and annotations.

Bottom portion of crutch could be regarded as form of homemade bludgeon as that term was used in state statute. Pauls v State (1984, **Del** Sup) 476 A2d 157.

Nightstick with knurled gripping surface on one end, but lacking an end which was heavier or thicker than the other, came within statutory class of object termed "billy." People v Fink (1982) 91 **Ill** 2d 237, 62 Ill Dec 935, 437 NE2d 623.

In asbestos products liability action, where defendants did not demonstrate that any of them were actually subjected to sufficient punitive damage judgments from multiclaimant litigation engendered by same products that in fact threatened their corporate existence, limitation on punitive damages for multiple personal injury plaintiffs was not justified. Hanlon v Johns-Manville Sales Corp. (1984, ND Iowa) 599 F Supp 376 (apparently applying **Iowa** law).

SUPPLEMENT 11 ALR4th 1272–1277

For latest cases, call the toll free number appearing on the cover of this supplement.

In prosecution for attempted possession of controlled substance seized pursuant to arrest for possession of billy club, term "billy" under statute prohibiting possession of one meant heavy wooden stick with handle grip which from its appearance was designed to be used to strike an individual and not for other lawful purposes; object which can be used as billy but which did not fit strict definition could still be prohibited under statute if there existed requisite intent to use object unlawfully against another; defendant in this case did not possess object that met statutory definition of "billy," where object was broom handle of 24-30 inches in length with tape wrapped around each end that provided handle grip. People v Talbert (1985, 3d Dept) 107 App Div 2d 842, 484 **NYS**2d 680.

65

For latest cases, call the toll free number appearing on the cover of this supplement.

recent cases on the subject you are researching as shown in Figure 7–7. Notice also that instructions are provided on how to find cases on this topic if you are using a computer-based research system.

Citators

Your research is not complete until you are satisfied that the rules and cases that apply to the legal problem in question are still valid law. This final task in the legal research process is commonly known as *shepardizing,* named after *Shepard's Citations,* a publication of Shepard's/McGraw-Hill Publishing Company.

Shepard's uses abbreviations as shown in Figure 7–8 to provide the researcher with parallel citations and references to precedent cases, as well as answers to essential research questions such as whether the precedent cases you have chosen to cite were subsequently affirmed, modified, or reversed.

Shepardizing requires that you have the case citation in order to complete your research project, and in most instances you will have that information. However, every now and then you might have only the name of a particular case. In that event, *Shepard's* provides you with another equally valuable research tool called *Shepard's Case Names Citator.* In this regularly updated

Figure 7–8 ***Shepard's Citations,*** **1986, Explanation of Codes used in Shepard's Citations.**

ABBREVIATIONS—ANALYSIS

History of Case		
a	(affirmed)	Same case affirmed on appeal.
cc	(connected case)	Different case from case cited but arising out of same subject matter or intimately connected therewith.
D	(dismissed)	Appeal from same case dismissed.
Gr	(granted)	Hearing or Rehearing granted.
m	(modified)	Same case modified on appeal.
r	(reversed)	Same case reversed on appeal.
s	(same case)	Same case as case cited.
S	(superseded)	Substitution for former opinion.
v	(vacated)	Same case vacated.
US	cert den	Certiorari denied by U.S. Supreme Court.
US	cert dis	Certiorari dismissed by U.S. Supreme Court.
US	reh den	Rehearing denied by U.S. Supreme Court.
US	reh dis	Rehearing dismissed by U.S. Supreme Court.

Treatment of Case		
c	(criticised)	Soundness of decision or reasoning in cited case criticised for reasons given.
d	(distinguished)	Case at bar different either in law or fact from case cited for reasons given.
e	(explained)	Statement of import of decision in cited case. Not merely a restatement of the facts.
f	(followed)	Cited as controlling.
h	(harmonized)	Apparent inconsistency explained and shown not to exist.
j	(dissenting opinion)	Citation in dissenting opinion.
L	(limited)	Refusal to extend decision of cited case beyond precise issues involved.
o	(overruled)	Ruling in cited case expressly overruled.
p	(parallel)	Citing case substantially alike or on all fours with cited case in its law or facts.
q	(questioned)	Soundness of decision or reasoning in cited case questioned.

Source: Reproduced by permission of Shepard's/McGraw-Hill, Inc. Further reproduction is strictly prohibited.

paperback resource, you can find the citation for a civil case by first locating the name of the case in the alphabetical index. Figure 7–9 is a reprint of one page from the *California Case Name Citator*. Shepard's publishes case name citators for nearly every state.

Suppose you decide to cite the precedent case of *People v. Grubb*, 63 Cal 2d 614 (1965) in the legal memorandum you are preparing and you want to be sure of its current status. You would first locate the proper volume of *Shepard's Citations*. In this example, it is the volume that reports California Supreme Court decisions, second series. You know which volume of *Shepard's* to pull from the shelf from the citation itself: Cal 2d. Since there are likely to be several different volumes of *Shepard's*, especially for the larger states, care should be taken to make sure you are working in the correct one. If you cannot find the citation you are looking for, chances are that you are simply in the wrong volume of *Shepard's Citations*.

Having located the correct volume, you next locate the page on which the volume of your cited case is listed. You are looking for Volume 63 Cal 2d 614, which happens to be on page 362 of this *Shepard's*. As you can see from Figure 7–10, in *Shepard's* the volume number of the cited case is boldly printed in the upper corner on each page. Next, as you scan down the page, you will find your case, 614, near the bottom of the column just to the left of the last column on the page.

Notice that the first citation is a cross-reference to the cited case in the regional reporter series given in the A.L.R. cite. This assures you that your work to this point has been accurate. The subsequent long list of citations indicates that the case of *People v. Grubb* has been cited frequently in other cases. Further examination of the citations relating to the history of the cited case indicates that the same case was cited in a dissenting opinion *(j)* in 67 C2d 482 and in 9 C3d 804, as well as in 112 CA 410. (Refer to Figure 7–8 to interpret abbreviations and to the tables in front of each *Shepard's* volume for a more extensive listing of symbols and abbreviations.) You will note the case was distinguished, *d*, in five citations, and followed, *f*, cited as controlling in two others. Most important, the case of *People v. Grubb* has not been reversed, overruled, or questioned, and you should feel reasonably safe in citing it, assuming that it is on point and will strengthen your case.

Shepardizing is usually the last step in the research process before you prepare the written memorandum of your findings. In this example, since the precedent case is still law, it is time to stop researching. Knowing when to stop researching is equally important as knowing how to do it. In this simplified example, only one case was used for the purpose of illustrating the research process from beginning to end. In most research assignments, you may very well be following these same steps with half a dozen or more citations until you locate the information you want.

Researching the Law Using West Publishing Co. Materials Few college libraries can afford to buy law books from both The Lawyers Cooperative Publishing Co. and West Publishing Co. Therefore, you must know how to research a topic if you are using West materials instead of Lawyers Coop books. The procedure is the same as outlined in the previous section, but the content and format of the books are slightly different.

Assume that you want to find out whether the use of a bow and arrow against another human is considered an assault with a deadly weapon. First, you would locate the topic digest (see Figure 7–4) to find an appropriate key word with which to begin your research. *Weapons* is listed under topic heading 1, Persons. Next, locate the alphabetically indexed volume in which *weapons* is a topic

Figure 7–9 *Shepard's California Case Names Citator.* 1985, Vol. 6, No. 4, page 185

CALIFORNIA CASE NAMES CITATOR — Kiz-Kon

Kizer, Grier v 219 Cal App 3d 422, 268 Cal Rptr 244 (1990)
Kizer v Hanna 200 Cal App 3d 882, 246 Cal Rptr 377 (1988)
Kizer v Hanna 48 Cal 3d 1, 255 Cal Rptr 412, 767 P2d 679 (1989)
Kizer, Newland v 209 Cal App 3d 647, 257 Cal Rptr 450 (1989)
Kizer v Ortiz 219 Cal App 3d 1055, 268 Cal Rptr 666 (1990)
Kizer, Reese v 194 Cal App 3d 885, 240 Cal Rptr 151 (1987)
Kizer, Reese v 46 Cal 3d 996, 251 Cal Rptr 299, 760 P2d 495 (1988)
Kizer v San Mateo 217 Cal App 3d 1477, 266 Cal Rptr 704 (1990)
Kizer v Sulnick 202 Cal App 3d 431, 248 Cal Rptr 712 (1988)
Kizer, Union of American Physicians and Dentists v 223 Cal App 3d 490, 272 Cal Rptr 886 (1990)
Kizer, Will v 208 Cal App 3d 709, 256 Cal Rptr 328 (1989)
Klee v Workers Compensation Appeals Board 211 Cal App 3d 1519, 260 Cal Rptr 217 (1989)
Klein v Oakland Raiders Ltd. 211 Cal App 3d 67, 259 Cal Rptr 149 (1989)
Klein v Superior Court of Santa Clara County 197 Cal App 3d 1217, 243 Cal Rptr 352 (1988)
Klein v Superior Court of Santa Clara County 198 Cal App 3d 894 (1988)
Kliger, Rojo v 205 Cal App 3d 646, 252 Cal Rptr 605 (1988)
Kliger, Rojo v 209 Cal App 3d 10, 257 Cal Rptr 158 (1989)
Kliger, Rojo v 220 Cal App 3d 412 (1989)
Kliger, Rojo v 52 Cal 3d 65, 801 P2d 373 (1990)
Kline, Rodriguez v 186 Cal App 3d 1145, 232 Cal Rptr 157 (1986)
Kline v Superior Court of Los Angeles County 227 Cal App 3d 512, 277 Cal Rptr 851 (1991)
Klingele v Engelman 192 Cal App 3d 1482, 238 Cal Rptr 199 (1987)
Klinger v Realty World Corp. 196 Cal App 3d 1549, 242 Cal Rptr 592 (1987)
Kloepfer v Commission on Judicial Performance 49 Cal 3d 826, 782 P2d 239 (1989)
Klugman v Gardner 188 Cal App 3d 1570, 234 Cal Rptr 176 (1987)
K-Mart Corp., California v 210 Cal App 3d Supp 1 (1989)
K-Mart Corp., Coats v 215 Cal App 3d 961, 264 Cal Rptr 12 (1989)
Knapp v Gardena 221 Cal App 3d 344, 270 Cal Rptr 524 (1990)
Knapp Development and Design v Pal-Mal Properties Ltd. 173 Cal App 3d 423, 219 Cal Rptr 44 (1985)
Knapp Development and Design v Pal-Mal Properties Ltd. 195 Cal App 3d 786, 240 Cal Rptr 920 (1987)
Knapp Press, Forman v 173 Cal App 3d 200, 218 Cal Rptr 815 (1985)
Knauer, California v 206 Cal App 3d 1124, 253 Cal Rptr 910 (1988)
Knauer, In re 206 Cal App 3d 1124, 253 Cal Rptr 910 (1988)
Knickerbocker v Stockton 199 Cal App 3d 235, 244 Cal Rptr 764 (1988)
Knight, California v 194 Cal App 3d 337, 239 Cal Rptr 413 (1987)
Knight, California v 204 Cal App 3d 1420, 252 Cal Rptr 17 (1988)
Knight, Encinitas Plaza Real v 209 Cal App 3d 996, 257 Cal Rptr 646 (1989)
Knight v Jewett 225 Cal App 3d 886, 275 Cal Rptr 292 (1990)
Knight v Public Employees Retirement System 223 Cal App 3d 527, 273 Cal Rptr 120 (1990)
Knighten v Sam's Parking Valet 206 Cal App 3d 69, 253 Cal Rptr 365 (1988)
Knights, California v 166 Cal App 3d 46, 212 Cal Rptr 307 (1985)
Knights, California v 167 Cal App 3d 102 (1985)
Knoell v Lompoc 195 Cal App 3d 378, 240 Cal Rptr 464 (1987)
Knoettgen v Superior Court of Los Angeles County 224 Cal App 3d 11, 273 Cal Rptr 636 (1990)
Knowlden, California v 171 Cal App 3d 1052, 217 Cal Rptr 758 (1985)
Knox, California v 204 Cal App 3d 197, 251 Cal Rptr 121 (1988)
Knox, In re 204 Cal App 3d 197, 251 Cal Rptr 121 (1988)
Koch, California v 209 Cal App 3d 770, 257 Cal Rptr 483 (1989)
Koch v Hankins 223 Cal App 3d 1599, 273 Cal Rptr 442 (1990)
Koch v Rodlin Enterprises Inc. 223 Cal App 3d 1591, 273 Cal Rptr 438 (1990)
Koch-Ash v Superior Court of Los Angeles County 180 Cal App 3d 689, 225 Cal Rptr 657 (1986)
Kodiak Industries Inc. v Ellis 185 Cal App 3d 75, 229 Cal Rptr 418 (1986)
Koehler, Hulsey v 218 Cal App 3d 1150, 267 Cal Rptr 523 (1990)
Koehrer v Superior Court of Riverside County 181 Cal App 3d 1155, 226 Cal Rptr 820 (1986)
Koenig, Prison Law Office v 181 Cal App 3d 737, 226 Cal Rptr 728 (1986)
Koenig, Prison Law Office v 186 Cal App 3d 560, 233 Cal Rptr 590 (1986)
Kohan v Cohan 204 Cal App 3d 915, 251 Cal Rptr 570 (1988)
Kohler v Aspen Airways Inc. 171 Cal App 3d 1193, 214 Cal Rptr 720 (1985)
Kohlruss, Mohn v 196 Cal App 3d 595, 242 Cal Rptr 110 (1987)
Koire v Metro Car Wash 164 Cal App 3d 298, 209 Cal Rptr 233 (1984)
Koire v Metro Car Wash 40 Cal 3d 24, 219 Cal Rptr 133, 707 P2d 195 (1985)
Koll Hancock Torrey Pines v Biophysica Foundation Inc. 215 Cal App 3d 883, 264 Cal Rptr 36 (1989)
Kolls-Wells-Bay Area, Summit Industrial Equipment Inc. v 186 Cal App 3d 309, 230 Cal Rptr 565 (1986)
Kolsky, LaForgia v 196 Cal App 3d 1103, 242 Cal Rptr 282 (1987)
Komara v Blair 199 Cal App 3d 161, 244 Cal Rptr 627 (1988)
Komatsu, California v 212 Cal App 3d 1, 260 Cal Rptr 253 (1989)
Kondor, California v 200 Cal App 3d 52, 245 Cal Rptr 750 (1988)

185

Figure 7–10 *Shepard's California Supreme Court Reports,* **2d Series, Vol. 63, page 362**

Vol. 63 CALIFORNIA SUPREME COURT REPORTS, 2d SERIES

66C2d^{5}491
66C2d502
66C2d^{9}557
66C2d^{4}558
f66C2d^{7}915
f66C2d^{9}917
j66C2d^{9}924
67C2d^{3}57
d67C2d^{1}369
d67C2d^{5}393
j67C2d^{2}450
68C2d^{3}568
68C2d^{4}568
68C2d^{5}568
68C2d^{6}568
68C2d^{7}568
68C2d^{9}568
70C2d^{9}765
e70C2d^{9}785
71C2d^{7}322
71C2d^{5}330
71C2d^{9}331
f71C2d^{9}1007
71C2d^{9}1110
f1C3d^{9}286
1C3d^{9}489
e1C3d^{9}509
e1C3d^{7}510
e1C3d^{5}719
e1C3d^{9}719
j1C3d^{9}741
d2C3d^{9}384
2C3d^{4}387
d2C3d^{7}387
j2C3d^{5}403
j2C3d^{7}407
3C3d^{6}805
e7C3d^{10}270
7C3d^{4}731
9C3d^{1}293
e9C3d^{5}315
d11C3d^{10}549
j11C3d^{11}551
11C3d^{6}622
15C3d^{1}441
j22C3d49
22C3d^{8}593
23C3d393
d28C3d^{5}306
34C3d^{16}100
34C3d^{14}357
35C3d^{10}668
238CÅ^{3}310
f238CÅ^{14}784
f238CÅ^{16}784
d239CÅ^{4}43
d239CÅ^{3}61
239CÅ^{3}726
e239CÅ^{5}745
240CÅ^{9}406
e241CÅ^{4}356
242CÅ^{2}484
244CÅ^{5}39
244CÅ^{9}39
244CÅ^{14}125
244CÅ^{5}332
d244CÅ^{5}583
d245CÅ^{5}688
247CÅ^{9}419
247CÅ845
d247CÅ^{5}845
249CÅ^{16}991
250CÅ^{4}524
f251CÅ^{1}11
f251CÅ^{7}18
f251CÅ^{3}19

f251CÅ^{9}20
251CÅ^{9}205
f251CÅ^{10}487
f251CÅ^{1}488
f251CÅ^{3}488
f251CÅ^{5}488
f251CÅ^{11}488
f251CÅ^{4}489
f251CÅ^{9}489
f251CÅ^{9}557
f251CÅ^{5}558
f251CÅ^{3}559
251CÅ^{14}856
251CÅ^{15}857
251CÅ^{9}923
d251CÅ^{5}989
251CÅ^{9}989
e252CÅ^{5}110
252CÅ^{6}853
252CÅ^{5}1058
253CÅ^{4}411
253CÅ^{9}414
d253CÅ^{5}505
253CÅ^{1}623
e253CÅ^{9}924
e255CÅ^{9}556
255CÅ^{9}702
255CÅ^{7}908
e256CÅ^{9}211
e256CÅ^{5}214
256CÅ^{2}221
256CÅ^{9}221
257CÅ^{1}54
d257CÅ^{9}89
259CÅ688
259CÅ^{9}692
d259CÅ^{5}714
261CÅ^{9}159
261CÅ^{10}576
d262CÅ^{5}419
263CÅ370
263CÅ^{4}374
d263CÅ696
d264CÅ^{9}722
e264CÅ^{9}764
e264CÅ^{5}937
265CÅ^{9}60
265CÅ^{3}790
f266CÅ^{1}534
d266CÅ^{3}887
d266CÅ^{9}887
266CÅ^{4}888
267CÅ^{9}143
e267CÅ^{9}605
268CÅ259
e268CÅ^{7}645
e268CÅ^{9}647
e268CÅ^{5}649
d268CÅ^{7}854
269CÅ^{6}203
269CÅ^{7}204
269CÅ^{1}589
270CÅ250
270CÅ^{14}254
d270CÅ^{1}258
270CÅ^{3}470
d271CÅ^{1}526
d271CÅ^{7}575
272CÅ^{9}219
272CÅ^{3}662
273CÅ^{17}485
275CÅ^{9}552
275CÅ^{6}591
276CÅ^{9}454
d276CÅ^{5}550
276CÅ^{14}558

d276CÅ^{5}570
d276CÅ^{9}571
276CÅ^{9}592
276CÅ^{16}752
276CÅ^{17}752
1CÅ^{1}32
1CÅ^{2}32
1CÅ^{2}235
1CÅ^{3}903
2CÅ^{9}213
f4CÅ^{9}49
e4CÅ^{9}497
d4CÅ^{5}603
5CÅ^{12}607
5CÅ^{15}607
f6CÅ^{1}279
f6CÅ^{4}279
7CÅ^{5}251
d10CÅ243
d10CÅ^{5}244
10CÅ297
10CÅ^{9}307
e10CÅ^{5}897
e10CÅ^{7}897
e10CÅ^{3}898
e10CÅ^{4}898
11CÅ^{14}989
d13CÅ^{9}617
e15CÅ^{5}23
16CÅ^{3}1006
16CÅ^{5}1006
17CÅ^{9}331
17CÅ^{3}669
17CÅ^{9}671
19CÅ^{4}346
19CÅ^{17}733
24CÅ879
d29CÅ^{9}972
29CÅ^{4}973
32CÅ^{9}458
d32CÅ^{6}459
32CÅ^{9}462
e34CÅ^{5}154
e34CÅ^{9}157
34CÅ^{5}896
d34CÅ^{9}897
e35CÅ^{9}825
f36CÅ^{5}679
f36CÅ^{9}680
d38CÅ^{18}410
38CÅ^{9}443
38CÅ^{9}742
40CÅ^{7}152
e41CÅ^{5}203
46CÅ^{3}70
46CÅ^{9}71
d47CÅ^{3}41
d47CÅ982
d47CÅ^{9}983
48CÅ^{9}601
f48CÅ^{7}604
49CÅ^{5}354
f53CÅ^{7}356
f53CÅ^{9}356
58CÅ^{10}743
d61CÅ^{9}150
68CÅ^{5}403
69CÅ^{1}1015
71CÅ79
74CÅ^{7}373
75CÅ^{9}771
75CÅ^{10}986
70CÅ^{7}656
79CÅ^{9}656
79CÅ^{5}657
d82CÅ^{9}555

83CÅ^{9}726
85CÅ^{5}602
d85CÅ^{7}604
90CÅ^{3}901
d92CÅ^{10}473
92CÅ^{11}474
d92CÅ^{9}562
j92CÅ564
92CÅ^{9}652
93CÅ^{17}731
94CÅ^{11}805
d95CÅ^{9}1001
d109CÅ^{9}707
d110CÅ^{2}38
e110CÅ^{4}42
f110CÅ^{9}614
110CÅ^{5}616
118CÅ^{9}383
e119CÅ^{7}654
e119CÅ^{8}654
121CÅ496
f121CÅ506
d128CÅ^{5}987
e133CÅ^{14}366
e133CÅ^{15}366
e133CÅ^{16}366
e133CÅ^{17}366
141CÅ^{16}332
141CÅ665
388US^{4}268
391US^{5}130
j402US^{1}632
18LE^{4}1183
20LE^{5}482
j29LE^{1}230
87SC^{4}1954
88SC^{5}1624
j91SC^{1}1729
365F2d^{5}217
j365F2d231
j367F2d^{9}996
374F2d^{1}351
422F2d^{9}323
540F2d738
e275FS^{9}269
303FS^{9}334
e324FS^{4}783
e324FS^{9}783
58CaAG780
59CaAG34
14CLA74
18CLA943
56CaL1042
56CaL1625
57CaL564
17CFW404
26HLJ368
45JBC323
49JBC265
10PLR51
16SAC34
9SFR266
79LF564
29LE993n
54AL^{2}830s
79AL^{2}1412s
7AL^{3}8s
81AL^{3}1021n

– 534 –
(407P2d289)
(47CaR377)
64C2d^{4}431
66C2d^{5}853
67C2d^{2}584
67C2d^{3}584

240CÅ^{2}218
260CÅ^{5}686
9CÅ^{4}400
40CÅ^{2}698
41CÅ^{1}740
65CÅ^{4}329
111CÅ^{6}611
127CÅ^{2}314
442F2d1186
306FS^{4}284
41JBC679

– 541 –
(407P2d282)
(47CaR370)
65C2d^{1}688
65C2d^{5}845
70C2d^{7}545
10C3d^{5}15
d19C3d^{4}108
238CÅ^{2}928
239CÅ^{1}585
239CÅ^{2}585
239CÅ^{6}725
239CÅ^{4}727
d250CÅ^{7}514
255CÅ^{4}467
e264CÅ112
268CÅ^{5}779
f271CÅ^{4}357
9CÅ^{5}569
13CÅ^{5}432
32CÅ^{5}545
40CÅ^{7}947
14CLA103
15CLA66
56CaL606
19AL^{3}779n
2AL^{4}1183n
2AL^{4}1201n

– 551 –
(407P2d649)
(47CaR473)
s224CÅ69
3C3d^{8}686
3C3d^{8}851
27C3d^{4}883
255CÅ^{6}525
6CÅ^{6}197
16CÅ^{6}413
28CÅ^{8}126
28CÅ^{6}177
32CÅ676
74CÅ^{1}918
82CÅ80
84CÅ^{2}1009
97CÅ^{2}741
97CÅ^{3}741
97CÅ^{4}741
523F2d813
555FS51
36CC189
45CC385

– 558 –
(407P2d659)
(47CaR483)
S264CÅ966
269CÅ^{1}21
j269CÅ23

– 561 –
(407P2d653)
(47CaR477)
65C2d^{2}688
66C2d^{2}166
66C2d^{2}340
66C2d^{2}449
66C2d^{2}725
67C2d17
68C2d^{2}430
70C2d^{1}722
240CÅ424
270CÅ^{2}721
58CÅ^{2}236

– 566 –
(407P2d661)
(47CaR485)
s61C2d210
s65C2d768
s71C2d13
65C2d^{1}688
66C2d^{4}723
70C2d490
71C2d^{4}510
1C3d295
1C3d538
240CÅ235
240CÅ^{2}371
242CÅ^{2}105
249CÅ^{2}694
250CÅ^{2}98
253CÅ^{3}455
267CÅ^{2}60
269CÅ^{2}595
d69CAÅ^{1}626
j392US^{2}627
j20LE^{2}1338
j88SC^{2}2267
14CLA107
99AL^{2}772s

– 574 –
(407P2d667)
(47CaR491)
65C2d^{1}688
66C2d^{3}557
69C2d^{1}251
69C2d^{2}251
70C2d^{2}723
f235CÅ^{1}590
239CÅ^{3}727
244CÅ^{2}128
79CÅ^{3}658
14CLA74

– 580 –
(407P2d656)
(47CaR480)
69C2d^{1}206
69C2d^{3}214
f70C2d^{3}160
254CÅ713
254CÅ^{3}717
c9CÅ^{1}751
9CÅ^{3}751
15CÅ^{3}711
51CÅ^{2}304
131CÅ^{2}484
131CÅ^{3}484
100AL^{2}325s

– 584 –
(407P2d857)
(47CaR553)
264CÅ^{2}884
268CÅ^{2}15
8CÅ^{2}461
22CÅ^{1}870
53CÅ^{3}1015
53CÅ^{4}1015
60CÅ791
139CÅ^{2}91
139CÅ200
20CLA242

– 598 –
(407P2d865)
(47CaR561)
12C3d308
j12C3d^{1}314
o12C3d^{1}314
240CÅ^{2}666
f240CÅ^{1}712
253CÅ857
266CÅ^{3}905
275CÅ^{3}690
276CÅ^{2}256
373F2d^{1}117
77PUC673
10LoyL781
17AL^{3}382n

– 602 –
(407P2d868)
(47CaR564)
s51C2d558
d3C3d^{3}562
3C3d^{3}565
238CÅ578
261CÅ^{1}396
271CÅ^{3}747
e5CÅ^{1}807
d12CÅ^{2}667
19CÅ^{4}924
43CÅ750
j43CÅ^{2}755
d56CÅ275
d79CÅ^{2}871
112CÅ^{3}219
471F2d^{1}1344
603F2d^{2}784
720F2d^{3}1018
392FS^{2}171
392FS^{3}172
576FS^{5}807
45AL^{2}994s
91AL^{3}927n
91AL^{3}937n
92AL^{3}527n

– 610 –
(407P2d993)
(47CaR681)
(18AL^{3}1403)
64C2d^{2}840
65C2d^{2}450
4C3d^{2}794

– 614 –
(408P2d100)
(47CaR772)
65C2d^{3}255
65C2d^{1}688
66C2d^{3}125
j67C2d^{2}482
4C3d705
5C3d^{3}860
6C3d41
7C3d^{6}273
j9C3d^{3}804
11C3d^{6}673
243CÅ^{6}555
250CÅ^{3}698
251CÅ^{3}29
d251CÅ^{7}842
255CÅ^{3}189
257CÅ^{3}684
258CÅ^{1}543
259CÅ^{4}85
259CÅ^{7}89
260CÅ^{1}609
261CÅ^{3}435
262CÅ^{3}900
264CÅ^{3}24
264CÅ^{3}265
264CÅ^{3}397
1CÅ^{3}464
d2CÅ^{3}308
4CÅ^{3}387
7CÅ^{7}19
7CÅ^{3}845
8CÅ^{4}500
d8CÅ^{7}501
20CÅ^{3}550
20CÅ^{3}752
30CÅ989
42CÅ^{7}993
50CÅ^{5}398
50CÅ^{6}398
64CÅ^{6}770
72CÅ^{7}55
d74CÅ^{3}368
81CÅ^{2}775
d86CÅ^{7}861
102CÅ^{6}701
103CÅ^{6}98
106CÅ^{7}727
f112CÅ^{2}404
j112CÅ410
116CÅ606
120CÅ^{4}644
f52CA3S^{3}9
53CaAG55
56CaAG507
58CaAG477
64CaAG331
65CaAG678
14CLA98
41JBC518
11AL^{4}1273n

– 624 –
(408P2d113)
(47CaR785)
54CaAG49
59CaAG46
10SwR814

– 629 –
(408P2d97)
(47CaR769)
s61C2d425
s70C2d480
cc62C2d803
63C2d^{6}866
65C2d^{6}688
66C2d^{1}723
66C2d^{1}810
67C2d^{6}14
240CÅ235
251CÅ^{1}372
253CÅ^{2}455
d260CÅ^{5}607
268CÅ^{2}648
d13CÅ^{1}725
14CLA79

– 635 –
(408P2d108)
(47CaR780)
Continued

362

Figure 7–11 47 Cal D 2d 795 Weapons

47 Cal D 2d—795

WEAPONS

References are to Digest Topics and Key Numbers

WEAPONS—Cont'd
ACTIONS for injuries. **Weap 18(2)**
AIR passengers' baggage, magnetometer search for weapons. **Const Law 319**
AIRCRAFT piracy, pistol concealed but empty. **Aviation 16**
ALIENS, possession, equal protection. **Weap 3**
APPEAL or error in criminal prosecutions. **Weap 17(7)**
ARREST—
Probable cause for arresting motorist when pistol observed in briefcase without search. **Arrest 71.1(9)**
Taking possession of gun on arrest of person for offense. **Arrest 71**
ARREST without probable cause—
Weapon found on person—
Illegal search and seizure—
Crim Law 394.4(1)
Searches 3.3(8)
ASSAULT, use of weapon in making, see this index **Assault and Battery**
ATOMIC weapons, detonation at proving grounds, damage to ranch buildings 150 miles away, liability of Federal government—
Em Dom 93
U S 78(10)
ATTORNEY fees, buyer, defense against stolen gun possession charge. **Sales 442(12)**
AUTOMOBILE glove compartment, cross-examination about gun, not prejudicial error or fundamental unfairness. **Hab Corp 45.2(1)**
AUTOMOBILES—
Concealment by guest, offense. **Weap 4, 10**
BAILEES, possession on unregistered firearm. **Weap 4**
BB guns, ordinance prohibiting parent from permitting child to possess or fire in city, validity. **Mun Corp 592(1)**
BEARING, right to. **Weap 1**
BOW and arrow, deadly weapon. **Assault 56**
BURDEN of proof—
Criminal prosecutions. **Weap 17(2)**
BYSTANDERS, police hitting bystander, res ipsa loquitur. **Weap 18(2)**
CARRYING in general. **Weap 5-13**
CHINESE throwing star, possession, specific intent not element—
Const Law 90.1(1)
Weap 3
CITY's use of force policy, unilateral change. **Labor 264**
CIVIL liability, sale or use. **Weap 18**
CONCEALED weapons, search of licensee—
Arrest 71.1(2)
Crim Law 394.4(9)
CONCEALMENT. **Weap 10**
Evidence in criminal prosecution. **Weap 17(4)**
Murder while possessing concealable weapon, degree on offense. **Homic 18(1)**
Pocket search without warrant, police officer. **Arrest 71**
CONFESSIONS procured through fear and threats on exhibiting weapons to accused. **Crim Law 522(4)**
CONSTITUTIONAL provisions. **Weap 3**
Commerce regulations. **Commerce 82.50**
CONTRABAND, forfeiture of vehicle used without authority, taking without just compensation. **Em Dom 2(1)**
CONVICTS—
Knowingly possessing sharp instrument, defense, overwrought condition. **Convicts 5**
CONVICTS carrying weapons, multiple prosecution, defenses. **Crim Law 29, 200(1)**
COURTHOUSE, entry condition, limited warrantless search for weapons. **Searches 7(10)**
CRIMINAL prosecutions in general. **Weap 17**

WEAPONS—Cont'd
CRIMINAL prosecutions in general—Cont'd
Statutes pertaining to weapons while committing an offense, applicability, principal offense includes weapon. **Crim Law 1208(6)**
DEADLY, see this index **Dangerous and Deadly Weapons**
DEADLY weapon offense of exhibiting, sentence to state prison improper. **Weap 17(8)**
DEFENSES in actions for injuries. **Weap 18(1)**
DEMONSTRATIVE evidence. **Crim Law 404(3, 4)**
DISASSEMBLED firearms, status as operable weapons. **Weap 8**
DISPLAY, rule and boisterous manner, pointing and firing at victims who saw weapon. **Weap 14**
DOUBLE jeopardy, misdemeanor under city ordinance as not includable in prosecution for burglary. **Crim Law 199**
EVIDENCE in criminal prosecution. **Weap 17(2–4)**
Burden of proof in criminal prosecutions. **Weap 17(2)**
Demonstrative. **Crim Law 404(3, 4)**
Presumption. **Weap 17(2)**
Weapon taken from prisoner on arrest for drunken driving. **Crim Law 395**
Rude, angry and threatening manner—
Offense necessarily included in offense of resisting public officer. **Crim Law 199**
Same offense as resisting public officer. **Crim Law 202(1)**
EXCISE tax—
Manufacturers. **Int Rev 4332**
EXCUSE for carrying. **Weap 13**
EXEMPTION—
From legal process. **Exemp 41**
From liability for carrying. **Weap 11**
EXHIBITING. **Weap 14**
FEDERAL questions in criminal prosecutions. **Courts 97(1)**
FELONS—
Firearm obtained in robbery, interstate commerce nexus 13 years earlier. **Weap 4**
Sister's revolver carried to pawnshop. **Weap 17(4)**
FELONY convicts, handgun possession forbidden—
Const Law 250.1(2)
Weap 3
FICTITIOUS statements, vagueness of statute forbidden in acquiring firearms. **Crim Law 13.1(2)**
FIRING range, explosion of shell after national guard demonstration, liability of state for injuries. **States 208**
FORFEITURES. **Weap 16**
Indian tribe, power, nonmember entering reservation and violating ordinance. **Indians 32**
FORMER jeopardy, single underlying incident, concealable revolver and loaded firearm in vehicle. **Crim Law 1209**
FRAUD—
Acquisition of firearm, validity of statute making false statement an offense. **Weap 3**
FRISK, police officer knowing defendant lacked respect for officers. **Searches 3.3(5)**
GIFTS. **Weap 4**
HAIR trigger, bullet hitting vehicle occupant, automobile and homeowner's insurance. **Insurance 435.16, 435.35**
HOMICIDE, means or instrument used, see this index **Homicide**
IDENTIFICATION, altering number, removing visible number from frame, hidden numbers remaining. **Weap 4**
INCRIMINATION, decision making defense to prosecution, possessing unregistered firearm, retroactivity. **Courts 100(1)**

Source: West's California Digest, 1985. Reprinted with permission.

(Figure 7–11). In the middle of the left column you will see the reference *BOW and arrow, deadly weapon,* followed by the word *Assault* and the number *56*.

West Publishing Co. uses a key-numbering system to help you locate the information you are researching. In this instance, *Assault 56* directs you to locate the alphabetical volume in which the topic of Assault is located and to turn to key 56 in that volume (Figure 7–12).

A quick reading of the headnotes in Figure 7–12b directs you to a specific case involving a bow and arrow, *People v. Garcia,* 79 Cal. Rptr. 833, 275 C.A.2d 517. The next step is to look up the *Garcia* case in either the *California Reporter* series or the California Appellate reports, second series. In Volume 275 of the *California Appellate* reports, the *Garcia* case is found on page 517 (Figure 7–13).

After reading the *Garcia* case, you decide it could be useful to your research. The next step then is to locate the citation in *Shepard's Citations* to find its current status. See Figure 7–14. The small *j* in front of the citation (see Figure 7–8) indicates that at least one judge did not agree with the opinion in this case and refers you to the case in which the dissenting opinion was rendered. You would most certainly want to locate and read the dissenting opinion case before deciding whether to cite the *Garcia* case.

It is important to note that in order to locate the *Garcia* case in *Shepard's Citations,* it was necessary to use the Cal. Rptr. citation rather than the C.A. cite. Publishers and publications vary in the scope and content of information they select for publication. Therefore, it is always a good idea to write down complete cites before putting the book back on the library shelf. You never know when it might be necessary to switch books or citations in order to complete your research.

Legal research is a time-consuming, labor-intensive part of the practice of law and is often assigned to a paralegal. As you become more proficient in legal research, you will find the process not nearly as overwhelming as it might seem in this introduction and overview. To have a successful paralegal career, it is imperative that you learn to perform this aspect of your job with particular skill and efficiency.

Computer-Aided Legal Research

As you can imagine, the process of legal research lends itself to computerization and no one is more aware of this fact that the major publishers of legal materials. Auto-Cite®, LEXIS®, and WESTLAW® are the current leaders in computer-aided legal research. Perhaps you are fortunate enough to be in a curriculum where you will be trained to use these programs. If not, these companies had the foresight to make their programs user-friendly. You will be able to become remarkably proficient with about a half-day's on-the-job training. Since the time involved in doing legal research on a computer is considerably less than doing it manually, only the smallest law offices are lacking some type of automated research system.

Auto-Cite® is the computerized equivalent of *Shepard's Citations.* Auto-Cite® verifies the citation you already have, provides parallel citations in the other reporters, indicates whether the case is still good law, and tells you if the case has been discussed in an A.L.R. annotation. When time permits, you are advised to check *Shepard's Citations* in addition to Auto-Cite® because one serves as a check against the other. Occasionally information obtained from one source will be different from another.

LEXIS® is the registered trademark for information products and services of Mead Data Central, Inc. and consists of an enormous group of libraries containing cases, statutes, codes, attorney general opinions, briefs, and other

Figure 7–12a Cover page from West's California Digest 2d, Vol. 4

WEST'S CALIFORNIA DIGEST 2d

Volume 4

ARMED SERVICES— ATTACHMENT

ST. PAUL, MINN.

WEST PUBLISHING CO.

Source: West's California Digest, 1985. Reprinted with permission.

Figure 7–12b Key 56 Assault and Battery 4 Cal D 2d 772

56 ASSAULT & BATTERY

4 Cal D 2d—772

For later cases see same Topic and Key Number in Pocket Part

carrying concealed dirk or dagger did not prejudice defendants. West's Ann.Pen.Code, §§ 245(a), 12020.

People v. Cabral, 124 Cal.Rptr. 418, 51 C.A.3d 707.

Cal.App. 1974. Pointing an unloaded gun at another person, with no effort or threat to use it as a bludgeon, is not an "assault with a deadly weapon." West's Ann.Pen.Code, § 245(a).

People v. Orr, 117 Cal.Rptr. 738, 43 C.A.3d 666.

Cal.App. 1974. An assault with a deadly weapon may be perpetrated without drawing or exhibiting weapon in a rude, angry, or threatening manner, or using it in a fight or quarrel. West's Ann.Pen. Code, §§ 245, 417.

People v. Escarcega, 117 Cal.Rptr. 595.

Cal.App. 1973. Requisite intent for commission of assault with a deadly weapon is the intent to commit a battery. West's Ann.Pen.Code, § 245(a).

People v. Lathus, 110 Cal.Rptr. 921, 35 C.A.3d 466.

Battery is not a lesser and necessarily included offense of assault with a deadly weapon and assault with a deadly weapon can be perpetrated without committing a battery.

People v. Lathus, 110 Cal.Rptr. 921, 35 C.A.3d 466.

Cal.App. 1972. To convict defendant of assault with a deadly weapon it was not necessary that prosecution introduce evidence to show that defendant actually made an attempt to strike or use the knife and only needed to prove that a deadly weapon was used and that defendant intended to commit a violent injury on another. West's Ann.Pen.Code, § 245.

People v. Gonzalez, 104 Cal.Rptr. 530, 28 C.A.3d 1091.

Cal.App. 1972. Although defendant could not be charged with robbing either boxboy or store manager, since the former had no dominion or control whatsoever over any money and since, with respect to the latter, a robbery charge (predicated on manager's constructive possession of money taken from cash registers) was precluded by reason of the fact that a robbery of those persons having control of the particular cash registers had also been charged, defendant's conduct with respect to the boxboy and store manager was nonetheless criminal, since all the elements of the lesser included offense of assault with a deadly weapon were charged and proved. West's Ann.Pen.Code, §§ 211, 245(a).

People v. Guerin, 99 Cal.Rptr. 573, 22 C.A.3d 775, certiorari denied 93 S.Ct. 145, 409 U.S. 859, 34 L.Ed.2d 105.

Cal.App. 1970. Specific intent is element of the crime of assault with deadly weapon, but such intent may be proved circumstantially from the act itself and from the surrounding circumstances. West's Ann.Pen.Code, § 245.

People v. Rocha, 86 Cal.Rptr. 837, 7 C.A.3d 909.

Cal.App. 1970. Where there was no question of an officer acting outside scope of his duties or of being unreasonably forcible, and defendant at time of being questioned suddenly pulled out loaded revolver and pointed it at questioning officer, essentials of an intent to commit an assault on police officer were sufficiently shown. West's Ann.Pen. Code, § 245(b).

People v. Livingston, 84 Cal.Rptr. 237.

Where arresting officers identified themselves to defendant and showed their badges, defendant knew or reasonably should have known that person who he assaulted with deadly weapon was police officer. West's Ann.Pen.Code, § 245(b).

People v. Livingston, 84 Cal.Rptr. 237.

Cal.App. 1969. A battery, or a wounding is not necessary in order to sustain a conviction for assault with a deadly weapon.

People v. Birch, 83 Cal.Rptr. 98, 3 C.A.3d 167.

Cal.App. 1969. Defendant committed assault with "deadly weapon" where he approached victim in front of victim's residence and shot an arrow into his arm. West's Ann. Pen. Code, § 245.

People v. Garcia, 79 Cal.Rptr. 833, 275 C.A.2d 517.

Defendant convicted of assault with deadly weapon did not abandon aggression nor remove victim's actual or apparent need to protect himself, so as to avail defendant of self-defense, where after argument with victim and following victim's challenge to fight, defendant left victim, returned with bow and arrow, and shot victim while victim was trying to disarm defendant to protect himself. West's Ann.Pen.Code, § 245.

People v. Garcia, 79 Cal.Rptr. 833, 275 C.A.2d 517.

Cal.App. 1968. It was not necessary that defendant actually fire shotgun in order to commit offense of assault with a deadly weapon. West's Ann.Pen.Code, § 245 and (a, b).

People v. Wheeler, 67 Cal.Rptr. 246, 260 C.A.2d 522.

Lack of intent to harm is defense to charge of assault with a deadly weapon.

People v. Wheeler, 67 Cal.Rptr. 246, 260 C.A.2d 522.

For legislative history of cited statutes

Source: West's California Digest, 1985. Reprinted with permission.

Figure 7–13a A page from *People v. Garcia*

[Crim. No. 16110. Second Dist., Div. One. Aug. 8, 1969]

THE PEOPLE, Plaintiff and Respondent, v. PHILLIP ANTHONY GARCIA, Defendant and Appellant.

[1] **Criminal Law—Appeal—Questions of Law and Fact—Consideration of Evidence by Appellate Court.**—On appeal from a conviction of assault with a deadly weapon involving the use of a bow and arrow, defendant could not successfully argue that he did not approach his victim with the bow ready for firing or in a threatening manner, or that the victim was the actual aggressor and that, in self-defense, defendant thrust an arrow by hand into the victim's shoulder; such argument, in effect, requested the appellate court to reweigh and reinterpret the evidence in a manner consistent with innocence, whereas at the appellate stage the test is not whether the evidence may be reconciled with innocence but whether there is substantial evidence in the record on appeal to warrant the inference of guilt drawn by the trier of fact.

[2] **Id.—Appeal—Questions of Law and Fact—Reasonable Doubt.**—It is the trier of fact, not the appellate court, that must be convinced of a defendant's guilt beyond a reasonable doubt; if the circumstances reasonably justify the trier of fact's findings, the opinion of the reviewing court that the circumstances might also be reasonably reconciled with a contrary finding does not warrant a reversal of the judgment.

[3a, 3b] **Assault—With Deadly Weapon—Evidence—Sufficiency.**—In a prosecution for assault with a deadly weapon, the evidence was ample to support conviction of the offense, where, after the victim refused a challenge to fight, defendant said he would be back, where, a half hour later, he approached the victim carrying a bow and arrow which he pointed at him, where the victim testified that he hit and kicked defendant to disarm him and then was shot, and where the clear conclusion from the circumstances was that the bow and arrow must have been held in a firing position and that only the pressure of a "loaded" bow could cause the arrow to go through the victim's arm.

[4] **Id.— Deadly Weapon.**— A bow and arrow held in a firing position with the arrow pointed at the victim in such a way

---

McK. Dig. References: [1] Criminal Law, § 1312; [2] Criminal Law, § 1314; [3] Assault and Battery, § 28(1); [5, 6, 9] Assault and Battery, § 4; [7, 8] Assault and Battery, § 33.

[4] See **Cal.Jur.2d, Rev.,** Assault and Battery, § 10; **Am.Jur.2d,** Assault and Battery, § 53.

Source: Bancroft-Whitney. Reprinted with permission.

that it can be fired in an instant constitutes a deadly weapon.

[5a, 5b] **Id.— Self-defense.**— In a prosecution for assault with a deadly weapon, the record showed that defendant was either an actual or apparent aggressor, and that the victim was justified in fearing imminent danger and believing that it was necessary to disarm defendant, where defendant had earlier challenged him to a fight, and where, at the time the victim struck and kicked him, defendant was "coming like that" with a bow and arrow; under such circumstances the victim was under no duty to retreat; in the exercise of his right of self-defense he could stand his ground and defend himself by the use of all force and means apparently necessary.

[6] **Id.—Self-defense.**—In order that a person may avail himself of the right of self-defense, it is sufficient that the appearance of his assailant be such as to arouse in his mind, as a reasonable man, a belief that his assailant is about to commit great bodily harm on him.

[7a, 7b] **Id.— With Deadly Weapon— Evidence— Self-defense.**— In a prosecution for assault with a deadly weapon, defendant could not justify his shooting of the victim with a bow and arrow as self-defense, where there was evidence that after arguing with the victim and challenging him to fight, defendant returned with the bow and arrow with the intent to commit an assault on the victim, and in fact carried out this intention while the victim was trying to disarm him to protect himself, and where, in any event, the victim's efforts to disarm defendant did not justify defendant's use of a weapon having a high potential for inflicting a mortal wound.

[8] **Id.— With Deadly Weapon— Evidence— Self-defense.**—One does not have the right to provoke a quarrel, go to it armed, take advantage of it, and then convert his adversary's lawful efforts to protect himself into grounds for further aggression against him under the guise of self-defense.

[9] **Id.—Self-defense.**—The use of excessive force destroys the justification for self-defense, but the question whether there was such an excess is ordinarily one for the trier of fact.

APPEAL from a judgment of the Superior Court of Los Angeles County. Paul G. Breckenridge, Judge. Affirmed.

Prosecution for assault with a deadly weapon. Judgment of conviction affirmed.

---

[7] See **Cal.Jur.2d, Rev.**, Assault and Battery, § 15; **Am.Jur.2d** Assault and Battery, § 69.

Figure 7–14 ***Shepard's California Reporter*, Vol. 80, page 39**

CALIFORNIA REPORTER — Vol. 80

259CaR[3]642
774P2d[3]671

– 528 –
f266CaR[7]919
31MJ144

– 542 –
55AL[4]537n

– 568 –
248CaR694

– 620 –
Alk
814P2d1372

– 645 –
Cir. 3
720FS1155
Cir. 9
719FS[1]940
30SAC478

– 649 –
245CaR[2]146
261CaR498

– 655 –
j245CaR202
276CaR[5]709

– 672 –
252CaR[6]778
281CaR[11]800
j285CaR255
j815P2d328
18WSR14

– 683 –
246CaR[10]903
d246CaR [11]903
d273CaR728
f273CaR[8]744
Conn
592A2d410

– 718 –
249CaR[1]218
269CaR[1]660

– 723 –
249CaR[1]193
254CaR[1]348
765P2d[1]510

– 753 –
49AL[4]92n
49AL[4]93n
49AL[4]205n

– 761 –
246CaR[2]429
262CaR[15]297
280CaR530
CF§2.07

– 785 –
254CaR[8]615
766P2d[9]30

– 797 –
Ariz
788P2d130

– 807 –
248CaR726

– 811 –
64AL[4]916n
64AL[4]936n

– 833 –
d259CAR[1]321
e260CaR[1]441
280CaR[3]576

– 864 –
272CaR[5]179

– 885 –
77AL[4]1048n

Vol. 79

– 1 –
270CaR[5]563

– 9 –
264CaR[2]542
61AL[4]1090n

– 12 –
20Pcf1045

– 18 –
j282CaR462
j811P2d754

– 23 –
f255CaR[11]65
259CaR[15]254
CCLM4
§7.06

– 33 –
d256CaR[3]472
d286CaR[3]333
57AL[4]351n

– 60 –
84AL[4]240n

– 77 –
270CaR81
271CaR697
272CaR[14]218
274CaR[8]452
276CaR201
276CaR239
277CaR83
279CaR890
283CaR634
j767P2d678

– 92 –
j245CaR202
280CaR[4]278

– 106 –
273CaR[17]12
281CaR[6]623
281CaR[9]623
281CaR[13]623
281CaR[14]623
f281CaR[18]623
Idaho
797P2d85

Kan
798P2d958
Mass
577NE293
64SCL7

– 123 –
262CaR882
262CaR[3]883
277CaR545

– 124 –
j279CaR589
j807P2d431

– 133 –
62AL[4]194n
62AL[4]227n

– 140 –
NOCA§13.48

– 155 –
281CaR800

– 168 –
d256CaR[8]593
286CaR176

– 187 –
249CaR900

– 194 –
59AL[4]79n
59AL[4]80n
59AL[4]85n
65AL[4]306n

– 208 –
d281CaR[4]227

– 229 –
22LoyL99

– 287 –
247CaR[1]667
247CaR[2]669
55AL[4]1123n

– 297 –
d250CaR[1]834
274CaR[1]214

– 313 –
253CaR654
270CaR866

– 319 –
283CaR[4]561
Cir. 9
876F2d[1]704
CCLM4
§1.13

– 326 –
248CaR692
259CaR387
261CaR[4]167
270CaR783
j287CaR486

– 337 –
246CaR[8]894
264CaR[2]675
284CaR[3]80
q284CaR81

j284CaR82
FL§5.53

– 369 –
266CaR[4]110
276CaR664
279Ca[13]75
Cir. 6
749FS[2]1476
749FS[15]1481
22Pcf48
66AL[4]94n
66AL[4]96n
PLPD§6.03

– 381 –
256CaR[13]510
q283CaR[5]590
q812P2d[5]937

– 388 –
Cir. 9
f762FS[6]1379

– 401 –
282CaR85
283CaR[8]57
1988IlLR197
CCLM4
§5.11
CRB§15.06

– 415 –
259CaR419
e259CaR[3]421

– 447 –
262CaR119

– 478 –
252CaR[8]592

– 508 –
281CaR[2]364

– 526 –
261CaR[1]722

– 529 –
j247CaR466
249CaR[2]87
251CaR[1]143
251CaR[4]143
257CaR[2]288
269CaR[4]481
f283CaR[1]118
f283CaR[2]118
f283CaR[3]118
f283Car[4]118
284CaR[4]886
756P2d[2]811

– 539 –
CF§6.15

– 543 –
254CaR[11]215
257CaR168
765P2d[11]377
Cir. 6
702FS1366
24LoyL65

– 555 –
CF§8.10

– 567 –
55AL[4]700n
76AL[4]212n

– 571 –
262CaR[4]696

– 579 –
258CaR[3]132
281CaR233

– 583 –
SD
450NW238

– 587 –
d284CaR[1]587
Cir. 3
f938F2d[1]412

– 622 –
51AL[4]43n

– 650 –
247CaR[3]399
253CaR[3]319
253CaR[1]526
256CaR[3]425
259CaR[2]130
259CaR[3]131
269CaR[1]101
e285CaR[3]507
32MJ67

– 662 –
j285CaR76
j814P2d1318

– 668 –
Md
544A2d804

– 671 –
92ALRF759n
92ALRF767n

– 677 –
Colo
778P2d1383

– 707 –
266CaR[4]562
d273CaR[2]612
284CaR[1]33

– 717 –
CF§5.10

– 723 –
250CaR[2]256
257CaR[2]872
257CaR[2]884
258CaR597
268CaR[2]329
273CaR[1]273
q273CaR278
q284CaR18
758P2d[2]583
771P2d[2]821
q771P2d830
771P2d[2]833
j771P2d836
772P2d1064

Cir. 6
763FS[2]226
d763FS227
DC
572A2d1071
La
556So2d565
Mo
799SW598
Ohio
545NE92
Pa
555A2d1312
24LoyL96

– 729 –
d282CaR[1]768
d284CaR[1]146
d284CaR[2]146
d284CaR[3]146
d286CaR434
d286CaR[2]435
Cir. 9
765FS[1]625
24UCD1076

– 733 –
cc106SC617

– 743 –
246CaR[8]697
251CaR[8]250
e253CaR[2]724
e257CaR[8]89
260CaR[2]589
263CaR[2]737
264CaR580
f285CaR[2]23
760P2d[8]447
e764P2d[2]1101
e770P2d[8]269
776P2d[2]291

– 757 –
265CaR[3]550
f284CaR[2]550

– 829 –
Cir. 3
937F2d857

– 833 –
j249CaR905
73AL[4]998n

– 848 –
Ohio
533NE352
FL§9.10

– 852 –
269CaR254
Wis
433NW281

– 872 –
263CaR[20]323
263CaR[24]324
269CaR[2]697
22LoyL817
24LoyL938
15PLR350

– 880 –
f245CaR[3]157
248CaR[3]908

f266CaR[3]920

– 893 –
284CaR[5]61

– 911 –
j261CaR72

Vol. 80

– 1 –
245CaR349
245CaR[5]350
245CaR[9]353
245CaR[11]353
245CaR[16]354
247CaR[9]231
247CaR[10]231
248CaR178
249CaR270
250CaR[4]671
252CaR[1]804
257CaR[25]555
j264CaR425
273CaR[9]727
277CaR[12]141
278CaR[11]322
284CaR[11]588
758P2d[4]1202
770P2d [25]1124
j782P2d666
802P2d[12]925
18WSR15

– 28 –
258CaR[3]410
266CaR[3]219

– 31 –
248CaR401
248CaR[7]865
d250CaR[8]868
254CaR[4]600
j258CaR260
756P2d[7]252
d759P2d[8]503
766P2d[4]14
j771P2d1348
Nebr
436NW134
78CaL642
24LoyL638

– 49 –
245CaR387
259CaR[1]685
j259CaR697
j273CaR578
276CaR[16]777
774P2d[1]714
j774P2d726
j797P2d602
802P2d[16]267
j110SC1732
Fla
527So2d809
27SDL543
74VaL1368

– 70 –
d254CaR[1]381
51AL[4]166n
51AL[4]185n

39

legal material for each of the states and the U.S. Additionally, LEXIS® has full-text articles from selected law reviews as well as various legal news services and other periodicals. Since its contents expand daily, only your local LEXIS® representative would be able to provide you with a detailed and complete list of the system's research capabilities.

WESTLAW® from West Publishing Company provides nearly the same information with its databases as LEXIS® with its libraries. That is, the majority of the legal material from all states and the U.S. is available from either source. The choice of whether to use WESTLAW® or LEXIS® is often influenced by the variety of databases available on each and how far back in time they go.

Both systems have recent parts of *Shepard's Citations*, various copyrighted books, some cases not yet in print, and unpublished opinions. Neither system is indexed. Instead, these computerized systems have the ability to read, in a matter of seconds, every word of every sentence in every paragraph of every case for the occurrence of particular words, numbers, phrases, or combinations of words, numbers, and phrases—something no human can possibly do. The legal researcher must become particularly creative in thinking up words and phrases for the computer to be able to perform its function.

Although the cost of computer-aided legal research is considerable, as the legal researcher becomes more accustomed to working with the system it is possible to cut the time spent in doing research by half. Since time is money to a law firm, being able to perform the research task in less time results in a win-win situation for everyone—the firm is more efficient and the client saves money.

7–3 Legal Writing

It is appropriate to interject at this point some thoughts about writing in general. The best writers always write with the reader in mind. Since you will probably not be present when your memorandum is read, your writing should strive to anticipate the reader's questions and provide the answers. For example, one mistake that students often make in answering essay questions is to assume that the reader knows as much as they know about the subject. Although it is usually an accurate assumption that your instructor knows what you are talking about, it is your duty as a student to make sure that you convince the instructor that you are thoroughly familiar with the topic. That means putting down everything you know about the subject going back to the beginning of time, if necessary.

Likewise, when you prepare a legal memorandum you should assume that the lawyer knows little, if anything, about the particular problem or its solution. It is your duty as a paralegal to communicate your thoughts clearly and concisely so that anyone who might be working on the client's file will be able to understand what is going on. Do not attempt to impress others with your vocabulary or your ability to construct long, complex sentences. Simplicity is best. Do not worry about your writing style. It will emerge with each memorandum you write. You should, however, pay attention to the image your writing portrays. If your basic written language skills—punctuation, spelling, grammar—could benefit from a brush-up course, do not hesitate to get these skills updated as quickly as possible. The primary tools you will use every day as a paralegal are words, words, and more words.

To achieve clarity in your written communication, you should expect to revise and edit your work several times. Lawyers and judges typically go through three or more drafts of any important written communication before they consider it acceptable. There is no reason to expect that your writing will be done with less effort. The purpose of the first draft is to get your words and ideas onto paper or your word processing screen, without regard to form or content. The second draft is to edit and revise the first version. Third and subsequent drafts are for the purpose of adding polish, that is, checking for clarity, understanding, content, and spelling errors. Even the best writers will tell you that any writing can always be improved. But since writers and paralegals alike have deadlines to meet, your goal should be for the reader to understand what you are trying to communicate.

Legal Research Memorandum

One of the main functions of paralegals is to assist lawyers in solving their clients' problems. A written memorandum of law is the most commonly used method to express and communicate ideas about the problem, to guide the work for the client, and to record the reasons for any actions taken in response to the problem. The legal memorandum is as valuable to the lawyer as blueprints are to an architect or the game plan is to a football coach. Because of its importance to both the lawyer and the client, the memorandum of law must provide a justifiable, conclusive response to the problem.

The legal research memorandum is concerned with the facts of the problem, the conclusion you have drawn as a result of your research, and how you arrived at that conclusion. Legal research memoranda are not argumentative. Rather, you should candidly present an evaluation of the facts, the strengths, and the weaknesses of the client's position. To attain this, you must become thoroughly familiar with the facts, locate and read the authorities, and become convinced of the most likely outcome. Thus, you become the expert in the office on this particular legal problem in the client's file. You will finally convey all your information to the lawyer, and subsequently to the client, in the form of a written memorandum.

Organization and Format

The legal memorandum is focused on the client's factual problem. The only appropriate discussion in the memorandum pertains to the codes, statutes, or precedent cases that apply to the problem. Do not relate any other peripheral information about the client, regardless of how interesting you think it might be. Avoid using cliches, vague adjectives, or any other stylistic writing techniques that might obscure the meaning of your memorandum. Since this document is the foundation on which the lawyer will build a successful case, its importance cannot be overemphasized.

You may find the format for presentation of the legal research memorandum will differ slightly from one law office to the next, based upon each lawyer's particular style. However, the major headings are likely to remain the same since the information contained in each one is the nuts and bolts of the memorandum. Figure 7–15 illustrates one way to organize and present information in a legal research memorandum.

Although the organization and format for a legal research memorandum presented in Figure 7–15 is intended for students' use, with slight modification it closely resembles those memoranda prepared by lawyers. Note that the organization of information is somewhat different from the format of most written material. That is, the conclusions and recommendations are presented before the facts of the case. The discussion of pertinent research information

Figure 7–15 Legal Research Memorandum

TO:	Course and section in which submitted; or name of attorney to whom submitted
FROM:	Your name
DATE:	Use the date on which the memorandum is due
RE:	A caption or summary of the contents of the memorandum; the name of the client, or the name of the lawsuit. **RE,** (ray) is an abbreviation of the Latin term, *in re,* meaning in the matter of and is an integral part of letters and memoranda pertaining to legal matters.
QUESTION:	State the legal issue(s) in question to keep the reader focused on the specific legal problem(s) arising from the facts.
CONCLUSIONS AND RECOMMENDATIONS:	Concisely answer the question(s) presented in the preceding paragraph. Include, if appropriate, what actions should be taken next, a suggested strategy to pursue, and any additional questions of fact that should be determined.
FACTS:	In your own words, include a brief but accurate discussion of the facts.
DISCUSSION:	Present an objective discussion of the information you found in the applicable codes, statutes, and precedent cases and indicate the likely outcome of the problem as demonstrated by this research information. Use subheadings to separate the various points being discussed and organize the subheadings in a logical manner to indicate the direction of your thoughts.

always follows your conclusion. In other words, you first present your conclusion and then you defend your position instead of presenting the facts and discussion first while building up to the conclusion. Students will become familiar with the preparation of various types of memoranda in other legal research and writing courses.

The objective of this chapter is to provide you with an overview of the foundation upon which to build your paralegal career and practice. It is not a complete and exhaustive study, nor the only way to perform the tasks of legal analysis, research, and writing. Because you will rarely, if ever, find the exact same set of circumstances and facts in one case to be present in another, each legal problem must be analyzed and researched from a unique perspective. It is the unique qualities of each case that will keep your work motivating and challenging. To be a part of the legal profession means that you are continually learning and dare not risk becoming complacent or inflexible, particularly in the area of legal research.

SUMMARY

7–1

Legal analysis is the process of applying rules of law or statutes to the given facts of a case. By comparing the relationship of a certain rule or statute to the facts, you can determine the strengths and weaknesses of the client's case. The process of legal analysis involves five steps: (1) locating and quoting the rule or statute; (2) stating the relevant facts and circumstances; (3) raising the questions or issues to be answered; (4) analyzing the key elements against the facts; and (5) stating a conclusion.

7–2

Legal research usually begins with a problem analysis. By identifying the key elements, categorizing them, and organizing the information in a logical format, the legal researcher is able to direct his or her efforts to the proper resources. Many research assignments begin by locating the subject matter in a digest or legal encyclopedia. This resource, in turn, leads the researcher to specific case law on point that must be updated by checking the supplemental pocket parts and by shepardizing. Many law firms are using computer-aided legal research programs to cut down on the time required when research is done manually. The most common computer-aided legal research programs are Auto-Cite®, LEXIS®, and WESTLAW®.

7–3

Preparing the legal research memorandum is the final step is the legal analysis and research process. It is from the legal research memorandum that the attorney will build the client's case and make decisions on how best to proceed in solving the client's problem. This important document must be prepared with accuracy, clarity, and sensitivity to any questions the reader is likely to have after reading the memorandum.

REVIEW

Key Terms

Before proceeding, review the key terms listed below to be sure you understand each one. If necessary, read over the corresponding section of the chapter. When you are ready to test your understanding, answer the Review Questions.

citation
cryptography
headnotes
legal analysis
re

Questions for Review and Discussion

1. Define the term *legal analysis* and explain its importance in legal problem solving.
2. What are the five steps in the legal analysis process?
3. Explain how you would use the "5Ws and an H" journalism technique to raise legal analysis questions.
4. What are the categories recommended for use in organizing facts into legal issues?
5. What procedure is followed in analyzing a legal problem?
6. What steps are involved in locating the law that is applicable to the legal problem in question?
7. Decipher the case citation: *State v Caples,* Neb. 1990, 462 N.W.2d 428, 236 Neb. 563.
8. Why is it important to update case citations, and what are two ways of performing this task?

9. How do computer-aided legal research programs work and how do they compare to performing research the old-fashioned way?
10. What are the typical headings of a legal research memorandum?

Activities

1. Research the applicable codes that apply to Polly's cockroach problem. Prepare a legal research memorandum of your findings using the suggested format.
2. Research and prepare a research memorandum for the Montgomery case.
3. Organize a field trip to the local law library and arrange a tour with the librarian.
4. Identify a legal issue problem that you, a friend, or family member have questioned. Write down the facts of the problem in a similar format as the Montgomery case or Polly's case. Proceed with the analysis and research. Prepare a written memorandum of your findings.
5. Locate a law office or law library with a computer-aided legal research program and arrange for a demonstration.
6. Contact a computer-aided legal research vendor and arrange for a demonstration.

PART THREE

LAW OFFICE PROCEDURES AND SYSTEMS

NOTES

CHAPTER 8 Law Office Administration

OUTLINE

8–1 Types of Legal Fees and Costs
- Retainer Fees
- Contingent Fees
- Other Types of Fees
- How Hourly Fees Are Determined
- Other Types of Billing Practices
- Legal Costs and Overhead Expenses

8–2 Keeping Track of Time
- The Importance of Timekeeping
- Timekeeping Systems

8–3 Keeping Track of Costs and Expenses
- Client-Related Costs
- Client-Related Expenses

8–4 Records Management
- Client Confidentiality
- Creating Files
- Records Management Systems
- Managing Inactive Files

COMMENTARY

The firm's administrator called you into his office yesterday and asked why your report of billable hours for the past two weeks was late. He was unsympathetic when you explained how much time you were spending in the law library and locating witnesses for Mr. Sweeney's trial next week. He even threatened to withhold your next paycheck if the reports were not turned in by the end of the day. It's now 4:55 p.m. and you still cannot locate a file that you must have for tomorrow's 8:30 a.m. client interview. While you were on the phone, the administrator left a note on your desk. It said, "No timesheets, no paycheck. No kidding." What is it with these people and their billable hours? And why are files never where they are supposed to be? Is paralegal work supposed to be this complicated? You think there must be something that can be done to make your working life less frustrating. Maybe a chat with the administrator to learn more about the firm's procedures and systems would shed some light on the practice of law from management's point of view. But first, you have timesheets to complete and a file to find.

OBJECTIVES

Each law firm has its own way of doing things; yet all have some administrative procedures and systems in common. After studying this chapter, you should be able to:

1. Discuss the common types of legal fees.
2. Explain how legal fees are determined.
3. Distinguish between legal costs and overhead expenses.
4. Explain the necessity for maintaining time records.
5. Discuss and describe types of timekeeping systems.
6. Define and discuss the term *trust account*.
7. Explain the reasons for and methods of tracking client-related costs and expenses.
8. Define the term *records management*.
9. Discuss ways to maintain client confidentiality.
10. Conduct a conflict-of-interest check.
11. Organize a filing system for active files.
12. Define and use a *tickler system*.
13. Suggest alternative ways of managing inactive client files.

8–1 Types of Legal Fees and Costs

Lawyers sell their services for a fee. The regular collection of fees ensures that the firm will have money available to meet overhead expenses and to provide an income for all employees of the firm. There are a number of types of legal fees. Prior to commencing work on a legal matter, the attorney and client will agree on how fees and costs will be handled. Many states now require that all fee and cost arrangements between attorney and client be in writing. Figure 8–1 is one sample of a written fee agreement published by the State Bar of California.

Retainer Fees

There are several types of retainer fees, as well as several meanings for the word *retainer*. The most common usage of the word retainer applies to the fee paid by a client at the beginning of a specified matter and is usually nonrefundable. The **case retainer** may be the entire fee due for the case or may represent only part of the fee. Case retainers are typical in litigated divorces and criminal cases, but firms may require a retainer in all situations to bind the client to the firm before work is performed.

A **retainer for general representation** is common for businesses, school boards, public entities, or anyone requiring continuing legal services. A flat annual amount is charged for general representation, with the services included and those excluded carefully spelled out in a written agreement. For example, some charges, such as for litigation matters or raising public funds, are not included in most general representation agreements. The general representation retainer provides the client with the ability to forecast annual legal expenses more accurately for budgeting purposes, and provides the law firm with a steady flow of cash.

Although relatively uncommon, the **pure retainer** binds the law firm to the client by including, among other things, the provision that the firm will not

Figure 8–1 Copy of Retainer Agreement

Sample Written Fee Contract #1
Hourly-Short Form—Litigation

DUNN & SWEENEY
2441 Baker Street
Los Angeles, CA 90012
(213) 608-9060

______________ ___, 19___

ATTORNEY-CLIENT FEE CONTRACT

This ATTORNEY-CLIENT FEE CONTRACT ("Contract") is entered into by and between William King ("Client") and Dunn & Sweeney ("Attorney").

1. **CONDITIONS.** This Contract will not take effect, and Attorney will have no obligation to provide legal services, until Client returns a signed copy of this Contract and pays the deposit called for under paragraph 3.

2. **SCOPE AND DUTIES.** Client hires Attorney to provide legal services in connection with ____________________. Attorney shall provide those legal services reasonably required to represent Client, and shall take reasonable steps to keep Client informed of progress and to respond to Client's inquiries. Client shall be truthful with Attorney, cooperate with Attorney, keep Attorney informed of developments, abide by this Contract, pay Attorney's bills on time and keep Attorney advised of Client's address, telephone number and whereabouts.

3. **DEPOSIT.** Client shall deposit $____________ by ____________. The sum will be deposited in a trust account, to be used to pay:

___ Costs and expenses only.
___ Costs and expenses and fees for legal services.

Client hereby authorizes Attorney to withdraw sums from the trust account to pay the costs and/or fees Client incurs. Any unused deposit at the conclusion of Attorney's services will be refunded.

4. **LEGAL FEES.** Client agrees to pay for legal services at the following rates: partners- ___/hour; associates- ___/hour; paralegals- ___/hour; law clerks- ___/hour; and for other personnel as follows, ______________________________. Attorney charges in minimum units of ___ hours.

5. **COSTS AND EXPENSES.** In addition to paying legal fees, Client shall reimburse Attorney for all costs and expenses incurred by Attorney, including, but not limited to, process servers' fees, fees fixed by law or assessed by courts or other agencies, court reporters' fees, long distance telephone calls, messenger and other delivery fees, postage, in-office photocopying at $__________ per page, parking, mileage at $__________ per mile, investigation expenses, consultants' fees, expert witness fees and other similar items. Client authorizes Attorney to incur all reasonable costs and to hire any investigators, consultants or expert witnesses reasonably necessary in Attorney's judgment, unless one or both of the clauses below are initialed by Client and Attorney.

______________ Attorney shall obtain Client's consent before incurring any cost in excess of $____________.
______________ Attorney shall obtain Client's consent before retaining outside investigators, consultants, or expert witnesses.

6. **STATEMENTS.** Attorney shall send Client periodic statements for fees and costs incurred. Client shall pay Attorney's statements within ______ days after each statement's date. Client may request a statement at intervals of no less than 30 days. Upon Client's request Attorney will provide a statement within 10 days.

7. **LIEN.** Client hereby grants Attorney a lien on any and all claims or causes of action that are the subject of Attorney's representation under this Contract. Attorney's lien will be for any sums due and owing to Attorney at the conclusion of Attorney's services. The lien will attach to any recovery Client may obtain, whether by arbitration award, judgment, settlement or otherwise.

8. **DISCHARGE AND WITHDRAWAL.** Client may discharge Attorney at any time. Attorney may withdraw with Client's consent or for good cause. Good clause includes Client's breach of this Contract, Client's refusal to cooperate with Attorney

---

These sample written fee agreement forms are intended to satisfy the basic requirements of Business & Professions Code Section 6148 but may not address varying contractual obligations which may be present in a particular case. The State Bar makes no representation of any kind, express or implied, concerning the use of these forms.

Figure 8–1 *continued*

or to follow Attorney's advice on a material matter or any other fact or circumstance that would render Attorney's continuing representation unlawful or unethical.

9. CONCLUSION OF SERVICES. When Attorney's services conclude, all unpaid charges shall become immediately due and payable. After Attorney's services conclude, Attorney will, upon Client's request, deliver Client's file to Client, along with any Client funds or property in Attorney's possession.

10. DISCLAIMER OF GUARANTEE. Nothing in this Contract and nothing in Attorney's statements to Client will be construed as a promise or guarantee about the outcome of Client's matter. Attorney makes no such promises or guarantees. Attorney's comments about the outcome of Client's matter are expressions of opinion only.

11. EFFECTIVE DATE. This Contract will take effect when Client has performed the conditions stated in paragraph 1, but its effective date will be retroactive to the date Attorney first provided services. The date at the beginning of this Contract is for reference only. Even if this Contract does not take effect, Client will be obligated to pay Attorney the reasonable value of any services Attorney may have performed for Client.

"Attorney"

DUNN & SWEENEY

By: ______________________________
Jeffrey P. Dunn

Address: ______________________________
____

Telephone: ______________________________

"Client"

____
William King

represent a competitor of the client and will keep the client advised of changes in laws or regulations that might have an impact on the client's business.

Contingent Fees

Contingent fees are conditional; they are paid only when a legal matter has been successfully resolved, whether by trial or settlement, and when the money has been received from the unsuccessful party to the lawsuit. Contingent fee arrangements are most common in plaintiff accident lawsuits, product liability matters, and collection cases. In contingent fee matters, if no money is recovered, there is usually no fee due.

The percentage amount to be paid to the law firm is agreed upon between the client and the firm prior to commencing legal action. Typically, contingent fees range from 25 percent to 50 percent of the total money awarded. Different percentage divisions may be agreed to, depending on whether the case is settled or goes to trial. For example, a contingent fee agreement might state that the lawyer's fee is 25 percent if the case is settled, and 33 ⅓ percent if the case goes to trial, or 50 percent if it is appealed.

Limits on the amount an attorney can charge in contingent fee matters have been imposed by some states; likewise, most states prohibit contingent fee arrangements in certain types of cases, such as family law matters and criminal cases.

Other Types of Fees

Fixed Fees Sometimes also called *flat fees*, **fixed fees** are usually associated with the standard services performed by most law firms. These include uncontested divorces, routine adoptions, preparation of a simple will, and forming a small business corporation. In addition, some firms might have a fixed charge for performing such services as making a court appearance, attending or taking a deposition, and preparing a motion or answers to interrogatories.

Statutory Fees Set by state legislatures, **statutory fees** vary from state to state and are most common in probate-estate and real-estate transactions. These percentage fees are calculated on a graduated scale based on the value of the assets being transferred.

Hourly Fees When a client is not being charged for legal services based upon a contingent fee, fixed fee, or statutory fee, then often they are billed according to an established **hourly fee** for time spent on their legal work. The hourly billing rate for attorneys and paralegals is determined after considering many factors, including education, experience, and geographic location of the firm.

How Hourly Fees Are Determined

Before determining how hourly rates are established, the subject of billable hours must first be addressed. **Billable hours** refers to time spent on client matters for which the client can be charged, such as researching a specific point of law or procedure and drafting pleadings. Most law firms have established a minimum number of annual billable hours that each partner, associate, and paralegal is expected to meet. Typically, that average minimum number is 2000–2400 hours for partners; 1600–2000 for associate attorneys; and 1200–1600 for paralegals.

To calculate how billable hours might affect your position as a paralegal, assume your firm operates on a 9 a.m. to 5 p.m. day. You are expected to be on the job 35 hours each week. Allowing for a two-week vacation and another ten days for sick leave, you will actually be present 1680 hours (35 hours per week × 48 weeks) during the year. If your firm requires that you bill a minimum of 1400 hours per year, you will have to bill a little more than 29 hours each week (1400 ÷ 48). No problem, you think. Think again.

You may be pressed to meet your billable hours quota because not every hour spent at work can be billed. For example, you cannot bill clients for a personal phone call, chatting with coworkers about the weekend, or acknowledging a birthday with a mid-afternoon cake and coffee break. Likewise, reviewing and organizing a client's file, updating the library, and looking for a misplaced document may not count toward your billable hours. Put another way, if you work a 35-hour week in order to meet your minimum billable hours quota, you only have 6 nonbillable hours left per week. Since most people spend at least two hours a day in mundane tasks, such as going through the mail, returning phone calls, dealing with interruptions, and engaging in the routine social obligations expected when working in an office, you can begin to comprehend some of the stress and pressures associated with being a paralegal trying to meet a performance standard.

The number of expected billable hours is only one important part of the equation in determining a firm's hourly fees for attorneys and paralegals. There are several ways and many factors to be considered in computing hourly fees, but for purposes of this illustration, we will use a simple expense-based formula that considers both the overhead expenses attributable to each attorney and the compensation they expect to receive.

$$\frac{\text{Overhead Expenses} + \text{Required Compensation}}{\text{Number of billable hours}} = \text{Hourly Rate}$$

For example, assume that a partner's share of annual overhead expenses is $55,000, personal income requirements are $225,000, and the partner typically bills a minimum of 2000 hours each year. Based on this formula, the partner's hourly rate would be:

$$\frac{\$55{,}000 + \$225{,}000}{2000} = \$140.00 \text{ per hour}$$

The actual billing rate, however, might be higher than this expense-based calculation suggests because, in determining hourly billing rates, factors such as reputation, years of experience, and community standards are also considered.

Leveraging Suppose that the custom in the community is a lower hourly billing rate than that calculated by the expense-based formula described above. In this case, the law firm or lawyer has several options: (1) move the practice to an area that would support the hourly rate; (2) cut overhead expenses; (3) lower personal income expectations; or (4) hire associate attorneys and paralegals to make up the difference through a concept known as **leveraging.** Leveraging is the process of making a profit from the services performed by others. For years, lawyers have been hiring associate attorneys not only to provide them with an on-the-job training opportunity, but also to provide the firm with a source of additional revenue. With the emergence of paralegals, law firms have found a valuable new resource that can also provide additional income for the firm.

When calculating the hourly rate for associate attorneys or paralegals, a third factor—profit—is added to the equation. Associate attorneys and paralegals are expected to produce a profit. If they do not, and are merely an additional expense, there is no reason to hire them. To calculate the hourly rate for a paralegal, assume the expense of providing office space and supplies, equipment, and secretarial support for the paralegal is $12,000; salary, employer tax contributions, and benefits are $36,000; and the firm's minimum profit requirement is equal to the expense of the paralegal, or $48,000. Also assume that the firm has established a standard for its paralegals of 1400 billable hours each year. According to our formula, the hourly billing rate for the paralegal, then, would be about $69 per hour:

$$\frac{\$12{,}000 + \$36{,}000 + \$48{,}000}{1400} = \$68.57 \text{ per hour}$$

Similarly, the hourly rate for an associate attorney might be:

$$\frac{\$30{,}000 + \$75{,}000 + \$105{,}000}{1900} = \$110.53 \text{ per hour}$$

Billing rates for associate attorneys and paralegals vary widely, just as they do with partners. It is quite common to find hourly rates for legal services higher in larger law firms and in major metropolitan cities than they are in smaller firms in suburban or rural areas.

There are, of course, other methods used to determine hourly rates, but this simple formula is surprisingly accurate for determining a base to which appropriate adjustments can be made.

Other Types of Billing Practices

Several events occurred during the 1980s that caused law firms to reconsider their old billing practices. Among these events was the increased competition from the growing number of lawyers entering the profession, the emergence of paralegals as an economic resource for the law firms that properly utilized their skills, and the dizzying rate with which firms discarded old equipment and installed computer systems.

Suddenly, lawyers found themselves competing to attract new clients and retain the old ones. Consumers are no longer in the passenger seat when purchasing legal services. They are now the force driving law firms to look at new ways to charge for their services. As a result, many firms now have added value billing and premium billing to their fee arrangement options.

Value Billing Task-based, or **value billing,** is a system in which the lawyer and the client negotiate an agreed-upon fee for a case. The relatively recent introduction of computerized systems and fierce competition into the legal profession have made value billing much more attractive to today's sophisticated consumer of legal services than the once-sacred practice of hourly billing.

Automating the law office eliminated the necessity to create each document from scratch. With the ability to store and retrieve agreements, briefs, pleadings, and corporate minutes, a task that once required several hours of attorney or paralegal time is now completed in a matter of minutes. The question is not whether to use a prior work product, but how much to charge for it.

For example, suppose Client A paid your firm $1500 for a job that required 10 hours of attorney and paralegal time. Then, Client B comes into your office with a similar situation. Because you are able to retrieve your work product performed for Client A and, with a few changes, are able to produce the same result for Client B in two hours instead of ten, how much should Client B be charged? Twenty percent of what Client A was charged, or $300? Would $750, or half the amount, be more reasonable? Or, should Client B pay the same as Client A? The problem is not a simple one.

Most attorneys are experiencing difficulty in agreeing on the application of value billing but few are having difficulty in realizing that increased competition has created the need for an alternative to hourly billing. Clients often choose a lawyer or a law firm based on the client's perception of how the services provided by that lawyer or the firm will best increase the value of the client's assets. From a client's perspective value is added to their assets when a benefit to which they are entitled is obtained, such as recovering damages for a breach of contract, or when the client is able to avoid a risk that would diminish his or her assets, such as being convinced that investing in a certain business venture is sure to lose money. But if the client must pay what he or she considers to be an excessive amount in legal fees, then the value of his/her assets has been diminished.

Consider all the various ethical and practical arguments that the concept of value billing creates and you will begin to understand the complexity of this latest administrative issue causing concern in many law firms.

Premium Billing Adding a surcharge to an amount determined by a firm's hourly rate when a good result is obtained, or charging a higher than usual rate for complex cases is known as **premium billing.** Not widely used, premium billing has been primarily restricted to law firms specializing in mergers and acquisitions. In these complex cases, often involving a hostile takeover, a law firm might turn down other cases and work around the clock for weeks at a time for just one client. If the firm's efforts result in a satisfactory outcome for the client, then an agreed upon premium is added to the previous agreement for legal fees.

Legal Costs and Overhead Expenses

Some costs are involved in all legal actions. These can include the court filing fees, process server's fees, fees for witnesses, and costs for transcripts of testimony. Costs associated with taking legal action are either advanced by the client prior to commencement of the action, with additional requests for costs submitted as they are incurred, or advanced by the law firm and repaid at the conclusion of the case. In either event, the costs associated with a legal action are paid by the client and are in addition to the legal fees.

In addition to the costs associated with taking legal action, many law firms also bill clients for *overhead expenses,* such as photocopies, postage, facsimiles, messenger service, telephone charges, secretarial services, and word processing. Overhead expenses appear either as itemized entries on the client's statement or as a surcharge. A surcharge is a percentage figure, usually no more than 5 percent, that is calculated on the total bill. This surcharge-percentage method for recapturing overhead expenses, although less costly to the firm than providing a record of itemized charges, can be unfair to some clients if the percentage figure is too high.

8–2 Keeping Track of Time

Regardless of the method used to determine the amount of a client's fees, the calculation must include the amount of time required to complete the task. Without good time records, law firms will experience continual cash flow problems because it is from these records that client bills are generated and management decisions are made, such as whether a certain paralegal needs more training in library research and whether certain types of cases are profitable for the firm.

Time is a paradox. Everyone wants more of it, yet we have all the time in the world. Getting the most from your daily 24-hour allotment requires good time-management skills and an equal amount of self-discipline. The problem in many law offices is that although everyone is conscious of the value of time, many are rather lax in recording how their time has been spent. Perhaps in no other profession does the axiom "time is money" hold more truth. Yet, time sheets are often submitted with large blocks of unaccounted time because the timekeeper is not diligent about recording time spent on client matters throughout the day. When timekeepers wait to record their time until the end of the week, their memories are rarely able to reconstruct a detailed analysis of their day-to-day activities. Law firms stand to lose hundreds of thousands of dollars each year from faulty timekeeping.

The Importance of Timekeeping

Time records provide the information from which some court documents, such as accountings in bankruptcy cases, and billing statements to clients are prepared. In addition, time records can provide the law office manager and the timekeepers with useful management information. For example, supervising attorneys can use time reports to review the work of associate attorneys and paralegals to see how long they are taking to perform certain tasks, on what projects they may be spending too much or too little time, and in which areas they may require more training, as well as to monitor their overall performance.

Time records are sometimes also used to motivate the timekeepers. For example, in some law firms weekly or monthly summaries of time reports are circulated in an effort to stimulate competition among the timekeepers and departments.

Since most people underestimate the amount of time involved in performing tasks or litigating a case, timekeeping is an important self-management tool. Keeping track of time will point out poor work habits and tasks that could be delegated and provide a realistic profile of how long projects actually take to complete.

From an administrative point of view, time records alone are the ultimate measure of profitability of any one case, a particular department, or any one attorney or paralegal. Based on time records, a firm might decide to revise its goals, make a change in long-range strategy, reward or terminate an employee, hire additional staff, or adjust its fee schedules.

Paralegals and attorneys are the income producers for the law firm. It is essential to your success that you learn the self-discipline required to record how you use your time throughout the day.

Timekeeping Systems

You can see that keeping accurate time records is one key to the success of the law firm. But just how do you go about keeping track of time? Here are some typical methods.

Converting Time into Decimals Most law firms convert time into decimals for ease and accuracy in recording based on the following conversion table:

0–6 minutes = .1 hour	31–36 minutes = .6 hour
7–12 minutes = .2 hour	37–42 minutes = .7 hour
13–15 minutes = .25 hour	43–45 minutes = .75 hour
16–18 minutes = .3 hour	46–48 minutes = .8 hour
19–24 minutes = .4 hour	49–54 minutes = .9 hour
25–30 minutes = .5 hour	55–60 minutes = 1.0 hour

With the converted decimal system, time can then be recorded using any of a variety of time-keeping systems.

The Time-Planning System The time-planning system is basically a daily or weekly appointment calendar with spaces provided for writing in appointments, things to do, and the amount of time spent for billing purposes. Some time planners, such as the one shown in Figure 8–2, also have spaces for assigning priorities to each item on your list, as well as a place to enter expenses and record memos.

The success of the time-planning system is dependent upon the timekeeper entering enough information so that the person who transcribes the planner will be able to prepare the client's statement from its contents. One advantage of the time-planning system is portability. For attorneys and paralegals who spend a great deal of their time away from the office, this type of system may be favored over other timekeeping methods.

The "One-Write" System Another type of manual timekeeping is the one-write system, which comes with or without carbons and is a convenient way to record billable hours and services performed. It is called a one-write system because each entry is made just once on self-adhering, perforated strips that are subsequently peeled off and attached to the accompanying client/case service record form.

If the timekeeper has legible handwriting, a photocopy of the service record form can be submitted with the client billing. Under these ideal circumstances no recopying or transcription is required, eliminating the opportunity for transposition errors as well as making this system one of the most efficient ways to record and bill for legal services. Most firms using this system require that billing statements be presented in a more professional, typed format describing the services performed but nevertheless find the one-write system ideal for keeping track of time. Figure 8–3 shows both the front and back sides of the one-write timekeeping system.

The Machine System Machine systems for recording time require that all client files have an assigned number and that the file number be available when the work is being performed. The machine system has a built-in clock to record time in decimal units, a numerical keypad for encoding the file number, and a

Figure 8–2 Sample of a Time Planner (discontinued product)

PRIORITY CODES

A. Urgent & Important
B. Important
C. Urgent
D. Low Priority
E. Routine

CONVERSION OF TIME INTO DECIMALS

6 Minutes =	.1 Hour	36 Minutes =	.6 Hour
12 Minutes =	.2 Hour	42 Minutes =	.7 Hour
15 Minutes =	.25 Hour	45 Minutes =	.75 Hour
18 Minutes =	.3 Hour	48 Minutes =	.8 Hour
24 Minutes =	.4 Hour	54 Minutes =	.9 Hour
30 Minutes =	.5 Hour	60 Minutes =	1.0 Hour

NOVEMBER 1992

S	M	T	W	T	F	S
1	2	3	4	5	6	7
8	9	10	11	12	13	14
15	16	17	18	19	20	21
22	23	24	25	26	27	28
29	30					

DECEMBER 1992

S	M	T	W	T	F	S
		1	2	3	4	5
6	7	8	9	10	11	12
13	14	15	16	17	18	19
20	21	22	23	24	25	26
27	28	29	30	31		

JANUARY 1993

S	M	T	W	T	F	S
					1	2
3	4	5	6	7	8	9
10	11	12	13	14	15	16
17	18	19	20	21	22	23
24	25	26	27	28	29	30
31						

INSTRUCTIONS: List all items to be done today, prioritize items according to importance, and number them in the order in which you will perform them.

Monday, December 28, 1992

363RD DAY – 3 DAYS LEFT

Priority Order Code	To Be Done	Time Estimate Hrs. 1/10s	Appointments	Hours	Memos & Expenses
				00 15 30 45 8	
				00 15 30 45 9	
				00 15 30 45 10	
				00 15 30 45 11	
				00 15 30 45 12	
				00 15 30 45 1	
				00 15 30 45 2	
				00 15 30 45 3	
				00 15 30 45 4	
				00 15 30 45 5	
				00 15 30 45	

Tuesday, December 29, 1992

364TH DAY – 2 DAYS LEFT

Priority Order Code	To Be Done	Time Estimate Hrs. 1/10s	Appointments	Hours	Memos & Expenses
				00 15 30 45 8	
				00 15 30 45 9	
				00 15 30 45 10	
				00 15 30 45 11	
				00 15 30 45 12	
				00 15 30 45 1	
				00 15 30 45 2	
				00 15 30 45 3	
				00 15 30 45 4	
				00 15 30 45 5	
				00 15 30 45	

Wednesday, December 30, 1992

365TH DAY – 1 DAY LEFT

Priority Order Code	To Be Done	Time Estimate Hrs. 1/10s	Appointments	Hours	Memos & Expenses
				00 15 30 45 8	
				00 15 30 45 9	
				00 15 30 45 10	
				00 15 30 45 11	
				00 15 30 45 12	
				00 15 30 45 1	
				00 15 30 45 2	
				00 15 30 45 3	
				00 15 30 45 4	
				00 15 30 45 5	
				00 15 30 45	

Source: Law Publications, Inc. Los Angeles, CA (1980). Reprinted with permission.

Figure 8–3 Sample of a Time Record

CODES FOR DESCRIPTION OF SERVICE

CLIENT TIME

A – Court Appearance, Hearings
C – Conference
D – Drafting
L – Letter or Dictation
R – Research
S – Study and Review
T – Telephone
V – Travel

NON-CLIENT TIME

E – Education and Reading
M – Management and Office Administration
X – Bar Association, Community Activities
P – Personal

DECIMAL CONVERSION

IN 6 or 12 MINUTE INTERVALS USE:		IN 15 MINUTE INTERVALS USE:
6 minutes = .1 hour	36 minutes = .6 hour	15 minutes = .25 hour
12 minutes = .2 hour	42 minutes = .7 hour	30 minutes = .5 hour
18 minutes = .3 hour	48 minutes = .8 hour	45 minutes = .75 hour
24 minutes = .4 hour	54 minutes = .9 hour	60 minutes = 1.0 hour
30 minutes = .5 hour	60 minutes = 1.0 hour	

TIME RECORD

	Date	Lawyer	Client & Case	File No.	Description of Service	Time		
							Hours	Decimal
Bend Tab Back						FROM TO		
Bend Tab Back						FROM TO		
Bend Tab Back						FROM TO		
Bend Tab Back						FROM TO		
Bend Tab Back						FROM TO		
Bend Tab Back						FROM TO		
Bend Tab Back						FROM TO		
Bend Tab Back						FROM TO		
Bend Tab Back						FROM TO		
Bend Tab Back						FROM TO		
Bend Tab Back						FROM TO		
Bend Tab Back						FROM TO		
Bend Tab Back						FROM TO		
Bend Tab Back						FROM TO		

FORM TR

Source: Cantor & Company, 110 Hopewell Road, Downingtown, PA 19335. Reprinted with permission.

Figure 8–3 ***continued***

Client
Matter

CLIENT SERVICE RECORD - PAGE

File No.
Attorney

INSTRUCTIONS: This form is for use with attorney Time Record supplies. Open one Client Service Record for each billable matter. Number each form behind the word "page". If more than one lawyer records time against the matter, use one of the three columns on the right of the form, and post each lawyer's time into a separate column. Monthly, or at the time of billing, multiply each lawyer's recorded hours by his billing rate, and enter the total time-dollar value of all attorneys in the "Dollar Balance" column. When a client is interim billed, subtract the amount of the bill (or the amount specified by the billing attorney) from the "Dollar Balance" column, and describe the billing beneath the last time strip pasted to the form.

PASTE TIME STRIPS HERE

Form CRS

Attorney →

Balance F'wd. →

Dollar Bal.

preestablished code for the work performed. Here is an abbreviated example of a work-performed code system:

Code	Work Performed
01	Telephone call to client
02	Telephone call from client
03	Prepare letter to client
04	Draft legal document
05	Attend deposition

The machine system offers the flexibility of assigning up to 99 coded work designations to fit almost any law-office task. Time is recorded on a roll of paper, similar to an adding machine roll. At the end of the timekeeping period, the codes must be transcribed for billing purposes by a secretary or billing clerk. When using the machine system, care must be taken to transcribe the codes accurately, and to remember to start the clock when commencing work on a file and to turn off the clock when finished. Otherwise, you might find a six-minute entry for preparing several pages of interrogatories or a five-hour telephone call appearing on the client's statement!

Computerized Timekeeping Systems The continuing proliferation of software packages designed specifically for law offices indicates a growing interest in using computers to record time. Most law office managers are excited by these programs because they often eliminate several steps, as well as errors, by combining the timekeeping and billing processes. For example, one software package allows you to turn on and off a stopwatch that tracks time and creates an electronic time slip for each billable activity. You simply enter the user's name, the client's name, an optional case number or name, and the activity performed. This program even allows you to keep track of billable telephone calls without changing programs.

Some programs interface with some PBX telephone systems, allowing for the metering of phone calls from the time the receiver is picked up to the time it is put down. With this type of software, the value of time spent is automatically calculated and inserted on the timeslip, as well as onto the several types of financial management reports it generates.

Both custom-designed and off-the-shelf software programs are gaining popularity among law-office managers and attorneys for keeping track of billable time. The reason is clear: When computerized systems are used by attorneys and paralegals, most time records—especially those kept on activities performed in the office—do not need to go through the additional step of being transcribed by a secretary or the billing clerk, thus eliminating errors and saving time.

The primary purpose of keeping time records is so the lawyers will know how much it costs them to provide legal services to clients, not to determine the fee to charge by multiplying the number of hours by the billing rate. In fact many recorded hours are not billed to the client. This can occur when a pleading needs to be rewritten because of attorney or paralegal error, or when a new paralegal takes twice as long to complete a task as would an experienced legal assistant. Whether or not your work can be billed to the client is a decision to be made by the attorney. But making sure that all your time is properly recorded is a decision and commitment that you make to yourself and to the firm.

8–3 Keeping Track of Costs and Expenses

It is important to the financial welfare of the law firm to keep records not only of time from which fees are determined but also records of client-related costs and expense items. The costs associated with litigation, such as court filing fees, witness fees, and transcripts of depositions, are often recovered by the prevailing party in a lawsuit. Some overhead expense items, such as long-distance telephone calls, faxes, and photocopies are often charged back to the client.

Client-Related Costs

Because of the increasing costs of taking legal action, most law firms today have abandoned the practice of advancing client costs. Instead, clients are usually required to advance court filing fees themselves and to reimburse the firm for any other costs incurred on the client's behalf as soon as they are billed.

In most instances, when a client agrees to retain a law firm he or she is required to place some money on deposit in the firm's client **trust account,** which is a checking account established for the specific purpose of holding money deposited by one party for the benefit of another. Trust account monies do not belong to the law firm until they are earned and are not to be used to pay the day-to-day operating expenses of the firm, such as salaries and rent. Rather, sums deposited into the firm's trust account belong to the client and are to be used to pay for court fees and other related items. Periodic accountings must be provided to the client indicating how his or her money has been spent and the amount of any balance remaining in the account. Any sums remaining after the close of the client's legal matter must be returned to the client.

Law firms always have at least one client trust account into which sums belonging to clients are deposited for safekeeping. Some firms have more than one trust account, but separate trust accounts need not be established for each individual client. Sums on deposit for individual clients are tracked through the firm's bookkeeping system. Both state and local bar associations take an active role in establishing guidelines for maintaining client trust accounts as well as punishing those who might abuse their fiduciary responsibility.

Client-Related Expenses

It is not unusual for expense items, such as long-distance telephone calls, photocopies, and messenger services, to be paid by the client. In order to charge expense items back to the client, however, the client must be aware that he or she will be billed for these, and accurate records must be kept.

Telephone Charges Preprinted long-distance call record forms, such as those shown in Figure 8–4, are used to track telephone calls. This manual record-keeping system usually recaptures only a minimal percentage of actual telephone expenses, because people who place the calls forget to write down complete information. If remembering at the end of the week how time was spent is difficult, trying to recall several telephone numbers and the reasons for the calls is virtually impossible.

Figure 8-4 Long-distance Call Record Form and Telephone Conference Record

LONG DISTANCE CALL RECORD

Date ______ Time Start ______ Time Stop ______ Total Time ______

CLIENT CASE ____________ FILE NO. ______

Place Called ____________ Phone No. ______

CALL ☐ To ☐ From ____________ Of ______

SUBJECT ____________

WHAT I SAID ____________

WHAT HE (SHE) SAID ____________

Amount $ ______

Charge To: ____________ TAX $ ______

TOTAL $ ______

Signature ____________

SAMPLE

TELEPHONE CONFERENCE RECORD

Date ______ Time Start ______ Time Stop ______ Total Time ______

CLIENT/CASE ____________ FILE NO. ______

CALL ☐ To ☐ From ____________ Of ______

SUBJECT ____________

WHAT I SAID ____________

WHAT HE (SHE) SAID ____________

Signature ____________

SAMPLE

Source: All-state Legal Supply Co. Cranford, NJ (1992). Reprinted with permission.

Another drawback to a manual system is that someone must compare the monthly telephone bill with all the call record forms to determine the actual amount of the call in order to bill the client. This is a time-consuming task producing only marginal results. Several companies, however, including some telephone companies, have electronic and computerized systems to track telephone charges. One popular device uses a numeric or alphanumeric data-entry terminal that records who is making the phone call and for whom. Without entering the proper input commands, the user is virtually locked out of the telephone system and cannot place outgoing calls.

Likewise, most local telephone companies, through their central switching location software system, can provide a monthly itemized list of telephone calls placed within their service area from each telephone in the firm. This type of call-tracking system provides more control over telephone charges because it monitors each individual telephone in the office.

A medium-sized law firm can spend $75,000 or more each year in telephone services. Assuming that 75 percent of these charges are directly related to client cases, when everyone is diligent about using the call record forms, the firm could expect to recover about $57,000 of its annual telephone expenses.

Facsimile Charges Perhaps not since the microwave oven has a technological device gained such wide acceptance so quickly and become a standard piece of equipment in the law office as the fax machine. Since even a small law firm can send and receive over 1000 facsimile pages each month, many firms now have more than one facsimile to keep work flowing.

There are several methods to track facsimile expenses. One way is to keep a log next to the facsimile machine to record the date, client case number, and number of pages sent or received. The client is then charged on a per-page basis, such as $1 or $2 per page. A data-entry terminal similar to the one for tracking telephone calls and using a numeric or alphanumeric code is another way to keep track of who is sending facsimiles and to whom.

Photocopy Expenses The modern-day law office cannot survive without at least one photocopy machine. Depending on the size of the office, most have one or more backup photocopiers for emergency or deadline situations. One of the more frustrating events in a law firm is to have work come to a halt because the photocopy machine has broken down or is being serviced.

Debit card cost-control systems, metered key-access systems, and coded data-entry terminals are common ways for law firms to control access to the photocopier and to record client account-billing information. Of course, it is also possible to record the information manually on a preprinted form, but this method is the least efficient and effective way to track photocopier usage.

A typically busy copier makes about 50,000 copies per month. With approximately 80 percent of these copies billable to clients at an average of 10 cents per copy, the firm may be able to recover about $4000 each month per copier.

Messenger and Courier Service Expenses Most law firms in major metropolitan areas are addicted to messenger services. Poor time management, procrastination, too many deadlines, and unreliable postal services have contributed to the rise in use of messengers and overnight couriers.

Figure 8–5 Messenger/Courier Service

Paralegals will sign for documents delivered by a messenger service. *Source:* Bob Mullenix.

Costs vary from company to company and are changed frequently, currently ranging from $10 and up for next-day air letters. All messenger and courier services provide the sender with a completed form that can be used to track a lost or delayed package. This same form can be used to reconcile the monthly statement and allocate charges to the appropriate client.

It is not uncommon even for smaller law firms to incur monthly charges of $300 to $500 for overnight or same-day delivery services.

8–4 Records Management

When PCs (personal computers) were first introduced there was great excitement about the dawning era of paperless offices. That didn't happen. Instead, the use of more computers in more law firms has generated more paper than ever before, resulting in the need to manage, store, and retrieve all that information more efficiently and effectively.

Arguably, a law office's most valuable resource is its clients' records or files. Proper management of these records and files—from creation to destruction—will save time, money, and frustration. **Records management** is the systematic storage of paper records for quick retrieval upon demand. Records management can be done manually, with a computer, or by using a combination of both systems. Regardless of the system used by your firm, the primary concern for everyone must be to protect the contents of the clients' files.

Client Confidentiality

When clients come to a lawyer, the matters to be discussed are often highly sensitive, personal, or emotional. Members of the firm must protect and preserve client confidences not only as a matter of courtesy but because the American Bar Association Rules for Professional Conduct require that client matters be held in strict confidence.

For clients to feel free to discuss all aspects of their case with attorneys, paralegals, and secretaries, they must believe that confidentiality is important to everyone in the law firm, starting with the receptionist. At the reception desk computer screens, client files, message slips, and scraps of paper that are being used by the receptionist must be hidden from view of anyone who might be in the reception area and then put away or disposed of properly when work on the file is finished.

Before inviting a client into your office, make sure that all files and documents have been removed from the top of your desk except those that pertain to the client's business. Adjust your computer screen so it is only visible to you. Put away any file folders or documents in the room that could be seen by a client.

Clients should be greeted quietly and their arrival discreetly announced without using their name, if possible. For example, the receptionist should use the intercom to let you know "Your 10:30 appointment is here" instead of "Jack Smith is here to see you about his divorce matter." By announcing the client's arrival in the former manner the receptionist has kept the client's identity confidential to anyone who might be in the reception area or your office.

When a client is calling the firm to speak with an attorney, paralegal, or secretary, the receptionist can also aid in protecting confidences by asking, "Will Ms. Jones know what this is regarding?" instead of, "May I tell Ms. Jones what this is regarding?"

Do not accept any calls while a client is in your office unless the call pertains to the client's business. Doing so is not only rude to the client who is sitting in your office but could result in an embarrassing breach of confidentiality of the caller.

At the end of the day, all client files should be put away, and in some cases locked away, in your desk, credenza, or filing cabinets. It may be unlikely that anyone from outside the firm would have an interest in your client files, but why take a chance? Espionage is not confined to spies from intelligence-gathering

Figure 8–6a A Traditional File Stack

A manual records management system can sometimes be time-consuming when trying to retrieve a file. *Source:* Bob Mullenix.

agencies. Messy divorce cases and corporate mergers have been known to generate a great deal of interest from parties who have huge financial stakes in the outcome. Making sure that files are locked up at night is one way to ensure that they do not fall into the wrong hands.

There is another benefit to keeping files in filing cabinets. Paper files are

Figure 8–6b Computer Disk Records System

File management has become more efficient with the use of the computer. *Source:* Mug Shots/The Stock Market. Reprinted with permission.

highly combustible. In the event of a fire, files outside their cabinets not only provide fuel for the flame but are more likely to be lost or damaged than those inside the cabinets, even if the cabinets are not fireproof.

Since client files are one of the firm's most valuable assets, everyone must take responsibility for protecting them.

Creating Files

There are several steps involved in creating a new file, whether the file is for a new client of the firm or for a current client. The first step involves completing a routine information sheet for the firm's records with such items as the client's name, address, and telephone numbers, as well as other parties to the action and their attorneys, fee arrangements, billing arrangements, and any noteworthy comments regarding the client or the case. Some firms create their own forms for this purpose. The new case memo form shown in Figure 8–7 is illustrative of the types available from supply houses.

Checking for Conflict of Interest Once all the pertinent information has been gathered, and before an actual file is opened, research of current and past clients must be conducted for a possible **conflict of interest.** A *conflict of interest* exists in a situation where regard for one duty leads to disregard of another. For example, an attorney representing both parties in a divorce action may discount the needs of one party in favor of the other; or, unknowingly, one attorney in your firm may have a financial interest in a corporation that asked one of the other lawyers in the firm to represent it in a litigation matter. The potential for a conflict of interest is particularly high when there are several lawyers in the firm. In all cases, once an actual conflict of interest exists, the attorney must withdraw and new counsel must be engaged. Since substituting counsel is costly and embarrassing, care should be taken to ensure that no possible conflict of interest exists before agreeing to represent any party in a legal action.

The process of checking for conflicts of interest usually begins with a paralegal, then continues through a records management clerk or the billing clerk, and ends finally with the lawyers themselves. You begin the conflicts check by searching the new file records for any other cases in which the firm has represented this same client, either as a plaintiff or defendant. Once that information is obtained, you then proceed to search the file records for any cases in which the firm might have represented or had another case against the adverse party. List any cases you find that might present a possible conflict of interest under the "Notes" section on the New Case Memo form before you pass it along to the billing department or the records management clerk. When the client is a corporation, the conflicts check should include the officers of the corporation, subsidiary corporations, and the parent corporation, if any.

Law firms that are fully automated will run a check on their client database for any of the names appearing on the new case memo form. Smaller firms without a computerized client database rely on their alphabetical client file card index, as well as on the memories of their attorneys.

Once the conflict check is completed, a physical file can be opened. Most law firms use some sort of a multipart, preprinted form with carbons attached, similar to the one shown in Figure 8–8 when opening new files. With one typing, copies of all relevant information regarding the case are provided to the attorney and secretary, bookkeeping, central filing, and the file itself.

The Client Database Information pertaining to a new client is also entered into the law firm's database as soon as the file is opened. Whether the firm is automated and all client records are accessed by computer, or whether the firm uses a manual index system to keep track of its clients, the integrity of any system is dependent upon the accuracy of the information in it. Accuracy, in turn, is largely a function of how often the system is updated to keep it current.

A computerized client database serves several functions. One is to provide

Figure 8–7 Sample of New Case Memo Set

NEW CASE MEMO SET

CLIENT INFORMATION

CLIENT ______ FILE NO. ______
ADDRESS ______ DATE OPENED ______
______ ☐ NEW CLIENT ☐ PRESENT CLIENT
PHONE(S): HOME ______ BUSINESS ______

CASE INFORMATION

FILE TITLE ______
MATTER ______
______
______
TYPE OF CASE ______
REFERRED BY ______ OBTAINED BY ______
RESPONSIBLE ATTORNEY ______ ASSIGNED TO ______
ADVERSE PARTY ______
ADDRESS ______
PHONE(S) ______
OPPOSING ATTORNEY ______
ADDRESS ______
PHONE(S) ______

FEE ARRANGEMENTS

☐ FIXED FEE OF $ ______ ☐ HOURLY RATE AT $ ______ PER HOUR
☐ HOURLY RATE AT $ ______ PER HOUR PLUS ______ % OF AMOUNT ☐ RECOVERED ☐ SAVED
☐ ESTIMATED FEE IN THE RANGE OF $ ______ TO $ ______
☐ CONTINGENT FEE OF ______ % OF AMOUNT ☐ RECOVERED ☐ SAVED ☐ OTHER ______
☐ FEE TO BE DETERMINED ON BASIS OF ALL RELEVANT FACTORS ☐ RETAINER OF $ ______ PER ☐ MONTH ☐ YEAR
NUMBER OF HOURS OF SERVICE COVERED BY RETAINER: UP TO ______ HOURS PER ☐ MONTH ☐ YEAR
EXCESS HOURS TO BE BILLED AT $ ______ PER HOUR.
☐ OTHER ______

BILLING ARRANGEMENTS

BILL ☐ MONTHLY ☐ QUARTERLY ☐ ON COMPLETION ☐ OTHER ______
☐ RETAINER OF $ ______ RECEIVED ON ______ ☐ TOWARDS FEE & COSTS
☐ $ ______ TOWARDS FEE
☐ $ ______ TOWARDS COSTS
☐ CLIENT'S DEPOSIT ACCOUNT OF $ ______ RECEIVED ON ______
TOWARDS FEES AND COSTS AS INCURRED. ACCOUNT TO BE MAINTAINED AT $ ______ UNTIL COMPLETION.

NOTES

______
______
______
______
______
______
______
______
______

Source: All-state Legal Supply Co. Cranford, NJ (1992). Reprinted with permission.

Figure 8–8 Sample of New Case Multipart Set

NEW CASE MULTIPART SET

©1974 by LAW PUBLICATIONS, A Division of All-state Legal Supply Co.
5910 Bowcroft Street, Los Angeles, California 90016
To reorder specify Form CS-1

CLIENT
MATTER
ADDRESS
PHONE
TYPE OF CASE
DATE OPENED:
ADVERSE PARTY:
ADDRESS:
PHONE:
FILE NO.
NOTES
OPPOSING ATTY.
ADDRESS:
PHONE:
RESP. ATTY.
REFERRED BY:
FILE NO.
CLIENT
MATTER
FILE NO.

SAMPLE

1. Snap set apart by removing stubs.
2. **White gummed sheet**—Moisten and attach top part on file folder; moisten and attach bottom part on file tab.
3. **Yellow sheet** — for attorney responsible for case.
4. **Pink sheet** — for office manager. File alphabetically by client's name.
5. **Green gummed sheet** — moisten and attach top part on client's ledger; moisten and attach middle part on type of case index; moisten and attach bottom part on either numerical index or on follow up "tickler."
6. **Blue sheet** — file numerically by file number; alphabetically by matter, adverse party's name, or by client's name as required.

Source: All-state Legal Supply Co. Cranford, NJ (1992). Reprinted with permission.

accurate information about clients to those in the law firm who may need the information. Most of the client database software programs include an activities file for each client, which will provide an up-to-date status report so that telephone calls can be returned or consultations held without chasing down a client's paper file. This results in a tremendous time savings for both attorneys and staff.

Records Management Systems

In most law offices you will find one of the three basic filing systems—alphabetic, numeric, and subject files—or combinations of the three, with the newest system for records management, barcoding, beginning to find its way into law firms.

Alphabetic Files Strict alphabetic filing is the arrangement of files or materials by the name of the client, organization, or title (when used for creating forms files). Precise rules exist for filing alphabetically, and unless everyone is familiar with them, unlimited opportunities exist for misplacing the files. Perhaps worse than the frustration caused by misplaced files, alphabetical filing destroys any attempt to maintain client confidentiality because anyone can locate files just by looking under the client's name, and the tabs of any files lying around can be seen and read easily.

Numeric Files Because using numbers is more accurate than using letters for filing purposes—most people can remember that 17 comes after 16, but many have difficulty remembering whether McDonald comes before or after Madison—most law firms today, especially those with a computerized billing system, use a numeric filing system.

Here is one example of a numeric filing system: A firm might choose to include the year in its numbering system, as a reminder of when the file was opened, as well as the sequential number of the file. The first file opened in 1993 would then be assigned the number 93-0001, the second file would carry the number 93-0002, and so on. This system has the added advantage of letting you know exactly how many new files were opened in any year.

Another example of a numeric filing system might be to assign each area of the practice a thousand series and number each new file sequentially in the series. For example, in one firm the litigation department files are in the 1000 to 1999 range, so file number 1067 means that the file is the sixty-seventh litigation file opened. If the firms wishes to track the number of cases brought into the firm annually, it can use the year as part of its numbering system, adding it at the end like this: 1067.93. Corporate clients with several files can be assigned their own numbers, still incorporating the basic numbering plan. For instance, all Jade Corporation files are in the 6000 series. Consequently, file number 6125.93 is the one hundred twenty-fifth file opened for Jade Corporation, and it was opened in 1993.

Some firms use a combination of digits and letters such as 93-0001 LT. This file number tells us that the first file opened in 1993 was a litigation file. 93-0025 EP would indicate that the twenty-fifth file opened in 1993 was an estate planning client. A quick periodic audit can tell the attorneys where the firm is, or should be, placing its marketing emphasis.

All numeric filing systems require also some kind of alphabetic client index, or you will not be able to locate the file using only the client's name. The multipart sets described in this chapter provide copies for filing in the attorney's and the secretary's alphabetic index. In addition, one notebook should be kept in a central location with each file number recorded as it is assigned to a file so that subsequent files will have the correct number in sequence. In most offices, one person is assigned the task of opening new files to eliminate the possibility of two or more files having the same number.

Subject Files Reference files, personal files, and form files may be maintained according to the subject to which they relate. In law firms, form files are the mainstay of the filing system since so much of legal work is repetitious. These "boilerplate" forms are usually filed according to categories such as family law, real estate, personal injury, and probate, with subdivisions for various forms within each subject category.

Using form files saves money for the client and the firm; but one major drawback with subject files is that there may be a problem in getting two people to agree on what to call the file. And, at times, even one person may have trouble deciding on a name. To be useful, then, subject files should also have a written, cross-referenced guide indicating under what subject certain materials are to be found.

Filing systems can also be arranged according to department, division, region, and geographic location, but these systems are more likely to be found in the law department of a large corporation than in private law firms.

Barcoding Files In just a few years barcoding has progressed from an obscure supermarket-based device to mainstream records management in organizations that must manage numerous paper files. Still underutilized in law firms, barcoding is one way to eliminate records management drudgery, promote efficiency, save money, and keep track of files. By applying barcodes to individual files, then scanning the barcodes of the files in use at the end of the day at the desk of their last location, keeping track of files is easy. Instead of spending hours locating a file, you simply enter the file number into the computer and its last known location will appear on the screen.

Implementing a barcode system requires a personal computer, a laser printer,

Figure 8–9 PC-Wand Barcode Emulator

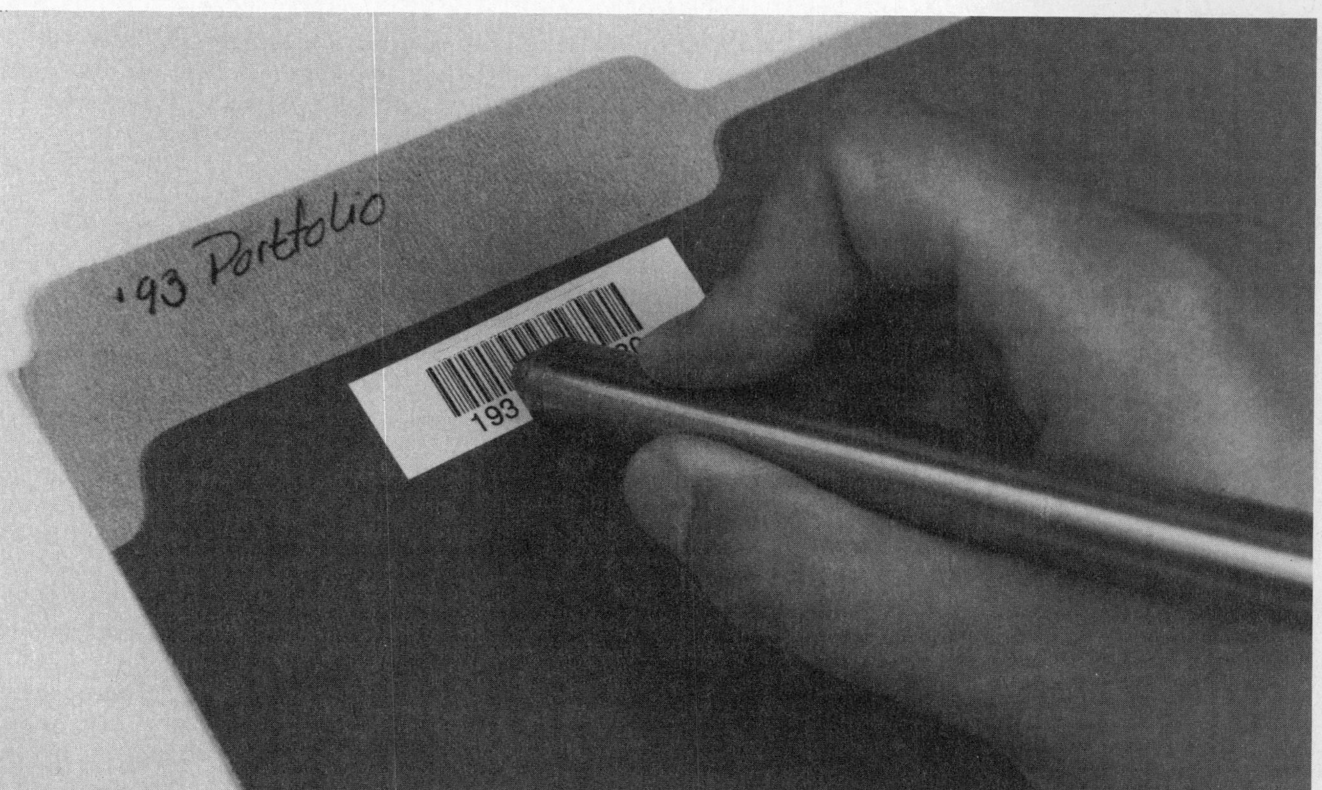

A PC-Wand is used to scan a file's barcode to identify the file and track its last location. *Source:* Aaron Haupt.

software, and a reader. Document-tracking equipment and software is now available from several distributors or can be easily programmed by a knowledgeable computer programmer. As the cost of this technology continues to fall, law firms will find barcoding particularly attractive, since it can be integrated with other administrative systems. For example, barcoded client files might be used in conjunction with barcoded employee identification cards to record billable time. Additionally, many courts nationwide are experimenting with barcoding court files, and at most test sites the results are encouraging. In the future using barcoded document-tracking systems in the law office may not be an option but a necessity.

Organizing Files Nothing presents a more unprofessional image than a client file full of loose papers. Disorganized files are inefficient and can be embarrassing to the person who must use them. Imagine appearing in court or before a client and not being able to locate important documents in the file or, worse yet, opening the file and having all the papers fall onto the floor.

All materials in the file should be punched and hung on metal fasteners in reverse chronological order so that the material on top is the latest material in the file. If the case is a relatively simple matter, all documents and correspondence pertaining to it may be kept in the same folder. In that instance, the correspondence is kept on one side of the folder, usually the left-hand side, and legal documents are placed on the right. In complex cases requiring numerous documents, individual folders are often created to hold exhibits, correspondence, pleadings, research memoranda, and attorney notes.

Many firms use a **docket** sheet to summarize the contents of the legal documents in the file and index tabs to make locating the document easy. The docket sheet usually contains several columns to be completed when a document is placed in the file. The far left column indicates the date the document is placed in the file; the next column summarizes the document's contents or the title of the document, such as Motion to Dismiss; the third column from the left is used to indicate the attorney's initials who prepared the document; and the last column shows the index tab number. With this system, anyone using the file can quickly access the required document without having to look through the entire file.

Tickler System A **tickler** is a memorandum book, calendar, or file to remind attorneys, paralegals, and secretaries of deadlines that must not be missed. A tickler system is not only the firm's first line of defense against client malpractice claims, but is required to be described in detail on applications for professional liability insurance.

The basic manual tickler system consists of index card drawers similar to those still found in the reference section of some libraries and reminder forms. The drawers are divided by tabs into all twelve months of the current year, as well as for three to five years in the future. Each month is further divided by tabbed cards into days 1 through 31. Deadlines, appearance dates, and other reminders are recorded on individual forms and placed behind the appropriate date and month.

Some law firms design their own forms to use with their tickler system. Others use index cards or commercially available preprinted forms. Regardless of the type of form used, it is imperative that you train yourself to use the tickler system. As a rule of thumb, nearly every piece of paper that comes across your desk will require at least two notations: on your desk calendar and on the tickler.

Figure 8–10 Sample of File Docket Sheet

DATE	TITLE OF DOCUMENT	ATTY	TAB #

For example, a letter from opposing counsel requesting a witness's deposition requires a response within a certain time period. The date the response is due should be recorded on your desk calendar, which is your personal version of a tickler, as well as a notation two or three days prior to the due date to give you time to take appropriate action. The same dates need to be entered on the tickler. If you are unavailable to take the required action, the file will still be pulled from the tickler reminder and given to someone else to follow through on. Here is a short list of items that are typically recorded on the tickler:

- Statutes of limitation
- Court appearance dates
- Due date on court pleadings

Figure 8–11 Sample of Tickler Reminder Form

REMINDER

REMINDER DATE: Month: ________ Day: ________ Year:

TO: ____________________

FILE NAME: ____________________ FILE NUMBER: ________

ACTION REQUIRED: ____________________

____

____

____

CRITICAL DATE: ____________________

This reminder prepared by: ____________ on ________

- Tax return dates
- Closing dates for real estate transactions
- Date to deliver a file to an attorney
- Corporation renewal dates
- Due dates on trial briefs

One or two secretaries or paralegals are usually given joint responsibility for managing the tickler system. At the beginning of each day, the designated individual pulls all the reminder slips for that day. If that day happens to be a Friday or a holiday, then reminder slips are also pulled for the following one or two days. The secretary or paralegal then locates the file indicated on the slip and takes appropriate action or forwards it to the person indicated on the reminder form.

When files are removed from the filing cabinet, most law firms use a checkout card to indicate who has possession of the file. Replacing a file with a checkout card also indicates that a file has been intentionally removed, not just misfiled. Once activity on the file is finished, a new slip is completed and returned to the tickler system, and the file is returned to its cabinet.

Some firms have purchased computer software that integrates a tickler system with a master calendar. The master calendar contains all the important court appearance dates and deadlines for each attorney in the firm. Master calendars are updated daily, usually by a paralegal, then printed and distributed to everyone in the firm at least once a week.

Figure 8–12 Sample of File Out Card

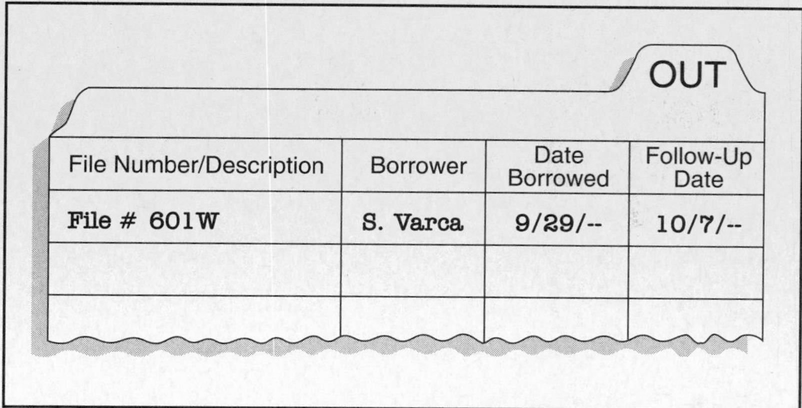
OUT

File Number/Description	Borrower	Date Borrowed	Follow-Up Date
File # 601W	S. Varca	9/29/--	10/7/--

Managing Inactive Files

Attorneys like to keep everything—forever. Although there may be a good reason to keep much of the documentation in a client's file for a period of time after the case has been resolved, the rising cost of office space and off-site warehousing facilities makes an equally good case for designing procedures for systematic file evaluation and review. Often it is best to give some, or all, of the file contents back to the client or to destroy them rather than pay for storage in some remote location for material never to be looked at again.

Records Retention Some documents, by law, must be retained for certain periods of time. The retention of other documents is left to the discretion of the firm. Figure 8–13 is a records retention guideline compiled by the Association of Legal Administrators. Finding suitable storage equipment and facilities for these items alone requires good planning and careful budgeting.

Micrographics Another way to store client files and documents is to use microfilm or microfiche. Just about everyone is familiar with **microfilm,** a process in which paper documents are put on a roll film cartridge or jacket of film, and **microfiche,** a sheet of microfilm containing rows of images in a grid pattern. These are the systems commonly found in libraries for storage of newspapers, magazines, and other print media. The user inserts the film cartridge or the sheet of microfilm into a reader to access the information, or a reader-printer if a photocopy of the information is required.

Plain-paper printing technology has now been incorporated by the major vendors in their micrographics systems, making microfilming a viable alternative in storing inactive files. It is now possible to store the information contained in one filing cabinet on a small role of film, and, if required, to produce a legible copy within minutes.

Micrographic technology is developing at a rapid pace. Soon reader-printers will be linked to computers to search the microfilm automatically upon command for the required documents, then transmit the image on the film to remote sites via facsimile or laser technology. As this technology is developed and becomes affordable, active files could also be kept on microfilm, thus greatly reducing the amount of office space needed to store client records.

Optical Disk Storage Because of its expense, optical disk technology is best suited for large law firms with huge databases and frequent retrieval activity.

Figure 8–13 Sample of Records Retention Guide

Type of Records	Retention Time
Accident reports/claims (settled cases)	7 years
Accounts payable ledgers and schedules	7 years
Accounts receivable ledgers and schedules	7 years
Audit reports	Permanently
Bank reconciliations	2 years
Bank statements	3 years
Capital stock and bond records: ledgers, transfer registers, stubs showing issues, record of interest coupons, opinions, etc.	Permanently
Cash books	Permanently
Charts of accounts	Permanently
Checks (canceled—see exception below)	7 years
Checks (canceled for important payments, i.e. taxes, purchases of property, special contracts, etc. Checks should be filed with the papers pertaining to the underlying transaction)	Permanently
Contracts, mortgages, notes, and leases (expired)	7 years
Contracts, mortgages, notes, and leases (still in effect)	Permanently
Correspondence (general)	3 years
Correspondence (legal and important matters only)	Permanently
Correspondence (routine) with customers and/or vendors	2 years
Deeds, mortgages, and bills of sale	Permanently
Depreciation schedules	Permanently
Duplicate deposit slips	2 years
Employment applications	3 years
Expense analyses/expense distribution schedules	7 years
Financial statements (year-end, other optional)	Permanently
Garnishments	7 years
General/private ledgers, year-end trial balance	Permanently
Insurance policies (expired)	3 years
Insurance records, current accident reports, claims, policies, etc.	Permanently
Internal audit reports (longer retention periods may be desirable)	3 years
Internal reports (miscellaneous)	3 years
Inventories of products, materials, and supplies	7 years
Invoices (to customers, from venders)	7 years
Journals	Permanently
Magnetic tape and tab cards	1 year
Minute books of directors, stockholders, bylaws, and charter	Permanently
Notes receivable ledgers and schedules	7 years
Option records (expired)	7 years
Patents and related papers	Permanently
Payroll records and summaries	7 years
Personnel files (terminated)	7 years
Petty cash vouchers	3 years
Physical inventory tags	3 years
Plant cost ledgers	7 years
Property appraisals by outside appraisers	Permanently
Property records, including costs, depreciation reserves, year-end trial balances, depreciation schedules, blueprints, and plans	Permanently
Purchase orders (except purchasing department copy)	1 year
Purchase orders (purchasing department copy)	7 years
Receiving sheets	1 year
Retirement and pension records	Permanently
Requisitions	1 year
Sales commission reports	3 years
Sales records	7 years
Scrap and salvage records (inventories, sales, etc.)	7 years
Stenographers' notebooks	1 year
Stock and bond certificates (canceled)	7 years
Stockroom withdrawal forms	1 year
Subsidiary ledgers	7 years
Tax returns and worksheets, revenue agents' reports, and other documents relating to determination of income tax liability	Permanently
Time books/cards	7 years
Trademark registrations and copyrights	Permanently
Training manuals	Permanently
Union agreements	Permanently
Voucher register and schedules	7 years
Vouchers for payments to vendors, employees, etc. (includes allowances and reimbursement of employees, officers, etc., for travel and entertainment expenses)	7 years
Withholding tax statements	7 years

Source: Association of Legal Administrators, Vernon Hills, IL (1987). Reprinted with permission.

Documents are put onto a disk with the use of a scanner. Information can then be retrieved on a computer screen and printed out on a printer. Some systems have **split-screen** capability. Documents can be retrieved in original form and displayed on the left side of the screen while modifications are performed to a copy on the right side of the screen. The integrity of the original document is preserved through a locking mechanism in the software. The split-screen technology works particularly well for long forms that require occasional modification, such as real estate leases and lengthy securities documentation. Since 13 or more file drawers of information can be stored on one disk, one of these systems would significantly decrease any firm's records storage space requirements.

Paper Shredders Many law firms have purchased paper shredding machines not only for the purpose of disposing of inactive files that they no longer wish to retain, but also for protecting client confidentiality. One look at the amount and content of paper filling the firm's trash can every day is usually reason enough to give serious thought to managing this waste more effectively.

The job of deciding how best to manage the firm's paper records is often delegated to a paralegal in law firms without a full-time records manager, because a paralegal should be able to tell which papers are important to keep and which can be destroyed. Likewise, other administrative tasks, such as updating the pocket supplements in the library and making sure that everyone's timesheets are turned in to the billing clerk on time are often the responsibility of a paralegal. The size of the law firm will often determine the breadth of the position's responsibilities, but you should not assume that the duties of a paralegal are limited to library research and drafting legal pleadings.

SUMMARY

8–1

There are several types of legal fee arrangements. Among them are retainer agreements, contingent fees, fixed fees, statutory fees, and hourly fee rates. Because of increased competition, the emergence of paralegals, and automation of the law office, many law firms are considering value billing and premium billing as alternatives to standard billing practices. Legal fees are determined in several ways. Contingent fees and statutory fees are percentage-based. Fixed fee and some retainer fee agreements are based upon an estimate of the amount of time to be spent on the client's legal matter. In determining hourly rates several factors, such as experience, reputation, and community custom are considered, as well as overhead expenses and individual income requirements. In addition to being charged a fee for services performed, clients are typically expected to pay all costs and expenses associated with their legal action.

8–2

Time is a valuable resource for the law firm. Time records provide the information from which some court documents such as accountings in bankruptcy cases and billing statements to clients are prepared. In addition, time records provide financial management information, indicate performance standard efficiencies or deficiencies, and are sometimes used to motivate attorneys and paralegals. There are several types of timekeeping systems, but personal commitment to systematically keeping time records is the key to the success of any timekeeping system.

8–3

In most cases the prevailing party is able to recapture costs advanced for litigation. Thus it is important that the law firm keep an accurate record of these costs. Many law firms also charge clients for certain overhead expense items, such as photocopies, faxes, telephone calls, and messenger services. Both manual systems and sophisticated, computerized cost-recovery systems are available to track and record this information.

8–4

Records management is the systematic storage and retrieval of paper records. It includes creating and organizing active files, as well as deciding how to manage inactive files. Records management can be done manually, with a computer, or by using a combination of both systems. Tickler systems are essential as reminders of important dates and deadlines and as the first line of defense against possible malpractice suits. Care must be taken to maintain client confidentiality when using client files and to avoid a conflict of interest when a client retains the firm.

REVIEW

Key Terms

Before proceeding, review the key terms listed below to be sure you understand each one. If necessary, read over the corresponding section of the chapter. When you are ready to test your understanding, answer the Review Questions.

billable hours
case retainer
conflict of interest
contingent fee
docket
fixed fee

hourly fee
leveraging
microfiche
microfilm
premium billing
pure retainer
records management
retainer for general representation
split-screen
statutory fee
tickler
trust account
value billing

Questions for Review and Discussion

1. Name the common types of legal fees.
2. Explain how legal fees are determined.
3. What are the differences between legal costs and overhead expenses?
4. Why must attorneys and paralegals keep accurate time records?
5. Describe some of the most common types of timekeeping systems.
6. What is a client trust account?
7. Explain the reasons for and methods of tracking client-related costs and expenses.
8. Define the term *records management*.
9. What steps can be taken to maintain client confidentiality in the law office?
10. When might a conflict of interest occur and what steps can you take to prevent it from happening?
11. What are some of the most common ways to organize a filing system for active files?
12. What is a *tickler system?*
13. Suggest alternative methods for a firm to handle inactive client files.

Activities

1. Construct a fictitious law firm with partners, associate attorneys, and paralegals. Using the expense-based formula and the custom in your community, determine the hourly billing rate for each group of timekeepers.
2. Read, complete, and discuss the attorney-client fee contract in Figure 8–1. Role-play yourself explaining the contents to a client who has never before been required to retain the services of a lawyer.
3. Record your time each day for one week in 15-minute intervals using the form provided in Figure 8–3.
4. Contact two or three software vendors for information on timekeeping programs. Invite them to demonstrate their programs to the class.
5. Discuss ways to motivate timekeepers to be more diligent in their timekeeping habits.
6. Contact a records storage facility to obtain information about their services and the costs of storing inactive files off-site. Also contact a micrographics vendor and an optical disk vendor for information about their records storage systems. Develop an argument for and against each type of records storage. Which would you recommend and why?

NOTES

CHAPTER 9 Information Management in the Law Office

OUTLINE

9–1 Introduction to Computer Hardware
- Types and Sizes of Computer Hardware
- The Central Processing Unit
- Memory
- Storage Capacity
- Auxiliary Storage
- Peripherals
- The Operating System
- Power Protection Devices

9–2 Introduction to Computer Software
- Integrated Data and Word Processing
- Deposition-Summary Software
- Case-Management Software
- Calendar Software
- Document-Assembly Software
- Document-Management Software
- Accounting and Billing Software

9–3 Preventing Computer-Related Management Problems
- Computer Viruses and Bugs
- Legal and Ethical Considerations of Software Usage
- Coping with the Industrial Injury of the Information Age
- Eight Problems a Computer Cannot Solve
- The Impact of Computers on Staff Positions

COMMENTARY

Dunn & Sweeney believes in high technology. The firm has every piece of equipment required to be a fully automated firm. The problem is you have acquired some word-processing skills but you do not really understand how a computer operates or how to speak "computerese." What is RAM capacity and why should you care? Should the firm upgrade its litigation-support software? Should they invest in document-assembly software? The attorneys have asked for your opinion on purchasing some new software packages. However, you are still trying to find out if it is true that computers don't make mistakes. You think the time has come for you to learn a little more about hardware and software.

OBJECTIVES

When hiring decisions are made, a paralegal with computer skills is more likely to get the job than one who lacks knowledge in this area. Minimally, a paralegal should be computer literate, possess keyboarding skills, and have an understanding of computer concepts and applications as they apply to the practice of law. After studying this chapter, you should be able to:

1. List the main components of a computer system.
2. Describe the functions of ROM and RAM.
3. Define the terms *kilobyte, megabyte, gigabyte.*
4. Discuss the two categories of printers.
5. Describe the functions of the operating system.
6. List the advantages of deposition-summary software and document-assembly software.
7. Explain the difference between a computer *virus* and a *bug* and understand how to guard against infection.
8. Explain when you can legally and ethically copy software.
9. Offer suggestions on ways to prevent CTD and carpal tunnel syndrome.
10. Describe how computers have changed the law office organization structure.

9–1 Introduction to Computer Hardware

Computer literacy is a desirable skill to possess for paralegals who work in today's technologically advanced law offices, but getting two people to agree on what computer literacy means is nearly impossible. Most people do agree, however, that a basic understanding of how computers work together with good keyboarding skills and a willingness to learn new software applications are key ingredients to becoming computer literate.

Few students today have experienced life without computers, yet computers themselves and their applications in the law office are relatively new developments. Figure 9–1 presents a microcosmic history of the personal computer.

In a short period of time, personal computers were integrated into businesses and law firms. The question is no longer whether to become computerized but which systems are going to make the practice of law more efficient and cost-effective.

A survey of law firms with 20 or fewer lawyers conducted in 1990 by the American Bar Association Legal Technology Resource Center revealed that 59 percent of the lawyers used a computer; 55 percent have terminals on their desks, and 39.5 percent use one outside the office; 17 percent of the lawyers have developed their own software, and 40 percent of these programs were designed by the lawyers themselves. Common uses for customized software are assembling documents, generating forms, and database and case management.

The first step in becoming computer literate is to understand how computers work. The following is a brief explanation of the "nuts and bolts" of computer systems.

Types and Sizes of Computer Hardware

Basically, there are three types and sizes of computer hardware: microcomputers, minicomputers, and mainframe computers.

Microcomputers The microcomputer, commonly called a desktop computer, a personal computer, or PC, was made possible by microchip technology, which began with the invention of the hand-held calculator in the late 1960s—and the

Figure 9–1 A Brief History of the Personal Computer

A BRIEF HISTORY OF THE PERSONAL COMPUTER

1975	The first personal computer is introduced in New Mexico by a company called Altair. Considered a hobbyist's device, it had no practical use. William H. Gates III and Paul Allen supplied the software system and laid the foundation for a company known as Microsoft Corp.
1977	Steven P. Jobs and Steve Wozniak launched the personal computer industry with the introduction of the Apple II. Commodore and Tandy introduced their own personal computer models the same year.
1981	IBM introduced its first PC. Forced to catch up with the early industry leaders, IBM purchased hardware and software from third parties rather than following the established tradition of manufacturing hardware and software that was incompatible with other systems. Many law firms that were using IBM's magnetic card word processing system began switching to computers.
1982	Compaq Computer introduced the first IBM-compatible "clone" made possible by IBM's use of widely available components.
1984	Apple introduced its Macintosh, which quickly gained acceptance because it is easy to use. IBM countered with its PC-AT model.
1986	Compaq introduced the first computer to use Intel's 386 microchip, which is now the standard for IBM-compatible personal computers.
1987	IBM announced the PS/2 system to counteract the flood of "clones" and also announced that it would work with Microsoft on a new, easier-to-use operating system called the OS/2.
1989	NEC and Toshiba lead the industry in the fastest-growing segment of the PC market—lightweight laptop and notebook PCs.
1991	IBM and Apple agree to work together to develop a new generation of PCs.

rest, as the saying goes, is history. A **microchip** is a wafer of silicon measuring about ¼″ square and less than four thousandths of an inch thick, that contains imprinted circuits through which electronic impulses travel. Through the development of microchip technology, it is now possible to capture massive amounts of data on a chip no larger than the fingernail on your little finger.

Most often used by one person and designed to perform one task at a time, such as word processing, microcomputers can be linked together in the law office in a **local area network** (LAN) for the purpose of sharing information and printers. Microcomputers are relatively simple to operate, cost less than other computer models, and can be moved about with ease. With these features, it is easy to understand why the microcomputer has become, for many, the first choice in office-automation equipment for law offices.

Minicomputers The next step up from the microcomputer is the minicomputer, which can be accessed by 100 or more users at the same time. Minicomputers have more memory and more storage capacity than micros and can perform multiple tasks simultaneously. The ability to perform complex tasks requires the firm to employ someone with enough technical knowledge and expertise to manage the minicomputer system.

Mainframe Computers The largest, most powerful, and most expensive computer is the mainframe, which can support a huge number of users and perform several complex tasks simultaneously. Only the largest law firms and corporate legal departments can justify the cost and size of owning a mainframe computer.

Without having to incur the cost of purchasing a mainframe, any law firm can still avail itself of the mainframe's size and power for the purpose of performing computer-aided research (discussed in Chapter 7). Service companies, or vendors, allow access to their mainframe's vast libraries through a process known as timesharing. It is likely that your law firm will not have a mainframe computer on the premises, but if the firm subscribes to one or more timesharing services, with a microcomputer, a telephone line, and a modem you will be able to access most of the information you need to conduct your research or investigation.

The Central Processing Unit

Commonly called the **CPU,** the **central processing unit** is the brains of the computer. The CPU is usually found on a single microchip and executes the program instructions to process data. Typically the most costly component of the computer, the CPU is divided into the *control unit,* which directs the computer to perform the necessary processes such as word processing, keeping the calendar, or tracking litigation, and the *arithmetic/logic unit (ALU),* which performs mathematical computations and allows the computer to make decisions pertaining to them. The ALU functions are performed in places on the chips called *registers* that are very small and, therefore, have difficulty storing vast amounts of information. Additional chips, called *memory,* are thus used for storage purposes.

Memory

Memory, or *main storage,* is an area for storing programs and data while you are working on a program. For example, while you are creating a new document using the word-processing software stored in memory, the new data you are entering is also being stored on the CPU's memory chip.

There are two major types of internal memory. **ROM,** or read only memory, is one type of internal memory. ROM means that the data is fixed—you cannot change it or destroy it by turning off the microcomputer. ROM integrated circuits are manufactured to store operating instructions permanently. When you turn on your PC and information appears on the screen, you know that ROM has done its job, and the micro is ready to go to work. **RAM,** or random access memory, is the second type of internal memory. Since new information can be stored and removed from RAM, the information in RAM is said to be *volatile.* In other words, any information in RAM can be lost when the power is turned off unless you have taken the steps required to save it before closing down the system.

Storage Capacity

Computer storage capacity is expressed by the number of memory cells on each chip. When the computer is operating, the CPU reads electronic signals that represent the binary number system, which is composed entirely of zeroes and ones. A **bit** refers to these individual binary digits, which will be either a zero or a one. Eight bits are required to make one **byte,** or character. For example, 01101001 might be read by the CPU as the letter *b.*

In the metric system, *K* is the symbol for 1000. However, a **kilobyte,** or K in computerese, actually represents 1024 bytes or characters of information in the memory of a computer. Therefore, when you hear that a computer has a 256K or 512K memory, that means that the computer has 256 × 1024, or 512 × 1024 locations for storage. A **megabyte** equals 1024K, or about a million-character storage capacity, and a **gigabyte** is 1024MB (megabytes), or about a billion characters.

Auxiliary Storage

The most popular forms of auxiliary storage for microcomputers are the diskette and the hard disk. **Diskettes,** also called *floppy disks,* are made of a thin, pliable, magnetically coated plastic on which data is stored. Floppy disks come in three standard sizes: 8-inch, 5¼-inch, and 3½-inch, and each can store about 180 pages of data on one side of the disk. Double-density diskettes can store about twice as much information as the single-density ones.

A **hard disk,** made from nonbending, rigid aluminum, can store about 5000 pages of data, and rotates within the CPU at a much higher rate of speed than floppy disks, thus providing faster retrieval and storage capabilities. Most hard disks are built into the microcomputer in an airtight, sealed unit and are not subject to the wear and tear of floppy disks. However, should the hard disk be damaged by a bounce on the desk or in being moved from one location to another, all data stored on the hard disk could be lost. For this reason, all data on a hard disk should be **backed up,** or copied onto another disk, regularly.

In a law firm where the computers are on a local area network, daily backup of the entire system is normal, often taking place automatically in the early morning hours when no one is likely to be using the system. Some of the more sophisticated computer systems automatically perform backup functions several times throughout the day without interfering with work flow. While there is no need to become paranoid about backing up your system, keep in mind that if the system "crashes" for any reason, you are likely to lose all the information that is not currently backed up. For a law firm, the possibility of losing all data created in just one morning is a grim thought.

Peripherals

The input and output devices connected to the microcomputer are called **peripherals.** The most popular input device is the standard keyboard, known as *Qwerty,* which was developed in the late 1800s by Christopher Sholes. Although other keyboards have been created and attempts have been made from time to time to recruit converts, the Qwerty keyboard has continued to be the standard, and certainly the one most familiar to typists.

Another input device is called the **mouse.** The mouse is a small desktop pointing device that, as it is moved across the desk, also moves the **cursor,** a blinking arrow, dash, or other symbol on the screen that tells the typist the system is ready for input or shows where typed characters will appear on the screen.

Output peripheral devices include the printer and the video monitor. Printers are classified according to the way printing is accomplished. Similar to old-model typewriters, *impact printers* have a mechanism that strikes a ribbon, transferring the characters onto paper. Types of impact printers include dot matrix, daisy wheel, thimble, and line printers. Some people refer to these types of printers as *letter-quality printers* because, even though they are slow and noisy, their quality is suitable for most office correspondence.

Nonimpact printers include ink jet printers, which deposit droplets of ink onto the paper; thermal printers, which use heat to produce characters on paper; and laser printers, which use a small laser beam to keep images on the paper. Laser printers are fast and quiet (although more expensive than the other types) and are favored by high-volume, paper-producing organizations such as law firms.

The CRT, cathode ray tube, or *video monitor,* displays computer input. These high-resolution television screens, or monitors, are either monochrome—typically green, amber, or white—or color, displaying a range of colors that are especially good for graphics but sometimes distracting for word processing. The CRT and the keyboard together are often referred to as the **terminal.**

The **modem** is another peripheral device that converts microcomputer-generated electrical digital signals into audio signals and transmits them via telephone lines over long distances. Actually, a modem is both an input and an output device that allows a microcomputer to communicate with another micro, a minicomputer, a mainframe, or other compatible office-automation equipment using telephone lines. Since messages can be transmitted across town or around the world, modems are standard equipment for law offices that subscribe to research or informational databases. Figure 9–2 illustrates some of the various computer components.

Figure 9–2 Computer Components

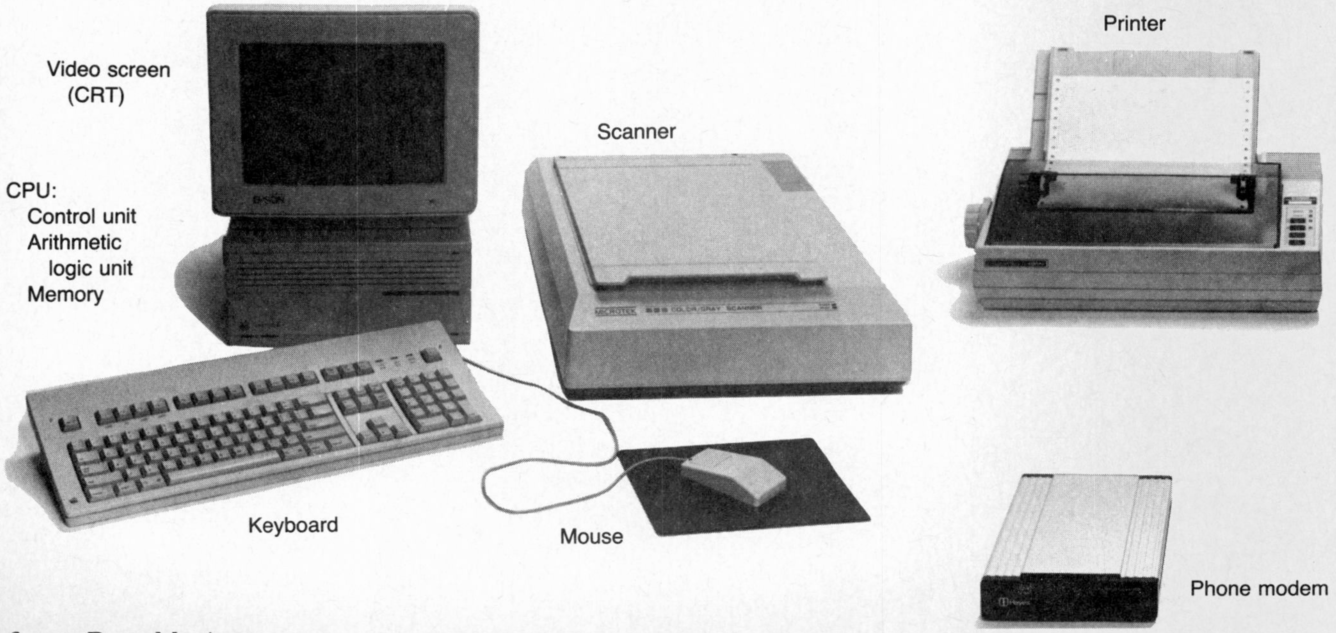

Source: Doug Martin.

The Operating System

The **operating system,** simply defined, is a software program that manages the operation of the microcomputer. It loads specific programs, oversees the storage of data, and controls all the peripheral devices. The *DOS*, or disk operating system, goes to work loading a portion of the operating system into memory as soon as the computer is turned on. There are several types of operating systems developed by different manufacturers. Some of the more familiar ones are MS-DOS, Apple-DOS, and UNIX.

Typical functions of a disk operating system might include library commands, which are single-word commands such as Clear (the screen) or Delete; a utility program to accomplish routine tasks such as backing up disks or *formatting* disks (preparing disks to store data); and the system operating routines that tell the microcomputer what to do.

Power Protection Devices

Since electrical power disturbances can cause a loss of data, or the creation of incorrect output data, power protection is of concern to all microcomputer users. Power disturbances can be caused by air conditioners and copiers being turned on and off, by lightning, or by a complete loss of power due to downed wires. Isolation transformers, surge suppressors, and transient suppressors are external devices that block or reduce potential power disturbances. Alternative sources of power such as generators or batteries can provide emergency electrical current when commercial power is unavailable. As law firms become more dependent upon computers, good power protection devices and alternative sources of emergency power will become increasingly critical.

9–2 Introduction to Computer Software

As a general rule, computer software should be purchased after hardware has been selected, because software is not designed to run on all hardware systems. For example, software designed to be used with an IBM computer system or a clone will not work on a Macintosh computer; IBM and Macintosh run on different types of operating systems.

New software specifically designed for use in law offices is now regularly introduced to the market and widely advertised. Some software will make your law firm operate more efficiently and some will not. Before succumbing to marketing hype, there are two important questions to be answered: Who is going to use the software, and what do they want it to do?

Lawyers, paralegals, secretaries, and word processors will no doubt want to use the computer system. Library personnel and facilities managers, as well as accounting and administrative staff are also likely to want computers. Some staff members might want a computer for home use, or a portable one to take to court or the law library. Once the users of the software are determined, the next question is, for what purposes will they be using it? What functions are expected of the software? What results are required? Some users will need to design spreadsheets and compute numbers. Others will require only word processing. Still others might want the capability of desktop publishing and graphics design.

Following is a brief descriptive overview of some of the tasks possible with different types of software specifically designed for use in a law office.

Integrated Data and Word Processing

An integrated system usually means that from any desktop unit, you can work with words or data, or both. Many legal secretaries and word processors, however, have no need for the ability to compute data or create spreadsheets because their work is often limited to creating documents with few, if any, figures. On the other hand, bankruptcy and probate paralegals, tax attorneys, and the firm's accounting personnel will require software capable of computing columns of figures and creating spreadsheets in addition to word processing.

Deposition-Summary Software

One of the most common uses for litigation support software is to summarize depositions, a task traditionally delegated to a paralegal. An automated litigation-support system can save an enormous amount of time by searching thousand of pages of transcripts for information pertaining to a particular subject, a task typically performed manually.

Recalling Chapter 5, a *deposition* is oral testimony given under oath that can be admitted as evidence at a trial. The original deposition is transcribed by a court reporter and notarized. The *deponent,* the person being deposed, is given the opportunity to read his or her deposition and make corrections. Corrections are noted and the transcript is then sealed. Attorneys use depositions to collect facts, to prepare a chronology of events, and to compare with the statements and testimony of other witnesses to spot inconsistencies or conflicts.

For a small additional fee, the court reporter will provide you with a copy of the deponent's testimony stored on a floppy disk. Once the data is loaded onto your computer, using the search function, you can freely move through the text to review, highlight, or extract pertinent information. The deposition (see Figure 9–3) can then be summarized easily in a choice of several format styles, depending on how the attorney is going to use the testimony and his or her individual preference.

Traditionally, deposition summaries follow three formats: the page/line index, which is keyed back to individual transcript pages as shown in Figure 9–4; the narrative, which presents the testimony in paragraph form as shown in Figure 9–5; and the issue summary, which is organized by issue and is the most analytical (see Figure 9–6). Some litigation support software allows you to search the transcripts of several deponents with one query using a key word, as illustrated in Figure 9–7.

When the computer system is integrated with a scanner, photographs, charts and graphs, letters, memos, and pencilled notes can also be stored and retrieved in their entirety. For example, if your firm is involved in a complex lawsuit, such as the Iran-Contra hearings, it might require a search for all letters and memos written by Ronald Reagan after May 1, 1985 addressed to John Poindexter that contain in the text the phrase *arms deal* or *Oliver North.* With fully integrated litigation-support software, you could browse through images of the original letters, including any notations pencilled in the margins, in just a few seconds on your microcomputer screen.

Litigation-support software can track a plaintiff's inventory of damages,

Figure 9–3 Two pages of a Deposition of Della Street

DEPOSITION OF DELLA STREET
08/01/92

Page 14

Q. All right. Let me ask you this. How many bank accounts did you have during the course of your relationship with Mr. Mason?
A. You mean like joint accounts?
Q. I mean like any bank accounts with your name on them, joint or otherwise.
A. Well, we had four or five over the years. We had a joint checking account at Bank of America in Milpitas.
Q. Okay, let's start with that. When was it opened?
A. About 1975, 1976.
Q. Whose money was used to open it?
A. Well, some of it was mine. I had about $4,000 in savings, and then—and then I'd sold my car for $800, and that went in too.
Q. Who else did the money come from, that was used to open the joint checking account?
A. Just Perry.
Q. And how much was that?
A. About—about $8,000.
Q. All right. Did you—"you" meaning you personally—put any more money into the joint account after that?
A. My child support checks.
Q. How much were those?
A. $100 a month.
Q. Okay. Anything else?
A. No, sir.
Q. Who else deposited monies into the Bank of America

DEPOSITION OF DELLA STREET
08/01/92

Page 15

joint checking account?
A. Just Perry.
Q. Okay. Did the two of you have any kind of agreement when the account was opened that the money you deposited would remain yours?
A. No, sir.
Q. Or that he would make contributions for all of your joint living expenses?
A. No, sir. We never talked about it that much. We just did it.
Q. Okay. What kind of expenses were paid from this account?
A. Expenses? Well, the down payment on the house on Jackson Street, for one. And the mortgage payments.
Q. Okay. What else?
A. Well, we paid Perry's medical bills from it when he was in the hospital in 1982, for his heart. I think that's all.
Q. When was the account closed?
A. Perry closed it right after he found out that I had taken some money out of it and opened another account at Security Pacific. That was in 1982.
Q. Why did you open another account?
A. Well, I was afraid if Perry died, the joint checking account would be frozen, and I wouldn't have any money to live on.
Q. How much did you withdraw from the joint account?
A. $20,000.

Source: Vol. 2, Issue 1, Jan-March 1990. These tables are reprinted with the permission of *California Paralegal Magazine*, P.O. Box 6960, Los Osos, CA 93412 (805)528-8705.

including original cost and replacement cost; match invoices and documents to inventory items; and index and store exhibits. In addition, the software can manage memos, letters, depositions, witnesses, exhibits, and other related material by providing rapid access to any data pertaining to a specific case.

Because litigation-support software is such a powerful tool for both attorneys and paralegals, it is a significant asset in pretrial case management as well as during the trial itself.

Case-Management Software

The definition of *case management* varies from one law firm to another. Most people agree, however, that case management begins with the creation of a database using dBase or RBase software. With a computerized case-management system, most of the pertinent information of a litigation client's file can be entered into the computer. After entering a few commands, you could pull up the name, address, and telephone number of the client's doctor, insurance provider, and the expert witness who will testify on behalf of your client at trial. Having this and other frequently used information at your fingertips is far more

Figures 9–4 through 9–7 Examples of Deposition Summary Formats

PAGE/LINE INDEX

14:8 Defendant had four or five bank accounts during relationship with decedent.

14:10 Bank of America joint checking account opened 1975/1976. Monies used:
1) From defendant: $4,800;
2) From decedent: $8,000.

14:21 Deposits:
1) By defendant: $100 monthly child support checks.
2) By decedent: all other monies.

15:3 No agreement that defendant's deposits would remain hers.

15:7 No agreement that decedent would make contributions for all of their joint living expenses.

15:11 Expenses paid from joint checking account:
1) down payment and mortgage payments on Jackson Street house;
2) decedent's medical bills from 1982 hospitalization.

15:19 Decedent closed account in 1982 after learning of defendant's $20,000 withdrawal.

15:19 Defendant opened new account at Security Pacific with $20,000.

NARRATIVE SUMMARY

Defendant had four or five bank accounts during her relationship with decedent. They opened a joint checking account at the Bank of America in Milpitas in 1975 or 1976, using $4,800 of defendant's money and $8,000 of decedent's money. Defendant deposited her $100 monthly child support checks into the account. Decedent made all other deposits.

There was no agreement that defendant's deposits would remain hers, or that decedent would make contributions for all of their joint living expenses. They used the monies from the joint checking account to make the down payment and mortgage payments on the Jackson Street house, and to pay decedent's medical bills from his 1982 hospitalization.

Decedent closed the account in 1982 after learning of defendant's $20,000 withdrawal. Defendant used the $20,000 to open a new account at Security Pacific.

efficient than having to run around and locate the file whenever you need to work on it.

In family law and collection work, the case-management database can keep track of payments received and automatically generate a letter for payments that are missed. Because collection law revolves around the calendar, a case-manage-

ISSUE SUMMARY

BANK ACCOUNTS

Bank of America, Milpitas branch. Joint checking account no. __________. Opened by defendant and decedent in 1975/1976. Closed by decedent in 1982. Monies used to open account came from defendant ($4,800) and decedent ($8,000). Deposits into account were made by defendant ($100 monthly child support checks) and decedent (all other). Withdrawals from account were made by defendant and decedent for real property payments and medical bills. Defendant also made $20,000 withdrawal from account in 1982.

Security Pacific Account no. __________ [...]

KEYWORD SEARCH DIGEST
("account")

DRAKE.DEP page 42, line 3

Q. So your sister-in-law never mentioned to you that she and Mr. Mason had a joint bank account?

A. No, she didn't. We never talked about money.

BERGER.DEP page 67, line 17

Q. And did Ms. Street tell you why she opened another bank account under her own name at Security Pacific while Mr. Mason was in the hospital?

A. She said if he died, she wouldn't have anything to live on for a while. She wouldn't be able to get anything out of their joint account. She was real worried about that.

HAMILTON.DEP page 96, line 27

Q. What else did Ms. Street say about the financial arrangement she had with Mr. Mason?

A. Well, she did say that Mr. Mason had told her over and over again that he would take care of her for the rest of her life. That he was putting money in an account for her.

Source: Vol. 2, Issue 1, Jan.-March 1990. These tables are reprinted with the permission of *California Paralegal Magazine,* P.O. Box 6960, Los Osos, CA 93412, (805)528-8705.

ment system can automatically generate pleadings to enforce payment, such as issuing garnishment writs and notices of judgment debtor hearings.

An optimally functioning case-management system can also keep track of work in process as well as work to be done in the future and issue periodic status reports on specific files as reminders to the attorney and paralegal assigned to the file.

Calendar Software

Calendar software programs are designed to keep everyone in the firm up-to-date on the whereabouts of attorneys and paralegals and the cases on which they are spending time. The calendar can include as little or as much information as desired. Some firms use their automated calendar to include *statutory dates,* the time fixed by law within which parties must take judicial action to enforce their rights. Others use the automated calendar to replace manual calendars and include only appointments and court appearances. Automated calendars are capable of keeping track of everyone's schedule, providing daily status reports with case reminders, appointments, and other pertinent information such as the status of a client's account. In smaller law firms, the automated calendar can even be used as a tickler, reminding attorneys and paralegals of impending deadlines. Since calendaring important dates is such a crucial part of the practice of law, using an automated calendaring system that requires only one entry is less likely to result in missing an important date than using a manual system, which usually requires an entry in several calendars—the attorney's desk calendar, the attorney's pocket calendar, the paralegal's calendar, and the secretary's calendar.

Document-Assembly Software

Creating a new document using parts of an old one is not a recent development in the practice of law. Early in their careers attorneys learned the value of being able to use a prior work product to service a client more efficiently. What is new is that document-assembly software has replaced the earlier cut-and-paste techniques used to create a new document from bits and pieces of an old one.

Document-assembly software has changed virtually every legal specialty, from probate, real estate, and family law to bankruptcy and litigation practices. For many applications, the power of the most recent high-end word-processing software is enough, but for complex documents, a document-assembly *engine,* as such software is called, is required.

Once installed, the document-assembly engine works with your processor to produce two drafts of a document, one for the author and another for the user, that can be stored, edited, and printed by your word processor. The most simplistic of the document-assembly programs generates *boilerplates,* fill-in-the-blank forms. This program is only slightly more capable than a word-processing system with mail-merge functions. The more sophisticated programs, however, have rudimentary artificial intelligence and are capable of generating finished documents, automatically incorporating information unique to a client, such as wills or contracts.

Document-Management Software

Document-management software was created to manage the production, storage, retrieval, security, and backup of documents generated on a PC. When

Figure 9–8 An Automated Calendar

A fully automated legal office will use calendar software to keep everyone in the firm up-to-date. *Source:* File Photo.

word processing was in its infancy, keeping track of documents was relatively simple. Many law firms used dedicated word processors such as Vydec and Lexitron where documents were stored on diskettes. If someone wanted a copy of a document, they made a copy of it and off they went. Because word processing was the exclusive domain of trained operators, document control was seldom an issue in those days. But now, with a personal computer on nearly every desk, it has become increasingly difficult, if not impossible, to know who worked on a document last and what changes may have been made to the original.

With the use of header information, which includes the name of the author of the document, the date, client information, and the type of document, document-management software allows everyone to know the whereabouts of documents as well as their provenance and pedigree. Disciplined users of document-management software find the advantages of taking the time to update the header far outweigh the few minutes required to enter the information. Here are just some of the document-management tools the software provides.

Tracking In a complex merger and acquisition deal, several people in the firm may be working on different parts of the same document simultaneously on a networked computer system. In this instance, it is extremely important that each person be working on the most recent version of the document. With its built-in clock and headers, document-management software allows everyone to keep track of various versions.

Managing Revisions With document-management software you can keep useful documents intact instead of erasing each earlier version. This allows anyone to retrieve language from an earlier version or to recreate the process of a heavily negotiated portion of a contract.

Backup Newly created files on the PC are automatically backed up to the central system with this software because it has the ability to store a second copy simultaneously.

Locking Documents When one person is working on a document, this software has the ability to lock others out, thus eliminating the risk of loss of control. Anyone attempting to retrieve the same document is advised by the computer who is working on the document, so that normal work can continue.

Locating Documents More PC users means more documents are being generated, which might save time and money for attorneys, paralegals, and clients if they knew of their existence and had a way to locate a particular document. With header information such as author, date, subject, and client, document-management software can help anyone track down an existing document.

Automatic Archives Document-management software can set up a small database of information on each file. It is possible to search the database periodically for all memoranda, letters, or other documents, and have them automatically transferred to the archive files. Doing so frees up disk-storage space on your computer.

Accounting and Billing Software

Even the smallest law firms today have computerized accounting and client-billing systems. In fact, software that performs these vital administrative functions is often the second type of software purchased, right after the word-processing program. Depending upon the needs of the firm and the type of computer system, reasonably priced software can be purchased from most computer vendors to handle nearly every bookkeeping and billing task.

Computerized billing systems greatly reduce billing time, as well as generate information about each client's account. Most systems are able to generate one bill at a time, or bills for the clients of a particular lawyer, or bills for clients whose balances exceed a certain amount. In addition, most computerized billing systems automatically update and generate financial management reports including aged accounts-receivable reports, aged work-in-progress reports, on-demand trust account reports, profitability reports by area of specialization, and performance reports on each timekeeper.

If the firm is using computerized expense-tracking systems to monitor photocopier, facsimile, and long-distance telephone calls, these systems can be integrated into some of the billing software programs and the charges automatically posted directly to client accounts at specified intervals. In addition, some accounting software will generate checks, receipts, and bank deposit slips; post entries to clients' accounts automatically; and prepare daily transaction reports on all the firm's accounts.

As you can see, the question is not whether a law firm should have a computer system but how much the firm must spend in order to provide client services in the most economical and efficient way possible.

9–3 Preventing Computer-Related Management Problems

As you might expect, along with the benefits of computers there are also some computer-related management problems. Awareness of some of these will help you prepare for handling them in the event they occur in your office.

Computer Viruses and Bugs

A computer **virus** is a program that replicates itself within the computer system. In the process, it uses up available memory and destroys existing data and programs. Although internal sabotage by a disgruntled employee is one way a virus can be introduced into a system, most viruses are introduced from outside the firm. One of the most publicized virus attacks occurred in 1987 when IBM was invaded by a virus that wished "Season's Greetings" to program users at IBM. The virus attached itself to the distribution lists of every IBM user who received it, and half a million copies of the virus program quickly spread throughout IBM's worldwide electronic mail network, causing operations to come to a halt. More recently, in March 1992, the Michelangelo virus, thought to have originated in the Netherlands, threatened to wipe out data in storage on computers around the world unless the users took precautions to prevent the virus from spreading.

A **bug,** on the other hand, is a basic flaw in the initial design of the software program. As software programs become more complex, particularly those for the personal computer, the chances are dramatically increased that the thousands of strings of binary codes required to make up a program will end up with a bug in them. Software bugs come in several forms, such as simple errors committed at the time the program was written—the equivalent of forgetting to dot an *i* or cross a *t*. Or a bug can be the result of a more complicated interaction between two or more parts of a program that do not quite mesh. In 1989

Ashton-Tate, the publishers of dBase IV, reported a $19.8 million quarterly loss attributed largely to bugs in the program.

There is one major difference between a virus and a bug: viruses are intentionally caused and bugs are programming mistakes. There is not much anyone can do about a bug, except return the software to the manufacturer. But there are some precautions law firms can take to prevent a virus from infecting their computer system. Here are some of them.

- Draft and implement a comprehensive security policy that emphasizes safe computing methods and covers all computer operations, including procedures for issuing and periodically changing access codes or passwords, and for terminating or discharging employees who have access to the computer system. Steps should also be taken to protect networks against unauthorized dial-ins from outside vendors or other personnel.
- Before using any off-the-shelf software, check to make sure the shrink-wrap packaging is intact. If the packaging has been removed, someone may have tampered with the program.
- Thoroughly test any new software on an isolated system before distributing it throughout the firm or installing it on a network.
- Check the directory information regularly, especially the file length and date of creation of files. If you do not know why a file's date has been changed or why its length has changed, pull it out of use until you find out.
- Make backup copies of all new programs immediately after opening them and securely store the originals. In the event a virus appears on your backup copy, you still have the virus-free original.
- Limit the sharing of files and software programs, and be particularly wary of shareware programs downloaded from electronic bulletin boards. If you are hooked into any network, particularly an external network, your system is vulnerable to infection.

Legal and Ethical Considerations of Software Usage

The *Copyright Act of 1980* states that software programs are eligible for the same copyright protection as other forms of original creativity and expression. Furthermore, the act prescribes damages of $10,000 for each illegally duplicated copy of the software, and an additional $40,000 per copy if the copyright holder can prove that the copies were made intentionally.

Many firms have written policies that ban **piracy,** or the unauthorized copying of software, in an attempt to protect themselves in court, should the need arise, and to remind personnel of the substantial penalties involved with the intentional duplication of software. Other firms have negotiated a **site licensing agreement** with vendors, which allows them to duplicate a specified number of copies of the program for use in the law firm. A site license also eliminates the ethical issue of whether a duplicate copy can be made legally, and, since a site license usually is about 25 to 50 percent less expensive than buying the same number of individual copies, it offers a more cost-effective way of providing all workstations in the firm with copies of the software.

The Copyright Act of 1980 does permit the duplication of one backup copy of each off-the-shelf program. The problem, however, is that this backup copy can then become the source of many more copies. When Lotus Development Corporation sued Rixon Incorporated for $10 million over this issue, more people became aware of the serious ramifications involved with using pirated copies of computer software. The suit alleged that Rixon had made unauthorized copies of its Lotus 1–2–3 software and distributed them throughout the company. Without admitting any wrongdoing, Rixon paid an undisclosed amount to Lotus to settle the matter. Subsequently, other software companies began actively pursuing those firms that violate licensing agreements.

Coping with the Industrial Injury of the Information Age

Although high technology has made many jobs in the law office easier, it has also afflicted countless numbers of workers with the industrial injury of the information age—**cumulative trauma disorder (CTD).** Cumulative trauma disorder is not a new phenomenon. However, until recently, it was usually found only in manufacturing environments where hand and arm motions are repeated continuously. As automation has continued to reduce jobs to simpler tasks, and the pressure to increase productivity has cut into or eliminated rest periods, CTD is affecting more and more office workers.

Here is the problem. When you work on a computer, shoulder muscles are tight to support the arms and eye muscles remain rigidly focused on the screen. Each time you punch a key, the muscle running from the elbow through the forearm contracts. The muscle is attached to tendons that slide back in lubricated sheaths through the wrist to lift the fingers. The muscle relaxes, the tendons slide forward, and the finger pushes down.

In the days before computers, when a secretary used a typewriter, she (they were nearly all women in those days) would periodically pause to roll out a finished page and insert a new one. There were many more hand and wrist motions involved with the typing process then. With computers, typists can move paragraphs and pages around without lifting a finger from the keyboard, and the result is a dramatic increase in the number of workers complaining of CTD.

CTD problems range from swollen tendons and muscle spasms to severe nerve damage, or a combination of symptoms. CTD at its worst can result in *carpal tunnel syndrome,* a potentially crippling injury that often requires surgery.

Here are some suggestions for preventing CTD problems.

- Review workstations. Poorly designed furniture leads to bad posture, which can affect the back, the neck, and the spine, as well as arms, wrists, and hands. Chairs and keyboards that are too high or too low may force users to work with their hands bent in peculiar positions. Stiff keyboards may require too much effort to push the keys. Screens that are too high, too low, or too far away require the users to crane their necks for hours on end.
- Arm tendons should be stretched before and after long typing jobs, just as a runner stretches leg tendons before and after exercising.
- Build upper-body strength with weights. The ability of the neck, shoulders and wrists to hold still for long periods is related to their strength.
- Take regular breaks. Although there is no consensus among experts as to how often and how long work breaks should be, there is agreement that they are necessary no matter how well-designed the workstation is. Some doctors recommend a 15-minute break every two hours, while others suggest five minutes every hour, a minute or two on the half-hour. Some states have laws mandating work breaks.
- When taking a break, allow focusing eye muscles to get a workout by looking at distant objects. Stand up and move around. Return phone calls or perform other tasks.

Eight Problems a Computer Cannot Solve

Because computer technology has greatly enlarged the scope of work performed by everyone in today's law offices, better understanding is required about what computers can and cannot do.

Here are a few problems that computers cannot solve.

1. *A computer will not solve vague, poorly defined problems.* You have to understand exactly what the problem is that you want the computer to solve. This requires thinking about and planning what you want the computer to do.
2. *A computer will usually not save money by eliminating staff.* Instead, a computer will create new ways of doing things and new jobs.
3. *A computer will not correct errors in your manual procedures.* Since automation begins with the direct transfer of data from a manual system to the computerized system, if you put "garbage in," you will get "garbage out"—GIGO, as computer people say.
4. *A computer will not be able to perform sophisticated functions until quite a few years after the system is up and running.* Before you can even think about getting your computer to perform sophisticated functions, you must spend an enormous amount of time keying information into the system. It is best to tackle only one area at a time to get the most from your investment. Like people, the computer must walk before it can run.
5. *A computer will not solve problems that call for a subjective evaluation.* Computers cannot think—but eventually they might. Even so, any decision that requires qualitative input is not appropriate for computerization. For example, the final decision to hire one legal assistant over another is arrived at by considering a broad range of personnel factors and issues that are difficult to quantify.
6. *A computer will not solve all your scheduling problems.* Even with automated calendaring, litigation-support systems, and gargantuan databases, there will still be scheduling problems. Automation can assist you in executing well-developed plans, but plans change frequently in the dynamic law-office environment.
7. *A computer's software will not take kindly to changes made by amateurs.* Don't even try it. If you do not end up completely trashing the program, remember that manufacturers refuse to service programs that have been tampered with.
8. *A computer will not always be right.* Although you might think your computer is infallible, systems can and do make errors. Faulty circuitry, a program with bugs, or a disk going bad can produce mistakes that often go undetected—for a time. Most systems function so flawlessly, you tend to stop checking up on them. Do not allow yourself to fall into the trap of complacency and dependency.

The Impact of Computers on Staff Positions

Technology has been gradually changing the way people work in law firms. But in just the past few years many firms have made significant changes in organizational structure, particularly in the administrative and paralegal areas. Many of these changes are no doubt the result of technology improvements in both computer hardware and software.

To keep up with the changes in technology, many offices have formed their own in-house training department to ensure that employees are properly trained on computer equipment, as well as routine office procedures. In addition, the use of firm-specific software programs has required many firms to recruit and train their own pool of temporary workers and floaters. In these firms, the manager of secretarial services works closely with the manager of the training department to coordinate and monitor the firm's daily support-staff requirements.

Powerful and sophisticated computer programs require on-site management of information systems. MIS (management of information systems) managers are often responsible for developing the firm's long-range technology plans as well as supervising all computer operations and associated personnel, whereas the systems administrator is responsible for the day-to-day systems operations and maintenance. Larger firms might also employ in-house software and hardware specialists who work with users to develop databases for a specific attorney, one area of specialization, or for purposes of practice management.

The impact of technology, however, is probably most evident at the paralegal level. Computers now make it possible for paralegals to do much of the work previously done by lawyers, such as assembling drafts of complex documents and researching in-depth obscure points of law. As a result, more than one litigation department has had to restructure its paralegal sector to include positions for document clerk, paralegal trainee, paralegal, senior paralegal, and paralegal supervisor.

The meshing of computer technology with paralegal skills has created many opportunities for growth and advancement in what was once considered a dead-end job. Paralegals today can chart a career path moving from an entry-level position to paralegal supervisor. Or, paralegals who develop computer expertise above and beyond the ordinary requirements now find themselves in positions as law firm MIS professionals. Still others go on to learn more about law-office management and become the firm's executive administrator. The opportunities for paralegals in today's dynamic legal profession are truly boundless and made possible largely through computer technology.

SUMMARY

9–1

Microchip technology, first introduced in the hand-held calculator, made possible the proliferation of microcomputers, or PCs. The three main components of PC hardware are: the CPU, or the brains of the computer, where information is stored in memory (expressed as bytes) on disks; the input devices, a keyboard, modem and mouse; and, the output devices, a video monitor and printer. The disk operating system is the software program that manages the operation of the PC through a library of preprogrammed commands. Information stored in memory can be lost in the event of an electrical power disturbance, but power protection devices can be used to block or reduce these potential problems.

9–2

Information management systems do not operate on hardware alone. Different types of software programs, such as litigation-support, document-assembly and document-management software, allow paralegals to locate and retrieve pertinent testimony, documents, and exhibits in half the time required to perform the same tasks manually. In addition, tickler and calendaring programs reduce the chances of missing important dates and deadlines, database programs facilitate conflict-of-interest checks, and accounting and billing programs provide important financial management tools for the automated law office.

9–3

The proliferation of computers brings new management problems to the law firm. Computer viruses, intentionally caused programs that replicate themselves within the computer, taking up available memory and destroying existing data and programs in the process, are usually an external problem occurring on networked systems. A bug, on the other hand, is a software programming mistake, which may go undetected for a period of time. Neither of these occurrences is frequent, but either can wreak havoc with your system. Other management problems can occur when software is illegally copied and passed around for use within the firm. Software is protected by copyright laws, and in the absence of a licensing agreement with the manufacturer it is illegal to make copies of programs. Cumulative trauma disorder and carpal tunnel syndrome are health problems related to computer usage. Everyone using a computer for extended periods of time should take regular breaks to prevent injury or health problems related to computer use. Computers should not be expected to solve all the information-management problems in the law office. They will, however, increase productivity as well as improve employee morale and job satisfaction when properly integrated into the law firm.

REVIEW

Key Terms

Before proceeding, review the key terms listed below to be sure you understand each one. If necessary, read over the corresponding section of the chapter. When you are ready to test your understanding, answer the Review Questions.

backed up
bit
bug
byte
central processing unit (CPU)
cumulative trauma disorder
cursor
diskette
gigabyte
hard disk
K
kilobyte

local area network (LAN)
megabyte
memory
microchip
modem
mouse
operating system
peripherals
piracy
RAM
ROM
site licensing agreement
terminal
virus

Questions for Review and Discussion

1. What are the main components of a computer system?
2. Define and explain the functions of ROM and RAM.
3. How much memory can be stored on a megabyte? On a gigabyte?
4. Printers are categorized into two groups. What are they? Give examples of each.
5. What is the function of the operating system?
6. What are the advantages of using deposition-summary software and document-assembly software?
7. Explain the difference between a computer virus and a bug. What steps can you take to guard against infection?
8. When might you legally copy software?
9. What can you do to prevent CTD and carpal tunnel syndrome?
10. How have computers changed the organizational structure of the automated law office?

Activities

1. Contact two or three software companies that design programs specifically for the legal profession. Ask them for brochures and product information to share with the class, or ask them to visit and present a demonstration of their products.
2. Invite an attorney who specializes in copyright law to discuss the Copyright Act of 1980 and its implications in software management with the class.
3. Organize a field trip to a local computer hardware vendor for the purpose of viewing types of input and output devices, scanners, printers, and other related products typically used in law firms.
4. Invite a worker compensation specialist to the class to discuss the impact of cumulative trauma disorders and carpal tunnel syndrome on law office employees.

PART FOUR

PERSONAL AND PROFESSIONAL CAREER DEVELOPMENT

NOTES

CHAPTER 10 Law Practice Specialties

OUTLINE

COMMENTARY

After working at Dunn & Sweeney for several months, you can now understand why it might be important to select one or two areas of the law in which to specialize. Just keeping up with the changes in procedure in any one specialty is enough of a challenge; staying abreast of changes in several areas is nearly impossible. But you are still uncertain which specialties might be best for you.

You want to explore a few of the areas that interest you and find out if one type of practice is more suitable for your personality than another.

OBJECTIVES

In Chapter 1 you learned how the paralegal position became an integral part of the U.S. legal system and the general routine duties and responsibilities associated with most paralegal positions. In this chapter, you are presented with more detailed information for a few selected fields of law in which paralegals are routinely employed.

The overviews, background information, and paralegal functions provided for the selected specialties presented in this chapter are purposely brief and far from all-inclusive. This chapter is intended to present a summary only of a few chosen fields of law—some of which are relatively new fields—and the more typical functions of a paralegal working in each. After studying this chapter, you should be able to:

1. Compare and contrast a Chapter 7, Chapter 11, and Chapter 13 bankruptcy proceeding.
2. Describe the difference between a voluntary and an involuntary bankruptcy.
3. Discuss three types of business entities: sole proprietorship, partnership, corporation.
4. Define the term *civil litigation.*
5. List the functions of the collections paralegal.
6. Discuss the duties of the criminal law paralegal.
7. Discuss the background of employee benefits law.
8. List the diverse subcategories of family law.
9. Describe the functions of the intellectual property law paralegal.
10. Discuss the three categories of probate court proceedings.
11. Discuss the relationship between client contact and selected fields of law.

10–1 Fields of Law

When most people think of a career in the legal field, they think of family law, real estate, and civil litigation. These are the fields of law in which many people have had a personal experience. The difficulties some people have experienced in a divorce settlement or child custody arrangements certainly can prompt their interest in how the law works.

Perhaps you were involved in a real-estate transaction in which everything that could go wrong did go wrong. This left you thinking you could have done a better job representing yourself. Or perhaps your legal experience was with a personal-injury litigation matter that ended up before a jury, and you were fascinated by the entire litigation process.

The practice of law, however, is not limited to a few fields. Rather, the list of specialties is nearly unlimited. In 1982 the Supreme Court ruled that a lawyer may list him- or herself under any field of law, provided that it is not misleading. Figure 10–1 lists over 300 generally recognized fields of law. As world economies become more interdependent, and as more sophisticated technologies are developed, look for opportunities in new specialty areas of law to emerge for both lawyers and paralegals.

Figure 10–1 Fields of Law

FIELDS OF LAW

The Supreme Court ruling *IN re RMJ*, 455 U.S. 191, 102 S. Ct. 929 71 L.Ed. 2d 64 (1982) established that a lawyer may list himself/herself under any field of law, provided that it is not misleading. *Subject to editorial consistency and legal ethics, we will review and consider any reasonable request for fields of law not on this list.*

Accident & Health Insurance Law
Accounting Malpractice Law
Acquisitions, Divestitures & Mergers Law
Administrative Law
Admiralty Law
Adoption Law
Advertising Law
Advisor on Laws of (State Nation)
Advisor on Laws of European Economic Community
Aerospace Law
Agriculture Law
Aircraft Title Law
Airplane Crash Litigation
Alcohol Beverage Law
Alternate Dispute Resolution Law
Antitrust Law
Appellate Practice
Arbitration Law
Architectural Malpractice Law
Arson and Insurance Fraud Defense Law
Art Law
Art Business Law
Asbestos Litigation
Association Law
Automobile Law
Aviation Law
Bad Faith Law
Banking Law
Bankruptcy Law
Bond Law
Business Law
Business Crimes Law
Business Development Law
Campaign Finance Law
Casino Law
Casualty Insurance Law
Cemetery Law
Chancery Practice
Charitable Trusts & Foundations Law
Church or Ecclesiastic Law
Civil Litigation
Civil Litigation—Defense
Civil Practice
Civil Rights Law
Civil Service Law
Class Actions
Coal Law
Collection Law
College Law
Commercial Collections
Commercial Law
Commercial Leasing Law
Commodities Law
Common Carrier Law
Communications Law
Community Property Law
Compensation, Deferred Law
Complex & Multi-District Litigation
Computer Law
Condemnation Law
Condominium Law
Conservatorship Law
Constitutional Law
Construction Law
Consumer Law
Consumer Credit Law
Contract Law
Conveyancing Law
Controlled Substances Law
Cooperative Law
Copyright Law
Corporate Financing Law
Corporate Reorganization & Insolvency Law
Corporation Law
Court Martial Law
Credit Union Law
Creditor Bankruptcy Law
Creditors Rights Law
Criminal Defense Law
Criminal Law
Criminal Tax Law
Crop Damage Law
Custody Law
Customs Law
Debtor/Bankruptcy Law
Debtor/Creditor Law
Defendants Law
Defense of DUI & Drug Cases
Dental Malpractice Law
Directors & Officers Liability
Divorce Law
Domestic Relations
Drainage & Levee Law
Drug Law
Education Law
Election Law
Eminent Domain Law
Employee Benefit Law
Employee Stock Ownership Plans & Financing
Employment Law
Employment Discrimination Law
Energy Law
Engineering Malpractice Law
Entertainment Law
Environmental Insurance Law
Environmental Law
Environmental & Industrial Disease Law
Equal Opportunity Law
Equine Law
Equipment Leasing Law
Equity Practice
ERISA
Estate Planning
Estate Planning & Probate
Export Law & Regulation
Fair Employment Law
Family Law
Farm Law
Federal Employers Liability Law
Federal Excise Tax Law
Federal Gas Law
Federal Income, Estate & Gift Tax Law
Federal Power Law
Federal Practice
Federal Tort Law
Fidelity & Surety Law
Fiduciary Law
Finance Law
Financial Institution Law
Firearms Law
Fire Insurance Law
Fishery Law
Food, Drug & Cosmetic Law
Foreclosure Law
Foreign Collaborations/Joint Ventures
Foreign Patent Law
Forestry Law
Franchise Law
Fraudulent Sales Law
General Negligence Trials & Appeals
Government (or Public) Contract Law
Guardianship Law
Handicapped Rights Law
Hazardous Materials Law
Health Care & Hospital Law
High Technology Law
Highway Design Law
Historic Preservation Law
Housing & Urban Development Law
Immigration & Nationality Law
Import & Export Law
Indian Affairs Law
Industrial and/or Intellectual Property Law
Industrial Revenue Bond Law
Insolvency Law
Insurance Law
Insurance Law—Bad Faith
Insurance Law—Catastrophe Losses
Insurance Defense Law
Insurance Policyholders' Law
Intellectual Property Law
International Business Law
International Commercial Law
International Law
International Trade Commission Law
Interstate Commerce Law
Invasion of Privacy Law
Investment Law
Japanese Negotiations Law
Juvenile Law
Labor Law
Labor Law—Management & Employees
Landlord & Tenant Law
Land Use Law
Legal Ethics & Discipline Law
Legal Research
Legislative Practice
Libel & Slander Law
Licensing Law
Life Insurance Law
Liquor Control Law
Literary Property Law
Litigation
Litigation—Trial & Appellate
Livestock Law
Malpractice Law—Architectural
Malpractice Law—Legal
Malpractice Law—Legal/Medical
Malpractice Law—Legal/Medical Defense
Malpractice Law—Medical
Malpractice Law—Professional
Marine & Inland Marine Insurance Law
Maritime Law
Maritime Negligence Law
Marketing Law
Matrimonial Law
Mechanics Lien Law
Media Law
Mediation Law
Medical Legal Law
Mental Health Law
Mergers & Acquisitions
Military Law
Mine Safety & Health Law
Mining Law
Mobile Home Law
Mortgage Law
Motion Picture Law
Motor Carrier Law
Municipal Bond Law
Municipal Finance Law
Municipal Law
Natural Resources Law
Negligence Law
Non-Profit Organizations Law
Nuclear (or Atomic) Law
Occupational Disease Law
Occupational Safety & Health Law
Offshore Injuries Law
Oil & Gas Law
OSHA Law
Partnership Law
Patent Law
Patent, Trademark & Copyright Law
Pension & Profit Sharing Law
Personal Injury Law
Personal Injury Trial Law
Petroleum Law
Pipeline Law
Post-Conviction Relief Law
Poverty Law
Premises Liability Law
Probate Law
Products Liability Law
Products Liability Law—Asbestos
Professional Corporations Law
Professional Ethics & Discipline Law
Professional Liablity Law
Project Finance Law
Property & Inland Marine Insurance Law
Public Authority Financing Law
Public Contract Law
Public Employment Relations Law
Public Housing Law
Public Improvement Law
Public Land Law
Publishing Law
Radiation Law
Radio Law
Railroad Law
Ranch Law
Real Estate Law
Real Estate Development and/or Syndications Law
Receivership Law
Reclamation Law
Regulatory Law
Re-Insurance Law
Rent Control Law
Reorganization Law
Retail Collection Law
Retirement Plans—Qualified RICO
Riparian Rights Law
Savings & Loan Law
School Law
Science Law
Secured Transactions Law
Securities Law
Selective Service Law
Sexual Abuse of Children Law
Sexual Assault Law
Shareholders Law
Shopping Center Law
Small Business Law
Social Security Disability Law
Space Law
Sports Law
State & Local Tax Law
Steamship Law
Subrogation Law
Surety Law
Taxation Law
Tax Certiorari Law
Tax Exempt Financing Law
Tax Litigation & Appeals
Tax Shelters Law
Technology Law
TEFRA (Tax Equity & Fiscal Responsibility Act of 1982)
Telecommunication Law
Television Law
Theatre Law
Timber & Logging/Lumber
Time Sharing Law
Title Insurance Law
Title Opinions Law
Tort Law
Tort Law—Defense
Toxic Torts
Trade Association Law
Trademark Law
Tradename Law
Trade Regulation Law
Trade Secrets Law
Traffic Law
Transnational Law
Transportation Law
Travel Law
Trial Practice
Trial Practice—Civil
Trial Practice—Criminal
Trust Law
Truth-in-Lending Law
UCC (Uniform Commerce)
Unemployment Compensation Law
Unfair Competition Law
Unfair Trade Practices Law
Uninsured Motorist Law
University Law
Urban Affairs Law
Utility Law
Venture Capital Law
Veterans Law
Wage Earner Plans
Wage & Hour Law
Water Quality Law
Water Rights Law
Welfare Law
Will Contests Law
Wills
Worker's Compensation Law
Workmen's (or Worker's) Compensation Law
Workmen's Compensation Law
Wrongful Death Law
Wrongful Discharge Law
Zoning Law

10–2 Bankruptcy Law

One unique aspect associated with specializing in bankruptcy law is the fact that all bankruptcy matters are under federal court jurisdiction. There are no state bankruptcy courts nor can there be, since the U.S. Constitution provides in Article I, Section 8, clause 4 that the Congress shall have the power "To establish . . . uniform Laws on the subject of Bankruptcies throughout the United States."

For the bankruptcy paralegal, this means that the federal laws regarding bankruptcy are the same from state to state. When you are faced with a massive bankruptcy filing, such as that of Federated Department Stores, involving law firms from all over the country and tens of thousands of claims from creditors, the fact that everyone is operating under the same system of laws takes on great significance.

A Brief History and Overview of Bankruptcy Law

The first bankruptcy laws date back to 1800, with subsequent acts passed in 1841, 1898, 1938, and 1978. Throughout the country, in each judicial district, a United States Bankruptcy Court has been created as an independent adjunct to the district court. Bankruptcy judges are appointed by the President of the U.S. for a term of 14 years.

From a purely pragmatic perspective, specializing in bankruptcy law may ensure your paralegal career. Businesses and individuals file for bankruptcy in good times and bad. Many industries such as the airlines, which were once regulated, are now subject to the whims of the free-market system. When these industries find themselves in trouble, they are often forced to file for bankruptcy.

Likewise, individual filings, which make up the bulk of bankruptcy cases filed each year, are increasing as more people turn to the bankruptcy courts as a way out when faced with unemployment, catastrophic health problems, or massive consumer debt.

Since 1980, the total number of bankruptcy cases filed has nearly doubled, with no downtrend in sight. During a one-year period from July 1989 through June 1990, the records of the Administrative Office of the United States Courts indicate that 725,000 bankruptcies were filed. In one year alone, 1991, a record 944,000 individuals and businesses filed for bankruptcy. The Administrative Office of the Courts predicts that 1992 will be another record year for bankruptcy filings. Because of the increase in individual and business bankruptcy filings in recent years, in April 1991 the chairman of the American Bankruptcy Institute asked Congress to establish a committee to revamp the nation's bankruptcy system once again. A similar committee was responsible for the report leading to the passage of the Bankruptcy Reform Act of 1978.

With the number of bankruptcy cases on the rise, the need for paralegals in this field will increase substantially in the foreseeable future.

Chapter 7 Bankruptcy

In general, a **debtor** is any person, partnership, or corporation with debts. However, banks, railroads, building and loan associations, insurance companies, savings and loan associations, homestead associations, and credit unions

Figure 10–2 Personal Bankruptcy in U.S.

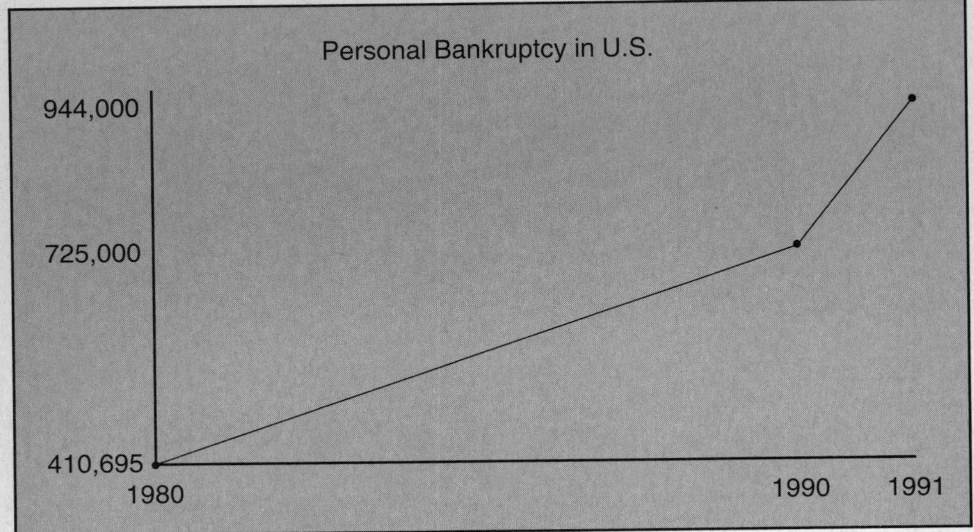

Source: Administrative Office of the United States Courts. Reprinted with permission.

are exempt from classification as a debtor under the federal bankruptcy laws and cannot file for bankruptcy.

A **Chapter 7** is a personal or business bankruptcy proceeding in which the debtor, who is also called a petitioner, is compelled to turn property into cash—to *liquidate* assets—to pay creditors. Filing for bankruptcy is the equivalent of calling a time out with creditors. **Wage garnishments,** a statutory proceeding whereby a portion of a debtor's wages are applied to the debt owed to a third person, are halted. Lawsuits are shelved. Foreclosures on a mortgage are postponed. Collection efforts cease while the debtor bares his or her financial soul to a federal bankruptcy trustee.

Secured debts, or debts against which property has been pledged as collateral, are paid from the liquidated assets after attorney's fees, court costs, and taxes are paid. If a secured creditor receives any payment, the amount is usually only a fraction of the total amount owed. Some *unsecured* debts may be discharged completely, such as credit cards and utility bills. However, the courts will not discharge debts of child support, alimony, student loans, court fines, taxes, and judgments resulting from drunken driving.

A Chapter 7 bankruptcy is designed to give petitioners who are overwhelmed by personal debts a fresh start. Therefore, petitioners often are able to keep their house and car, as long as the payments are made, as well as their household furniture and furnishings and any books or tools used in making their living. However, if there is too much **equity** in the house—the difference between what the property is worth and what is owed on it—the court might force a sale. There are both federal and state laws that limit the value of exempt property. Debtors can file for bankruptcy under Chapter 7 only once every six years.

Chapter 13 Bankruptcy

Chapter 13 is the second type of personal bankruptcy proceeding. Unlike a Chapter 7 bankruptcy, which requires the liquidation of nonexempt assets, a Chapter 13 proceeding is specifically designed for a debtor with a stable income.

Under a Chapter 13, the petitioner, with the help of a bankruptcy trustee, works out a repayment plan with the creditors, extending in some cases for up to five years. During the plan period, the debtor pays the trustee as agreed and the trustee makes payments to the creditors. The trustee has the authority to make any necessary and reasonable adjustments to the plan, but except for a medical emergency, the debtor is not allowed to apply for credit without approval from the court.

In some cases, a Chapter 13 bankruptcy proceeding is a win-win solution for both the debtors and the creditors. For example, under a Chapter 13 the debtors will find it easier to hold on to the family residence, their cars, family heirlooms, and other valued items than under a Chapter 7 filing, since the purpose of Chapter 13 is to pay off credit obligations without having to liquidate assets. In addition, the creditors greatly improve their chances of collection with a Chapter 13 proceeding, even though they may not receive the full amount due and it may take longer to collect.

Chapter 13 petitioners usually find it easier than Chapter 7 filers to obtain credit again once the plan is complete. This could be an important decision-making factor, considering the value placed on having a good credit rating by lenders and others.

Chapter 11 Bankruptcy

Businesses are no longer permitted to file a straight liquidation bankruptcy. They may, however, file a **Chapter 11** bankruptcy proceeding to reorganize. The purpose of a Chapter 11 reorganization is to attempt to ensure that the creditors will not be harmed and to forestall or eliminate the chances of the enterprise going out of business. Eastern Airlines and Federated Department Stores are well-known examples of Chapter 11 business reorganization bankruptcies.

The bankruptcy courts have traditionally refused to let individuals file for Chapter 11 bankruptcy, reserving that right for businesses alone. However, in June 1991 the U.S. Supreme Court ruled in *Toibb v. Radloff*, 111 S. Ct. 2197 (1991) that individual debtors can file for Chapter 11.

A Chapter 11 works much the same way as a Chapter 13. In both cases, the goal is to pay off the creditors without having to liquidate all the assets. In a Chapter 11, instead of automatically appointing a trustee to work out a repayment plan, a bankruptcy trustee's office appoints a committee from a list of the business's seven largest creditors. However, if there is sufficient cause, upon motion and a hearing, the court may appoint a trustee to oversee the debtor's affairs. Sufficient cause might include fraud, dishonesty, incompetence, or gross mismanagement of the business; or, if the creditors believe it is in their best interests they may request that a trustee be appointed.

In the absence of the appointment of a trustee, the creditors' committee, together with the debtor and the debtor's attorney, work out a plan to pay the creditors. Remedies could include selling property belonging to the debtor, retaining the services of turn-around specialists to run the business, or seeking a buyer for the business. It is not unusual for the major creditors in a Chapter 11 proceeding to retain their own counsel to represent their interests, nor is it unusual for companies to successfully emerge from a Chapter 11 proceeding.

Involuntary Bankruptcy

Although most bankruptcy filings are voluntary actions on the part of the debtor, in some situations an involuntary Chapter 7 (personal liquidation) or

Chapter 11 (business reorganization) bankruptcy proceeding may be initiated against a debtor by a group of creditors.

In an **involuntary bankruptcy** proceeding, three or more creditors with claims totaling $5000 over and above any lien on the debtor's property may force the debtor into bankruptcy. If there are fewer than 12 creditors, any one creditor may institute bankruptcy proceedings if claims against the debtor total $5000 or more. Farmers and nonprofit organizations are exempt from involuntary bankruptcy actions.

Functions of the Bankruptcy Paralegal

The services of paralegals are so valuable in a bankruptcy practice that Section 330 of the new Bankruptcy Code provides for compensation of paralegal services. This section provides, in part, for "reasonable compensation for actual, necessary services rendered by such trustee, examiner, professional person, or attorney, as the case may be, and by any *paraprofessional person employed by such trustee, professional person, or attorney,* as the case may be, based on the time, the nature, the extent, and the value of such services" (emphasis added)

In addition to having a thorough understanding and knowledge of bankruptcy law, paralegals are responsible for tasks such as the following.

1. Interviewing and working with clients to obtain all the information required to file the bankruptcy petition and the accompanying schedules of financial information.
2. Assembling client's financial documents including tax returns, deeds of title to property, and life insurance policies.
3. Compiling a list of assets.
4. Compiling a list of debts.
5. Arranging searches under the Uniform Commercial Code and with title companies for secured property transactions.
6. Ordering asset appraisals.
7. Communicating with client on general bankruptcy court procedures.
8. Drafting petitions and schedules.
9. Filing proofs of claims from creditors.
10. Handling routine calls and correspondence to and from creditors, the chairperson for the creditors' committee, the attorneys, the trustee, and the client.
11. Attending court hearings with attorney and client to facilitate the flow of paperwork.
12. Maintaining a calendar of critical dates.
13. Drafting, filing, and serving the debtor's monthly financial statement in a Chapter 11 proceeding.
14. Drafting, filing, and serving complaints in any adversary proceedings.
15. Drafting and filing attorney's fee applications.
16. Drafting and filing the discharge application when the case is completed.

10–3 Business and Corporate Law

In many urban and suburban areas, business and corporate law practices employ paralegals to perform a variety of tasks. Both new business startups and established corporations require ongoing legal services.

Background and Overview of Business and Corporate Law

There are three categories of business entities: a **sole proprietorship,** which is a business owned by one person; a **partnership,** a business owned by two or more persons; and a **corporation.** A corporation is more than a business entity. It is a legal entity, a creation of law, formed primarily for the convenience of those people who have invested money in the corporation, its **shareholders.**

Corporations, whether *domestic* (formed under the laws of your state) or *foreign* (organized under the laws of another state) have a major advantage over a sole proprietorship or a partnership. That advantage is the corporation's limited liability. Since a corporation, in the eyes of the law, is a separate legal entity, its liabilities extend only to the value of its assets. Likewise, an individual shareholder's liability is limited to the amount of his or her investment in stock of the corporation. If a corporation encounters financial difficulty or is enjoined in a lawsuit, it is unlikely that the shareholders will be required to liquidate their personal assets to pay the corporation's debts or any judgment against it.

Most partnerships and sole proprietorships do not enjoy the limited liability protection of a corporation. If a partnership or proprietorship finds itself in financial trouble, the partners or owner are personally liable for the business's debts.

In the past, corporations also were entitled to certain federal and state tax advantages. For example, a corporation was taxed at a lesser rate than individuals. In addition, the fees for incorporation by many states were relatively low, resulting in a strong growth in the number of corporations being formed. However, recent federal and state tax-reform acts have eliminated some of the attractiveness of a corporation. Business owners need expert advice on how best to organize.

Functions of the Business and Corporate Paralegal

Much of the legal work associated with a new business startup is often handled by a paralegal. Likewise, once a business is established, the owners or shareholders need continuing help with their legal matters. Partners come and go, requiring new partnership agreements, buy-sell agreements, and payouts. Corporate minute books must be kept current to reflect the major decisions of the officers and directors. Paralegals familiar with business and corporate law find themselves in demand in most parts of the country.

The typical functions of a business and corporate paralegal include the following.

1. Researching the availability of the proposed name and reserving same.
2. Drafting and filing Articles of Incorporation or drafting Partnership Agreements.
3. Drafting corporate by-laws, notices of meetings, and minutes.
4. Drafting shareholder agreements, buy-sell agreements, and banking resolutions.
5. Preparing necessary documents for opening business bank account(s).
6. Drafting employment agreements for corporate officers and other key employees.
7. Completing and filing application for employer identification number.
8. Completing and filing applications with appropriate state and federal tax authorities and administrative agencies.

9. Completing and filing applications for appropriate licenses from specific agencies.
10. Completing and filing trade name applications, copyright applications, and financial statements.
11. Ordering corporate minute book, stock book, and seal.
12. Issuing and transferring stock, preparing and maintaining shareholder register.

10–4 Civil Litigation

Litigation is the action or process of carrying on a suit in law or equity. **Civil litigation** is the action or process of carrying on a lawsuit governing private rights and remedies, as opposed to criminal law, military law, or international law. In other words, when a private party sues another private party, corporation, or public agency to remedy a private right, the action is a civil litigation action. Product liability, personal injury, breach of contract, and wrongful termination of employment are common types of civil litigation lawsuits.

Functions of the Civil Litigation Paralegal

Because civil litigation is often complex, litigation paralegals work more closely with attorneys than in some other areas of specialization and perform a wide range of tasks that might include the following.

1. Interviewing clients, gathering facts, and checking statute of limitations.
2. Drafting pleadings, arranging for signature, filing, and service.
3. Conducting investigations, obtaining documentary evidence, and taking witnesses' statements.
4. Maintaining contact with client and providing instructions and information.
5. Drafting discovery documents including interrogatories, requests for admissions, or answers to interrogatories and requests for admissions.
6. Arranging for depositions, giving notices, and drafting questions.
7. Taking notes during depositions and summarizing depositions.
8. Preparing motions and settings for trial and pretrial conferences.
9. Preparing for trial; organizing exhibits, evidence, witnesses, subpoenas, and investigation of jurors.
10. Drafting findings of fact or objections (as requested) and proposed judgment.
11. Preparing and serving of releases, settlement documents, or judgment.
12. Obtaining payment of judgment or arranging to levy execution, including examination of judgment debtor.
13. Conducting legal research for appellate briefs, if appeal is taken.

This list of functions is not all-inclusive, since civil litigation matters may take a number of years to resolve. During the period of a civil lawsuit, any number of pleadings, motions, and discovery documents may be required. This list, however, does include the usual functions performed by a civil litigation paralegal.

10–5 Collections

Unfortunately, some individuals and businesses choose not to pay their debts or any judgments against them. When this happens, the matter often winds up on an attorney's desk for action. Paralegals are often assigned many of the tasks involved with collection matters.

Overview of Collections

Debt collections cases are brought to the law firm by individuals, businesses, corporations, and organizations. Insurance companies and banks typically assign their debt collection work to outside law firms. However, the key to a successful collections practice is locating and attaching the debtor's assets.

Paralegals who enjoy working in the collections field are usually good detectives with a great deal of patience and persistence. Debtors tend to be quite clever at concealing assets, and the paralegal must be equally clever at locating them. Many collection firms regularly employ the services of private investigators and professional asset locators, but it is often the paralegal who uncovers the debtor's assets, the clue to which may be buried in the paperwork.

Functions of the Collections Paralegal

In addition to serving as liaison between a private investigator or asset locator and the attorney, a collections paralegal often works directly with state and local administrative agencies to ascertain information regarding the financial background and current status of the debtor.

Functions of the collections paralegal include the following.

1. Interviewing the client and reviewing client's documentation of the debt.
2. Drafting demand letter to debtor.
3. Conducting preliminary asset investigation.
4. Drafting, filing, and serving summons and complaint.
5. After hearing or default, drafting judgment, cost bill, and other support pleadings.
6. Drafting, filing, and serving documents for judgment debtor examination.
7. Preparing and serving wage garnishment writ on debtor's employer.
8. Arranging for notice of sale posting or publication.
9. Communicating with sheriff on levy against personal property.
10. Preparing and filing abstracts of judgments in all counties and states where debtor may own property.
11. Preparing and filing satisfaction of judgment when debt is collected.

10–6 Criminal Law

Only a comparatively small number of lawyers in private practice specialize in criminal law. Subsequently, a relatively small number of paralegals find themselves working in the criminal law field. The majority of criminal law paralegals are employed by a district attorney's office, a public defender's office, or some related public-sector group.

Figure 10–3 A Courtroom Consultation

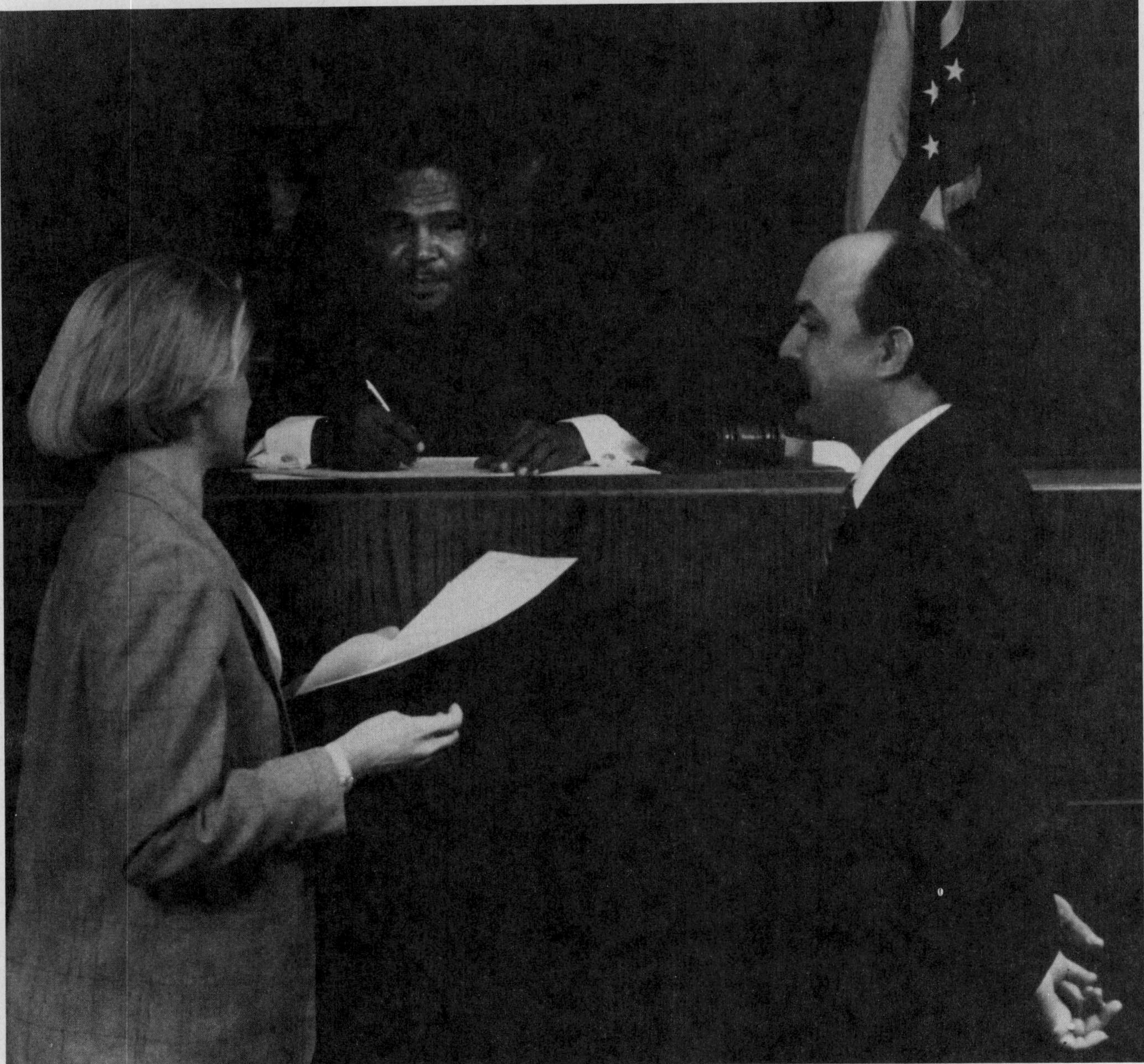

The public defender and the district attorney will discuss a point of law with the judge during a trial. *Source:* Ted Rice

Overview of Criminal Law

The outbreak of white-collar crimes in the last decade has made criminal law specialists out of many attorneys who never thought they would be involved in the criminal justice system. Businessmen and -women, stockbrokers, attorneys, doctors, and accountants have been charged with crimes ranging from fraud and embezzlement to insider trading and failing to warn patients of a potentially life-threatening illness.

Representing those accused of a crime is a most serious business, since the accused may be in danger of losing all of his or her rights to life and liberty. In a small office, when a call is placed to an attorney from jail, frequently the legal assistant is the one who takes it, because criminal law attorneys spend a great deal of time in court. It is then up to the legal assistant to obtain accurate information, including the full name of the person being held, the address and telephone number of the jail, the nature of the charge, the time and place of arrest, whether a warrant for the arrest had been issued, and whether bail has been set.

The attorney should be quickly notified and arrangements made to see the client as soon after the arrest as possible.

Functions of the Criminal Law Paralegal

Although some of the duties of the criminal law paralegal vary depending on whether you are working in a private law firm, the district attorney's office, or the public defender's office, many functions remain the same regardless of place of employment. The duties of the criminal law paralegal include the following.

1. Interviewing the client with the attorney.
2. Arranging for bail.
3. Investigating facts, and obtaining the police report and warrants.
4. Gathering information to plea bargain, to prepare charges, or to plead for arraignment.
5. Preparing for preliminary hearing or grand jury hearing.
6. Researching the law for filing of pretrial motions.
7. Interviewing and issuing subpoenas to witnesses.
8. Photographing the alleged crime scene and examining physical evidence.
9. Arranging for and coordinating investigators and experts.
10. Attending pretrial conferences with attorney.
11. Drafting jury instructions.
12. Attending and assisting at trial.
13. Researching the law for appealable issues.
14. Drafting assignments of error and arguments for appeal.

10–7 Family Law

Many people become interested in paralegal studies after firsthand experience with a family law matter. Nationwide the divorce rate remains at or near the 50 percent mark. Since the social stigma once attached to divorced people has diminished, no longer is it uncommon for an individual to have been divorced more than once. Arguably, in no other field of law does the paralegal play such a vital and encompassing role as in the family law practice.

Background of Family Law

Prior to the 1960s, the general attitude and expectation of married couples was that the marriage would last until one of them died. Few people now in their 40s or older had divorced parents; even fewer had divorced grandparents. The same cannot be said for more recent generations. As a whole, U.S. society has come to accept divorce as a relatively easy way to end a relationship. Nevertheless, the process of terminating a marriage is never a pleasant experience.

In the late 1960s and throughout the 1970s many states adopted their own version of a family law act. These various acts changed prior laws pertaining to marriage, divorce, legal separations, separate maintenance, annulments, child custody and support, spousal support, and the division of property. In many instances, the effects of these changes in family laws were not what the legislators intended when the laws were enacted.

One major change resulting from the new laws was to eliminate the term *divorce* in some states. In California, for example, a divorce action was replaced with *dissolution of marriage proceeding*, which is initiated by the *petitioner*, who files a *petition for dissolution*. The *respondent* is given an opportunity to file his or her *response*. In addition to this major change in terminology, grounds for dissolution or divorce in most *no-fault* states are irreconcilable differences or incurable insanity. In other words, one party is not required to blame or find fault with the other in order to terminate the marriage.

The field of family law is by no means limited to the issues involving the dissolution of a marriage, child custody and support, spousal support, and property division. The modern-day family law practice is diverse and includes paternity actions, surrogate-parenting rights, fetal rights, adoptions, child abuse and neglect concerns, juvenile delinquency problems, crimes between family members, clarifying the definition of the family unit, civil lawsuits for emotional distress filed against former spouses, premarital agreements, and the property rights and financial responsibility of unmarried persons who live together.

Functions of the Family Law Paralegal

Understandably, family law clients are often emotionally distraught, requiring a great deal of handholding and a sympathetic listener. Thus, the family law paralegal not only acts as the principal liaison between the client and the attorney, he or she is often called upon to provide emotional support to the client.

In addition to a working knowledge of the law and court procedures, the well-informed family law paralegal is also current on federal, state, county, and local support systems, as well as the appropriate counselors, government agencies, and authorities to which clients may be referred for various needs and purposes.

In addition to assuming the roles of confidant and friend, the functions of the family law paralegal include the following.

1. Interviewing the client and collecting background information and financial data.
2. Participating in discussions of alternative options to divorce including counseling, mediation, separation, or reconciliation.
3. Drafting and arranging service of appropriate legal documents to commence legal proceeding.
4. Assisting client in preparing monthly income and expense calculation.
5. Determining spousal- and child-support needs.
6. Arranging for real and personal property appraisers.
7. Obtaining court hearing dates.
8. Drafting settlement agreement.
9. Preparing final decree of dissolution and accompanying documents.

10–8 Intellectual Property Law

Largely as a result of the proliferation of computer software, there has been a concurrent interest and growth in intellectual property law. Once associated primarily with inventors and engineers, the intellectual property law practice may include clients from the music industry, authors, playwrights, and other innovative and creative people. The intellectual property law practice is research-intensive, with cases often winding up in the courtroom for decision by a jury.

Overview of Intellectual Property Law

Although it has always been difficult to protect an idea that could make millions for you, recent changes in the copyright laws have kept many lawyers busy in courtrooms across the country. For example, the *Copyright Act of 1980* states that computer software programs are eligible for the same copyright protection as other forms of original creativity and expression. Furthermore, the act prescribes damages of $10,000 for each illegally duplicated copy of software and an additional $40,000 penalty per copy if the copyright holder can prove that the copies were made intentionally. Similar protection applies to authors of materials that are duplicated for use in classrooms.

Recent courtroom trials have focused on the entertainment industry, where individuals and companies have been accused of stealing the ideas presented by someone else and turning them into hit movies or gold recordings without compensating the idea generator.

Intellectual property law covers a diverse range of clients, and paralegals are an integral part of this practice specialty.

Functions of the Intellectual Property Law Paralegal

Although not as emotionally intense as the family law practice, this field of law has its highly charged moments. Imagine the emotional state of a client who has seen his or her work presented as the work of someone else. Or imagine the state of mind of the inventor who has worked day and night to develop a truly better mousetrap, only to find it cannot be patented. Intellectual property law is far from routine or boring. Intellectual property paralegals are likely to have a great deal of contact with clients and will perform much of their work autonomously.

The functions of the intellectual property law paralegal include these tasks.

1. Conducting patent and trademark searches.
2. Conducting on-line computer database searches for technical information relating to particular patents and trademarks.
3. Drafting trademark or service mark applications, renewal applications, and affidavits.
4. Drafting copyright applications.
5. Researching case law, procedural law, and unfair competition matters.
6. Maintaining files of new products and invention developments.
7. Reviewing patent filings with engineers.
8. Drafting licensing agreements relating to proprietary information or technology.
9. Communicating with foreign trademark attorneys and agents regarding foreign trademarks.
10. Assisting in trial preparation, including arranging for visual aids and models for trial use.

Figure 10–4 A U.S. Copyright Form

FORM TX
UNITED STATES COPYRIGHT OFFICE

REGISTRATION NUMBER

TX TXU

EFFECTIVE DATE OF REGISTRATION

Month Day Year

DO NOT WRITE ABOVE THIS LINE. IF YOU NEED MORE SPACE, USE A SEPARATE CONTINUATION SHEET.

1

TITLE OF THIS WORK ▼

PREVIOUS OR ALTERNATIVE TITLES ▼

PUBLICATION AS A CONTRIBUTION If this work was published as a contribution to a periodical, serial, or collection, give information about the collective work in which the contribution appeared. **Title of Collective Work ▼**

If published in a periodical or serial give: **Volume ▼** **Number ▼** **Issue Date ▼** **On Pages ▼**

2

a **NAME OF AUTHOR ▼** **DATES OF BIRTH AND DEATH** Year Born ▼ Year Died ▼

Was this contribution to the work a "work made for hire"? ☐ Yes ☐ No

AUTHOR'S NATIONALITY OR DOMICILE Name of Country OR { Citizen of ▶ ______ Domiciled in ▶ ______

WAS THIS AUTHOR'S CONTRIBUTION TO THE WORK Anonymous? ☐ Yes ☐ No Pseudonymous? ☐ Yes ☐ No If the answer to either of these questions is "Yes," see detailed instructions.

NATURE OF AUTHORSHIP Briefly describe nature of the material created by this author in which copyright is claimed. ▼

b **NAME OF AUTHOR ▼** **DATES OF BIRTH AND DEATH** Year Born ▼ Year Died ▼

Was this contribution to the work a "work made for hire"? ☐ Yes ☐ No

AUTHOR'S NATIONALITY OR DOMICILE Name of country OR { Citizen of ▶ ______ Domiciled in ▶ ______

WAS THIS AUTHOR'S CONTRIBUTION TO THE WORK Anonymous? ☐ Yes ☐ No Pseudonymous? ☐ Yes ☐ No If the answer to either of these questions is "Yes," see detailed instructions

NATURE OF AUTHORSHIP Briefly describe nature of the material created by this author in which copyright is claimed. ▼

c **NAME OF AUTHOR ▼** **DATES OF BIRTH AND DEATH** Year Born ▼ Year Died ▼

Was this contribution to the work a "work made for hire"? ☐ Yes ☐ No

AUTHOR'S NATIONALITY OR DOMICILE Name of Country OR { Citizen of ▶ ______ Domiciled in ▶ ______

WAS THIS AUTHOR'S CONTRIBUTION TO THE WORK Anonymous? ☐ Yes ☐ No Pseudonymous? ☐ Yes ☐ No If the answer to either of these questions is "Yes," see detailed instructions

NATURE OF AUTHORSHIP Briefly describe nature of the material created by this author in which copyright is claimed. ▼

NOTE

Under the law, the "author" of a "work made for hire" is generally the employer, not the employee (see instructions). For any part of this work that was "made for hire" check "Yes" in the space provided, give the employer (or other person for whom the work was prepared) as "Author" of that part, and leave the space for dates of birth and death blank.

3

YEAR IN WHICH CREATION OF THIS WORK WAS COMPLETED **This information must be given in all cases.** ______ ◀ Year

DATE AND NATION OF FIRST PUBLICATION OF THIS PARTICULAR WORK **Complete this information ONLY if this work has been published.** Month ▶ ______ Day ▶ ______ Year ▶ ______ ______ ◀ Nation

4

COPYRIGHT CLAIMANT(S) Name and address must be given even if the claimant is the same as the author given in space 2.▼

See instructions before completing this space

TRANSFER If the claimant(s) named here in space 4 are different from the author(s) named in space 2, give a brief statement of how the claimant(s) obtained ownership of the copyright.▼

DO NOT WRITE HERE OFFICE USE ONLY

APPLICATION RECEIVED

ONE DEPOSIT RECEIVED

TWO DEPOSITS RECEIVED

REMITTANCE NUMBER AND DATE

MORE ON BACK ▶ • Complete all applicable spaces (numbers 5-11) on the reverse side of this page. • See detailed instructions. • Sign the form at line 10.

DO NOT WRITE HERE

Page 1 of ______ pages

Figure 10–4 continued

EXAMINED BY

FORM TX

CHECKED BY

☐ CORRESPONDENCE Yes

☐ DEPOSIT ACCOUNT FUNDS USED

FOR COPYRIGHT OFFICE USE ONLY

DO NOT WRITE ABOVE THIS LINE. IF YOU NEED MORE SPACE, USE A SEPARATE CONTINUATION SHEET.

5

PREVIOUS REGISTRATION Has registration for this work, or for an earlier version of this work, already been made in the Copyright Office?
☐ **Yes** ☐ **No** If your answer is "Yes," why is another registration being sought? (Check appropriate box) ▼
☐ This is the first published edition of a work previously registered in unpublished form.
☐ This is the first application submitted by this author as copyright claimant.
☐ This is a changed version of the work, as shown by space 6 on this application.
If your answer is "Yes," give: **Previous Registration Number** ▼ **Year of Registration** ▼

6

DERIVATIVE WORK OR COMPILATION Complete both space 6a & 6b for a derivative work; complete only 6b for a compilation.
a. **Preexisting Material** Identify any preexisting work or works that this work is based on or incorporates. ▼

b. **Material Added to This Work** Give a brief, general statement of the material that has been added to this work and in which copyright is claimed. ▼

See instructions before completing this space.

7

MANUFACTURERS AND LOCATIONS If this is a published work consisting preponderantly of nondramatic literary material in English, the law may require that the copies be manufactured in the United States or Canada for full protection. If so, the names of the manufacturers who performed certain processes, and the places where these processes were performed **must** be given. See instructions for details.
Names of Manufacturers ▼ **Places of Manufacture** ▼

8

REPRODUCTION FOR USE OF BLIND OR PHYSICALLY HANDICAPPED INDIVIDUALS A signature on this form at space 10, and a check in one of the boxes here in space 8, constitutes a non-exclusive grant of permission to the Library of Congress to reproduce and distribute solely for the blind and physically handicapped and under the conditions and limitations prescribed by the regulations of the Copyright Office: (1) copies of the work identified in space 1 of this application in Braille (or similar tactile symbols); or (2) phonorecords embodying a fixation of a reading of that work; or (3) both.
a ☐ Copies and Phonorecords b ☐ Copies Only c ☐ Phonorecords Only

See instructions.

9

DEPOSIT ACCOUNT If the registration fee is to be charged to a Deposit Account established in the Copyright Office, give name and number of Account.
Name ▼ **Account Number** ▼

CORRESPONDENCE Give name and address to which correspondence about this application should be sent. Name/Address/Apt/City/State/Zip ▼

Area Code & Telephone Number ▶

Be sure to give your daytime phone ◀ number.

10

CERTIFICATION* I, the undersigned, hereby certify that I am the
Check one ▶
☐ author
☐ other copyright claimant
☐ owner of exclusive right(s)
☐ authorized agent of ______
Name of author or other copyright claimant, or owner of exclusive right(s) ▲

of the work identified in this application and that the statements made by me in this application are correct to the best of my knowledge.

Typed or printed name and date ▼ If this is a published work, this date must be the same as or later than the date of publication given in space 3.

date ▶

Handwritten signature (X) ▼

11

MAIL CERTIFICATE TO

Name ▼

Number/Street/Apartment Number ▼

City/State/ZIP ▼

Certificate will be mailed in window envelope

Have you:
- Completed all necessary spaces?
- Signed your application in space 10?
- Enclosed check or money order for $10 payable to *Register of Copyrights*?
- Enclosed your deposit material with the application and fee?

MAIL TO: Register of Copyrights, Library of Congress, Washington, D.C. 20559

* 17 U.S.C. § 506(e): Any person who knowingly makes a false representation of a material fact in the application for copyright registration provided for by section 409, or in any written statement filed in connection with the application, shall be fined not more than $2,500.

* **U.S. GOVERNMENT PRINTING OFFICE: 1984: 421-278/10,006**

October 1984—50,000

10–9 Labor Law

Opportunities for paralegals to work in legal environments relating to employment matters exist with private law firms who specialize in labor law, within labor unions, with the in-house corporate counsel of large corporations, or within the personnel department of companies.

Overview of Employee-Employer Relationships

Just as the value systems and attitudes of employers and employees have changed over the last 30 years, so, too, have the federal and state laws governing these relationships.

Beginning with Title VII of the Civil Rights Act of 1964, employers were prohibited from discriminating against employees or potential employees on the basis of race, creed, color, sex, religion, and national origin. Subsequent amendments expanded Title VII, and new federal legislation now prohibits discrimination based upon pregnancy, age, or disabilities.

In addition to discriminatory practices and policies, employers must now also be concerned with equal pay, sexual harassment in the workplace, employees with life-threatening illnesses, and drug and alcohol abuse, as well as providing a safe and healthful working environment. Some states have more liberal laws protecting the rights of employees than others. These states have seen a dramatic increase in the number of wrongful-termination lawsuits filed by employees against employers, as well as an increase in claims for stress-related illnesses.

Functions of an Employee Benefits Paralegal

During the last decade, policy shifts at federal and state levels liberalized the benefits that employers can offer to employees. *Cafeteria plans,* from which employees may select and personalize their benefits program, became popular in many companies and government agencies. Whether elaborate and complex or simple and straightforward, all employee benefit plans require recordkeeping and administration. As a result, paralegals who were already working in corporate legal and personnel departments began to focus their skills on the administration of employee benefit plans.

Soon private law firms specializing in business, corporate, or labor law saw an additional service that they could provide to clients by bringing the employee benefit work into the firm to be handled by a paralegal. In addition, paralegals with employee benefit backgrounds work for major financial planning institutions, with actuarial consultants, and with private business firms that administer benefit programs for other companies.

Much of employee benefits work entails working with numbers, calculations, and charts and graphs. Meticulous bookkeeping and recordkeeping skills are a must for this position. Computer software programs perform many of the tedious functions involved with this type of work, but a labor law paralegal, especially one administering employee benefits, should have an above-average background in basic accounting procedures and not be entirely dependent upon a computer.

Paralegals who specialize in employee benefits are responsible for researching, implementing, and maintaining all the benefit programs offered to employees, including health, dental, and life insurance programs, cafeteria programs, and the firm's retirement program.

The functions of an employee benefits paralegal include:

1. Drafting the qualified plan documents, including trust agreements, custodial agreements, 401(k) documents, and employee stock-purchase agreements.
2. Monitoring new laws and regulations and drafting plan-amendment documents as required.
3. Drafting deferred compensation plans, including nonqualified executive-compensation plans, stock-option agreements, medical and other executive-benefits reimbursement plans.
4. Drafting notification of participation, election to participate, and beneficiary designation.
5. Drafting board of directors' resolutions and other required corporate records for plan adoption.
6. Preparing and filing of IRS application for determination letter.
7. Preparing and filing annual report.
8. Monitoring new legislation and coordinating and mailing notices to clients regarding impact of legislation on plans.
9. Calculating employer contributions and allocating to participant accounts.
10. Calculating years of service for eligibility and vesting for participants.
11. Calculating benefits for terminated participants.
12. General plan maintenance, including payment of termination benefits to terminated or retiring employees; tracking employee loan repayments; depositing employer and employee contributions to accounts; and reviewing, updating, or revising accounts to comply with new tax laws.

Functions of a Labor Law Paralegal

Labor law is not limited to employee benefits administration. Rather, this specialty covers a wide range of employee and labor-related issues, such as legal action for wrongful termination; discriminatory practices in hiring, promoting, and terminating employees; and sexual harassment.

Labor law paralegals may perform the following tasks.

1. Interviewing clients and witnesses.
2. Taking witness statements.
3. Investigating the alleged facts and circumstances surrounding the complaint.
4. Drafting performance evaluation forms for the client.
5. Leading training workshops on how to conduct a legal interview.
6. Leading training workshops on how to conduct a performance evaluation.
7. Screening job candidates for clients.
8. Monitoring the interview process for the client.
9. Developing the employee policy manual.
10. Monitoring state and federal regulations such as OSHA and Americans with Disabilities Act compliance.

10–10 Probate and Estate Planning

The probate and estate-planning paralegal is given a wide variety of duties, from interviewing clients and drafting wills and trusts to preparing federal and state estate-tax returns. Experienced freelance paralegals specializing in this field occasionally work for several lawyers or law firms at the same time, as independent contractors.

Overview of Probate

The purpose of an estate **probate** proceeding is to gather the assets and property of the deceased, pay any outstanding debts or federal or state taxes owed by the decedent, and to distribute the remainder of the deceased's property to those who are entitled to receive it either by law or by the provisions of a will. Proceedings in the probate court fall into three categories: (1) estate proceedings, (2) guardianships, and (3) conservatorships.

There are two types of estate proceedings. A **testate** proceeding takes place when a person dies leaving a valid will; an **intestate** proceeding takes place when a person dies leaving no will. Basically there are two types of wills: a **holographic will,** which is written entirely by hand by the decedent, and a **witnessed will,** which is usually typewritten and witnessed by two or more witnesses. Some states recognize as valid both holographic wills and witnessed wills, as well as other types of wills. Likewise, some states do not require that a holographic will be witnessed, as long as the entire contents of the will are in the deceased's own handwriting. Paralegals must check their own state statutes to determine the requirements for individual states.

A **guardianship** proceeding is held for the purpose of having a court-appointed guardian to take care of the person or property of a minor. Guardians are agents of the court appointed by the court to act in the place of a parent of minor children. In some instances, such as when a minor child is a party to a lawsuit, one or both of that child's parents may be appointed as *guardian ad litem* to represent the child's interest during legal action. But in probate proceedings, the parents of a minor child or children may nominate a guardian of the person and property of any minors in a will. Should the parents die, the court will usually acquiesce to the wishes of the parents and appoint the parents' nominee as guardian of any living minor children.

Conservatorship proceedings are held for the purpose of appointing an adult to take care of the person or property of any person who is unable to provide for his or her own personal needs for food, clothing, shelter, and other physical needs, or for any person who is unable to manage his or her financial affairs. Any individual of sound mind and good health may nominate his or her own conservator to act on his or her behalf when the nominator is no longer able to take proper care of him- or herself. Once an individual is incapacitated, the selection of the conservator is left solely to the court's discretion.

A Brief Look at Estate Planning

Many estates may be subject to a variety of taxes, including federal estate and income taxes, state inheritance and income taxes, and real-property taxes. However, in order to reduce estate-tax liability, many people are engaging in estate-planning practices prior to or as a part of will preparation.

Establishing one or more trusts has become an acceptable and affordable way to transfer property in an estate from the decedent to the beneficiaries and, in most cases, greatly reduce or eliminate probate proceedings and some estate taxes. Paralegals should be aware of the tax implications of any decisions regarding an individual's estate and incorporate the client's desires into a total estate plan. The more a paralegal knows about taxes, the more valuable he or she will be to the estate-planning attorney.

Functions of the Probate Paralegal

Depending upon the level of expertise of the probate paralegal, she or he might be expected to perform a variety of functions such as those that follow.

1. Interviewing clients and collecting information and documents.
2. Obtaining certified copies of the death certificate.
3. Preparing and publishing appropriate notices of death.
4. Assisting estate representatives in opening estate bank account and safe deposit box and transferring money and securities to be sold.
5. Reviewing creditors' claims, presenting them to estate representative for approval, and transmitting claims to the court.
6. Filing life insurance claims and other death-benefit claims.
7. Preparing Form 706 (federal estate tax), if required, and final income tax returns.
8. Arranging for sale of real property.
9. Preparing accountings for court.
10. Arranging with representative for distribution of property to heirs.
11. Preparing receipts of distributees.
12. Preparing and filing papers for final discharge.

10–11 How to Choose Areas of Specialization

Because of space limitations, several fields of law in which paralegals are known to function successfully are not included in this chapter. These fields include real estate law, landlord-tenant disputes, worker's compensation and other administrative agency matters, securities and municipal bonds, and tax law.

From the various lists of functions provided, you can readily discern that each specialization has some function similarities and some differences. For maximum job satisfaction, it is important for you to give some thought to the area or areas in which you would like to specialize. For example, some paralegals gain expertise in related fields, such as business and corporate law and tax law. Probate, estate planning, and tax law are also related fields. The same is true of worker's compensation, unemployment benefits, and Social Security administration matters.

Characteristics of Selected Fields

As you explore the different fields of law, you will want to consider how your personality fits with a particular area of specialization. For example, are you a "people person"? Or do you prefer to work in solitude? Does working closely with others motivate and stimulate you? Or does having other people around while you are working annoy and distract you?

Specializations with Heavy Client Contact If you like working directly with the client in one-on-one situations, the fields of family law, criminal law, and problems involving an administrative agency are just right for you. Typically, these practices center around emotional, intense issues and people. Frustration and anxiety often reach high levels.

The paralegal must be able to remain calm when under stress, to react unemotionally to occasional outbursts from clients, attorneys, agency workers, and others. Above all, the paralegal must not become emotionally involved with his or her clients and be able to leave the work behind at the end of the day.

Working in client-intensive practices can be a challenging and rewarding career for legal assistants who are able to control their stress, anxiety, depression, and general attitude.

Specializations with Some Client Contact The fields of bankruptcy, business and corporate law, and probate and estate planning require some limited contact with the client. The paralegal usually interviews the client to obtain the required information for completing any documents and other paperwork. With the exception of a phone call or two, the legal assistant may then have no further contact with the client until the client returns to the office to sign documents.

Not only do these fields of law require less contact with the client, they typically are not as emotionally intense as some other areas. Individual stress levels in these businesslike practices are usually more acceptable. You are not as likely to receive distress calls at midnight, nor threats on your life from clients or ex-spouses of clients.

Specializations with Little Client Contact Intellectual property law, employee benefits, collections, and civil litigation are fields in which the paralegal may never deal directly with the client after the initial interview. In some instances, it would not be unusual for the legal assistant never to have direct contact with the client, since the client is often a company or large organization, and not an individual.

These fields of law are seen by some legal assistants as cold and impersonal. They do tend to be research-intensive and require the production of prodigious amounts of paper documents. Stress levels are usually low, and the general atmosphere of the office is more relaxed than in some other areas of specialization, except when preparing for trial.

It is important that you give some thought to your personal style and preferences before embarking on a career path.

SUMMARY

10–1

The practice of law is not limited to a few fields. The U.S. Supreme Court lists over 300 generally recognized fields of law. As world economies become more interdependent and more sophisticated technologies are developed, it is reasonable to expect new specialty areas of law will emerge, providing even more opportunities for paralegals.

10–2

The U.S. Constitution gave Congress the power to establish uniform laws on the subject of bankruptcy to be administered in the federal court system. Subsequently, U.S. Bankruptcy Courts were created in each judicial district throughout the country as independent adjuncts to the district court. Judges in the bankruptcy courts are appointed by the President of the U.S. for a term of 14 years. Chapter 7 is one type of personal bankruptcy proceeding, which requires the debtor to liquidate all assets to pay creditors. Chapter 13 is another type of personal bankruptcy proceeding specifically designed for a debtor with a stable income. With the help of a trustee, a repayment plan is worked out with creditors; the debtor is usually not required to liquidate assets as long as scheduled payments are being made. A Chapter 11 bankruptcy proceeding is no longer reserved just for the reorganization of businesses. Since the U.S. Supreme Court's June 1991 decision, individuals may also file Chapter 11 proceedings. A Chapter 11 bankruptcy attempts to ensure that creditors will not be harmed when a business or individual experiences financial difficulties. Businesses are no longer permitted to file a straight liquidation bankruptcy. The services of paralegals are so valuable in a bankruptcy practice that the court allows law firms to be compensated for the services provided by these paraprofessionals.

10–3

There are three categories of business entities: a sole proprietorship, which is a business owned by one person; a partnership, which is a business owned by two or more persons; and a corporation, which is created and governed by laws primarily for the convenience of the investors, or shareholders. One major advantage a corporation has over a proprietorship or a partnership is its limited liability protection for shareholders. In the past corporations were also taxed at a lower rate than individuals, but recent federal and state tax-reform acts have eliminated, for the most part, any tax advantages to being incorporated. Paralegals perform many tasks in a business and corporate practice and often work with little direct supervision from an attorney.

10–4

Civil litigation is the action or process of carrying on a lawsuit governing private rights and remedies. Parties to civil litigation suits can include individuals, corporations, and public agencies. Product liability, personal injury, breach of contract, and wrongful termination of employment are common types of civil litigation lawsuits. Litigation paralegals work closely with attorneys, performing a variety of tasks including drafting pleadings, obtaining documentary evidence, summarizing depositions, preparing for trial, and conducting legal research.

10–5

Debt-collection cases are brought to the law firm by individuals, businesses, corporations, and private organizations for action on outstanding obligations and judgments obtained against a debtor. Paralegals work closely with asset locators and private investigators to locate the debtor's assets, then proceed to prepare and file legal documents in order to seize or attach those assets. Paralegals specializing in debt collection often work with little direct supervision from an attorney.

10–6

Compared to other fields of law, only a small number of lawyers in private practice specialize in criminal law. Criminal law paralegals, therefore, usually are employed in district attorney's offices, in the Department of the Treasury, and in public defenders' offices. However, the proliferation of white-collar crimes has made criminal law specialists out of many attorneys who never thought they would be involved in the criminal justice system. Criminal law paralegals work closely with the client, the attorney, the police department, and investigators gathering information, facts, and evidence.

10–7

Many paralegals first become interested in the field of family law because of personal experience in a divorce proceeding. During the last two or three decades, family law acts introduced in many states have redefined the entire family law practice. The field of family law is no longer limited to the issues involving the dissolution of a marriage, child custody and support, spousal support, and the division of property. The practice of family law now may include paternity actions, surrogate-parenting rights, fetal rights, adoptions, child abuse and neglect concerns, juvenile delinquency problems, crimes between family members, clarifying the definition of the family unit, civil lawsuits for emotional distress, premarital agreements, and the property rights and financial responsibilities of unmarried persons who live together. The paralegal in the family law practice is the primary liaison between the client and the attorney and performs many functions, including providing emotional support for the client. Family law paralegals work closely with clients in this field of law and must guard against becoming overly involved with the clients' problems. This field is known to produce a high level of job burnout and stress-related illnesses. Nevertheless, it is usually a rewarding and challenging experience.

10–8

The intellectual property law field is research-intensive, with cases often winding up in the courtroom for decision by a jury. Often at issue are copyright protection and infringement matters, patent protection and violations of patent rights, trademark and service mark searches and registration. Intellectual property law is often an international practice, since individuals and companies often desire to protect their creative ideas in other countries as well as within the United States. Paralegals in this field perform a variety of functions including research and drafting of legal documents, often working with little direct supervision.

10–9

Paralegals can find employment in employee benefits and labor law with private law firms that specialize in this field, with labor union groups, with in-house corporate counsel of large corporations, within the personnel department of companies, in major financial-planning institutions, and with private actuarial consultants who administer the benefit programs for their client companies. Many paralegals become expert in administering employee benefit plans, drafting plan documents, monitoring new laws and regulations that may require amending plans, preparing and filing Internal Revenue Service forms, and overseeing the payment of termination benefits to employees.

10–10

The purpose of a probate proceeding is to gather the assets and property of the deceased, pay any outstanding debts and any federal or state taxes owed by the decedent, and to distribute the remainder of the deceased's property. In addition to estate proceedings, probate courts also hear matters concerning guardianship and conservatorship matters. Estate planning provides for the disposal of property before death by will, the establishment of a trust, and other methods for transferring estate property. Proper estate planning may reduce estate-tax liability and speed up the transfer of property to the heirs. Paralegals are often involved in the estate-planning and probate process from beginning to end and usually work with little direct supervision.

10–11

In choosing an area of specialization, one major consideration should be whether your personal style is compatible with the field of law in which you are interested. Family law, criminal law, and problems involving administrative agencies typically involve heavy client contact. Bankruptcy, business and corporate law, and probate and estate planning require some client contact, but there is less likelihood of becoming emotionally involved with the clients and their legal matters. Intellectual property law, employee benefits, collection work, and civil litigation often require very little client contact. Some paralegals like working closely with the clients whereas others prefer to have less client involvement. Your preferences in this regard will help you determine the fields of law in which you are most likely to find career satisfaction.

REVIEW

Key Terms

Before proceeding, review the key terms listed below to be sure you understand each one. If necessary, read over the corresponding section of the chapter. When you are ready to test your understanding, answer the Review Questions.

Chapter 7
Chapter 11
Chapter 13
civil litigation
conservatorship
corporation
debtor
equity
guardianship
holographic will
intestate
involuntary bankruptcy
litigation
partnership
probate
secured debts
shareholders
sole proprietorship
testate
wage garnishment
witnessed will

Questions for Review and Discussion

1. What are the similarities and differences in a Chapter 7, Chapter 11, and Chapter 13 bankruptcy proceeding?
2. What is the difference between a voluntary and an involuntary bankruptcy proceeding?
3. What are three common types of business entities?
4. What does the term *civil litigation* mean?
5. What are some of the functions performed by a collections paralegal?
6. What are the duties of a criminal law paralegal?
7. Why do you think there is increasing interest in employee benefits and labor law specialties?
8. How has the practice of family law changed during the last two or three decades?
9. What are the typical functions of an intellectual property law paralegal?
10. What are the three categories of probate court proceedings and what is the purpose of each?
11. How might you proceed in selecting one or more fields of law in which to specialize?

Activities

1. Select the fields of law in which you have an interest and arrange for an informational interview with a paralegal or attorney in these fields to gather more information on the functions performed by a paralegal and job opportunities in the field. Report your findings to the class.
2. Invite a paralegal to speak to the class on "A Day in the Life of a Paralegal."

NOTES

CHAPTER 11 Ethics for Legal Assistants

OUTLINE

11–1 Discussion and Overview of Ethics
  Ethics
  Morals
  Professional Ethics
11–2 The American Bar Association Canons of Ethics and Model Rules of Professional Conduct
11–3 Ethics and Legal Assistants
  American Bar Association Model Guidelines for Legal Assistants
  National Association of Legal Assistants Guidelines
  State and Local Bar Association Rules for Legal Assistants

COMMENTARY

One paralegal, who has been with Dunn & Sweeney for several years, was commiserating in the coffee room with another paralegal about her new billable hours quota. "What they are asking is just not fair! After all, I'm not an attorney and will never be a partner in the firm. If I'm to bill the number of hours they're asking, I'll have to live here—or be more creative in keeping track of billable hours. There are one or two clients who wouldn't complain if they were charged for a few more hours each year. They can afford it."

Overhearing this conversation troubled you. You have known the difference between what is right and what is wrong since you were a child. You were taught that it is wrong not to tell the truth or to steal from others. But obviously some people do not share your ethical principles or moral values. Working at Dunn & Sweeney has proven that some people who do the wrong thing get away without being caught or punished, whereas others who live exemplary lives are sometimes punished for doing the right thing. It seems that in many instances ethical principles and moral values are a matter of convenience, subject to change depending upon the situation. You decide to find out immediately what ethical guidelines are available for lawyers and for legal assistants.

OBJECTIVES

In previous chapters you learned that the paralegal role is not only an accepted part of the legal profession but that the paralegal is relied upon more and more by attorneys, clients, and the public to provide legal services. After studying this chapter, you should be able to:

1. Define and discuss the terms *ethics* and an *ethic*.

2. Discuss the crux of the ethics dilemma.
3. Define the term *morals*.
4. Discuss the crux of the morals dilemma.
5. State the reason for adopting a code of ethics.
6. List the primary areas for concern covered by the American Bar Association's Canons of Ethics.
7. Compare the American Bar Association's Model Code of Professional Responsibility with its Canons of Ethics.
8. Discuss how the code applies to paralegals.
9. Formulate a model of ethical guidelines for your paralegal career.
10. Answer the most common questions regarding ethical practices for paralegals.

11–1 Discussion and Overview of Ethics

Regardless of the field of law in which you specialize, everyone who works in the legal profession is routinely faced with making ethical and moral decisions. No one is exempt from the opportunity to make these choices. Secretaries, paralegals, attorneys, and judges must always be aware of the implications and consequences of their decisions and actions.

Ethics

Ethics is the field of moral science and an **ethic** is a set of moral principles. Having a sense of ethics is to know how people *should* behave. However, the crux of the ethics dilemma is not in knowing what you should do, but reconciling that belief with what you actually *do*. Nearly everyone has had some experience dealing with what you should have done in a certain situation versus what you actually did.

Perhaps it helps to know that in general, human behavior is strongly motivated toward needs fulfillment, and to satisfy your needs you are likely to act first in your own self-interest. That is, you will tend to make decisions that are most likely to get you what you want or satisfy your needs, even if your decision is not what you think you should do.

For example, if you are like most people you like to feel good about yourself. Suppose you find out one of your coworkers is padding her timesheets. She also alleges that her action is justified because everyone else does it. In this type of situation you are faced with an ethical dilemma. You know you should report her dishonesty to management. However, you then put your friendship at stake, and you can be reasonably sure she will no longer be willing to help you out when you find yourself up against a deadline. The action you take will undoubtedly be based upon whether you need the goodwill of management more than the goodwill of your coworker. Thus, you will be putting your own self-interest ahead of your personal ethic.

Morals

Unlike ethics, which is knowing what you should do, **morals** refer to the perception of what is right and wrong. The crux of the moral dilemma lies in the definitions of right and wrong. Most people think they know right from wrong, but judgment in some circumstances is purely subjective, and the path taken is often the one that will result in the least negative consequences. In other words, what is right for one set of events and people may be wrong for another.

For example, what is the right thing to do with an eight-year-old child from a good neighborhood whose middle-class parents get caught using and selling cocaine? What will be the long-term consequences of removing the child from the home pending legal action? Will incarcerating the first-time offender parents be more or less harmful to the child and society than leaving the family intact and imposing alternative penalties? Since the perception of what is right and wrong often varies from one individual to the next, there is always ample opportunity for discussion about what is considered to be moral behavior under the circumstances.

Here is another example of a moral and ethical dilemma. Everyone knows that it is wrong to drink and drive. Yet many people still choose to have a few drinks and then get behind the wheel. In doing so, the drinking driver has chosen to ignore his or her ethical standard of behavior—knowing what action should be taken—and has also chosen to ignore his or her morals—knowing what is right and wrong.

Professional Ethics

Because of the abundant opportunities to disagree on what is ethical and moral conduct, many businesses and professions attempt to define for their members the parameters of acceptable behavior by establishing a written code of ethics. The legal profession is no exception, since it is well known that the practice of law routinely presents ethical and moral challenges to everyone who works with any branch of the legal system. Since the turn of the century, the American Bar Association has taken an active role in establishing guidelines and standards by which lawyers, legal assistants, and everyone working in the legal profession is expected to conduct him- or herself.

The American Bar Association (ABA) adopted the first canons of professional ethics in 1908. In 1969 the ABA presented a completely revised version of the lawyer's ethics code called the Model Code of Professional Responsibility (MCPR). Virtually every state adopted all or most of the MCPR's provisions, resulting in something close to uniformity. Then in the early 1980s, recognizing the need to expand the rules of professional conduct to reflect the changes occurring within the profession and society, the ABA once again undertook the process of drafting and debating new provisions. In 1984, a significantly different code, known as the Model Rules of Professional Conduct (MRPC) was adopted by the ABA to be used in place of the 1969 version. To date, 36 states have patterned their codes on the MRPC.

Although joining the American Bar Association is not mandatory, its rules of ethical conduct are seldom ignored even by those lawyers who choose not to become members because of the ABA's influence in local legal communities. Regardless of whether a lawyer is a member of the ABA or simply a member of the local bar association, if a lawyer finds him- or herself in trouble with a client or other members of the legal community, resolving the problem follows a similar pattern. That is, when a lawyer engages in unethical behavior and a complaint is filed with the state or local bar association, an investigation is conducted and a hearing held, if warranted. If the lawyer is found to have violated the ethics code, sanctions may be imposed. Disciplinary sanctions can range from the payment of a fine and/or a temporary suspension of the lawyer's license to practice law to lifetime disbarment.

Even though legal assistants and other nonlawyer employees cannot be full members of any bar association, they are indirectly held accountable to the same standards of ethical behavior as lawyers. If a paralegal or any other employee engages in unethical conduct while employed by the lawyer, it is the lawyer who will be disciplined. Therefore, it is important that you know the standards to which lawyers are held accountable.

11–2 The American Bar Association Canons of Ethics and Model Rules of Professional Conduct

Because they are historically significant, the original nine Canons of Ethics are presented here together with the updated Model Rules of Professional Conduct. The entire MRPC runs about 40 pages and can be found in the *Martindale-Hubbell Law Digest*. It is not the intention of this text to present and discuss all of the rules. Therefore, some of the rules that are obviously applicable only to attorneys, such as how to structure fees for services, have been left out of this discussion. The purpose of presenting both the nearly century-old canons together with the modern rules is to give you a perspective on how the legal principles continue to change to reflect a changing profession and to illustrate the foundation on which many of the modern principles are based.

As you read through the original Canons of Ethics and their modern counterparts, remember that these standards and guidelines also apply to you and everyone else who works in the legal profession.

> **Canon 1:** A Lawyer Should Assist in Maintaining the Integrity and Competence of the Legal Profession.
>
> *MRPC 1.1: A lawyer shall provide competent representation to a client. Competent representation requires the legal knowledge, skill, thoroughness and preparation reasonably necessary for the representation.*
>
> *MRPC 1.16(2): . . . a lawyer shall not represent a client, or where representation has commenced, shall withdraw from the representation of a client if: . . . the lawyer's physical or mental condition materially impairs the lawyer's ability to represent the client. . . .*
>
> *MRPC 8.3: A lawyer having knowledge that another lawyer has committed a violation of the Rules of Professional Conduct that raises a substantial question as to that lawyer's honesty, trustworthiness or fitness as a lawyer in other respects, shall inform the appropriate professional authority.*
>
> *MRPC 8.4: It is professional misconduct for a lawyer to . . . violate the Rules of Professional Conduct, knowingly assist or induce another to do so . . . commit a criminal act . . . engage in conduct involving dishonesty, fraud, deceit or misrepresentation . . . imply an ability to influence improperly a government agency or official.*

One of the basic principles of the U.S. legal system is that every person who wants or needs legal assistance should have access to the services of a lawyer and can expect to be protected from anyone who is not qualified to practice law or who is incompetent. Lawyers and legal assistants are expected to maintain high standards and to encourage the same from their colleagues. Continuing education, paying close attention to details, and receiving or providing feedback on performance are a few ways to maintain professional integrity and competence.

> **Canon 2:** A Lawyer Should Assist the Legal Profession in Fulfilling its Duty to Make Legal Counsel Available.
>
> *MRPC 6.1: A lawyer should render public interest legal service. A lawyer may discharge this responsibility by providing professional services at no fee or a reduced fee to persons of limited means or to public service or charitable groups or organizations, by service in activities for improving the law, the legal system or the*

legal profession, and by financial support for organizations that provide legal services to persons of limited means.

MRPC 6.2: A lawyer shall not seek to avoid appointment by a tribunal to represent a person except for good cause, such as: . . . (b) representing the client is likely to result in an unreasonable financial burden on the lawyer; or (c) the client or the cause is so repugnant to the lawyer as to be likely to impair the client-lawyer relationship or the lawyer's ability to represent the client.

Expanding the use of paralegals is one way in which the legal profession can provide competent and affordable legal services to a wider range of people. Educating the public to recognize a legal problem and providing information on how to resolve it through seminars, workshops, lectures, and civic programs, as well as providing ***pro bono publico*** services, a Latin phrase meaning "for the public good or welfare," are ways in which lawyers and paralegals can make the law more accessible to the general public.

Canon 3: A Lawyer Should Assist in Preventing the Unauthorized Practice of Law.

MRPC 5.5 A lawyer shall not: . . . (b) assist a person who is not a member of the bar in the performance of activity that constitutes the unauthorized practice of law.

Actions that might constitute the unauthorized practice of law remain unresolved. Assisting someone in filling out a legal form might be viewed as practicing law by some people, but others regard this action as simply providing a service. Protecting the public remains the primary concern of the ABA and state bar associations, yet a diploma from law school and a license to practice does not guarantee competency. Yet, the practice of law is limited to those who are admitted to the bar and licensed to practice after meeting certain state requirements. However, it is well known that legal secretaries and paralegals with several years' worth of practical experience are often as knowledgeable, or in some cases more knowledgeable, about certain laws and procedures than a lawyer might be. Regardless of the lack of agreement on what acts constitute the practice of law, most attorneys do delegate certain tasks to nonlawyers, such as drafting legal documents, that were done previously only by lawyers. A lawyer must supervise the work performed by nonlawyers and accept responsibility for the work product.

Canon 4: A Lawyer Should Preserve the Confidences and Secrets of a Client.

MRPC 1.6: (a) A lawyer shall not reveal information relating to representation of a client unless the client consents after consultation, except for disclosures that are impliedly authorized in order to carry out the representation except as stated in paragraph (b).

(b) A lawyer may reveal such information to the extent the lawyer reasonably believes necessary: (1) to prevent the client from committing a criminal act that the lawyer believes is likely to result in imminent death or substantial bodily harm; or (2) to establish a claim or defense on behalf of the lawyer in a controversy between the lawyer and the client. . . .

In order to properly represent a client, the attorney must know all the facts and information pertaining to the client's legal matter. One of the worst situations in which a lawyer might find him- or herself is to be surprised or caught unaware by new evidence or a witness's testimony. These events make good television drama, but in real life lack of information may destroy a client's life or career. In order to create an atmosphere where the client is free to tell the whole truth, everyone working on the client's matter must maintain the client's confidence.

Maintaining client confidence often creates stress for legal professionals. You are working in an exciting, challenging environment with interesting people and situations yet you cannot talk about your work outside the office without violating the client's confidence.

Canon 5: A Lawyer Should Exercise Independent Professional Judgment on Behalf of a Client.

MRPC 2.1: In representing a client, a lawyer shall exercise independent professional

> *judgment and render candid advice. In rendering advice, a lawyer may refer not only to law but to other considerations such as moral, economic, social and political factors, that may be relevant to the client's situation.*

Clients are entitled to straightforward advice expressing the lawyer's honest assessment even when that advice involves unpleasant facts and alternatives that a client does not want to confront. When matters that go beyond strictly legal questions, such as family matters that can involve psychiatry, psychology, or social work, and business problems that may require accounting and financial expertise, the lawyer should exercise independent professional judgment and, if necessary, refer the client to someone more qualified to handle a problem that may be beyond the lawyer's legal knowledge.

> **Canon 6:** A Lawyer Should Represent a Client Competently.
> *MRPC 1.7 (a): A lawyer shall not represent a client if the representation of that client will be directly adverse to another client . . . (b) A lawyer shall not represent a client if the representation of that client may be materially limited by the lawyer's responsibilities to another client or to a third person, or by the lawyer's own interests. . . .*
> *MRPC 1.8: A lawyer shall not enter into a business transaction with a client or knowingly acquire an ownership, possessory, security or other pecuniary interest adverse to a client . . .*
> *MRPC 1.9: A lawyer who has formerly represented a client in a matter shall not thereafter represent another person in the same or a substantially related matter in which that person's interests are materially adverse to the interests of the former client unless the former client consents after consultation.*

When a client retains a lawyer, the client expects that the lawyer has a certain amount of competence and will be able to represent his or her interest. In agreeing to represent the client, the lawyer has created a **fiduciary** relationship. That is, the client has entrusted the lawyer with information and property and the lawyer has a duty to protect the client's interest. The lawyer must not compromise the client's needs or wishes by succumbing to any pressure from outside influences or other loyalties. A conflict of interest may be present when the lawyer's personal interests interfere with professional judgment; when the lawyer attempts to represent multiple clients in the same matter; and when the interests of third parties might interfere with professional judgment or the relationship between the lawyer and the client.

> **Canon 7:** A Lawyer Should Represent a Client Zealously Within the Bounds of the Law.
> *MRPC 1.2(a): A lawyer shall abide by a client's decisions concerning the objectives of representation . . . and shall consult with the client as to the means by which they are to be pursued. A lawyer shall abide by a client's decision whether to accept an offer of settlement of a matter. In a criminal case, the lawyer shall abide by the client's decision, after consultation with the lawyer, as to a plea to be entered, whether to waive jury trial and whether the client will testify. . . . (d) A lawyer shall not counsel a client to engage, or assist a client, in conduct that the lawyer knows is criminal or fraudulent, but a lawyer may discuss the legal consequences of any proposed course of conduct with a client. . . .*
> *MRPC 4.4: In representing a client, a lawyer shall not use means that have no substantial purpose other than to embarrass, delay, or burden a third person, or use methods of obtaining evidence that violate the legal rights of such a person.*

When an attorney agrees to represent a client, he or she must do so in good faith and to the best of his or her ability but not to the detriment of others. The U.S. legal system ensures that every person is entitled to a day in court—to have his or her conduct judged and regulated in accordance with the law—even those who commit a heinous crime. When an attorney or paralegal who is part of the team fails to vigorously and diligently pursue the client's best interests, the constitutional guarantee of due process is violated.

Canon 8: A Lawyer Should Assist in Improving the Legal System.
MRPC 1.3: A lawyer shall act with reasonable diligence and promptness in representing a client.
MRPC 1.4: A lawyer shall keep a client reasonably informed about the status of a matter and promptly comply with reasonable requests for information. . . .
MRPC 3.1: A lawyer shall not bring or defend a proceeding . . . unless there is a basis for doing so that is not frivolous. . . .
MRPC 3.2 A lawyer shall make reasonable efforts to expedite litigation consistent with the interests of the client.

One way to improve the legal system is to decrease the number of frivolous lawsuits. A frivolous lawsuit is one in which the client desires to have the action taken primarily for the purpose of harassing or maliciously injuring another person or one in which the lawyer is unable to make a good-faith argument on the merits of the action.

Another way to improve the legal system is to do everything possible to expedite litigation, rather than engaging in dilatory practices that delay moving the lawsuit along merely for the convenience of the lawyers or for the purpose of frustrating the opposing party.

Using the services of paralegals is yet another way to improve the legal system, since paralegals can make legal services affordable to a greater number of people. Writing legal documents in words and terms familiar to the layperson and taking action to protect the public from unscrupulous or incompetent legal representatives are yet other ways in which lawyers and legal assistants can improve the legal system.

Canon 9: A Lawyer Should Avoid Even the Appearance of Professional Impropriety.
MRPC 1.14(b): A lawyer may seek the appointment of a guardian or take other protective action with respect to a client, only when the lawyer reasonably believes that the client cannot adequately act in the client's own interest.
MRPC 1.15(a): A lawyer shall hold property of clients or third persons that is in a lawyer's possession in connection with a representation separate from the lawyer's own property.
MRPC 4.1: In the course of representing a client a lawyer shall not knowingly: (a) make a false statement of material fact or law . . . (b) fail to disclose a material fact . . .
MRPC 7.1: A lawyer shall not make a false or misleading communication about the lawyer or the lawyer's services . . . if it . . . (b) is likely to create an unjustified expectation about results the lawyer can achieve . . . or, (c) compares the lawyer's services with other lawyers' services, unless the comparison can be factually substantiated.
MRPC 7.5(a): A lawyer shall not by in-person or live telephone contact solicit professional employment from a prospective client with whom the lawyer has no family or prior professional relationship when a significant motive for the lawyer's doing so is the lawyer's pecuniary gain. (b) A lawyer shall not solicit professional employment from a prospective client by written or recorded communication. . . .

In recent years, lawyer-bashing has been elevated to an art form. In reality, many accountants, doctors, business leaders, church leaders, and others have violated the rules of professional conduct. Inappropriate or poor choices in judgment and behavior are not the exclusive domain of the legal profession.

Even though the Model Rules of Professional Conduct attempt to anticipate and write a rule for every possible situation that might occur in a profession as dynamic as the practice of law, Canon 9 warns lawyers and paralegals to avoid doing anything that might possibly be construed as inappropriate or unethical behavior. More emphasis is being placed in law schools and legal assistant programs on legal ethics. Yet a very basic question remains: Can ethical behavior be taught, or is it something you should know?

Often the most innocent acts may take on the appearance of impropriety. A paralegal with good intentions may inadvertently overstep the bounds of professionalism and find the road back to a good reputation to be long and arduous. A good rule to follow: If you have the slightest doubt about whether your action may be interpreted as a breach of professional impropriety, don't do it.

The purpose of the ABA's Canons of Ethics and Model Rules of Professional Conduct are to provide guidelines for ethical behavior and to protect the public. However, in many instances the guidelines raise additional questions. Perhaps "let your conscience be your guide" is enough in most circumstances, but what maxim is appropriate for those people who do not have a conscience? Which brings us back to the question of whether ethics can be taught and, if so, who is responsible for teaching ethics?

11–3 Ethics and Legal Assistants

Even though legal assistants cannot become full members of the American Bar Association or state and local bar associations, they are encouraged to become associate members in those organizations that have opened membership to them. Membership in professional organizations provides networking opportunities, access to the latest information having an impact on the profession, and the opportunity to take part in certain activities.

However, whether a member or not, paralegals are expected to adopt the codes and rules of ethical conduct required by the ABA and their state and local bar associations.

American Bar Association Model Guidelines for Legal Assistants

In August 1991, after an exhaustive process, the American Bar Association's House of Delegates adopted Model Guidelines for the Utilization of Legal Assistant Services. These standards are to serve as a guide to attorneys nationwide on the use and supervision of legal assistants. The model was developed with the viewpoint that having written guidance for lawyers on the utilization of legal assistants would encourage their use and ensure that both legal assistants and the lawyers who supervise them have a clear understanding of the areas in which legal assistants can work under the supervision of a lawyer without encountering professional responsibility conflicts or unauthorized practice of law problems.

The ten guidelines presented by the ABA are not intended to contradict or override any state or professional guidelines now in place. Rather, they are intended to assist states in adopting or revising such guidelines and to clear up any ambiguities or misunderstandings held by legal assistants, attorneys, educators, or students. The ABA's model guidelines for the utilization of legal assistants are:

> **1.** *A lawyer is responsible for all of the professional actions of a legal assistant performing legal assistant services at the lawyer's direction and should take reasonable measures to ensure that the legal assistant's conduct is consistent with the lawyer's obligations under the ABA Model Rules of Professional Conduct.*
>
> **2.** *Provided the lawyer maintains responsibility for the work product, a lawyer may delegate to a legal assistant any task normally performed by the lawyer except those tasks proscribed to one not licensed as a lawyer by statute, court rule, administrative rule or regulation, controlling authority, the ABA Model Rules of Professional Conduct, or these Guidelines.*

3. *A lawyer may not delegate to a legal assistant:*
   a) *Responsibility for establishing an attorney-client relationship.*
   b) *Responsibility for establishing the amount of a fee to be charged for a legal service.*
   c) *Responsibility for a legal opinion rendered to a client.*

This guideline does not mean that a legal assistant cannot take part in establishing an attorney-client relationship, or communicate the fee to a client, or relay a legal opinion. It does mean, however, that the lawyer must take responsibility for any of these actions on the part of a legal assistant.

4. *It is the lawyer's responsibility to take reasonable measures to ensure that clients, courts, and other lawyers are aware that a legal assistant, whose services are utilized by the lawyer in performing legal services, is not licensed to practice law.*

The ABA committee that developed these guidelines emphasizes the lawyer's responsibility for the disclosure of the legal assistant's status but leaves to the lawyer's discretion whether to communicate directly with the client in writing or by some other means, or to require the legal assistant to make the disclosure of his or her status.

5. *A lawyer may identify legal assistants by name and title on the lawyer's letterhead and on business cards identifying the lawyer's firm.*

The committee's objective regarding this guideline is consistent with the objective of disclosing the legal assistant's status and provides the legal assistant with recognition as part of the legal services team. The committee notes, however, that the states of Kansas, Michigan, New Hampshire, New Mexico, and North Carolina are some of the states that do not permit attorneys to list legal assistants on their letterhead.

6. *It is the responsibility of a lawyer to take reasonable measures to ensure that all client confidences are preserved by a legal assistant.*
7. *A lawyer should take reasonable measures to prevent conflicts of interest resulting from a legal assistant's other employment or interests insofar as such other employment or interests would present a conflict of interest it if were that of the lawyer.*

The most common example of a conflict of interest referred to in this guideline occurs when a legal assistant has experience or information in a specific area, such as in asbestos or other type of specialized product-liability case, or with a specific opposing client. Unless the legal assistant, who obtained this specialized knowledge while employed by another law firm, is screened from working on a similar case in his or her current firm, the legal assistant's former or current involvement can be dangerous to the firm. The legal assistant's new firm could be barred from performing any work in a certain legal area because of the legal assistant's prior employment in a similar area.

8. *A lawyer may include a charge for the work performed by a legal assistant in setting a charge for legal services.*

The expected overall effect of this guideline is to lower the total cost of legal services by encouraging the use of legal assistants to perform some services that were previously performed by lawyers.

9. *A lawyer may not split legal fees with a legal assistant nor pay a legal assistant for the referral of legal business. A lawyer may compensate a legal assistant based on the quantity of the legal assistant's work and the value of that work to a law practice, but the legal assistant's compensation may not be contingent, by advance agreement, upon the profitability of the lawyer's practice.*

This guideline does not prohibit a lawyer who has had a particularly profitable period from recognizing the contribution of the legal assistant with a bonus. Nor does it prohibit a lawyer who engages in a particularly profitable specialty from compensating a legal assistant who contributes materially to the success of that practice more handsomely that the compensation generally awarded to other legal assistants in that geographic area who work in less lucrative law practices.

> **10.** *A lawyer who employs a legal assistant should facilitate the legal assistant's participation in appropriate continuing education and in* pro bono publico *activities.*

The ABA committee recognizes that the improvement of formal legal assistant education will generally improve the legal services rendered by lawyers employing legal assistants and provide a more satisfying professional atmosphere in which legal assistants may work.

Whether the persons employed by the lawyer are secretaries, law clerks, law student interns, investigators, paralegals (freelancers or employees), or any others who are acting under the direction or supervision of a lawyer, all are bound by these collective model codes and model rules for ethical behavior. The lawyers must take responsibility for directing and supervising the work performed by all nonlawyers in their employ, as well as be held responsible for their professional conduct.

Because the lawyer is held responsible for your behavior and your work, you can be assured that most lawyers will provide close supervision and intense scrutiny of your work. There is tremendous pressure on everyone to continually perform ethically and without error. Anything less than perfection may have dire consequences.

National Association of Legal Assistants Guidelines

In 1984 the National Association of Legal Assistants (NALA) adopted their own Model Standards and Guidelines for Utilization of Legal Assistants. NALA's guidelines, which were also updated in 1990 to reflect the changing profession, are similar in some ways but different in others from the ABA's. NALA's guidelines represent a statement of how the legal assistant may function in the law office. They are not intended to be a comprehensive or exhaustive list of the proper duties of a legal assistant. Rather, they are designed as guides to what may or may not be proper conduct for the legal assistant.

Although NALA's guidelines, which follow, may not have universal application, they do form a basis for the legal assistant and supervising attorney to follow in the operation of a law office.

> **I.** PREAMBLE Proper utilization of the services of legal assistants affects the efficient delivery of legal services. Legal assistants and the legal profession should be assured that some measures exist for identifying legal assistants and their role in assisting attorneys in the delivery of legal services. Therefore, the National Association of Legal Assistants, Inc., hereby adopts these Model Standards and Guidelines as an educational document for the benefit of legal assistants and the legal profession.
>
> **II.** DEFINITION Legal assistants (within this occupational category some individuals are known as paralegals) are a distinguishable group of persons who assist attorneys in the delivery of legal services. Through formal education, training, and experience, legal assistants have knowledge and expertise regarding the legal system and substantive and procedural law which qualify them to do work of a legal nature under the supervision of an attorney.
>
> **III.** STANDARDS A legal assistant should meet certain minimum qualifications. The following standards may be used to determine an individual's qualifications as a legal assistant:

1. Successful completion of the Certified Legal Assistant (CLA™) examination of the National Association of Legal Assistants, Inc.;
2. Graduation from an ABA approved program of study for legal assistants;
3. Graduation from a course of study for legal assistants which is institutionally accredited but not ABA approved, and which requires not less than the equivalent of 60 semester hours of classroom study;
4. Graduation from a course of study for legal assistants, other than those set forth in (2) and (3) above, plus not less than six months of in-house training, as a legal assistant;
5. A baccalaureate degree in any field, plus not less than six months in-house training as a legal assistant;
6. A minimum of three years of law-related experience under the supervision of an attorney, including at least six months of in-house training as a legal assistant; or
7. Two years of in-house training as a legal assistant.

For purpose of these Standards, "in-house training as a legal assistant" means attorney education of the employee concerning legal assistant duties and these Guidelines. In addition to review and analysis of assignments the legal assistant should receive a reasonable amount of instruction directly related to the duties and obligations of the legal assistant.

IV. GUIDELINES These guidelines relating to standards of performance and professional responsibility are intended to aid legal assistants and attorneys. The responsibility rests with an attorney who employs legal assistants to educate them with respect to the duties they are assigned and to supervise the manner in which such duties are accomplished.

V. Legal assistants should:

1. Disclose their status as legal assistants at the outset of any professional relationship with a client, other attorneys, a court or administrative agency or personnel thereof, or members of the general public;
2. Preserve the confidences and secrets of all clients; and
3. Understand the attorney's Code of Professional Responsibility and these guidelines in order to avoid any action which would involve the attorney in a violation of that Code, or give the appearance of professional impropriety.

VI. Legal assistants should not:

1. Establish attorney-client relationships; set legal fees; give legal opinions or advice; or represent a client before a court; nor
2. Engage in, encourage, or contribute to any act which could constitute the unauthorized practice of law.

VII. Legal assistants may perform services for an attorney in the representation of a client, provided:

1. The services performed by the legal assistant do not require the exercise of independent professional legal judgment;
2. The attorney maintains a direct relationship with the client and maintains control of all client matters;
3. The attorney supervises the legal assistant;
4. The attorney remains professionally responsible for all work on behalf of the client, including any actions taken or not taken by the legal assistant in connection therewith; and

5. The services performed supplement, merge with and become the attorney's work product.

VIII. In the supervision of a legal assistant, consideration should be given to:

1. Designating work assignments that correspond to the legal assistant's abilities, knowledge, training and experience;
2. Educating and training the legal assistant with respect to professional responsibility, local rules and practices, and firm policies;
3. Monitoring the work and professional conduct of the legal assistant to ensure that the work is substantially correct and timely performed;
4. Providing continuing education for the legal assistant in substantive matters through courses, institutes, workshops, seminars and in-house training; and
5. Encouraging and supporting membership and active participation in professional organizations.

IX. Except as otherwise provided by statute, court rule or decision, administrative rule or regulation, or the attorney's Code of Professional Responsibility; and within the preceding parameters and proscriptions, a legal assistant may perform any function delegated by an attorney, including but not limited to the following:

1. Conduct client interviews and maintain general contact with the client after the establishment of the attorney-client relationship, so long as the client is aware of the status and function of the legal assistant, and the client contact is under the supervision of the attorney.
2. Locate and interview witnesses, so long as the witnesses are aware of the status and function of the legal assistant.
3. Conduct investigations and statistical and documentary research for review by the attorney.
4. Conduct legal research for review by the attorney.
5. Draft legal documents for review by the attorney.
6. Draft correspondence and pleadings for review by and signature of the attorney.
7. Summarize depositions, interrogatories, and testimony for review by the attorney.
8. Attend executions of wills, real estate closings, depositions, court or administrative hearings and trials with the attorney.
9. Author and sign letters provided the legal assistant's status is clearly indicated and the correspondence does not contain independent legal opinions or legal advice.

NALA's guidelines and standards for utilization of legal assistants were developed from generally accepted practices, but each supervising attorney and each legal assistant must be aware of the specific rules, decisions, and statutes applicable to legal assistants within his or her jurisdiction.

State and Local Bar Association Rules for Legal Assistants

Since the 1960s legal assistants and lawyers have worked to find answers to specific questions pertaining to the legal assistant position. Many state and local bar associations have formed committees on legal assistants or the unauthorized practice of law to investigate complaints of rule violations, draft new rules, and interpret current ones. Some of the most common questions regarding the utilization of legal assistants and the generally accepted answers are summarized here. Caution is advised as you read the following material. Each state and local bar association has its own standards and rules for ethical conduct for paralegals. You are strongly encouraged to contact the bar association for your state and county for a copy of their guidelines, rather than rely on this summary.

Use of Name on Firm's Stationery Some states now allow a paralegal's name to be printed on the law firm's stationery, as long as it is clear to the reader which names are those of attorneys and which are those of paralegals. Other states, however, have been reluctant to follow along for fear of offending the dignity of the profession. A quick telephone call to your state bar will tell you its current position on this issue.

Business Cards Most states allow legal assistants to have a business card. The legal assistant's nonlawyer status must be clear and, if the legal assistant is employed by a law firm, the firm must approve the format and content of the card. However, the business card must not be used to solicit business for the law firm. For example, the card must not be given to someone who has not asked for legal help.

Signature on Correspondence Only a small number of states restrict paralegals to signing routine or administrative correspondence. Most states agree that a paralegal can sign letters to clients and opposing counsel written on the firm's letterhead using his or her own name, as long as the letter does not give legal advice or involve the application of legal knowledge and the status of the paralegal is clear. A general rule to follow is to make your paralegal status clear in both oral and written communication.

Listing on Legal Documents The legal assistant's role in litigation is often now recognized in some court opinions printed in the reporter volumes, and the names of the paralegals who played a major role in preparing appellate court briefs are sometimes printed along with the names of the lawyers involved. The number of states that oppose including the names of paralegals on legal documents is rapidly diminishing.

Listing on the Door Most states have concluded that it would be improper to list paralegal names on the office door.

Partnerships and Sharing of Fees Paralegals and lawyers must not enter into any partnerships involving the practice of law, nor can they share fees, since sharing fees with a lawyer would be the same as having a partnership interest in the practice. Instead, full-time paralegals employed by law firms are paid a salary and may participate in the firm's benefits and retirement programs. Freelance paralegals or part-time paralegals are usually paid on an hourly basis for their work.

Appearance at Hearings and in Court Paralegals may appear and represent clients in administrative hearings when the agency has specifically authorized such representation. When authorization has been given, the paralegal may also advise and draft documents for clients with administrative agency problems. In addition, in some states paralegals can represent clients in some lower courts, such as in small claims court and justice of the peace courts. A few states allow paralegals to appear in other courts to set dates on cases and perform other administrative duties.

Appearance at a Real Estate Closing Some states will allow a paralegal to appear at a real estate closing in place of the supervising attorney, so long as the paralegal does not give legal advice or become involved in negotiations. Other states do not allow a paralegal to attend without an attorney, and in some other states neither lawyers nor paralegals are involved in a routine real-estate closing.

Drafting Documents and Conducting Depositions Legal assistants routinely draft documents under the supervision of an attorney that are presented as the work of the attorney. Although a paralegal may be asked to attend a deposition, he or she may not ask any questions during a deposition, since doing so is construed as practicing law.

Interviewing Clients Legal assistants routinely interview clients without an attorney being present. However, the paralegal should discuss the purpose and content of the interview with the attorney prior to meeting with the client and should be receiving regular supervision from the attorney.

With the rapid changes taking place in the status and duties of paralegals, it is imperative that you stay in contact with your state and local bar associations to keep informed of the latest changes affecting you. The information presented in this chapter on guidelines for ethical conduct are a summary only of the issues and questions that are usually of interest to people with little or no prior working knowledge of the legal profession. New questions and problems that have not yet been raised about what is moral or ethical behavior will no doubt be presented to you during your career in law. To resolve them you will need to refer to all the adopted rules, guidelines, and standards; seek the advice of wise men and women; and search your own soul for the answers.

SUMMARY

11–1

Everyone associated with the legal profession is routinely faced with making ethical and moral decisions. The crux of the ethics dilemma is reconciling knowledge of what you should do with what you actually do. Similarly, the crux of the morals dilemma is in defining right and wrong. Both ethics and morals are largely a matter of individual perception. Thus, the opportunity exists for differing perceptions of the same issues and situations.

11–2

The American Bar Association adopted its first canons of professional ethics in 1908 to define the parameters of acceptable behavior for members of the legal profession. These canons were revised in 1969 and became the Model Code of Professional Responsibility. Another revision in 1984 resulted in the current Model Rules of Professional Conduct. Although membership in the American Bar Association is voluntary, its ethical code is the standard by which all members of the legal profession, including legal assistants, are judged.

11–3

Paralegals are expected to be knowledgeable about and to conform to the same ethical standards as lawyers because the lawyer is ultimately held responsible for the conduct and behavior of all of his or her employees. In addition, the American Bar Association and the National Association of Legal Assistants have adopted guidelines and standards for the utilization of legal assistants to help clarify for everyone the status and duties associated with the position. Further, each state and local bar association has adopted a code of ethics for lawyers and legal assistants in their respective areas. Most states allow a paralegal's name to be printed on the firm's stationery, have a business card, and to sign correspondence, as long as the paralegal's status is clearly indicated. Most states prohibit a paralegal's name from being listed on the firm's door, sharing fees with attorneys, or appearing at hearings and in court. Hearings before most administrative agencies are exceptions where paralegals may appear and represent clients in many situations. Paralegals are advised to check with their state and local bar associations for clarification on ethical conduct in their own states.

REVIEW

Key Terms

Before proceeding, review the key terms listed below to be sure you understand each one. If necessary, read over the corresponding section of the chapter. When you are ready to test your understanding, answer the Review Questions.

ethic
ethics
fiduciary
morals
pro bono publico

Questions for Review and Discussion

1. Define the terms *ethics* and an *ethic*.
2. What is the crux of the ethics dilemma?
3. Define the term *morals*.
4. What is the crux of the morals dilemma?
5. Why do associations and businesses adopt a code of ethics?
6. List the primary areas for concern covered by the American Bar Association's Canons of Ethics.

7. Compare the American Bar Association's Model Code of Professional Responsibility with its Canons of Ethics.
8. Discuss how the code applies to legal assistants.
9. What items would you specifically include in your own code of ethics as a paralegal?
10. What are some of the most common questions regarding ethical practices for paralegals?

Activities

1. Contact your state bar association and your local bar association for copies of their rules for ethical conduct.
2. Invite a member of the bar association's ethics committee to speak to the class on common ethical dilemmas facing lawyers and paralegals today.
3. Ask the class to share recent ethical dilemmas they have faced, such as drinking and driving, cheating on an exam, or assisting someone else in a situation where their own sense of ethics or morals played a part in their decision.

NOTES

CHAPTER 12 Interpersonal Communication Skills

OUTLINE

COMMENTARY

Some days you wonder about the kind of career you have chosen for yourself. You always believed the Golden Rule was a good one to live by, but many times it seems you are the only one following it. Yesterday one of the attorneys yelled at you for absolutely no reason other than you were standing in her office when she received a troubling phone call. Mr. Dunn is as nice as can be one day, but the next day will take on the characteristics of Attila the Hun. One of the secretaries is always sweetness personified, but has yet to complete one of your typing assignments on time. Is it you? Is it they? What is going on?

OBJECTIVES

Your career as a paralegal is likely to be more satisfying and rewarding if you have a basic understanding of interpersonal styles. After studying this chapter, you should be able to:

1. Define the three interpersonal styles.
2. Define the concept of *basic human rights.*
3. Describe the role of basic human rights in assertive communication.
4. Give examples of assertive, nonassertive, and aggressive communication.
5. List the factors involved in selecting an interpersonal style.

6. Describe and discuss the different ways to be assertive.
7. Describe the fundamentals of effective listening skills.
8. List the components of constructive criticism.
9. State the criteria for making ethical interpersonal decisions.
10. List the principles of interpersonal ethics.

12–1 Interpersonal Styles

Most people find lawsuits and dealing with lawyers unpleasant. Few people come to your office to see you when they are happy. Instead, they seek you out when they have a problem and want you to solve it. Regardless of the reason that forced a client to seek the services of an attorney, the outcome is the same: there will be winners and losers. No one likes to lose. Yet people seeking the services of a lawyer are sometimes forced into an adversary relationship simply because they have decided to exercise their right to justice. Once the decision has been made to take legal action, above all they want to win!

If you purposely selected a career that would afford you one of the best opportunities to study human behavior and the impact of communication on behavior, you could not make a better choice than law. Lawyers, paralegals, and everyone else working in the legal profession must master the art of interpersonal communication in all its various forms or find themselves eventually forced out of law. It is with words that lawsuits are commenced, judges and juries are persuaded, legal briefs are written, and lives are forever changed.

The focus of this chapter is on developing an effective verbal interpersonal style that will help you find satisfaction and success as a paralegal. You need to deal comfortably with angry, frustrated, aggressive lawyers and clients without becoming emotionally involved or overly sensitive. Likewise, you need to develop the skills of listening with empathy, stating your opinions without hesitation, and relating positively to clients and coworkers.

Basic Human Rights

Before exploring the three interpersonal styles—nonassertive, assertive, and aggressive—it is important first to understand a basic principle and concept in developing interpersonal skills. The concept pertains to **basic human rights** and the principle is: whatever rights you claim for yourself you must also grant to other people.

Several decades ago the United Nations issued a Universal Declaration of Human Rights. In this declaration, a *basic human right* is defined as anything that *all* people are entitled to be, have, or do by virtue of their existence as human beings. In other words, basic human rights are those rights to which all human beings are entitled and that are necessary in order to live a decent life. Figure 12–1 lists only a few of over 200 basic human rights.

Although there is no formal declaration of basic human rights, nevertheless most people agree that everyone is entitled to these rights. Some rights, such as the right to have and express your own opinion, is legally protected in the United States; others are so much a part of our daily lives that we simply take them for granted. The important thing to remember about basic human rights is that they apply to everyone. Therefore, any rights you claim for yourself, you must also grant to others. For example, if you want the right to express your

Figure 12–1 List of Basic Human Rights

Basic Human Rights		
The right to be independent The right to your opinion The right to not feel guilty The right to speak up The right to be happy The right to take time out to think before responding The right to not explain or justify your decisions	The right to be left alone The right to your feelings The right to make mistakes The right to privacy The right to change your mind The right to accept responsibility for your decisions The right to be treated with respect	The right to be successful The right to refuse requests The right to make choices The right to your own space The right to ask for what you want The right to not be publicly humiliated or embarrassed

opinion and make your own decisions, then you must allow others to express their opinions and decide what is right for them.

Responsibilities When you assume rights, you also assume responsibilities. For example, when you assume the right to make your own choices and decisions, you must also assume responsibility for the results of your choices. Let us say that you know for certain that another paralegal has been padding his timesheets to make himself look good, yet you decide to take no action. Two months later, this same paralegal is singled out for a promotion and a huge bonus that you expected to receive. You are furious with yourself for not speaking up sooner. But doing so now would only make you look bad, so you must live with the result of your prior decision to take no action.

Likewise, when you decided to become a paralegal your choice resulted in more responsibilities for you. For example, in addition to your usual responsibilities, you are now expected to attend class regularly, complete homework assignments, pass exams, earn a degree or certificate, then start a new life.

Some people take on too many responsibilities. They think they are responsible for everyone and everything so they take on responsibility for the behavior and feelings of others. However, unless you use a great deal of force, you cannot control the behavior or feelings of other people, nor can you make them change. What other people do or how they feel is completely up to them. You are not responsible. The only person you can control is yourself. Your responsibility begins and ends with that over which you have control.

In developing your interpersonal skills, your responsibility is to communicate your ideas, needs, and feelings with others in such a way that they can then decide how to respond. If you withhold information because you think they will be hurt, you are denying them the right to make their own decisions and taking responsibility for their feelings.

Knowing that you have certain rights and responsibilities does not mean you can do as you please, nor does it guarantee that you will always get what you want. Since everyone has the right to make his or her own choices and decisions, you can only hope that by treating others with respect and granting them their basic human rights you will be able to establish better interpersonal relationships.

Conflicting Rights At times there will be a difference of opinion as to who has rights in a given situation, or the boundaries of where your rights end and the other person's rights begin may be unclear. For example, you have the right to use your own judgment in deciding whether a request is reasonable, no matter who made the request. That is, you have a right to say "no" without feeling guilty even if the person making the request is your boss, a client, a relative, or a friend.

However, although you also have the right to change your mind, it is unclear whether you have the right to change your mind midstream about fulfilling commitments you have made. If the other person will be seriously inconvenienced by your change of mind, you may have the responsibility to fulfill your commitment.

Role Rights Role rights are sometimes confused with human rights. Whereas basic human rights are applicable to all people, **role rights** are those a person holds by virtue of function, status, or position. These include the role rights existing between an employer and employee, parent and child, lawyer and client. For example, an employer has the right to hire and fire; the employee does not. The employer, however, does not have the right to treat employees with disrespect or to ask them to do something that might be unethical. An easy way to distinguish between human rights and role rights is to ask yourself whether the right in question should be granted to everyone.

Owning a Belief System It is one thing to be able to identify human rights and role rights and another to have enough confidence to act on them. Most people have a fairly well-defined belief system. In order to be assertive it is important that your belief system supports the idea of basic human rights—enough so that you have confidence in owning specific rights. For example, many people have difficulty believing in their right to express their opinion honestly to the boss or to someone who may choose to feel hurt.

Another example of lacking belief and confidence in a right may occur when you want to ask for a raise. You know you have the right to ask for what you want and for what you think you deserve. Yet you struggle with accepting this right because your belief system is telling you that (a) you must not be working hard enough, because if you work hard your efforts will be rewarded; (b) the boss might not agree with you and it is best not to make a request and be turned down; and (c) if the boss thought a raise was in order, it would be given—to ask for it would be to question the boss's judgment.

The struggle taking place between your rights and your beliefs is the result of cultural programming, which can stop you from claiming your rights. It is important to reevaluate these old programming messages for validity in today's world. They may be holding you back in your career and keeping you from developing your interpersonal skills. It is your right to take responsibility for yourself and for your happiness, which is often dependent upon the effectiveness of your communication style.

Owning Feelings Everyone has feelings and everyone is responsible for how he or she is going to feel about a person or event. No one can make you feel anything you do not choose to feel, since no one has control of your feelings except you. Therefore, you alone decide to feel angry, sad, happy, used, intimidated, or any way you want to feel.

Lawyers are generally known for their aggressive, intimidating personalities. But paralegals must learn to maintain a professional style in the presence of adversity. This means you must control your feelings and learn not to take personally the outbursts or intimidating behavior of others, even when it is directed toward you.

The equation $A + B = C$ can be used to illustrate how feelings develop. In this emotion equation, the letter A represents an event, the letter B represents how you perceive the event, and C is how you decide to feel about the event. How you perceive the event, or B, is the factor you can control, which, in turn, controls your feelings.

For example, your supervising attorney has just lost a big case. She comes into your office, slams the file down on your desk, and tells you that the case was lost because of something you neglected to do. In other words, losing the case is all your fault. Whether or not this is true, you have several choices concerning how you perceive what has happened and how you will feel about what has happened.

Typically, when faced with aggressive, intimidating behavior the response is first to defend yourself, then feel angry, followed by humiliation. Thoughts run the gamut from "She shouldn't treat me this way," to denial, to looking for someone else to blame.

However, if you decide not to react immediately to her outburst in the typical fashion, you will be taking control of and owning your feelings instead of responding to and being controlled by the attorney's outburst. If you change your perception of the incident from a personal attack on you to how the attorney is feeling, you can change the way you respond. You can feel sad that she lost the case, empathy for how upset she is, and the frustration of losing. These are legitimate feelings, and the appropriate ones for you to express. There is no need for you to feel guilty, angry, abused, or intimated unless you choose to feel that way. Substituting *empathy,* or understanding of what the other person is feeling, is usually a positive interpersonal technique for everyone involved in this type of situation.

Defining Interpersonal Styles

The three most common interpersonal styles are nonassertive, assertive, and aggressive.

Nonassertive Being **nonassertive,** or passive, means that you fail to stand up for your basic human rights or you do so in an ineffective way. For example, a nonassertive person is not likely to speak up when she or he is being treated with disrespect. Worse yet, the nonassertive person is more likely to get even by spreading gossip, rather than by speaking directly to the person who is being disrespectful. He or she may also resort to manipulative behavior, such as conveniently forgetting to pass along an important message, which proves to be embarrassing to the other person.

When you fail to act in ways that honestly express your feelings and beliefs or when you are apologetic, unsure, or hesitant, others can easily disregard

Figure 12–2 The Emotion Equation

The Emotion Equation

A = The event
+ B = How you perceive the event
C = Your feelings and behavior

Source: Albert Ellis, Ph.D.

Figure 12–3a A nonassertive person usually will not express his or her feelings and beliefs honestly.

"I hate to bother you, but. . . ."

Source: Dennis Zimmermen.

what you have to say. In behaving so, you have allowed your rights to be violated. The nonassertive person wants to please others and avoid conflict at all costs, even if it means relinquishing a few rights.

Typically, the nonassertive person believes that his or her feelings are not as important as another person's. Although they often feel used and mistreated, nonassertive people will not speak up because they are afraid to hurt someone else's feelings. Likewise, nonassertives think their opinions are not important, but they pay attention to what everyone else has to say. Since they have a great need to be liked by others, these passive people will not readily offer an opinion until they hear what the other person has to say. By holding back, they can change their opinion if needed to be in agreement, thus satisfying their desire to please others.

Although often very likable, nonassertive people are master manipulators. They get their needs met by making others guess what those needs are and then punishing them if they guess wrong. For example, ask a nonassertive person where they want to go for lunch and they typically respond with "I don't care; wherever you want to go is fine." Then they punish you with silence, whining, or complaining when you choose a Chinese restaurant because they really wanted Mexican food.

In the office, nonassertive people can sabotage management decisions. When asked their opinion about a subject that concerns them, they will either offer none or say what they think the other person wants to hear. More often than not, they will then either do as they please or use the office grapevine to communicate their true feelings.

Nonassertive people take no responsibility for their feelings or actions. Instead, they are the victims of their failure to stand up for their basic human rights. Nonassertion indicates not only a lack of self-respect and self-esteem, it also indicates a lack of confidence in the other person's ability to cope with disappointments, to handle problems, or to take responsibility for their decisions.

There are few positive outcomes to an interpersonal style that has as its goal the masking of feelings, thoughts, and beliefs. Busy people pay little or no attention to the nonassertive style. There is just not enough time to figure out what these people really want.

Assertive Being **assertive** means that you stand up for your basic human rights and show respect for the rights of others. Assertive people have a high level of self-confidence and **self-esteem;** they like and feel good about themselves. They feel no need to put down others or be disrespectful.

Because they like themselves enough to know they deserve to be treated with respect, assertive people refuse to be the victim of anyone's bad temper or ill manners. Unlike nonassertives, the assertive person goes to the source of the problem and deals with the person and the problem directly. Assertive people dislike and will not tolerate subterfuge, intrigue, manipulation, or gossip.

The assertive style is based on mutual respect and understanding, always leaving room for compromise when personal needs and rights might conflict with those of another person. There is no compromise, however, when it comes to self-respect. Assertive people know that if you do not respect yourself enough to go after what you want and to stand up for your rights, you will not receive respect from others.

The assertive style is easy to relate to and to maintain because it is honest, forthright, and tactful. You always know exactly where assertive people stand on any subject. That does not mean they say whatever they feel like without considering anyone else. On the contrary, they usually think through and evaluate the impact of their communication or behavior before taking action. They may not tell you everything they are thinking or feeling, but what they do say is honest. Assertive people are tactful, not stupid. On the other hand, assertive people will not withhold information just to make themselves look good or because they think you will not be able to handle the truth. These people assume you want to and are willing to take responsibility for your rights and feelings.

Aggressive When you stand up for your rights but put down others, are disrespectful, or violate their rights, you are being **aggressive.** The implied message is: This is what I want or think; what you want or think does not matter. My feelings are important; yours are not.

At one time or another, everyone acts aggressively and is the victim of aggressive behavior. The lawyer who interrogates an employee instead of asking a question for clarification, or the nonassertive person who explodes in anger are both acting out aggression.

There are several similarities between aggression and nonassertion. One is that both aggressive and nonassertive behavior indicate a lack of self-confidence and self-esteem. Another similarity is the attempt to gain power through

Figure 12–3b Assertive people deal directly with the person and the problem.

"Let's work this out; I think. . . ."

Source: Dennis Zimmermen.

manipulation. The aggressive person can manipulate by humiliating, belittling, degrading, and overpowering others. The nonassertive person tries to gain power by remaining silent, causing others to use the process of elimination in guessing the true meaning of his or her behavior. People who use either style can become abusive—verbally and/or physically—when they feel powerless or out of control.

Because these two styles have several common characteristics, you can readily see how a nonassertive person could become aggressive when pushed too far. Hence the psychological term *passive-aggressive.* Sometimes passive or nonassertive people become frustrated or angry and explode with a temper tantrum or diatribe, or even throw anything at hand. Since all human behavior is directed toward fulfilling a need, nonassertive people who will not stand up for themselves are more likely than others to have difficulty in getting their needs met. At some point these usually complacent individuals may become aggressive, and the resulting behavior is never pleasant.

Likewise, people who are typically aggressive—hostile, angry, demeaning, disrespectful—can on occasion be passive. Unfortunately, when an aggressive person becomes passive it is usually a sign for you to be more alert. Aggressives use charm and seeming acquiescence to manipulate others. However, relating to the aggressive style is often easier than dealing with the nonassertive. At least you usually know what they like and dislike and where you stand. With the passive style, you are always having to guess.

Figure 12–3c Aggressive people stand up for their rights but put down others.

"You had better. . . ."

Source: Dennis Zimmermen.

Choosing Your Interpersonal Style

By now you should be able to distinguish among the three interpersonal styles. In some situations you would be wise to be nonassertive and not express your opinion. At other times, aggressively raising your voice might be the only way to get someone's attention. You always have the right to choose whichever style is best for you under the circumstances.

How do you decide which style to choose? Ask yourself these questions.

1. How important to me are the people involved in the situation?
2. How much risk am I willing to take?
3. On what, if any, issues am I willing to compromise?
4. Which style is most likely to improve this situation?
5. What effect will my choice have on my self-respect?
6. What are the likely consequences of my choice for which I will be responsible?

In most situations your best choice is the assertive style, since it is honest and respectful. More important, your choice of style tells others how to treat you. When you fail to stand up for your rights, you are giving tacit approval to others to manipulate, dominate, and exploit you. Most people respond positively to assertiveness. They might not always agree with you or like you, but they will respect you for standing up for yourself. Assertiveness makes interpersonal relationships less stressful and more productive.

Figure 12–4 Common Characteristics of Interpersonal Styles

Common Characteristics of Interpersonal Styles

	Words and Phrases Used	Nonverbal Clues
Nonassertive	I may be wrong but... ; I don't know; what do you think? Well... you know... um... ; If it's not too much trouble, would you mind... ; I hate to bother you but...	Poor eye contact; nervousness; hesitant; quiet voice tone; poor posture; keeps to self; does not attract attention to self; dresses conservatively; lacks confidence; manipulative; avoids conflicts; will not express opinion; needs to be liked by others.
Assertive	I want... ; What do you want?; I need... ; I prefer... ; I choose to... ; I will... ; Let's work this out; I think... ; What do you think?; What would you like to see happen? I can see how you would think that and I disagree.	Good eye contact; calm; relaxed; good posture; presence; pleasant demeanor; confident; strong, even voice tone; dresses appropriately; interacts confidently with others; dependable, reliable; honest; honors commitments; trustworthy; works for harmony; respects self and others.
Aggressive	You should... ; You ought to... ; You must... ; You have to... ; You've got to... ; You'd better... ; You've got to be kidding!; Stupid! Dummy! No way! My way is the only way.	Glaring, piercing eye contact; hyperactivity; pacing; slamming doors; tossing or throwing things; rude gestures; name-calling; loud voice tone; intimidating behavior; abusive; hostile; tells jokes that are demeaning; interrupts others; condescending; disrespectful; lacks self-esteem and self-confidence.

12–2 How to Be Assertive

Since the situations calling for the assertive style vary widely, you need to be familiar with several different ways to assert yourself in order to choose the appropriate one(s) for the occasion.

I-messages

When you use **I-messages,** statements beginning with "I," instead of **you-messages,** statements beginning with "you," you set up fewer barriers. After all, the point of developing good interpersonal skills is to get through the listener's barriers, not create more. When you stick to expressing your own thoughts or feelings honestly and avoid criticizing others, you are more likely to be heard.

An I-message is a personal statement that describes you. It is a reflection of how you think and feel or what you need from others. It is authentic and honest and does not contain evaluations or judgments. I-messages build confidence that comes through to others as a sign that you are to be taken seriously and treated with respect.

If you have problems making I-statements, review your programming tapes.

No doubt you were told that it is not nice to call attention to yourself or to boast. However, assertiveness requires that you focus on yourself instead of others, since not doing so is a violation of the other person's basic human rights.

For example, think about your reaction to this you-message: "You talk too loudly," versus the I-message, "I have sensitive hearing. Please speak more softly." The you-message is aggressive, judgmental, and a put-down. The I-message is authentic and honest. Most people turn off, tune out, or respond defensively to a you-message. With the possible exception of a direct compliment, such as "You look wonderful!" most you-messages are aggressive and often lead to arguments.

Here are the various types of assertive I-messages and some situations in which they can be effective.

Declarative I-messages These messages disclose your feelings, ideas, likes and dislikes, and attitude. Some examples are: "I'm excited about taking on this new assignment." "I appreciate the support you gave me on this research project." "I'm confused about what steps to take next on this case. I would like your guidance. Is now a good time to talk?"

Responsive I-messages When you need to respond with a "yes" or "no" answer, a responsive I-message will clearly state your true feelings. Here are some examples: "No, I will not be able to get that rough draft to you by Monday because I am preparing for the Peterson trial that starts on Wednesday. I can have the draft to you by Friday. Will that work for you?" Or, "Yes, I will be happy to run over to the clerk's office for you to check the register of actions. I could use a break."

Although sometimes you may want to give an explanation for your response to a request, it is not necessary to justify your decisions. In fact, unless you are particularly skilled at being assertive, saying no to a request and giving an explanation might be perceived by the listener as an invitation to argue with you in an attempt to get you to change your mind. You do have the right to say "no" or "yes" to any request without offering an explanation.

Preventive I-messages These messages let people know ahead of time what you want or need and can prevent conflicts and misunderstandings. For example, "I want to set up a time with you to coordinate our calendars so I will be better informed about your time commitments for the coming week." Or, "I would like us to figure out how many top-priority deadlines we have this week so we can make sure we have time to get them done."

General Assertive I-messages Here are some examples of common situations and an assertive response. You are put on the spot with a question or statement that has caught you completely off guard. Instead of blurting out something you may later regret, remember you have the right to take time out and think when put in this situation. Your assertive response might be: "I need to think over what you just said. I'll get back to you before the end of the day." Or while you are trying to express your opinion, your boss interrupts you. Your assertive response could be: "Please let me finish making my point."

Showing Empathy When you show **empathy** you recognize the other person's point of view while standing up for your rights. This technique is particularly useful in situations where you are likely to overreact in an aggressive way or be resentfully nonassertive.

Here are two examples. Another paralegal asks you to put in a good word for him with an attorney with whom he has a personality clash. Your empathetic-assertive response might be: "I can understand why you want me to help you resolve this problem, but the two of you will have to work this out on your own. I don't want to get involved in this."

The boss has asked you to stay late to work on a report she needs early tomorrow afternoon. Your empathetic-assertive response could be: "I understand you need this report by tomorrow afternoon but I cannot stay late to work on it. I will come in early tomorrow and get it to you as quickly as possible."

Assertion with Increasing Firmness

Most often a simple, assertive statement is all that is required to get your point across. However, sometimes you will have to deal with people who are persistent and will ignore your response. The following is an example of how you can state and restate your position with increasing firmness and not be aggressive.

A client keeps asking to take you to dinner. You do not want to accept the invitation. Your first response is: "Thank you for the invitation. That's very nice of you, but I never go out socially with a client." The client is not willing to accept your response and says, "Oh, come on. You have to eat and I would like to thank you for your help." Your second response: "No, thanks. I feel strongly about not accepting social invitations from clients." The client persists. Then you say: "The answer is 'no.' Please do not ask me again."

Some people just cannot take "no" for an answer and will believe you are serious only when you have repeated your response several times. Until you state your position more than once, they think there is a chance you will change your mind. State your position calmly and rationally, using a matter-of-fact tone of voice. In the third response, it is appropriate to state the consequences if the problem is not satisfactorily resolved. Using the last example, you could say, "The answer is 'no,' and if you persist you will be jeopardizing our working relationship." Including consequences will usually take care of any further argument on the subject.

Confronting Broken Agreements

Confrontive assertion is appropriate when someone fails to keep his or her agreements with you. Confronting others assertively involves describing specifically and nonjudgmentally what the other person said they would do, what they actually did, and what you want. Again, a matter-of-fact tone of voice is important.

For example, "I thought we agreed that when I took on the extra responsibilities created when John left the firm that you would make sure that the performance review committee was informed so that my compensation could be adjusted accordingly. Yet, two months have now gone by and no one on the committee seems to be aware of my increased responsibilities. I want to know why you have not kept your end of the agreement."

In addition to honestly expressing your thoughts and feelings, being assertive puts you in control over your behavior and communication. You always have the right to choose how you are going to respond in any situation. There is no

Figure 12–5 Communication Effectiveness Assessment

Rating Scale: 4–Always; 3–Often; 2–Sometimes; 1–Seldom; 0–Never.

_______ 1. I am open and honest when I have something to say and do not hesitate to tell others what I think or how I feel.
_______ 2. I choose my words carefully, knowing that words have different meanings to others.
_______ 3. I recognize that I may interpret a message differently than it was intended.
_______ 4. Before I open my mouth, I consider the receiver and the likely impact of my message.
_______ 5. I continually look for indications that I am being understood when communicating.
_______ 6. Usually my messages are brief and to the point.
_______ 7. I avoid using jargon with anyone who might not understand it.
_______ 8. I avoid using slang words, cliches, or colloquial expressions.
_______ 9. I do not choose words to intentionally upset or distract others.
_______ 10. I am aware that how I say something is as important as what I say.
_______ 11. My nonverbal messages are congruent with my verbal message.
_______ 12. I carefully consider whether my message would best be understood in person, over the telephone, or in writing.
_______ 13. My opinion about what someone says is based on what I hear them saying rather than on what I think of them as a person.
_______ 14. When I don't agree with someone else's ideas, I listen extra carefully.
_______ 15. I pay particular attention to being a better listener.

_______ Total Score

INTERPRETING YOUR SCORE

Score	
50–60	If you were being honest, you are a very effective communicator and rarely contribute to any misunderstanding.
40–49	Occasionally you contribute to breakdowns in communication. For the most part, however, you are communicating effectively.
30–39	As an average communicator, you share equal responsibility for any misunderstandings.
20–29	Many people fall into this category (when they are being honest). There is room for improvement in your communication skills.
10–19	As a frequent source of communication problems, you will see a remarkable improvement in your interpersonal skills if you are willing to work on communicating.
0–9	Give yourself a pat on the back for being honest. Read some books, attend workshops, go to seminars—do anything to improve your communication skills. You won't regret it.

reason why you need to accept treatment from anyone that is less than satisfactory to you. The choice is always yours.

12–3 How to Be an Effective Listener

Being able to express your beliefs, feelings, and needs is important to your interpersonal skills. Equally important is the need to listen to others. To be an effective listener is to have an accurate understanding of the message at the end of the conversation. To achieve this goal, an effective listener is one who strives for clarification and understanding, rather than making assumptions about the speaker's intent and content.

Effective Listening Techniques

Effective listeners are assertive listeners. That means you must actively participate in the conversation in ways that are designed to keep the communication flowing rather than shutting down, turning off, or putting the other person on the defensive. Here are some of the techniques you can use to become an effective listener.

Active Listening An **active listener** is one who shows involvement with the speaker by maintaining eye contact; indicating interest with appropriate, alert, open body language; concentrating on what the speaker is saying; responding with comments such as "I see" and "Uh-huh," or an affirmative nod of the head; or by restating and summarizing parts of the conversation for clarity and to signify an accurate understanding of the message.

Active listeners are aware that words have different meanings to different people and questions are often necessary to clarify meaning. In addition, you must be able to recognize and overcome your particular biases, prejudices, and stereotypes in order to give each speaker the attention he or she deserves.

Reduce or Eliminate Distractions Distractions come from a variety of sources. One source is the environment itself, such as when a radio is playing too loudly, telephones are ringing, or the temperature is too hot or too cold. Physical barriers such as a desk between the speaker and listener are also environmental distractions to good communication.

In the perfect communication environment listeners are also able to suspend judgments and get beyond the speaker's accent, mannerisms, and appearance, giving full attention to the message the speaker is attempting to communicate. To remain totally objective and rise above all the inevitable distractions takes more skill than that possessed by most listeners.

Let Others Do the Talking You cannot hear what others have to say if you are talking. Good listeners do just that—they listen. They do not attempt to control or manipulate the conversation by jumping in with unsolicited advice, nor do they deflect the conversation to call attention to themselves by recalling similar situations. Good listeners also avoid the temptation to fill up the air space when the speaker has paused to collect his or her thoughts or catch a breath. "Dead air" should be a concern only in radio or television programming, not in interpersonal communication.

Pay Attention to Nonverbal Cues Listening to the words themselves is only one part of the listening process. Effective listeners pay attention also to the speaker's tone of voice, placement of emphasis, speed of delivery, pitch, and volume for clues to the speaker's feeling about the topic.

In addition, the speaker's face, eyes, posture, gestures, and general appearance tell you about his or her overall attitude and feelings. You want to be especially aware of the relationship between the nonverbal and the verbal messages. If they are not supporting one another and instead are sending mixed messages, you will want to ask the speaker for clarification.

Take Responsibility Poor listeners are those who think that the speaker is solely responsible for getting the message across to the listener. Effective listeners realize that communication is a two-way process requiring effort on the part of both participants to reach understanding. Until you understand both the intent and the content of a message, there is no communication.

Here are the steps to becoming a better listener.

Step 1: Learn to *concentrate*. Shut out both the external and internal distractions and open yourself up to actually hearing the message. You must be determined to understand what the other person is saying.

Step 2: Probe for better understanding by asking for clarification. "I'm not sure I understand." Or, "Please repeat that." And, "Is this what you mean?"

Step 3: Reflect the speaker's comments to extend and amplify as a way to gain understanding. "This is what I heard you say. . . . Is that what you meant?" Or, "If such and such is true, would it mean that . . . ?

Step 4: When you think you have heard and understood the message, *summarize* it by paraphrasing and giving feedback to the speaker. This is the process that allows you to determine whether you have indeed understood the message. If your impression of the conversation accurately reflects the speaker's intent, then you have succeeded in being an effective listener. "As I understand it, you want me to . . . " or, "I think I understand how you feel. You feel sad to know that your friend took advantage of you when you were most willing to help if he had asked you directly."

In summary, here are the techniques that can help make you an effective listener.

1. Listen actively.
2. Minimize distractions.
3. Talk less and listen more.
4. Pay attention to nonverbal cues.
5. Take responsibility for making sure that you understand the intent and content of the message.

12–4 How to Give Constructive Feedback

Providing feedback is an integral part of the interpersonal process. Without feedback there is no way to tell whether your message has been received and understood. When you listen actively, ask questions to clarify, and summarize an interpersonal exchange, you are providing feedback. In addition, there are other forms of feedback that are used less often but are nevertheless an integral part of the interpersonal process—giving positive and negative feedback.

Positive Feedback

Kenneth Blanchard and Spencer Johnson wrote a best-selling book called *The One-Minute Manager* (New York: Morrow, 1982) for the purpose of providing a simple way to get positive behavior results. One of their suggestions is to catch people doing things approximately right and encourage the continuance of that behavior with a few words of specific praise. "Nice going, Jack" will not do the job. Specific praise would be, "Jack, you did a great job on getting all those exhibits assembled and marked on time. Thanks."

Why do you, in your job as a paralegal, need to praise others? It is as much a part of your interpersonal skills as expressing your ideas or developing your listening skills. Most people do not receive enough recognition for the work they do and the effort they put into their jobs. The tendency, unfortunately, is to withhold praise for good work but to quickly point out mistakes. The more you acknowledge the contributions made by your coworkers and your boss, the better your interpersonal relationships. Taking the lead in praising and complimenting others is another way of being assertive and lets others know how you want to be treated.

Negative Feedback

Few, if any, people enjoy being criticized. Yet giving and receiving critical feedback is a part of life and necessary for growth. It can be an effective way to improve interpersonal relationships or provide the impetus to change behavior.

It is important for you to keep in mind that you cannot change the behavior of another person. Only they can make the decision to change. You can, however, provide them with the information from which they will decide whether or not to make a behavior change.

There are some general ideas about criticism written by Hendrie Weisinger, Ph.D., in his book *Nobody's Perfect* (Los Angeles: Stratford Press, 1981) that are designed to put criticism in a new perspective. Dr. Weisinger points out that the word *criticism* is a derivative of the word *critique*. One definition of *critique* is to give information. If you can change your way of thinking about criticism and look at it from Dr. Weisinger's perspective, you will see that the person who is criticizing you is giving you some valuable information. He or she is merely exercising one of the basic human rights—the right to express an opinion. You do not have to agree or argue or feel embarrassed, intimidated, or threatened. Since you are in control of your feelings and behavior, you decide what happens next. The same is true when you criticize others—you are expressing your opinion and other people have the freedom to choose how they will respond.

It's true that some people provide criticism more skillfully than others, but for most of us constructive criticism wounds just as deeply as destructive criticism. However, when you are on the receiving end of the criticism and you remember that you are free to choose how much importance to give the information and how to respond to it, you will find that critical feedback can lead to closer relationships and improved performance. For example, think how good you will feel when you can go into your boss's office and ask, "How can I improve my performance?" and it isn't even close to performance review time.

When someone takes the time to criticize your work or to tell you that you have a habit that drives him or her crazy, that person cares enough about you to deal with a negative subject, never a pleasant experience for anyone. Perhaps this person could just fire you or divorce you. The least you can do is hear him or her out without getting defensive. When he or she has finished, the appropriate response is simply, "Thank you for telling me that." Then go away, think about the information you were given, and decide what you want to do with it.

How to Give Constructive Negative Feedback

When the tables are turned and you need to criticize someone, be sure to provide the feedback as soon as possible after the incident to which it refers, and focus your critique only on that particular incident. Check your emotional state before you open your mouth and be sure your motives are honorable. If you are very emotional and your intention is only to put down, humiliate, or embarrass the receiver, then take no action until you are more in control.

All feedback should be specific and descriptive of the incident, not simply reflecting your evaluation or judgment. Most important, constructive feedback pertains only to situations or events over which the receiver has some control to make changes. If the receiver is criticized for faults or shortcomings over which he or she has no control or is unable to act upon, the receiver will only become frustrated by your feedback. For example, it makes no sense to criticize someone for being too short or too tall, too young or too old. There is nothing anyone can do to change that situation. But when someone repeatedly makes a mistake or does not get to work on time, constructive criticism is appropriate.

Here is Dr. Weisinger's model for giving constructive negative feedback. It is designed to provide information to the receiver while showing respect for him or her as a human being and without making him or her defensive.

1. *Be descriptive.* Constructive feedback describes specifically the situation or behavior. It is not evaluative nor judgmental; it is focused on behavior, not the individual.
2. *Show empathy.* Your feedback should indicate understanding, concern, and respect for the person receiving it and express your feelings about the situation or behavior.
3. *Be specific.* Clearly state the specific situation or behavior you want to see changed. If you are vague, most receivers will pay no attention to your requests.
4. *State consequences.* State the positive consequences should the receiver choose to accept and act upon the feedback, and the negative consequences on which you are prepared to follow through if the receiver chooses not to take action. If you do not follow through on the consequences, you will lose all credibility. It is therefore a good idea to give some prior thought to the consequences before you state them.

To test your understanding of the elements of critical feedback, complete the assessment in Figure 12–6.

Because constructive feedback requires thought and skill, Dr. Weisinger suggests using this model script for giving feedback.

1. Start by describing the situation or behavior you want to see changed. Begin your statement with the word *when,* not *you.* For example, "When you are late for work day after day . . . " Statements that begin with *you* have aggressive undertones and most people become defensive when a you-statement is directed to them.
2. Next, express your feelings using an assertive I-statement. "I feel angry/sad/confused/happy/frustrated/confused." You might also show empathy by saying, "I understand why you have trouble getting to work on time. The traffic is unpredictable. Nevertheless, I feel frustrated and angry because everyone else is able to get here on time every day."
3. Then, describe the behavior you want to see and use an assertive I-statement here too. "I want you to take responsibility for getting here every day at 8:30 a.m."

Figure 12–6 Assessment of Critical Feedback

Assessment of Critical Feedback

Below are several statements of critical feedback. After reading each one, indicate the missing elements of constructive feedback on the space following each statement.

1. You are always complaining about everything and it upsets me. ____________
2. You have a bad attitude. ____________
3. All you need to do is work harder and you will succeed. ____________
4. Get real! Life isn't fair! ____________
5. Everyone here likes working with you. I just wish you had more skills. ____________
6. Your clothes don't reflect the image of this firm. ____________
7. Too bad your brief was full of typing errors. Otherwise, it was okay. ____________
8. Others would probably take you more seriously if you were taller. ____________
9. Why are you so sensitive? ____________
10. You are one of the best paralegals in the firm. It is not like you to overlook checking the citations in a brief. I know something must have been bothering you. Tell me what happened. ____________

4. Do not forget to state the positive or negative consequences associated with action or inaction. "If you will take that responsibility then we will be happy to have you be a part of our legal services team. If you choose not to take that responsibility, then I have no alternative but to ask for your resignation."

Here is another example using Dr. Weisinger's model: "When you make promises to me and don't keep them, I feel disappointed and upset. I understand that sometimes unforeseen things happen. But this behavior seems to have become a pattern. I need you and depend upon you. I want you to take responsibility for keeping your commitments. If you are willing to show me that you can be trusted, then we will be able to maintain our reputation as a winning team. If you choose not to take responsibility for honoring your commitments, then I will no longer feel obligated to cover for you."

With this information, the receiver can then decide what action to take. This constructive feedback model allows the receiver to stay in control. It does not put down, insult, or embarrass anyone since it deals only with facts and behavior. Since you cannot make choices for others, you may not get the result you want from this or any other method of feedback. Using this model, you have a better chance of a successful outcome.

One last suggestion when giving negative feedback. Sometimes you might want to get feedback from the receiver after you have stated the consequences. You can ask the receiver for feedback by saying, "What do you think about this?" or, "How do you feel about what I have said?" or, "Do you think you can do what I asked you to do?" This allows the receiver to take part in the discussion. The more feedback that takes place between the giver and the receiver, the more likely you are to be able to resolve any issue to your mutual satisfaction.

12–5 Ethics and Interpersonal Style

Ethical principles and concepts were discussed at length in Chapter 11. But the opportunities to make ethically responsible choices are not limited to your professional duties. They extend to routine situations and everyday dilemmas. For example, how do you use the firm's time—to take care of their business or yours? Do you arrive for work on time even though no one clocks you in? Are breaks and lunch periods extended a few minutes here and there?

Decisions you make about telling the truth provide additional examples of everyday ethical situations. Perhaps you and another paralegal were assigned to work on a research project. Your level of involvement was limited but your boss doesn't know that. When he compliments you on the role you played, do you explain that your role was limited and that your coworker deserves most of the praise? Suppose you overhear someone making an untrue remark about a coworker. It would be embarrassing for you to counter the remark. Do you let the incident pass? One of the secretaries is looking for another job because she cannot get along with the other people in the office. She has given your name as a reference. You cannot be held legally liable for the information you give out. When asked about the situation, will you answer honestly?

Ethics in Communication

In his book *Organizational Communication*, 2d ed. (New York: Longman, 1990), Gary L. Kreps presents three general criteria for making ethical decisions in everyday situations: (1) honesty, (2) avoiding harm, and (3) justice. Let's look at how these criteria apply to you as a paralegal.

1. *Members of the firm should not intentionally deceive one another.*

Most people would not argue against the value of honesty, but in some situations, if you are completely candid the results might be damaging. In reality, you may defend the principle of honesty yet find it difficult to live by it. The ethical dilemma here is that most situations are more than just facts. There are feelings, needs, desires, and images to consider. Do you stick to just the facts, or do you add your opinion and present it as fact? You have a responsibility to check inferences and references before discussing issues involving others, as well as a responsibility to state clearly that your opinion is an opinion and not a fact.

2. *Members of the firm should not purposely communicate anything that would harm any other member.*

Members of the firm have a responsibility to determine whether any harm might befall others as a result of the communication. For example, your supervising attorney has been stealing from the firm for the past several months by adding personal expenses to his business-expense report. You are aware of this because you have been preparing the monthly report while he is preparing for trial. Is it ethical for you to say nothing, since if you were to bring the matter to the attention of certain individuals it would cause harm? Do you wait to be asked and then say something? Should you bring the matter to someone's attention? If so, whose? You would be wise to assess all aspects of the situation before taking action.

The principle of purposeful harm applies without question to those occasions where you could say something about someone else that should not be said. But sometimes you might make a statement without having all the information. To speak out when you are not sure would fall under this principle of doing harm to another member of the firm.

3. *Members of the firm should be treated justly.*

The interpretation of justice is often dependent on individual points of view. Within the context of the law firm, justice and fairness will differ from one level of employment to the next. For example, typically those members of the firm with a higher status will receive more fringe benefits than those at the lower levels. From an ethical point of view, you must determine what is just within a particular context. Employing the harm rule in criterion 2 is useful here for clarification.

In the interest of being just, you might be required to tell the truth even though it may cause harm. For example, justice requires that you tell what you know about the attorney who is stealing from the firm. Although Principle 2 says you should not purposely harm a member of the firm, Principle 3 calls for justice.

Interpersonal Ethics

When you are choosing your interpersonal style, consider this: the only ethical interpersonal style is assertiveness. To communicate ethically requires that you respect the rights of others to take a position that may be different from yours, that you treat others as worthy human beings, and that you encourage free choice.

In addition, ethical communication requires that you present yourself authentically. That is, you are direct, honest, and straightforward in communicating information and feelings. Being authentic does not mean that you communicate everything; it means that your communication is relevant and legitimate.

The ethical interpersonal communicator assumes responsibility for taking part in the process as both the sender and receiver and works to understand the other person's point of view without violating the person's right of free choice. When the time comes, the ethical person presents information accurately and candidly.

Three principles of interpersonal ethics and specific behaviors are presented by Charles T. Brown and Paul Keller in their book *Monologue to Dialogue: An Exploration of Interpersonal Communication*, 2d ed. (Englewood Cliffs, N.J.: Prentice-Hall, 1979):

1. *Ethical communication shows respect for the other person.* Respect for others suggests that lying and distortion of facts and figures are not ethical behaviors.
2. *Ethical communication shows respect for the other person's ideas.* Respect for others' ideas suggests that another person feels free to disagree with you if his or her position is different from yours.
3. *Ethical communication encourages (or at least does not inhibit) another person's ability to make free choices.* Preserving the right of free choice requires refraining from extreme emotional appeals. Manipulative strategies of all kinds restrict the other person's choice and fall into the area of questionable ethical interpersonal behavior.

SUMMARY

12–1

The three interpersonal styles are assertive (standing up for your basic human rights without violating the rights of others), nonassertive (failing to stand up for your basic human rights), and aggressive (standing up for your rights while violating the rights of others). Basic human rights are those rights to which everyone is entitled in order to live a decent life. They are to be honored and granted to everyone. One of those rights is the right to choose how you are going to feel and respond in any interpersonal situation. When making this decision you will want to consider the importance of the relationship, the risks involved, the issues on which you will compromise, which style is most likely to improve the situation, the effect of your choice on your self-respect, and the consequences of your choice for which you will be held responsible.

12–2

Assertive communication is an authentic, honest, direct, yet tactful expression of your thoughts, feelings, and beliefs. It involves the use of various types of I-messages, showing empathy and increasing firmness for those who refuse to get the message, and confronting others who have failed to keep agreements or commitments. Choosing an interpersonal style is always your choice but most people respond positively to the assertive style, since it is based on self-confidence, self-respect, and self-esteem.

12–3

Most knowledge is acquired by listening, yet most of us do it poorly. There are several barriers to effective listening, including both environmental and psychological distractions; physical barriers; and not being able to overcome individual biases, prejudices, and stereotypes. Active listening requires that the listener take an equal responsibility in the communication process by asking questions for clarification, summarizing for agreement of understanding, and paying attention to the sender's nonverbal clues. When you let others do the talking while you concentrate on effective listening there is less likelihood of misunderstanding.

12–4

Giving and receiving criticism and feedback is an important component of the communication process. When recognized as a way to communicate information to others in a way that enables them to use it for their advantage and benefit instead of as a way to find fault or place blame, criticism can be a powerful tool in developing interpersonal skills.

12–5

Ethical principles apply to interpersonal communication as well as to the practice of law. Three criteria to apply in making ethical communication decisions are: honesty, avoiding harm, and justice. In addition, three principles of interpersonal ethics are showing respect for the other person, showing respect for the other person's ideas, and encouraging another person's ability to make free choices by refraining from manipulation. The assertive interpersonal style satisfies these ethical criteria.

REVIEW

Key Terms

Before proceeding, review the key terms listed below to be sure you understand each one. If necessary, read over the corresponding section of the chapter. When you are ready to test your understanding, answer the Review Questions.

active listener
aggressive
assertive
basic human right
empathy
I-messages
nonassertive
role rights
self-esteem
you-messages

Questions for Review and Discussion

1. What are the three styles of communication and how are they different?
2. What is the principle behind the concept of basic human rights?
3. What part do basic human rights play in being assertive?
4. Give one example of each style of communication.
5. When selecting a communication style, what factors do you want to consider?
6. There are several ways to be assertive. What are some of them?
7. What are the fundamentals of effective listening?
8. List the components of the constructive criticism model.
9. What are the general criteria for making ethical interpersonal decisions?
10. List the principles of interpersonal ethics.

Activities

1. Take the statements of criticism from Figure 12–6 and make them into constructive feedback statements. Script out (write down) your new statements. You will need to make up some of the information in order for the statements to conform to the model. It is important, however, that you follow the format of the feedback model. That is, begin with a *When* statement; follow with an *I*-statement to express your feelings and to show empathy. Then use another *I*-statement to describe the behavior you want to see, and state the consequences. Include both a positive consequence and a negative consequence for each statement.
2. Write out a script to give constructive criticism to someone at work or someone in your personal life.
3. In groups of two students, role-play the following situations:
   a. Asking for a raise.
   b. Criticizing someone who fails to keep a commitment.
   c. Being asked to take on more tasks that are not your responsibility and that you do not want to do.

   Respond nonassertively, assertively, and aggressively to each situation.

NOTES

CHAPTER 13 Career Development

OUTLINE

13–1 Ten Techniques for Managing Time
  Use a To-Do List
  Focus on One Task at a Time
  Use Energy Wisely
  Be Neat
  Learn to Say No
  Use Dead Time Effectively
  Minimize Interruptions
  Delegate
  Communicate
  Separate Your Personal Life and Your Office Life
13–2 Projecting a Professional Image
  First Impressions
  Dress for Success
  Good Manners
13–3 How to Write a Resume
  Contact Information
  Work Experience
  Work History
  Education
  References
  Miscellaneous Information
13–4 Preparing for an Interview
  Types of Interviews
  Typical Interview Questions
13–5 Guidelines for Building a Satisfying Career
  Be Thorough, Dependable, and Consistent in Your Work
  Learn to Ask Questions and Communicate
  Take Initiative
  Remember You Are Part of a Team
  Pay Attention to the Bottom Line
  Do Not Overstep Boundaries
  Never Breach Confidentiality
  Choose the Position You Accept Carefully

COMMENTARY

You have noticed that there is more to being successful as a legal assistant than just knowing how to research and draft legal documents. With all the assignments and projects that are routinely assigned, it seems you could spend all your time working and never be finished. You know that employers are concerned about billable hours, but you worry that you may not be able to meet performance standards. Occasionally you wonder whether the way you look and dress is projecting the appropriate image for the job you want. But the big questions on your mind are: How do you get the job you want in the first place, and what do you need to do to be successful once you get it?

OBJECTIVES

After studying this chapter, you should be able to:

1. List ten techniques to get control of your time.
2. Discuss ways to minimize interruptions.
3. Describe what dressing for success means in the legal profession.
4. Discuss the impact on others of first impressions and good manners.
5. List the categories of information that are essential for a resume.
6. Compose your resume.
7. Describe the three types of interviews.
8. Answer the typical interview questions.
9. Explain the value of teamwork in the law office.
10. Discuss ways to build a satisfying career.

13–1 Ten Techniques for Managing Time

Time management is as much a learned skill as researching and drafting documents. Yet, perhaps because time is taken for granted, most of us manage it poorly. We pay too little attention to how we spend our time, then suddenly the realization hits us that time is running out and the pressure is on to make up for the time we lost. Reacting to the pressure to make up for lost time results in mistakes in judgment, errors in decisions, and disappointing ourselves and others.

A legal assistant cannot afford to be a poor time manager. She or he must be able to account for most of the hours spent on the job. Paralegal time is a valuable resource for law firms, and paralegals are expected to produce profits for the firm. Therefore, the goals of a good time-management program for legal assistants are (1) to ensure that you meet or exceed your billable hours quota, (2) to reduce stress, and (3) to increase the number of discretionary hours in which you can do whatever you wish.

Good time-management skills are largely a matter of self-discipline. When you take responsibility for putting your goals ahead of everything else and for keeping the commitments you made to yourself, to the firm, to the clients, and to your career you will find that you are managing your time wisely. Here are some of the most effective tools to help develop your skills for managing time.

Use a To-Do List

If you don't plan your day, your day will be planned by others. That is, if you do not have a written schedule of activities to guide you, you will find yourself spending time putting out fires and reacting to your coworkers' priorities instead of attending to your priorities.

The first step to getting control of your time is to make a list of tasks for each day. Some people make their lists the first thing in the morning; others prefer to make a list for the next day before leaving the office. Next, rank each task on your list in order of priority. When tasks are not ranked in order of priority, most people will do the things they like to do first and put off the other tasks even though those tasks may have a higher priority.

Many paralegals find the week-at-a-glance and month-at-a-glance calendars the most effective in helping to establish long-term priorities and schedule activities, because these types of calendars provide a continual overview of coming events. For the short-term, however, the daily to-do list is a must.

There are printed forms available, such as the one shown in Figure 13–1, or you can develop one of your own. Regardless of the type you choose, the secret of the to-do list is to actually *use* it. Refer to the list frequently to make sure you are managing your time wisely and check off each item as you complete it.

To keep from feeling like a slave to the list, periodically reward yourself when you complete an assignment. Rewards can be simple, such as returning a phone call, savoring a fresh cup of coffee, or taking a walk around the block. Do not expect others to acknowledge the little jobs you do every day; this is something you should learn to do for yourself. The better you treat yourself, the more motivated you will be to move from one goal to the next.

Focus on One Task at a Time

When you are faced with accomplishing several tasks within a given time frame, you must train yourself to concentrate only on the task at hand. Because you have ranked your priorities on the to-do list, you will not forget your other assignments but can instead focus on the current one.

Break down large projects into small, individual tasks so that you can focus on the immediate task instead of the entire project, which may seem overwhelming. Estimate the amount of time each task will require and set deadlines. Eliminate internal and external distractions as much as possible and work toward the reward you have promised yourself.

Use Energy Wisely

Your energy level has a great impact upon the pace at which you are able to accomplish tasks, as well as your attitude toward your work. When possible, schedule activities that require the most concentration, creativity, analysis, and decision making during your high-energy hours. For some, this peak energy time is early morning; for others, it may be midday, late afternoon, or early evening. If your high-energy hours do not coincide with the busiest part of your workday, you may be able to modify your peaks by changing your sleeping or eating habits, or, if possible, by working on a flexible hours schedule.

Be Neat

You will find that an uncluttered desk and office will improve your efficiency as well as your mood, and will be a great stress reducer. Work toward getting papers off your desk and onto someone else's, organized in files, or even into the wastebasket when warranted. The mounds of paper generated and received in a law office are reason enough to attempt to follow Alan Lakein's famous time-management principle—handle a piece of paper only once—as discussed

Figure 13–1 Daily Action Sheet (discontinued product)

DAILY ACTION SHEET

PRIORITY CODES

A. Urgent & Important
B. Important
C. Urgent
D. Low Priority
E. Routine

CONVERSION OF TIME INTO DECIMALS

6 Minutes = .1 Hour	36 Minutes = .6 Hour
12 Minutes = .2 Hour	42 Minutes = .7 Hour
15 Minutes = .25 Hour	45 Minutes = .75 Hour
18 Minutes = .3 Hour	48 Minutes = .8 Hour
24 Minutes = .4 Hour	54 Minutes = .9 Hour
30 Minutes = .5 Hour	60 Minutes = 1.0 Hour

INSTRUCTIONS: List all items to be done today, prioritize items according to importance, and number them in the order in which you will perform them.

Date: ______________________

Priority Order	Priority Code	To Be Done	Time Estimate Hrs.	Time Estimate 1/10s

Source: Law Publications, Inc., Los Angeles, CA (1980).

in his book *How to Get Control of Your Time and Your Life* (New York: Peter H. Wyden, 1973).

Learn to Say No

You must learn to say "no" to some tasks, meetings, lunches, and other time-consuming activities in which you are asked to participate, or you will end up managing your time in accordance with other people's priorities instead of your own. Occasionally, you may even need to say "no" to your boss—tactfully, of course—or at least discuss with him or her how the requested activity fits in with your other priorities.

Use Dead Time Effectively

Every day you have a certain amount of "dead time" when you are not doing anything that directly leads to accomplishing a top-priority goal—time spent commuting, waiting for someone or something, lunch, coffee breaks, or early-morning inertia. You can liven up this dead time by reading low-priority mail, tackling some quick tasks, checking your to-do list, or catching up on journal and magazine articles. Or you can use this time just as effectively to relax and renew yourself for the tasks ahead. Dead-time periods are little windows of free time during your day to be used as you prefer. Use them wisely.

Minimize Interruptions

If you can get control of the telephone and drop-in visitors, you can control your life. Here are some suggestions for getting control of telephone time.

- Establish a certain time each day to make and receive telephone calls. By telling others when you will be available to take calls, you will automatically cut down on interruptions. And by returning calls during one block of time, you will be operating much more efficiently. Or, if you find this suggestion completely out of the question, at least have your calls screened or recorded on an answering machine during certain parts of the day to give you some quiet time. Remember to turn off the bell on your phone so you won't be tempted to answer it.
- Do little jobs such as reading, writing short notes, opening the mail, or checking your to-do list while you are "on hold" for someone else. A speaker phone will allow you to move about the office while you are on hold.
- Know what you want to accomplish before you pick up the phone. Make notes of the points you want to cover and the amount of time you want to spend on each. Keep the conversation moving along by directing the other party to your next point when you feel you have sufficiently covered the topic. When the objective of the call has been met, courteously end the conversation.
- If you must leave a message, let the other party know exactly what you need or want. The other party can then be prepared when he or she returns your call.
- To avoid unnecessary call-backs, make sure you have all the information you need and that you and the other party understand each other. The best way to check for clarity and thoroughness is to summarize the conversation and ask the other party to validate your summary.

Handling drop-in visitors is sometimes easier than coping with telephone interruptions. A "Please Do Not Disturb" sign hung on your doorknob will usually keep most people from intruding. Likewise, simply letting others know that you are working against a deadline will, in most instances, get you the uninterrupted time you need to complete your tasks.

Figure 13–2 A Method to Minimize Interruptions

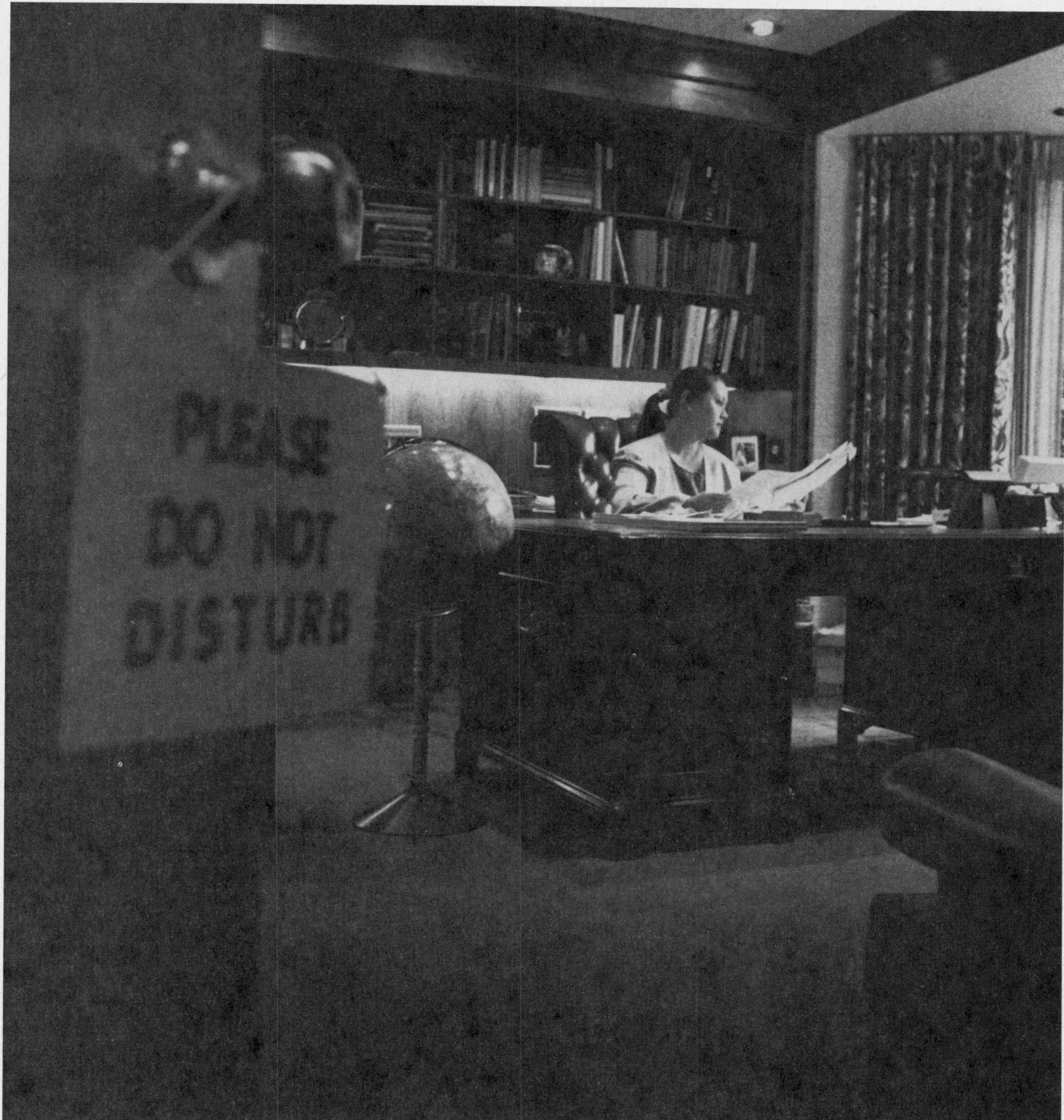

A "Do Not Disturb" sign will get you uninterrupted time to meet work deadlines.
Source: Bob Mullenix.

Delegate

Delegating work to others is often difficult for paralegals to do, because they tend to be detail-oriented people and want to control every aspect of an assignment. Yet assigning certain tasks or portions of a project to others is one of the best ways to manage your time. Every item on your to-do list should be questioned. Which ones can be delegated to a secretary? To the copy center? To the file clerk? To an outside service? Keep in mind that your hours are billable and that you have a responsibility to the client, to the firm, and to yourself to make sure that the time you spend on a task is billable time.

Communicate

Take responsibility for keeping your attorney informed of your work schedule. Some paralegals make it a practice to spend a few minutes at the beginning of each day going over their to-do list with the attorney. These few minutes in the morning can save hours of time during the day when you find, for instance, that you each have different ideas of which tasks have priority.

Before reorganizing your priorities to accept a rush assignment, ask for specifics about what is to be done and when it is really due. Give the attorney an estimate of how much time you think the project will take and what other tasks you will have to put aside in order to take on the new assignment. Then ask the attorney to decide which task has priority. More than one legal assistant has rushed to finish a project only to find it still sitting in the attorney's in box three weeks later.

Separate Your Personal Life and Your Office Life

Keeping your personal life separate from your office life may seem impossible, but with some help from your friends and family you can do it. For example, do not accept personal telephone calls at the office that are not emergencies. Instead, ask your friends and family to leave messages on your home answering machine. You can return the calls later.

Make medical and other personal appointments on weekends, or before and after your normal office hours. Have your salary check deposited automatically to your checking account, mail it to the bank, or use the bank's automatic teller machine instead of standing in the teller line. Bring a lunch to work a couple of days a week and eat it with your coworkers while you chat about personal matters rather than take time away from your billable hours.

One major advantage to keeping your two lives separated: if you do not bring your personal life into the office, you need not take your office life home. Everyone benefits from this practice.

13–2 Projecting a Professional Image

Whenever you come into contact with other people, you project an image. Before anyone has the opportunity to get to know you, they already have a picture in mind of who you are and what you know. The picture you present may set the stage for success or failure.

First Impressions

Although judgments made on first impressions may seem irrational, they occur nevertheless and, once formed, are difficult to change. Anyone anticipating a

Figure 13–3 Judgments will be made about you based entirely on your appearance.

Source: Bob Mullenix.

career in the legal profession must expect to adopt the law professional's wardrobe. Typically, lawyers and paralegals wear conservative business suits or dresses as the uniform of choice. The general public's expectation is that people who work in the legal profession should look like professionals, and one of the quickest ways to separate the paralegal staff from the support staff is by dress.

If you expect to command the respect necessary to carry out your legal assistant duties with clients, court personnel, attorneys, and other professionals in your field, it is necessary for you to look the part and to project an image that matches the expectations of those who are working with you and for you. It is important that you make a positive first impression so that other people will continue to have an open mind and be able to discover your skills and abilities.

Dress for Success

The clothes you wear are a cue to others and help in establishing your credibility, likability, and sense of professionalism. When you enter a room, even though no one in the room may know you or have seen you before, each person will make at least ten decisions about you based solely on your appearance. According to William Thourlby, author of *You Are What You Wear—The Key to Business Success* (Kansas City: Sheed Andrews and McMeel, 1978), many decisions may be made about you, but at the very least judgments will be made about your economic and educational levels, trustworthiness, and level of sophistication, based entirely on your appearance.

It is particularly important for the newly trained legal professional to present a favorable first impression to potential employers and to clients. Knowing how to use clothing to establish yourself in your new role will help you become successful more quickly.

Clothing Guidelines A business suit is the accepted form of dress for both females and males in the legal profession. To project authority and success, choose conservative, well-tailored styles made of natural fibers. This means that you will probably spend more than you want to spend and possibly more than you can afford at first, but high-quality fabrics such as wool and silk in conservative styles will last longer and look better than lesser-quality fabrics and fad fashions. In selecting professional clothing, remember that a high front-end investment will pay out long-term dividends if you make wise choices.

John T. Molloy first wrote *The Woman's Dress for Success Book* (New York: Warner Books) in 1978. Although Molloy has written several subsequent books on success dressing, the guidelines set forth in his first book for selecting appropriate clothing still apply to both men and women:

1. Establish personal dress and grooming standards appropriate for the firm where you wish to work. Before you apply for a job, try to find out what the people who work there are wearing. If you are in doubt, dress conservatively. If you find out the dress code is more relaxed, you can adjust to it later. When you actually begin work, identify the most successful people in the organization and imitate their manner of dress.
2. Dress for the job you want, not the job you have. If you are currently a secretary and desire to move up in the firm, do not continue to dress like a secretary. Employees can communicate with their clothing that they are satisfied with their position. Some image observers say they can walk into an office and see who is ready for a promotion.

3. Avoid wearing the newest dress fad in a business setting. In most cases, the world of business is more conservative than the college environment, the arts, or the world of sports. If you are a "fashion setter," you might be viewed as unstable or lacking in sincerity. To be taken seriously, avoid clothing that is too flashy!
4. When you select a wardrobe, consider regional differences in dress and grooming standards. Geography is a major factor in how people dress. What may be suitable business attire for a paralegal in Los Angeles may be too casual in New York. Pay attention to local customs and traditions when establishing your personal dress and grooming standards.

The money you spend on career clothing should be viewed as an investment, with each item carefully selected to fit properly and look attractive on you. If you concentrate on two or three key colors that can be interchanged, you will have a more extensive wardrobe, rather than a closetful of clothing that does not go together. The less money you have to spend, the more important it is for you to buy quality clothing.

Accessory Guidelines Accessories such as jewelry, handbags, briefcases, neckties, wallets, personal organizers, and luggage are closely related to clothing in terms of establishing your image. Women should choose understated jewelry such as a pin, one gold bangle bracelet, and small earrings. Avoid wearing jewelry that sparkles, makes noise, or dangles. Both men and women should wear an attractive, good-quality watch.

Handbags, briefcases, wallets, and luggage also make a definite statement. Like shoes (no sandals, open-toes, or sports shoes) and clothing, accessories should look serious and professional. Avoid pastel colors and flowered patterns in favor of something made of good-quality leather with a conservative design. Do not overload any accessory that you are going to carry. Doing so will make you look weighed down and out of control. Keep handbags and briefcases highly organized. There is nothing more unprofessional or inefficient-looking than rummaging around trying to find something in your handbag or briefcase.

General Grooming Guidelines Short, shiny, clean hair is preferred for both men and women in the legal profession. Long hair has a collegiate image; short hair is more professional. If you must keep your long hair, pull it back and pin it up for work.

Long, brightly colored fingernails detract from your professional image. Nails should be regularly manicured, kept short, and coated with clear or pale polish. Men, too, need to pay close attention to nail grooming, since the hands are constantly in view. Dirty, ragged nails are not the appropriate image for a paralegal.

There are no substitutes for daily bathing, regular dental hygiene, and use of a good deodorant. Working in a law office is often stressful, and stress produces body odors. Nothing turns off people more quickly than body odor or bad breath. Keep a deodorant stick and mouthwash in your desk and briefcase to avoid offending others.

Good Manners

Good manners and knowledge of proper business etiquette are just as important to your professional image as the way you look. In recent years some people have neglected good manners and proper business etiquette in favor of a more relaxed approach to living and working with others. However, the display of good manners in the business environment is so important that manners and etiquette are receiving renewed attention from executives and the press. It is safe to assume that without good manners your professional image will suffer.

There are several recent books on the subject of proper business etiquette. Listed here are only a few of many tips from corporate etiquette consultant Letitia Baldridge, author of *Letitia Baldridge's Complete Guide to Executive Manners* (New York: Rausen Associates, 1985).

1. Making others feel comfortable is the secret of good manners.
2. When you are the host at a restaurant, allow your guest's order to be taken before your own. To avoid confusion over payment of the check, either present your credit card prior to presentation of the check or instruct the server to give the check to you.
3. When making introductions, a young person should be introduced to an older one, and a person of no rank should be introduced to a person of high rank.
4. Whoever reaches the door first should hold it open for others who are close by.

In addition, do not address a client by his or her first name unless he or she has insisted that you do so. Never refer to an attorney by his or her first name when talking with a client. Likewise, in front of clients, you should be addressed as Mr., Ms., or whatever title is appropriate or preferred. Even though it may be the custom in some parts of the country to address everyone by his or her first name immediately upon meeting, in the business environment this custom is often interpreted as rude and unprofessional.

When you look and act like you mean business, you are creating an image of professionalism and self-confidence to which others will relate in a positive way. In turn, you will feel more professional and self-confident. The end result of this self-fulfilling prophecy is that you are more professional and self-confident.

13–3 How to Write a Resume

A resume is a summary of your career and educational accomplishments. The purpose of a resume is to generate enough interest in the person who reads it that you will be called in to an interview. A resume will not get you a job; but a well-written, interesting resume will get you an interview. The rest is up to you.

When preparing a resume, keep the following fact uppermost in your mind: a help-wanted ad for a highly desirable position is likely to generate several hundred responses. If you prepare only one resume, print a hundred copies, and send a resume to every employer, you will probably never be called for an interview. Your resume should be written to appeal to one particular reader at a time and must address the duties and responsibilities of the position to which you are applying.

Although there are several different acceptable formats for putting your resume together, be sure to include the following categories of information in every resume you prepare.

Contact Information

At the top of your resume provide all pertinent information to make it easy for the reader to get in touch with you. Include your full name, address with apartment number and zip code, and both daytime and evening telephone numbers. If you do not want to be called during the day on your current job, for example, give a daytime number where the caller may leave a message for you. Since most business is conducted during daytime hours, it is important that potential employers be able to reach you or leave a message for you during normal work hours.

Work Experience

Employers are primarily interested in your skills and work experience. Tell the readers of your resume as soon as possible what you can do for them. Do not make them read through pages of information, only to discover that you do not have the skills and experience required for the position.

Be honest about what you have done. You will not be able "to bluff your way" through an interview. The people who will be interviewing you are experts and professionals in their field. They have seen hundreds of job candidates during their careers and are adept at separating truth from fiction.

If you do not have much experience, or if your experience has been in another field, the challenge for you is to be able to relate your previous experience honestly to the position for which you are applying. For example, a woman who is reentering the workplace after being a homemaker has performed the five functions of management—planning, organizing, staffing, directing, and controlling—as a regular part of her occupation as homemaker. She needs only to use the language of management to translate her homemaking skills into easily recognizable job functions.

Likewise, a newly graduated student may have worked part-time while going to school and/or participated in group activities that allowed him or her to gain experience in taking responsibility for completing various projects. By thinking of these activities in business terms and using active verbs such as *planned, researched, developed, wrote,* and *implemented,* your resume will take on a completely different tone, as well as be an honest representation of the skills you will bring to the job.

One way to state your work experience in an interesting and readable way is first to think about each job you have had in these terms: (1) what problems you had to solve, (2) how you solved each one, and (3) the measurable results. Employers hire employees because they have a problem to be solved and the employer wants to find out from your resume and the interview whether you are the problem solver they should hire.

To translate your problem-solving capabilities into a resume, do not tell the reader what problems you solved, only how you solved them and the results. Make an extensive list of action verbs, such as *planned, organized, supervised,* and *researched,* and use these verbs to describe what you did. You do not need to phrase your experience with "I" in a resume.

Then tell the reader the results of your efforts in some measurable or quantifiable form. For example, "saved the firm $10,000 in employment-agency fees"; or, "increased billable hours by 20% over the previous year."

Employers are primarily interested in two things: (1) what you can do for them, and (2) how hiring you will increase the firm's profits. If you cannot do the job and hiring you will only increase their expenses, there is no reason to give you the job.

Work History

This category is a chronological summary of your work experience. In some styles of resumes work experience is separated from work history, since employers are often more interested in what you did than for whom you did it. The work experience section, in that case, is composed of two or more paragraphs of two to four sentences each, highlighting just your prior work experience.

The work history section, then, lists in reverse chronological order the positions you have held for the last ten years only. In addition to dates (month and year are enough), include the name and address of your employers and your job title at each one.

Education

Most employers are interested in your educational background—not grammar school or high school, but in your postsecondary, technical school, private business school, or college work. Again, list your educational work in reverse order; that is, list the highest degree or certificate earned first. Include any seminars, workshops, or conferences you attended that relate to the position you are seeking. You do not need to include your dates of graduation or attendance in these programs, but do include the names and locations (city and state) of the institutions or programs on your list.

References

"References will be submitted upon request" is all you need to say on the resume unless you are specifically instructed to include a list of references. When the time comes, you should choose your references carefully. Obviously, do not give out the names of references without their permission. Choose people who know you well and can speak about your character, habits, and values as well as your skills and ability to do the job. It is more important to choose people who are well acquainted with you than those who might look impressive.

Employers may or may not check your personal references. Because of increasing numbers of fraudulent resumes in recent years, employers have become more diligent about checking education and employment records to verify dates, fields of study, and employment history.

Miscellaneous Information

Hobbies, community activities, organization memberships, career objective statements, and personal data do not belong on your personal resume. Remember the function of a resume is to create enough interest in the reader to prompt a personal interview. Only information about your work experience, work history, and education will accomplish the interview objective.

Employment laws were created to keep everyone focused on the job itself, and what you do in your spare time or who you live with is not a reliable indication of whether you can do the job. Nonetheless, during the interview you may decide to reveal some of your hobbies, activities, and memberships. However, you should be aware that doing so is not a condition of employment and volunteering the information may have a negative effect, since you do not know the interviewer's personal preferences and biases. You will have the opportunity to divulge this information at the appropriate time.

Once the job has been offered to you and you have accepted it, the employer is then entitled to personal information about you, as might be required by various government agencies and insurance companies.

Figure 13–4 is one sample of a resume that follows the outline suggested. There is no one right way or wrong way to put a resume together. You should check several current books on the topic of resume writing and select a few samples that will work for you.

13–4 Preparing for an Interview

Being interviewed is the most important step in the hiring process. For both the law firm and for you, the candidate, the personal interview provides a variety and volume of information about one another that could not be obtained in any other way. The purpose of this face-to-face meeting is to gather enough information to determine whether there is a match between the candidate and the firm.

Types of Interviews

In general, there are three types of interviews: structured, semistructured, and unstructured. The interviewer in a structured interview has a prepared list of questions and does not deviate from the list. The interviewer focuses on job-related questions and then completes a standardized evaluation. Structured interviews are used most often in firms under pressure from the Equal Employment Opportunity Commission to document their interviewing practices and procedures in the event anyone questions why one applicant was hired instead of another. Structured interviews are also used when candidates are interviewed by a panel or committee, when there are time pressures, or when several candidates are being interviewed.

A limited set of questions prepared in advance forms the basis for a semistructured interview. This type of interview is used when there are fewer candidates, since it offers more flexibility for the interviewer to ask follow-up questions than the structured interview.

Little advance preparation is required for the unstructured interview except for the development of a few topics to be discussed. The interviewer asks general questions to prompt the candidate to discuss her- or himself and then forms the next question based on the candidate's response. The unstructured interview resembles an information-gathering conversation between two people who have recently met and may cover a broad range of topics. Although an unstructured interview appears to be relaxed and informal, it is nonetheless designed to gather extensive information from the candidate. The candidate should not be lulled into giving more information than is requested, nor think that this informality is in any way a signal that he or she is the favored candidate.

SAMPLE RESUME

Kelli Johnson
1910 N. Barrington, #12
Dallas, Texas 75206

(214) 992-5788 (day)
(214) 992-2711 (evening)
(214) 895-3756 (FAX message)

WORK EXPERIENCE

Supervised and managed paralegal staff of five including preparation of performance evaluations, awarding of bonuses, and budgeting for salary and staff increases. Reduced paralegal turnover by 100 percent.

Wrote job description, placed advertising, paper screened applicants, interviewed, hired and oriented three experienced paralegals to firm's staff. Developed training program, interviewed, hired and trained two inexperienced paralegals. Increased paralegal staff by five and firm's billable hours by 5,000 annually during last two years.

Interviewed clients, wrote intake memoranda, created client database and follow-up system which saved the firm approximately ten attorney hours per week in performing routine client services tasks.

WORK HISTORY

1990 - Present *Legal Assistant Manager*
Foxcroft & Barney, Richardson, Texas

1986 - 1990 *Civil Litigation Paralegal*
Adams, Little & Brown, Gainesville, Florida

1984 - 1986 *Legal Secretary*
Smith, Williams & Associates, Gainesville, Florida

EDUCATION

Currently enrolled, Business Management program
University of Texas

Associate of Arts degree in Legal Assisting
Gainesville Community College, Florida

Certificate of Legal Secretarial Procedures
Gainesville Business Institute, Florida

Seminar on interpersonal skills
CareerTrak Seminars, Miami, Florida

REFERENCES

Submitted upon request

Typical Interview Questions

Be prepared! Good interviewers and interviewees have perfected their interviewing skills over time. Too often job applicants see the interview as something that is being done to them and do not take an active part in the process. The gathering of information is a two-way process in which both the person conducting the interview and the applicant are sizing up each other to determine whether there is a good fit.

Applicants should spend at least as much time preparing answers to typical questions as the interviewer does in formulating the questions. The following is a list of questions, in no particular order, you should be prepared to answer in a personal interview.

1. What type of job are you most interested in?
2. Why do you want this job?
3. What jobs have you had in the past? Why did you leave?
4. Why did you choose this particular field of work?
5. What do you know about our firm?
6. Why do you feel you have received a good general education?
7. What qualifications do you have that will make you successful in this field? How do they relate to the position for which you are applying?
8. What personal characteristics do you think are necessary to be successful in this position?
9. Why do you think you would like this job?
10. Do you prefer to work with others or by yourself? Why?
11. How would you describe your decision-making style?
12. How do you react under pressure?
13. What kind of boss do you prefer? Why?
14. What have you learned from your previous job that might help you in this position?
15. What are your unique skills and abilities?
16. What have you done that demonstrates initiative and a willingness to work?
17. Will you describe a conflict you had with a boss or coworker and how you resolved it?
18. What is your major strength and your major weakness? Why do you consider your weakness to be a weakness?
19. Would you describe yourself as analytical, creative, or emotional? Why?
20. If you could have any job in the world, what would it be?
21. Will you tell me a little bit about yourself?
22. Why do you want to leave your current position?
23. What did you accomplish in your last job that you are most proud of?
24. What do you want to be doing five years from now?
25. Why should I hire you?

Remember, interviews are for the purpose of gathering information about you, your values and attitudes, your ability to think under pressure, and your ability to summarize information and present it in a rational and coherent way. You should expect that some of the questions listed will be asked in one form or another. The answers you prepare should relate entirely to the job for which you are interviewing. You do not need to divulge any personal information about your family life or your hobbies or outside interests during this interview.

Employers are looking for energetic, enthusiastic, motivated employees who will be a positive influence on and addition to the firm. All information you present should reflect your enthusiasm and desire to become a part of the firm and a longstanding employee.

13–5 Guidelines for Building a Satisfying Career

Although it might seem somewhat premature to be discussing ways to build a satisfying career, most experienced paralegals will agree that it is never too early to learn some of the basic techniques that will contribute to your personal and professional growth. The following are a few basic career guidelines that have been helpful to other paralegals.

Be Thorough, Dependable, and Consistent in Your Work

Everyone has an off-day now and then when something obvious is overlooked. If this situation occurs too frequently, do not expect to keep your job. Paralegals are expected to be professional in their work and that means checking and rechecking until you are certain beyond doubt that the work product for which you are responsible is complete and accurate.

Being thorough in your work means that not only are the facts accurate, but that you meet all your deadlines, keep track of everything you need to keep track of, and use your time wisely. When you build a reputation for thoroughness, you also build a reputation for dependability. Everyone will know that when you are given an assignment he or she can count on you to follow it through to completion without being concerned about the quality of the finished work product.

Thoroughness and dependability lead to consistency, and possessing these attributes will make lawyers seek you out as a prized legal assistant. Nothing is more frustrating than not knowing from one day to the next whether a certain paralegal is having a good day or a bad one. If a lawyer develops confidence in your ability to be consistently thorough and dependable in your work, and you disappoint him or her, you may have difficulty in rebuilding that confidence. You should adopt the attitude that every day is going to be a good day the minute you step through the office door.

When the odd mistake occurs you must acknowledge it as soon as you know about it and accept responsibility for correcting it. Most mistakes that are made can be corrected if caught soon enough. This is particularly true for errors in procedure. For example, if you failed to follow a court rule the error can usually be rectified by filing a corrected document or by a motion before the court. Procedural mistakes are always embarrassing, because it is your job to know and follow court procedure, but they are not fatal.

Responsibility and accountability extend to any work that you delegate to someone else. You should thoroughly check over any work that is sent to word processing or delegated to a secretary before you send it on to the attorney. As a general rule, the attorney is held responsible for the final work product outside the office but the paralegal is held responsible for the accuracy of that work inside the office.

Learn to Ask Questions and Communicate

Inexperienced legal assistants tend to ask fewer questions than those with more experience. The reason is simple: less experience means less confidence, and asking questions is sometimes falsely associated with lack of knowledge. The only dumb questions are those that are repeatedly asked and to which the same answer is given each time, and the ones not asked when something is not understood.

Good communication skills are difficult to develop, and even the best communicators sometimes have difficulty in making themselves understood. The attorney giving you instructions may be in a hurry, may assume that you know exactly what is to be done, or may be testing you. If you fail to ask enough questions so that you can do the job, you will fail to do the job. The responsibility rests with you to get all the information you need to succeed.

Never assume that you can read your attorney's mind even after you have worked together for years. You may guess correctly most of the time, but you will never be right all the time. It is always preferable to let others make their own decisions and not assume that you know a person so well that you will make the same choice as he or she would.

Do not put yourself in the position of having to make a choice between attorneys who make conflicting demands on your time. Instead, when two attorneys are competing for your time, go over your to-do list with them, and ask them to decide whose work has priority.

Keep your attorney informed of your work load. In some offices, this is handled with weekly status report meetings but in others, daily briefings are preferred. It is up to you to keep current on the status of projects and events for both you and your attorney.

Take Initiative

Paralegals who take initiative are preferred over those who wait to be asked. Taking the initiative means that when you see something that needs to be done, you do not wait for someone to ask you to do it.

Look for new ways to do things more efficiently. Volunteer to draft a document or research a point of law. Ask for the opportunity to take on more responsibility. Sign up for continuing education seminars and attend conferences, even if it is on your own time and at your own expense. Join a professional organization and get actively involved in committee work and building your professional network. Speak up. The most successful paralegals are not afraid to offer a countersuggestion or another point of view.

Remember You Are Part of a Team

The practice of law is a cooperative effort. Attorneys bring in the clients and secretaries process much of the paperwork. The paralegal is often the liaison between the attorney and the support staff, and in this position must develop a cooperative spirit among the members of the team.

Being a team player indicates a willingness to work together for the benefit of the team rather than for the aggrandizement of any individual member. The team's goals should be the same as the firm's goals. The goals of the individual members of the team should be the same as the team's. Team members cover for each other in a pinch, and they put the team's demands ahead of their own. For a paralegal whose status in the firm places him or her in the often uncomfortable middle, being part of the team means that you must develop a good working relationship with the support staff as well as the attorneys in order to be successful. Every member of the team has an important part to play, and without the full cooperation of each team member, no one will succeed.

Pay Attention to the Bottom Line

Paralegals are expected to produce profits for the law firm. Be advised that the firm's management team will pay close attention to whether the paralegals, individually and collectively, are contributing to the bottom-line profits or are an additional expense.

Paying attention to the bottom line for you means that you must keep complete and accurate records of your time on the job. Too many paralegals wait until the end of the day to record their time, only to find that reconstructing the day is impossible. These people then find that they have spent eight hours in the office but can only account for five. This is not fair to you or the firm.

Train yourself early in your career to record your time throughout the day, even when you are working on something that will not be billed to a client, such as straightening up the library or redrafting a document to correct a clerical error. The lawyer will decide what time to write off and what time to bill. The main problem that all paralegals have with time sheets, regardless of their years of experience, is self-deprecation. That is, you might think that it should have taken only two hours to locate a document at the courthouse but, because of traffic problems on the way there and a new clerk at the front desk, it took twice as long. If you decide to put down only the two hours it should have taken, you have just cheated yourself. The attorney will understand, under the circumstances, how a two-hour project could take four hours, but the firm's management team will not be able to understand why your timesheets are short and why you are making decisions that should be made by the attorney.

In order for the firm to make a profit, you must put in the hours. When you are given a nonbillable job, the first thing to ask is what portions of the job can be delegated to a secretary, a copy clerk, or the filing room. Most attorneys will respond positively when you pay attention to the bottom line and appreciate it when you point out, "This task is nonbillable. Is it okay to ask the secretary to work on it?"

Do Not Overstep Boundaries

Be sure to get a clear understanding of what your attorney expects from you when dealing with the clients. Some attorneys do not have a problem when you tell a client what he or she can or cannot do; but other attorneys may see this as overstepping the boundaries and giving legal advice. Clients will often call you and expect to get the same information that they would get from the attorney because you are as familiar with the case as the attorney and know the law. If you have not discussed the boundaries with the attorney, you could find yourself in hot water. With the best of intentions, you answer the client's question only to find that you have crossed over from providing facts into the unauthorized practice of law. When a client calls you and asks, "What should I do now?" the best thing for you to do is say you will find out and call the client back. Then, take a few minutes and think about the best way to handle the situation. Let the attorney decide how to respond to the client.

Overstepping the boundaries also applies to the firm's organizational structure, and how you handle interpersonal problems that might come up. If you have a problem with the attorney to whom you have been assigned, it is best to speak directly to the attorney and try to work out a solution with him or her. You should not discuss the problem with other paralegals or secretaries. This would be a serious breach of professional courtesy and ethics. Nor should you take the problem to someone higher up in the organization without first attempting to resolve it with the individual him- or herself. As a member of the firm's professional staff, you are expected to develop your communication and problem-solving skills so that you can handle interpersonal conflicts in a professional way.

Never Breach Confidentiality

One of the most frequent problems that occurs for paralegals is the unintentional breach of client confidentiality. It is not just the client's secrets that must remain confidential, but their identity as well. Regardless of how interesting or exciting your work is, you must not talk about a client or a case outside the office, even if you attempt to disguise the identity of the individual or the facts of the case.

Maintaining the client's confidence can be particularly difficult when the results may affect family members or friends. For example, you might work for a law firm that represents a savings and loan, and you have learned that the FSLIC is probably going to close down the S&L in which your mother has an account. Two attorneys in your office and you are the only people who know about the closing. The information is being withheld from the media to forestall a run on the institution. It will be very difficult for you not to warn your mother, but you must learn to draw the line between what you know because of your job and what is public knowledge. The information you have because of your job is confidential.

Choose the Position You Accept Carefully

Many paralegals are so eager to find a job, particularly their first job, that they accept the first position offered to them. This can be a big mistake. Before you accept any position, you should first spend some time deciding what specialty area you want to work in and seek work only in that area. If you take a position outside your chosen area, you will not be happy. You will always be looking for another position in your area and will not be able to give your full energy and attention to your current position. In addition, it is not as easy as you might think to switch from one specialty to another once you have gained some knowledge and expertise in one area. For example, if you spend a year or more in family law and then try to switch to bankruptcy, you may be taking a step back in your career instead of moving forward. This is because you will have to learn new procedures and systems and will not be as productive as you were in the former specialty until you learn the new one. When you change from one specialty to another, you may be required to take a cut in pay.

You should also take some time to check the reputation in the community of the law firm in which you are considering a position. If the firm's reputation is questionable, that reputation could follow you if you ever want to leave. A future employer might assume that your reputation is questionable, too, if you work there for any length of time.

Entry-level paralegals should try to find a position in an established law firm with an excellent reputation in the community and in which there are other paralegals or attorneys who are willing to provide the guidance and supervision that most new paralegals require, particularly during the first few months on the job. Although it is true that a smaller firm will provide more job diversification than a larger firm, the amount of responsibility thrust upon a paralegal in a small firm can be overwhelming to someone without experience.

Unfortunately, there are no fail-safe methods in career planning and development. Making mistakes and errors in judgment are inherent in humans and should not be considered a sign of failure. If you learn from your mistakes and do not repeat them, you have not failed, because you gained new knowledge from the experience. Failure occurs only when you fail to learn from your mistakes and continue to repeat them.

With experience you will learn that most of the career mistakes you will make can be corrected and do not cause permanent damage, but you must be willing to take responsibility for and be held accountable for all the decisions and choices you make both now and in the future.

SUMMARY

13–1

Time management is an essential skill for legal assistants because billable hours are a valuable resource for the law firm. The goals of a good time-management program are to meet or exceed the billable hours quota, to reduce stress, and to increase the number of discretionary hours. Some techniques to get control of your time include using a to-do list, focusing on one task at a time, using energy wisely, being neat and organized, learning to say no, using dead time effectively, minimizing interruptions, delegating work to others, communicating, and keeping personal life and office life separated.

13–2

Projecting a professional image is important to creating good first impressions, gaining confidence, and building credibility with coworkers, clients, and others. Choosing clothing and accessories considered professional and appropriate for the legal community in which you work is as important as always being well groomed. Using good manners and treating others with respect and courtesy are equally essential to your professionalism.

13–3

A resume will not get you a job, but an interesting and well-written resume will get you an interview. Your resume should contain information on where you can be contacted to schedule an interview, how your past work experience has prepared you for the job you are seeking, highlights of your educational background, and your work history. Employers are interested in how you solve problems and the results you are able to obtain, not in your hobbies or the organizations to which you belong. Direct the information in your resume to show why the firm should hire you and what they can expect from you once you are on the job.

13–4

There are three types of interviews: structured interviews, where the interviewer does not deviate from a list of prepared questions; semistructured interviews, where the interviewer has prepared a few advance questions but also relies on follow-up questions to the candidate's answers to elicit information; and unstructured interviews, which are designed to put the candidate at ease but nevertheless gather enough information to determine whether the candidate can do the job and should be hired. All candidates should be prepared to answer questions about their strengths and weaknesses, their ability to solve problems, their interpersonal skills, and how they work on a team. Candidates should also be prepared to ask questions about the firm's goals, management philosophy, reputation in the community, and strengths and weaknesses. The interview is a two-way process during which both the interviewer and the interviewee have the opportunity to gather information on one another.

13–5

There are many ways in which legal assistants can build a satisfying career. Some of those ways include developing a reputation for being thorough, dependable, and consistent in their work; learning to ask questions and to communicate with the attorneys; taking the initiative; being part of the team; paying attention to the bottom line; not overstepping the boundaries in dealing with clients, attorneys, or coworkers; never breaching confidentiality; and carefully choosing the firm in which they work.

REVIEW

Questions for Review and Discussion

1. What are ten techniques that will help you get control of your time?
2. What are some techniques for handling telephone and drop-in visitor interruptions?
3. Describe what dressing for success means in the legal profession.
4. Why are first impressions and good manners important to your professional image?
5. List the categories of information that are essential for a resume.
6. Describe the three types of interviews.
7. In general, what is the purpose for an interview, and what types of questions should you be prepared to answer?
8. Many people feel that they are more productive when they are allowed to work on their own. Explain the value of teamwork in the law office.
9. What can you do to build a satisfying career as a legal assistant?

Activities

1. Keep records of your time for a two-week period. What is the biggest time waster for you? Interruptions? Procrastination? Lack of clear direction or instruction? List ways to handle these time wasters in the future. Discuss with others ideas on how to manage time more productively.
2. Keep records of your time for another two-week period, using the ideas and techniques generated from Activity No. 1. Compare before and after records. Were you able to use any of the techniques to get more control of your time? Which time wasters are still causing problems for you, and what can you do about them?
3. Invite an image consultant to talk about techniques for developing a professional image appropriate for the legal profession in your area when you have a limited budget.
4. Prepare two versions of your resume on separate papers. Submit them to your instructor and an employment counselor for review and suggestions for improvement.
5. Role-play different types of job interviews to experience the process, how to formulate answers to interview questions, and to gain confidence.

GLOSSARY

Active listener: One who demonstrates involvement with the speaker.

Agenda: List of items to be covered or things to do; goals.

Aggressive: Standing up for your basic human rights without regard or respect for the rights of others.

Agreement: Requires an offer and an acceptance.

Answer: The defendant's response to a complaint that has been filed and served.

Appellant: The party bringing an appeal.

Appellate jurisdiction: The ability to review decisions of a lower court.

Appellee: The person against whom the appeal is brought.

Arbitration: The dispute-settling process that does not involve going to court, in which the parties agree that an impartial third party, the arbitrator, will act as a judge and make the decision, to which the parties will be bound.

Arraignment: The appearance or proceeding whereby the defendant is brought before an officer of the court and formally charged with having committed an offense.

Arrested: Taken into custody.

Assault: Any word or action that is intended to cause the person to whom it is directed to fear or have apprehension of immediate physical harm, or any offensive touching.

Assertive: Standing up for your basic human rights with regard and respect for the rights of others.

Assumption of risk: Applies when a plaintiff voluntarily enters into a risky situation knowing the risk involved. Several states have abolished the assumption of risk defense in lawsuits for negligence.

Backup: To copy data onto another computer disk.

Bail: The posting of cash or other form of security in exchange for the release of someone who has been accused of committing a crime.

Bail bond: The signed document that secures the release of an individual in custody; sometimes also called an *appearance bond*.

Basic human rights: Anything that all people are entitled to be, have, or do by virtue of their existence as human beings.

Battery: Unconsensual, harmful, or offensive physical contact intentionally performed.

Bench: A synonym commonly used to refer to the court.

Bench warrant: An order from the court empowering the proper legal authorities to seize a person.

Bilateral contract: A promise in exchange for another promise.

Bill of particulars: A legal document designed to elicit more factual details pertaining to the subject of a lawsuit; may be used instead of or in addition to interrogatories.

Billable hours: Time spent on client matters for which the client can be charged.

Bit: Individual binary digit, either a zero or a one, that, when put together with other bits, represents characters in the computer.

Body language: Elements of nonverbal communication including facial expression, eye contact, gestures, touch, appearance, posture, use of space and time, and physical movement.

Booking: The process whereby the accused is photographed, fingerprinted, and charged with committing a crime.

Breach of contract: When a party does not fulfill a contractual obligation.

Bug: A basic flaw in the initial design of a computer software program.

Business tort: Wrongful interference with another's business rights.

Byte: Eight bits, or binary digits, that represent one character in the computer.

Capacity: Being of legal age and mentally competent to enter into a contract.

Case retainer: The entire fee due for a case, or only part of the fee (common in litigated divorces and criminal cases).

Causation in fact: When the plaintiff's injury would not have occurred without the defendant's act.

Cause of action: A claim in law or fact sufficient to demand judicial attention.

Central processing unit: A component of a computer that executes the program instructions to process data.

Certiorari: A Latin word (pronounced sir-she-rare-ree) referring to a means of gaining appellate review of a case through the use of a writ.

Challenge for cause: A request to excuse a juror who does not meet the state statute requirements for jurors or who indicates that he or she may be prejudiced toward the defendant or prosecution.

Chapter 7: One type of bankruptcy proceeding, in which the debtor is compelled to turn property into cash to pay creditors.

Chapter 11: A type of bankruptcy proceeding that reorganizes a business and its finances to ensure that creditors will not be harmed and forestalls or eliminates the chances of the enterprise going out of business. Prior to June 1991, when the U.S. Supreme Court ruled that individual debtors can file for Chapter 11, this bankruptcy proceeding was reserved for businesses alone.

Chapter 13: A type of personal bankruptcy proceeding in which a petitioner with a stable income and a bankruptcy trustee work out a repayment plan with creditors.

Citation: The series of letters and numbers that comprise a code that identifies court decisions.

Civil cases: Actions brought before a trial court to settle disputes involving individuals, the state or federal government, business entities, individual states, or any combination thereof.

Civil law: Laws concerned with acts against individuals for which compensation or other relief is sought.

Civil litigation: The action or process of carrying on a lawsuit governing private rights and remedies.

Common law: The system of jurisprudence that originated in England when judges in small towns and villages resolved disputes based upon common sense, fairness, and social custom.

Comparative negligence: A defense in negligence lawsuits where the parties are assigned a percentage of negligence representing the degree to which each was at fault.

Complaint: The first pleading filed by the plaintiff in a lawsuit.

Conflict of interest: Where regard for one duty leads to the disregard of another.

Conservatorship: A proceeding held for the purpose of appointing an adult to take care of the person or property of any person who is unable to provide for his or her own personal needs or to manage his or her own finances.

Consideration: The inducement to a contract.

Constitution: The written instrument that sets forth the structure of laws by which a government is created and according to which a country or state is governed.

Contingency fee: A fee arrangement between a lawyer and a client whereby the lawyer receives a fee based upon a percentage of the amount the lawyer is able to recover for the client; if no amount is recovered for the client, then no fee is due.

Contract: A legally enforceable promise or set of promises.

Contributory negligence: A defense in negligence lawsuits where both parties have been negligent and their combined negligence caused the injury that is the subject of the lawsuit.

Conversion: When someone takes personal property owned by another and places it into service or otherwise deprives the owner of its use.

Copyright: A statutory right granted for life plus 50 years to authors, originators of artistic productions, and developers of computer programs; commonly denoted by the symbol © .

Corporation: A legal entity; a creation of law; formed primarily for the convenience of those people who have invested money in the corporation.

Counterclaim: An action filed by the defendant stating that he or she has a cause of action against the plaintiff.

Court: The branch of government that is responsible for the resolution of disputes arising under the laws of the government; frequently used as a substitute for *judge,* i.e., "The court stated its opinion."

Courts of record: Courts in which proceedings are recorded by a court reporter.

Crime: An act that violates the law and is a serious offense against morality.

Criminal cases: Actions brought in a trial court against individuals by the federal, state, or local government to punish them for breaking the law.

Criminal justice system: The method or procedure a society develops to handle those who are alleged to have committed a crime.

Cross-examination: The process in which a witness first examined by the prosecuting attorney is questioned by the defense attorney, or vice versa.

Cryptography: Code, as used in case citations.

Cumulative trauma disorder: An industrial injury, usually to the hands and wrist area, that affects people who perform repetitive tasks.

Cursor: A blinking arrow, dash, or other symbol on the computer screen that tells the user the system is ready for data input and where characters will appear on the screen.

Damages: The punishment in a tort action; usually the payment of monetary compensation by the individual or entity found to have injured another.

De novo: A Latin term meaning *new,* i.e., a *de novo* trial when a case is retried.

Debtor: Any person, partnership, or corporation with debts.

Defamation: The publication or oral communication of a statement that is injurious to the name or reputation of another.

Defendant: The person(s), entity, business, corporation, or branch of government being sued or charged with criminal conduct.

Deliberates: When the jury considers all the evidence and arguments presented and renders its opinion or verdict.

Demurrer: A legal pleading that contains a statement that admits the facts but asserts that the plaintiff failed to state a sufficient cause of action on which to base a claim.

Deposition: An in-person question-and-answer session conducted under oath and recorded by a court reporter or on videotape, during which counsel for both sides are present and have the opportunity to question the individual being deposed. Depositions may be taken of parties to a lawsuit and of witnesses. Testimony taken in a deposition may be used in court.

Direct examination: The process in which each witness is first examined by the side presenting that witness.

Discovery: The pretrial procedure by which one party gains information, facts, and documents held by the other party.

Diskettes: Thin, pliable, magnetically coated plastic on which data is stored; sometimes also called *floppy disks.*

Dismissed: Thrown out of court, as when a complaint fails to state a proper cause of action.

Diversity jurisdiction: The federal court's power to hear and determine cases involving controversies between citizens of different U.S. states or between citizens of a U.S. state and a foreign country, its citizens, or subjects.

Docket: A list of cases on the court's calendar; a sheet that summarizes the contents of the legal documents in a file.

Double jeopardy: A provision in the Fifth Amendment to the Constitution that provides that no person shall be tried twice for the same offense; to be tried twice for the same offense.

Due process: A course of legal action according to rules and principles that have been established by our legal system for the protection and enforcement of private rights.

Empathy: Understanding another person's point of view.

Equity: The difference between what property is worth and what is owed on it.

Ethic: A set of moral principles.

Ethics: The field of moral science.

Exclusionary rule: The rule that provides that evidence obtained without a warrant must be excluded at trial.

Executed: Signed.

Express contract: When all the terms and conditions of an agreement are fully and explicitly stated, either orally or in writing.

False imprisonment: The unjustified, intentional confinement, restraint, or detention of another person without that person's consent.

Family court: Hears matters involving issues relating to a family and its members, i.e., divorce or dissolution, adoptions, custody, and juvenile delinquency. Sometimes also known as *matrimonial court, domestic relations court*, and *juvenile court*.

Federal question jurisdiction: The federal court's power to hear and determine cases involving the meaning or application of something in the Constitution, in federal law, or in a treaty.

Felony: An offense punishable by forfeiture of certain rights; the generic term for certain high (serious) crimes, such as homicide, arson, rape, robbery, burglary, larceny, escape from prison, and treason.

Fiduciary: A duty to protect the interests of another who has entrusted you with information and/or property.

Fixed fee: A set rate for a standard service, e.g., an uncontested divorce, preparing a simple will, and forming a small business corporation; sometimes also called a *flat fee*.

Formal contract: A contract that requires a special form or method of creation to be enforceable.

Generalist: A legal assistant who is competent in several fields of law.

Gigabyte: Refers to 1024 megabytes, or about a billion-character, storage capacity in the memory of a computer.

Grand jury: A group of people, usually about 23 in number, drawn, summoned, and selected according to law to investigate and inform a court of criminal jurisdiction on crimes committed within its jurisdiction and to indict persons for crimes when it has discovered sufficient evidence to hold a person for trial.

Guardianship: A proceeding held for the purpose of appointing a guardian to take care of the person or property of a minor.

Habeas corpus: A Latin term meaning *you should have the body;* in a criminal proceeding, refers to the determination of whether the petitioner is being legally confined.

Hard disk: Nonbending, rigid aluminum disk on which about 5000 pages of data can be stored in a computer; rotates at higher rate of speed than a floppy disk.

Headnotes: One-sentence summaries of a particular point of law in a precedent-setting case.

Hearsay: Secondhand testimony or evidence.

Holographic will: A will written entirely by hand by the decedent.

Hourly fee: A billing rate for attorneys and legal assistants determined after considering many factors, including overhead, expected compensation, education, experience, and geographic location.

Hung jury: A jury whose members cannot reach a verdict by whatever degree of agreement is required.

I-messages: Statements that begin with the pronoun *I;* usually assertive statements.

Impaneling: The process by which jurors are selected and sworn in.

Impeachment: The process of charging a public official with wrongdoing while in office.

Implied by law: A type of contract in which the law imposes requirements on the parties even when they have not entered into a contractual obligation.

Implied in fact: When the conduct of the parties indicates that they intended to form a contract and that conduct creates and defines the terms of the contract.

In pro se: A Latin term meaning *on one's own behalf,* without the representation of an attorney; sometimes also known as *in propria persona* or *in pro per.*

Indicted: To be accused by a grand jury of having committed a crime.

Indictment: A formal, written accusation from a grand jury charging a person with a crime.

Infliction of emotional distress: An intentional act of such extreme and outrageous conduct that it goes beyond the bounds of human decency and causes another to experience severe emotional distress.

Informal contract: Type of contract based on substance rather than on form, that is not required to be in writing.

Intentional tort: An act that the tortfeasor made a conscious decision to perform with the expectation that the intended victim would in some way be harmed or injured.

Interrogate: To question or examine.

Interrogatories: Written questions addressed to a party in a lawsuit pertaining to the subject of the litigation.

Interview: To gather information.

Intestate: When a person dies leaving no will.

Investigation: An observation or inquiry into allegations, circumstances, or relationships in order to obtain factual information.

Involuntary bankruptcy: When three or more creditors with claims totaling $5000 over and above any lien on the debtor's property force the debtor into bankruptcy.

Judgment: The written version of a judge's decision.

Jurisdiction: The court's power to hear and determine a case.

Jurisprudence: A philosophy, science, or system of laws.

Jury instructions: Written memoranda to the jury that set forth the questions of fact that the jury must decide.

K: The metric symbol for 1000.

Kilobyte: Represented by the metric symbol *K;* represents 1024 characters of information in the memory of a computer.

Last clear chance: A defense in negligence lawsuits that allows the plaintiff to recover full damages despite the plaintiff's failure to exercise care in the face of certain danger. Because it is difficult to apply, this defense is no longer used in those jurisdictions where the comparative negligence rule has been adopted.

Law: The legislative pronouncement of the rules that should guide one's actions in society; the official rules and principles of conduct established by legislative authority, court decisions, or local custom.

Legal analysis: The process of applying rules of law or statutes to the given facts of a case.

Legal assistant: A person with legal skills beyond the secretarial level who works under the supervision of an attorney; sometimes also called a *paralegal.*

Legal technicians: Nonlawyers who provide out-of-court legal services directly to consumers without direct supervision of an attorney. Consumer rights organizations and various states are currently looking into the possibility of licensing legal technicians, but to date no state has begun this licensing.

Leveraging: The process of making a profit from the services performed by others, e.g., a law firm makes a profit from work done by a legal assistant.

Libel: A breach of the duty to refrain from making false, defamatory statements in writing about other people.

Litigation: The action or process of carrying on a suit in law or equity.

Local area network: Computers that are linked together for the purpose of sharing information and/or another piece of equipment, such as a printer.

Magistrate: An officer of the court.

Mandamus: Latin for *we command;* requires a public servant or official to perform a ministerial act that the law considers an absolute duty.

Mayhem: Maliciously maiming or dismembering another person.

Mediation: The dispute-settling process that does not involve going to court and which is merely advisory in nature (nonbinding). Instead of making a decision for the parties, the mediator attempts to work out an agreeable resolution of the controversy.

Megabyte: Refers to 1024K, or about a million-character, storage capacity in the memory of a computer.

Memorandum opinion: A document in which a judge's decision and the law on which he or she relied is set down in detail.

Memory: An area of a computer for storing programs and data while you are working on a program; also called *main storage.*

Microchip: A wafer of silicon measuring about one-fourth inch square and less than four-thousandths of an inch thick that contains imprinted circuits through which electronic impulses travel.

Microfiche: A sheet of microfilm containing rows of images in a grid pattern.

Microfilm: A process in which paper documents are put on a roll of film cartridge or jacket of film.

Miranda warning: "You have the right to remain silent. Any statement you make may be used against you in a court of law. You have the right to have an attorney present. If you cannot afford an attorney, one will be appointed for you." This extended privilege against self-incrimination to cover preliminary and routine questioning by police officers resulted from a U.S. Supreme Court decision in *Miranda v. Arizona,* 384 U.S. 436 (1966).

Misdemeanor: A class of criminal offenses usually considered less serious than felonies and for which punishment is less severe.

Modem: A peripheral device for a computer that converts electrical digital signals into audio signals and transmits them via telephone lines over long distances.

Morals: The perception of what is right and what is wrong.

Motion: A request submitted by an attorney to the court for a ruling on a pending action or a point of law.

Motion for Summary Judgment: A pleading in which the defendant requests that the court end the case without a full trial because, on the evidence presented to date, the court should find that the plaintiff cannot win and there is no need for a trial.

Mouse: A data-input device for a computer; a small desktop pointing device that moves a cursor on the computer screen.

Negligence: Failure to exercise the degree of care that a reasonable person would exercise under the same circumstances.

Nolo contendere: A Latin phrase meaning *I do not wish to contest it.* A *nolo contendere* plea is neither an admission of guilt nor a claim of innocence, and may not be used in any other case against the defendant as proof of guilt. In all other respects, a *nolo contendere* plea is treated the same as an admission of guilt.

Nonassertive: Failing to stand up for your basic human rights, or doing so in such a way as to be ineffective.

Nuisance: In tort law, a wrong arising from an unreasonable or unlawful use of property to the discomfort, annoyance, inconvenience, or damage of another.

Operating system: A system that manages the operation of a microcomputer.

Original jurisdiction: The ability to hear and decide all issues of fact and law.

Overruled: When objections to questions are raised but not allowed by the judge; requires the witness to answer the question.

Own recognizance: When the defendant agrees to appear in court as required without posting bail.

Paralegal: A person with legal skills beyond the secretarial level who works under the supervision of an attorney; sometimes also called a *legal assistant.*

Partnership: A business owned by two or more persons.

Patent: A grant from a government that allows an inventor who has satisfactorily demonstrated to the patent office that the invention is genuine and novel the exclusive right to make, use, and sell the invention for a period of 17 years.

Peremptory challenge: A request to excuse a juror that requires no specific reason or cause.

Peripherals: Input and output devices connected to a microcomputer.

Piracy: The unauthorized copying of computer software or other copyrighted properties.

Plaintiff: The one who initiates a lawsuit.

Plea bargain: The process whereby the accused and the prosecutor negotiate a mutually satisfactory disposition of the case.

Pleading: A formal paper filed with the court by the parties in a lawsuit containing their positions on the issues in dispute.

Precedent: Something that was said or done previously that provides a pattern for similar cases.

Premium billing: Adding a surcharge to an amount determined by a firm's hourly rate when a good result is obtained, or charging a higher-than-usual rate for a complex case.

Private judges: For-profit dispute-resolution businesses that offer private judging services by retired justices. Parties in a pending civil lawsuit may enter into a stipulation agreeing to a trial by a private judge of their own choosing, rather than wait their turn in the courts.

Private sector: In law, refers to those services selected and fully paid for by individuals or corporate clients.

Privilege against self-incrimination: No person shall be compelled to be a witness against him- or herself in a criminal case.

Pro bono publico: A Latin phrase meaning *for the public good or welfare;* sometimes also called *pro bono.*

Pro tempore: A Latin term meaning *for the time being;* commonly shortened to *pro tem,* as in "judge *pro tem.*"

Probate: The gathering of assets and property of the deceased to pay any outstanding debts and federal or state taxes owed, and to distribute the remainder of the deceased's property to those who are entitled to receive it either by law or by the provisions of a will.

Probate court: Hears proceedings regarding the estates of deceased or incompetent persons and matters pertaining to guardianship of a minor; known in some states as *surrogate court* or *orphan's court.*

Procedural due process: The rights and privileges granted by the Bill of Rights.

Procedural law: The sets of rules that establish the mechanics or steps that people who are involved in a lawsuit or criminal procedure must follow.

Promise: A declaration to do something or to refrain from doing something in the future.

Prosecutor: A person, usually a public official such as a district attorney or the

United States Attorney, who pursues a lawsuit or criminal trial on behalf of the public.

Proximate cause: A legal term used to describe the extent of the defendant's liability.

Public sector: In law, refers to legal problems that are not usually handled by a private attorney.

Pure retainer: A type of agreement between a client and a lawyer that binds the lawyer's firm to the client by including a provision that the firm will not represent a competitor of the client.

RAM: Random access memory; one type of internal memory where data can be stored and removed in the microcomputer.

Re: In the matter of; an abbreviation of the Latin term *in re*.

Reasonable person standard: A guideline for determining appropriate behavior in the circumstance, i.e., would a reasonable person have reacted the same way in the same circumstance?

Records management: The systematic storage of paper records for quick retrieval upon demand.

Referendum: A legislative process that gives the citizens the right to vote directly on any proposed legislation.

Regulate: To control the conduct of legal assistants and paralegals.

Request for admissions: A pleading in which one side asks the other to admit that certain facts are true so that they do not have to be proven at trial.

Request for the production of documents and things: A pleading requesting that one side be allowed to review and inspect before trial any documents or other evidence expected to be presented at trial by the other side.

Retainer: The fee paid by a client at the beginning of a specified legal matter; usually nonrefundable.

Retainer agreement: A contract between a lawyer and a client for the payment of fees and costs.

Retainer for general representation: A flat annual amount charged for general representation, with the services included and those excluded carefully spelled out in a written agreement; common for business clients, school boards, public entities, or anyone requiring continuing legal services.

Rights: Individual liberties either expressly provided for in state or federal constitutions, or that have been found to exist as those constitutions have been interpreted. *Legal rights* are those that a person is entitled to have, do, or receive from others, within the limits prescribed by law.

Role rights: Those rights a person holds by virtue of his or her function, status, or position.

ROM: Read only memory; one type of internal memory where data is fixed and cannot be changed or destroyed by turning off the microcomputer.

Rules: The standards, regulations, guidelines, or methods of proceeding that are enforceable only by the institution, organization, agency, or entity that made them.

Secured debts: Debts against which property has been pledged as collateral.

Self-esteem: The degree to which you like and feel good about yourself.

Sentence: The punishment ordered by a court to be inflicted upon a person found guilty of a crime.

Sequestered: When a jury is separated from others until the trial is over.

Service mark: Denoted by the letter S within a circle, used to distinguish the services of one person or company from those of any other.

Shareholders: People who invest money in a corporation.

Site licensing agreement: An agreement with a software vendor that allows the software purchaser to duplicate a specified number of copies of the program for the purchaser's own use.

Slander: A breach of the duty to refrain from making false, defamatory statements orally about other people.

Sole proprietorship: A business owned by one person.

Split screen: When documents on a computer can be retrieved in original form and displayed on one side of the screen while modifications are performed to the same document on the other side of the screen.

Split sentence: When a sentence for a crime involves both a period of incarceration and a period of probation.

Stare decisis: A Latin term meaning *to stand by that which was decided.*

Statute of limitations: The time fixed by law within which to bring a legal action.

Statutes: Acts of a legislative body; commonly referred to as *legislation.*

Statutory fee: Fees for legal service that are set by state legislature; common in probate procedures and real estate transactions.

Strict liability: A category of torts known as *liability without fault;* uses reasons other than fault in determining liability for injury and is most often applied in abnormally dangerous activities.

Substantive laws: Laws that create, define, and regulate the rights and duties of individuals, as well as the circumstances under which a court will grant one person the right to sue another.

Summons: The official notice that a civil action has been filed.

Suppress the evidence: A motion that asks a court not to allow certain evidence that was illegally seized to be introduced at trial.

Surety: A friend, family member, or bail bondsman who posts bail for the accused.

Suspended sentence: A sentence that places a convicted person on a fixed term of probation without having to serve any time in prison.

Sustained: When objections to questions are raised and approved; the witness is not allowed to answer the question.

Terminal: A video monitor and a computer keyboard together.

Testate: When a person dies leaving a valid will.

Tickler: A memorandum book, calendar, or file that serves as a reminder of important deadlines.

Tort: A private or civil wrong or injury.

Tortfeasor: A person who commits a tort.

Trade name: Distinguishes a company, business, or partnership, rather than a product or service, i.e., Kleenex, Xerox, and Scotch Tape are trade names that have acquired secondary meanings and are often used generically.

Trademark: Any word, name, symbol, emblem, motto, or device used by one manufacturer or merchant to distinguish its goods or products from those produced by another. The symbol ® indicates that the trademark is protected by law.

Treaty: An international agreement between two or more countries.

Trespass: When a person enters onto land owned by another or causes anything to enter onto land, remains on the land, or permits anything to remain on it without permission from the owner.

Trial courts: Responsible for receiving evidence and determining the application of the law to facts.

Trust account: A checking account established for the specific purpose of holding money deposited by one party for the benefit of another.

Unilateral contract: A promise for an act.

Value billing: A system in which a lawyer and a client negotiate a fee for a case.

Venue: The geographic location where a case is to be tried.

Verdict: The opinion of a jury given after considering all the evidence and arguments presented.

Virus: A program that replicates itself within the computer system, taking up storage space and destroying information.

Vital statistics: Routine personal data, e.g., full name, address, telephone number.

Voir dire: The examination of prospective jurors by the court and attorneys for the plaintiff and defendant to determine whether an individual exhibits an attitude that would keep him or her from serving as a fair and impartial juror in the case before the court.

Wage garnishments: A legal proceeding whereby a portion of a debtor's wages are applied to a debt owed to another.

Witnessed will: A will, usually typewritten, that is witnessed by two or more witnesses.

Writ: A written order issued by the court with directions about what is to be done.

You-messages: Statements that begin with the pronoun *you;* usually aggressive statements.

INDEX